THE VALLEY OF THE SHADOW

Jeremy slung his heavy backpack onto his shoulder and pulled the zipper on his Polarfleece top to his chin. It had been unusually damp and cold for April, and the walk from his apartment to campus had gotten to be a real pain in the ass. At least his roomie was out for the week — some rock-hunt or whatever it was that geology majors did. Probably having a rip-roaring time, finding some cute grad assistant to keep his sleeping bag warm. Bastard, he thought as he hiked up his collar in response to the mist that was descending.

He paused at the fridge, like he always did, noting the photo of him and his siblings, all five of them together — Kenneth, the oldest; Colleen, the pretty one; Stephen, his personal favorite and the one who had gone for the priesthood; Jenny, the teacher and another favorite; Colin, who was just graduating college and being a pain about it; and himself. He paused a little more on Jenny and Stephen — neither had been home in two years, and their messages to Mom and Dad had been a little strange. Were they not such straight arrows, he might have wondered if they'd joined the Family.

He made his way through the deepening evening, down the little side streets past duplexes and small apartments that made up the old town side of the college. Lights glowed cozily in the windows as residents and students went about their evening's work. Sacred Grounds, the coffee-bookstore beside campus, looked to be doing a brisk business, as students sought warmth and company in response to the miserable night. He thought longingly about ditching the library, then remembered he'd been ditching the library for three nights running, which was why he was out.

He rounded the corner to go in the side entrance, and noticed a man sitting on one of the marble benches beside the bike racks. Cripes, that's gotta be cold on the ass, he thought, then he did a double-take. Something about the man's posture, the way he held his hands were so familiar to Jeremy. He considered the man, and then he stared, unable to look anywhere else. He didn't even want to blink, or he'd realize he was hallucinating.

It was his brother Stephen, staring at the drizzle-slicked parking lot. Stephen, who had gone out to CA to look for their sister Jenny when she didn't come home for Christmas, and who hadn't written since then. He looked completely out of keeping for his profession — a sailor's peacoat, jeans, hiking boots, instead of the usual blacks and collar that had marked him as a Jesuit. What was he doing here? Why here? If he was in town, why didn't he look him up? Jeremy felt cold sweat soaking through his T-shirt, and his fingers were turning pruney from it. He forced himself to take a single step forward, then another, and another, telling himself the whole while that he wouldn't learn anything if he just sat on his ass.

"Stephen?" he whispered to himselfHe ventured closer, staring at the wisps of blond hair under the cap, the profile, and he felt surer. He took a breath and spoke audibly: "Stephen?"

The man turned sharply and Jeremy's certainty crystallized. "Steve!" he yelled with delight, crossing the few remaining steps with a bound.

Stephen smiled in recognition and stood up to hug his younger brother. "Jesus, Steve, where've you been?! Why didn't you tell me you were coming?"

Stephen's hug felt a little stiff, as if he weren't used to the action, then he seemed to relax. "Missed you too, baby brother," he said quietly before releasing Jeremy and stepping back.

"So — um, jeez — Speedy, what's up?" It sounded completely lame, but he couldn't find another thing to say.

"I've... been better," Stephen replied, and his voice sounded tired. He gave the parking lot a glance, then added, "I've been sitting out in the damp a while. Any place inside we can go?"

"Sure," Jeremy replied, noticing the duffel bag on the ground nearby. He started to heft it, but Stephen quickly retrieved it. Something clanked inside. Jeremy wanted to ask, but his brother was looking a bit anxiously for another venue. Guess the library would wait another night.

•••

"...And that pretty much covers it, I guess," Stephen said, fingering his coffee mug.

Now sitting back in Jeremy's living room, surrounded by the wreckage of a McDonald's supper, Jeremy considered his brother carefully. "Um, Speedy, not to burst your bubble or nothing, but you're not making a lot of sense."

"Look, I realize that, but I can't tell it any other way. You asked me where I've been for the past year, and this is it. And don't call me Speedy." Stephen took another swig of coffee. He looked strangely old to Jeremy, like he hadn't slept well in a long time.

"Okay, let's go over this again. Jenny went out to CA to teach, right? And you say her letters started getting funny about a year ago, then quit, right?"

"Yes. Which is when I went out."

"And then what? I want you to say this part, because it sounds so frickin' weird and you don't seem to get that," Jeremy snapped.

Stephen put down the mug and spoke in the same even tone he had used all night. "When I got to CA, I started asking around for Jenny. All I was able to find was that

Jenny had been seen with a few people, in particular a man. At first I thought, she was in trouble in the usual way — bad relationship, maybe pregnant. But the more I looked, the more I *couldn't* find. Jeremy, when someone disappears, usually there's peole who can say when they saw her last, if she was happy, that kind of thing. *No one* wanted to talk about seeing her. She had mentioned joining some church group that would allow her to help people, but every Catholic church I talked to acted like they didn't know who she was or what she was talking about. That's when I decided to hunker down and start combing the underside. And that's when they came to me."

"This was the group that Jenny was with."

"They called themselves the Society of Leopold. I'd never heard of it, but I was willing to figure there were a few little fringe groups that maybe I hadn't heard of. When I asked them about her, they seemed rather coy about it." Stephen grimaced. "I didn't like the vibe, but I thought I'd play along and see what came of it. They got really interested when they found out I was a Jesuit. In a few weeks, they were taking me along on these little reconaissance missions into San Francisco, telling me to watch out for people who didn't look right. They said Jenny had been doing this sort of thing when she vanished. So I went looking, and one night, I ran into…something."

Stephen paused and shivered, closing his eyes as memory took over. "He just didn't feel right to me when he walked past — I don't know how to describe it. I followed him, got close to him in the crowd, and started to reach out for his shoulder. Something made him turn around — My God, Jeremy, he wasn't even human! He didn't *look* human — more like… like he had a disease. And the worst part was he *knew* that I knew. He knew that I could see what he looked like."

Stephen's hands shook, and Jeremy was suddenly very nervous. Steve wouldn't pull his leg like this — he was honest-to-God scared. He ventured onto the couch next to Stephen and reached out a tenative hand. "Easy, Steve, it's cool," he said, wishing that it really was.

"I don't remember what happened after that, but apparently it was what they wanted. Next thing I knew, they were asking me to join. Like I said, I thought they knew something about Jenny they weren't telling, so I went in."

Jeremy stood up and paced the room a few times, trying to let the story sink in. "And they weren't telling what?"

"That she was part of them. That something didn't work out and she had left. That the guy she was seen with was a vampire."

Jeremy stopped dead and did a double-take. "A what?!"

"You heard me the first time I told this."

"Jeezus-pleezus, Steve, listen yourself! A vampire? This is not frickin' 'Buffy', okay?! I know there's some weirdoes out there, but vampires are not one of them, okay?"

"And I've seen plenty of weirdoes, and believe me, I know the difference." Stephen replied with quiet conviction.

"Big brother, these guys are obviously not all there. They convinced Jenny, they convinced you, talking about vampires. What comes next? You going to tell me that these guys go out vampire-hunting?"

Stephen didn't answer immediately, and Jeremy howled. "Mother MacGeary, I don't believe this! Steve, you believe this shit?!"

At that, his brother stood up and looked him straight in the eye. The room seemed to fill with his presence — indeed, Stephen either grew an inch or two or something else was taking up space. Jeremy felt it and wanted to shrink. His brother's face was stern, filled with conviction and strength, his blue eyes were clear, all-seeing. This was not his brother who had gone loony from the strain of trying to find Jenny. This was his brother, who very much believed in what he had seen and was trying to bust it through his thick skull. "Jeremy, if you had been out where I've been and seen what I've seen, you wouldn't ask that. I didn't believe it either, not at first. But the longer I've been here, the more I realize that I can't afford *not* to believe. Not if it means Jenny's life. Please, Jeremy — I came here thinking that maybe you would at least listen, if not understand. I don't like being called crazy, and I've had my fill of it for the past year."

"Look, Jenny's missing. When someone's missing, you call'.he polkÌe, you don't run around with this baloney!"

"And sometimes, when the police have no leads and aren't talking to you, you start taking chances, because that may be the only chance she's got. For God's sake, Jeremy, do you understand? At the very least, think about this — why in hell would I make up a lie like this?"

"You got a point." Jeremy finally nodded. "Fine. I reserve the right to think something's fishy, but that something isn't you. Deal?"

Stephen sighed, and seemed to shrink slightly, growing more wan and tired. "Deal." He sank back onto the couch, and the room returned to normal.

"Soooo, what happens now?" Jeremy ventured.

"I've got some leads back this way, and I wanted to check them out. And hey, you were in the neighborhood, and it's been a while, so I thought—"

Jeremy managed a grin. "Sure thing, Steve. Adam's out playing rock-hunter, so it's cool."

Stephen tried to smile, but on his worn face it came out more like a rictus. "Thanks, Jer." He leaned back on the couch, his eyes drifting shut as Jeremy rattled off his plans.

"I'll make a grocery run tomorrow, or I can show you the way and give you the cash and you can do it while I'm in class. I got class from nine till two tomorrow, and after that, we've got the afternoon. There's a great trail for running, hope you brought your shoes...."

Jeremy's voice trailed off when he turned and noticed Stephen fast asleep on the couch. He sighed, "Or it can wait till tomorrow, I guess."

He collected the supper wreckage and found an afghan and pillow for Stephen. No sense in waking him if he was that tired. Figuring the evening was over, he started for the kitchen to dive into some reading, and nearly tripped over Stephen's duffel bag, lying near the kitchen partition. Grumbling, Jeremy picked it up to heave it aside, and heard something clank within. This time, his curiosity was getting the better of him, what with all the talk about vampires and the like. Sneaking a glance at Stephen (who was still very sound asleep), he carefully pulled the zipper open and moved aside a few layers of shirts, sweaters and jeans.

A well-worn Bible with Apochrypha. A silver flask inscribed with a cross. A chalice for Mass. And two well-honed wooden stakes with a heavy mallet.

Mind's Eye Theatre™
LAWS
of the
HUNT

CREDITS

Written by: Jason Carl, Earle "Glas" Durboraw, Edward MacGregor, Peter Woodworth, Duncan Wyley

Additional writing by: Cynthia Summers

Developed by: Cynthia Summers

Previously published material has appeared in: Laws of the Night, Laws of the Ascension

Art direction by: Aaron Voss

Art by: Laura Robles

Layout and typesetting by: Eric Ross

Mind's Eye Theatre design: Mark Rein•Hagen, Ian Lemke and Mike Tinney

World of Darkness created by: Mark Rein•Hagen

SPECIAL THANKS TO:

Laura "Llewellyn" Middleton, for being a beacon in the night.

Bruce "Brother Shane" Hembree, the best brother a sister could have

And all the rest of the "mere mortals" — *Carpe diem*!

735 PARK NORTH BLVD.
SUITE 128
CLARKSTON, GA 30021
USA

Contents

Mind's Eye Theatre LAWS of HUNT

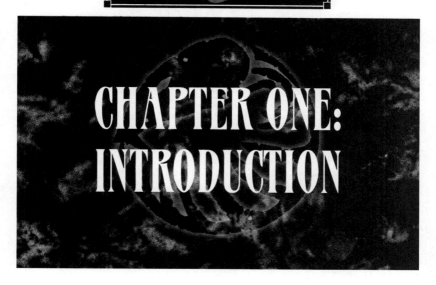

CHAPTER ONE: INTRODUCTION

THE FORESTS OF THE NIGHT

Once upon a time, long before television or computers or even books, people sat around the fire and told stories for entertainment. Whether it was a ballad of a hero's latest exploits or a cautionary tale about dealing with the hidden creatures of the world, storytellers were a valued part of the community as teachers and entertainers. And tale-telling was hardly a passive art — the storyteller relied on his audience for reaction to his tale as he spoke. How else would he know if they were enjoying the story, or if they were getting bored?

Time marched on, and technological developments began to change, if not interfere with, the storyteller's art. Books (and the development of greater literacy among people) meant that someone could simply read a story whenever he liked, instead of hunting down a storyteller to tell it. Radio and television remade the storyteller into an impassive creature that did not encourage audience participation. Stories were still told, and in great quantity, but they were largely sterile, unliving things.

Now we come to the 1970s, and the era of roleplaying. A group of players sits around a table, listening to their leader describe scenes of dank dungeons and dark cities, and they choose which path to take next. At one of these sessions, someone gets the idea to start standing up, moving and thinking as her character might. Over time, more players do the same, creating what will become known as live-action roleplaying (or LARP). In fact, this "new" entertainment is a return to the oldest — the leader was the storyteller, taking his listeners on a new journey, and the listeners were responding in kind, taking on the roles of the characters in the story, telling this new tale to the storyteller, the other player-listeners and to themselves.

WHAT IS MIND'S EYE THEATRE?

This game is probably unlike anything you have played before. In many ways, it's not really a game, because it doesn't have a lot of the trappings of games — such as cards,

dice or a playing board. It's also far more concerned with the stories to be told along the way than "winning." It's far more like the make-believe of childhood than what most people typically think of when they imagine "games." This book contains all the information you'll need to start playing and telling your own stories. You create the action, you choose the path to follow, you decide what risks to accept. We call this style of game **Mind's Eye Theatre**.

Playing **Mind's Eye Theatre** is like being in a movie. You and your friends are the characters, but there is no script. There may be a framework or setting that determines the parameters of the world around you, but you and the others around you are creating the story as you play. The "director" of this movie is the Storyteller, assisted by Narrators. The Storyteller creates the stage and the minor characters that the players interact with to tell this story.

Most scenes in **Mind's Eye Theatre** are played out in real-time — an hour in the make-believe world is 60 minutes long, and it takes up 60 minutes in the real world — and always in character. Players always remain in character during the game unless there is a rules dispute.

CHARACTERS

When you play **Mind's Eye Theatre**, you take on another persona, here a human who may be be gifted with unusual powers or who hunts the supernatural. Your character can be almost anything — from any walk of life, age, creed, race or sex. The only limit is your imagination. When you create this character, you decide what she says or does. You decide where she goes and what choices she makes. During the game, you speak as your character, unless you're resolving a rules dispute or talking to the Storyteller. Because most of what a **Mind's Eye Theatre** player perceives around him depends on the other players, all players must be vivid and expressive.

While the characters may direct the plot through their actions, the plot reacts in ways that direct the characters. For example, a character decides she wants to create a coffeehouse with space for people to perform, and she invites a well-known local group to perform for an evening — here, the characters are directing the plot through their actions. However, the plot reacts to this direction — the Storyteller tells the characters that the performance has aroused some suspicious attention. It seems that one of the performers reminds one of the characters of a singer who was supposed to have died about two years ago. Thus is a story built in **Mind's Eye Theatre**.

Creating a character for **Laws of the Hunt** is easy, and it takes just a few minutes. Only a few things become necessary to define the basic capabilities of a character, and when they're done, you can start playing. There's another phase to creating a character, though. A character is, by and large, like a person, and people aren't just flat cardboard cutouts with a few numbers to represent what they can do. People have pasts, likes and dislikes, goals and dreams — all the intangible things that make a person into what other people see when he walks into a room or talks to them. It's not much different from all the care that an actor or author takes when creating a character. So as you're creating your character, think a little about where she comes from, what she wants out of her existence, what she'll do to get it, what she loves and hates. Does your character love thunderstorms and watch them from the window, or have they frightened her ever since she was a small child? Does your character want revenge on the person who killed a loved one, and he'll bargain with the Devil himself to get it? While certain personality quirks

and details will emerge as you play, it's a good idea to have the basics in place for the first time you walk into a room and meet the other characters.

Characters are the heart and soul of the story. Without them, all the efforts of the Storyteller would be for nothing, and there would be no stories to tell.

THE STORYTELLER

The Storyteller is the one who creates the world that the players move through. She creates a skeletal framework of setting and plot, then turns the characters loose to put flesh on its bones. More than that, she acts as an impartial judge when the rules are questioned, describes scenes that can't be staged and even plays the parts of antagonists or other people with whom the characters interact. The Storyteller is usually assisted by Narrators, who play their own characters but are ready to answer rules questions when necessary.

Storytelling is a demanding (and occasionally exhausting) task. A Storyteller must oversee the events to be certain that people have a good time, that the rules are being followed and that the story is running smoothly. Sometimes she must create plot elements on the spur of the moment or adjudicate between several quarreling players. In spite of all this responsibility, there is something immensely satisfying about watching the players create something remarkable with the plot elements given them. It really makes the headache all worthwhile.

ELEGANTLY SIMPLE

This game was designed to be easy to play and easier to start. Character creation takes only a few minutes. The basic rules are simple, and they cover most of the encounters a new player will enter. Even very new players who have never played **Mind's Eye Theatre** or LARP before will find that this game takes little effort to pick up.

HOW TO USE THIS BOOK

This book gives you all the basic rules that you'll need to start playing or Storytelling mortals in the World of Darkness.

Chapter One: Introduction — The introduction to both **Mind's Eye Theatre** and the World of Darkness.

Chapter Two: The Hunters — Describes the organizations who hunt the supernatural, from the Inquistion to the Dauntain.

Chapter Three: The Gifted — Describes those mortals who are set apart by dint of their unusual gifts, whether to cast sorcerous spells or speak with the dead.

Chapter Four: Character Creation — Everything that you'll need to create a character to start playing.

Chapter Five: Numina and Powers — Here are the unusual powers that mortals and other hunters can wield in their quests against the supernatural.

Chapter Six: Rules, Systems and Drama — All the necessary rules and details to help the game run.

Chapter Seven: Storytelling — Whether you're a veteran Storyteller, or picked it up for the first time, this chapter will show you all the ropes and the special nuances of mortal games.

THE RULES THOU SHALT NOT BREAK

In the end, these are the only rules of the game that must always be obeyed. These help to keep everyone — other players, law enforcement, curious onlookers and you — safe and happy with the game. They're not intended to limit fun, only to be sure that everyone plays safely and has a good time.

NO TOUCHING

That means none. Even when everyone's being careful, accidents can happen.

NO STUNTS

No climbing, running, jumping or other dangerous stunts during a game. Let the rules cover actions like jumping from rooftops and the like. If you can imagine you're a no-nonsense federal agent who hunts vampires in his spare time, you can surely imagine swinging from a chandelier.

NO WEAPONS

That means none whatsoever, not even as props. Even obviously fake or silly toy weapons can look like the real thing in dim lighting, and might give the wrong impression about the game. Use item cards instead.

NO DRINKING OR DRUGS

Well, duh. Drugs and alcohol do not create peak performance. A player who's drunk or stoned is a danger to others and the game. There's nothing wrong with *playing* a character who is drunk or stoned, but bringing the real thing to a game is a very poor choice. At best, it's tasteless; at worst, it's illegal. Don't do it.

BE MINDFUL OF OTHERS

This one has become very important in the past couple of years. Always remember, especially if you play in a public place, that not everyone around you is involved in the game. Make sure that your actions do not frighten or disturb others — this includes conversations. In this age of terrorism, discussing the gory details of infernalism, torture and the like in a public place where non-players might overhear and misinterpret what's happening makes for a *very* bad combination. If a curious bystander from outside the game asks what's going on, drop out of character and explain politely.

THE RULES ARE FLEXIBLE

We at White Wolf like to call this "the golden rule." If there's some ruling herein (other than these listed here) that doesn't work for your group, then by all means change it if it means a smoother-running game. Just be consistent and fair — rulings that change weekly or that result in no-win situations upsets the fun.

IT'S ONLY A GAME

If a rival wins the day, if a plot falls apart, if a character dies — it's only a game. At the end of the day, it's still a game that is played to have fun. Don't spoil the fun for others by taking it too seriously. Leave the game behind when it ends. Playing **Mind's Eye Theatre** is fun, and getting together with a few other players afterward to discuss the night's work is great, but calling the player of the cenacle leader and demanding a meeting when he's studying for exams signals the need for some down time.

HAVE FUN

Not "Win". Not "Go out and kill everything else." Just have fun. The goal of **Mind's Eye Theatre** is to tell stories about the hero's journey and what happens along the way.

THE WORLD OF DARKNESS

On the surface, the World of Darkness doesn't seem to be different from our own. People are born, grow up, work and die every day. Plants and skyscrapers compete for space. The same newspapers are sold on the corner, and television is the same vast wasteland. But there is something else in the World of Darkness — an element fed from the violence and despair that permeates the world. This is what the monsters feed on, and the monsters are all too real.

The World of Darkness is not simply our own with a coating of black paint and some random monsters stirred in. It is about a world that has become too beaten down by violence, coarseness, social ills and emotional pain to rouse itself these days. The gulf between the haves and the have-nots is great and widens daily. Hope and compassion are all too rare, but all the more precious for their scarcity. The people look for some light in their lives, but even faith is a commodity. Those who do manage to lift themselves often do so through violent means, doing whatever it takes to make a dent in the walls. And in the midst of all this, unknown to the masses, move monsters and spirits and creatures of myth.

THE HUNTERS

Not everyone is blind to the threat in the midst of the world. Some brave men and women learn the truth, and make the decision to take up the fight against those who would misuse the mortals around them. Some believe that there is no hope for this enemy — only a swift death will ensure the safety of the masses. Others want only to study the supernatural, believing that knowledge truly is power. Some rare few ally themselves with "the enemy", whether due to previous attachments, or because they believe that the supernatural community is not evil but in need of help.

Taking up the cause is not for those who desire fame and glory. This is a world that denies belief in the supernatural, believing superstition and myth to be backward, and those who openly profess belief are usually ridiculed and shunned. Many times, these unfortunates lose their jobs or families because of their attachments. Some hunters and scholars find it difficult to maintain their motivation from night to night, when the fight is neverending and the recipients seem so ungrateful. Others may not have chosen their course, but rather have had it choose them — perhaps a beloved family member or friend has been touched by the supernatural in some way, and in this way reluctant hunters are born.

Humans are not perfect — far from it. They are subject to the frailties of the mortal condition, from sickness to hunger to sleep deprivation. They suffer crises of spirit, and find themselves struggling to maintain their devotions. Most of the supernatural community dismisses mortals as ultimately weak and worthless. But humans have remarkable resiliency in the face of trouble, deep wells of spiritual strength, and,

15

ultimately, their very nature as humans to sustain them through their difficult choice. There is nothing "mere" about mortals who have turned their energy on the creatures of the night — each is a potent reminder of what would happen should humanity's collective might turn its eye on the hidden parts of the world.

THE CREATURES OF THE NIGHT

These are the targets for the mortals herein, whether to hunt them or study them. They slip unseen through mortal society, taking innocents to use as tools, companions or prey. Wise in survival and hiding their existence, they do not appreciate efforts to stalk them, and the best hunters discover they must learn quickly or die trying.

VAMPIRES

Cursed with undeath and eternal hunger, vampires are the most common foes hunters face. As pale mockeries of the mortals they were, they stalk the night in search of prey. To pass the centuries, they play elaborate political games, using humans as pawns against their enemies. Some of these games can last for decades or even centuries, through move and countermove that might utilize generations of a single family. While some seem content to slip through the night, others are ravening bloodthirsty monsters that treat human life very cheaply indeed, leaving a trail of bloodless corpses and wreckage in their wake. Few hunters have encountered ancient vampires, but whispers claim that such jaded creatures are no longer remotely human, with equally inhuman desires and tastes.

Vampires are among the most dangerous prey that a hunter can face — mind control, blood magic, incredible strength, preternaturally sharp senses and rapid healing only part of vampires' repertoire of tricks. Even the Society of Leopold, the most active vampire-hunters in the world, finds that it must face them with fire and faith if there is to be any hope of success. Worse yet, many vampires turn the tables on their hunters, manipulating them into hunting the undead's own rivals. Vampire-hunters often have good cause to wonder who is hunting whom.

For more about these dark stalkers, see **Laws of the Night**.

SHAPESHIFTERS

Legends around the world tell of men and women who could change their shapes and become one with the animals. The legends do not lie — there are many who bear this gift, walking among both animals and men with ease. Stories speak of some who can become like bears, ravens, great cats or even serpents at will, but the shapeshifter that a hunter is most likely to encounter is the werewolf. The werewolves of the World of Darkness appear as normal humans or wolves, but change freely between a variety of shapes, including a nine-foot-tall half-wolf. They seem most at home in the wild places and fight to defend these spots fiercely, calling on a mix of incredible natural speed and strength, and shamanistic beliefs that enable them to summon spirits for aid. Close-knit, like pack animals, to take on one werewolf is to risk taking on all its kin.

Werewolf-hunters are very rare, and with good reason. Not only is the half-wolf form a very effective battle machine, but a strange terror clouds the minds of those who encounter such a creature. The folk-legends are quite correct to say that silver will dispatch a werewolf, but most would-be hunters die trying out other remedies first.

For more about werewolves, see **Laws of the Wild**, and the **Changing Breeds** books for other kinds of shapeshifters.

MAGES

Mages are mortals who can manipulate reality through the force of their will alone.

Mages rarely attract the notice of hunters for a variety of reasons. As they are for all intents and purposes mortal, they don't tend to stand out in a crowd. Indeed, some have gotten very good at not being noticed, whether through calling on mystical powers or just being lucky at avoiding attention at the right moments. However, they are not without their share of enemies, and have a talent for making enemies that are often just as skilled in the mystical arts.

For more about the willworkers, see **Laws of Ascension**.

WRAITHS

What happens when we die? Some believe that souls pass on to whatever punishment or reward they have earned in life, while others believe that souls return some great well of spirit to await rebirth. But what of those spirits that do not go quietly into the good night, who are tied to the living world by unfinished tasks or personal attachments? This is the fate of wraiths, those trapped in the shadowy spirit-world where passions call more strongly than the grave. Many wish only to finish their business and move on, but not a few twisted spirits have darker agendas in mind. Worse, they have a variety of powers at their disposal, ranging from classic poltergeist knockings and hauntings to full-blown possession or even physical harm, and can manifest these powers while remaining safely in the spirit lands. Mortals victimized by a haunting soon learn how powerful a malicious ghost can be.

Most mortals only witness wraiths through their mischief, as a barrier exists between the lands of the living and dead. Some mortals are lucky (or unlucky) enough to be able to see and hear the dead quite clearly, and wraiths prize such individuals. Those who hunt wraiths are nearly always proficient in the occult, and have discovered how to strike an arrogant ghost by damaging some tie he has to the living world.

See **Oblivion** for more about wraiths in Mind's Eye Theatre.

CHANGELINGS

Long ago, the boundaries between this world and the hidden one were thinner, and creatures of dream walked among men. Dream and wonder were common things, feeding the faerie folk. Now in this modern age of science, dreams are stifled and starving. In the midst of such famine, the faeries clothe themselves in mortal flesh to survive. They seek dreams where they can find them and bring wonder to the shrinking corners of the world. Not all dreams are pleasant, though, and some dark ones find horror to be a preferable substitute for wonder.

Few mortals actively hunt the fae, partly because the fae usually blend in with humanity and partly because they do not actively prey on humanity in the manner of vampires or werewolves. For every changeling that only wishes to inspire a child's dream, though, there is one who takes malicious pleasure in tormenting that child, and such activity usually draws angry attention. While most hunter and scholarly organizations ignore the fae, there is a special group of hunters (who are often fae-blooded themselves) who make up for any apparent lack of attention.

The Shining Host contains more information about changelings in Mind's Eye Theatre.

The next morning, Jeremy blinked awake to the smell of coffee and eggs. Groggily he rolled out of bed and fumbled for a sweatshirt. What a night — he kept dreaming about vampire-hunters, seeing his brother armed with a cross and stake, ready for action.

In the kitchen, Stephen read the paper, occasionally circling items. He glanced up at Jeremy's approach; he definitely looked better than last night. "Good morning."

"What's good about it?" Jeremy grumbled good-naturedly as he poured himself a cup of coffee and munched a piece of toast. Breakfast continued in silence a few minutes before Jeremy ventured, "Hey, about last night—"

Stephen put down the paper with a small smile. "I dumped a lot on you last night, baby brother. I'm sorry. I just... I just wanted you to understand."

"Steve, I still don't, but I'm willing to let you have it for now. You say that this is all part and parcel of why Jenny went AWOL, right?"

"Yes."

"Well, Steve, I want her back. I want her back home for next Christmas, so I can change that picture on the fridge. And I want you with her, *capiche*? And if that means that monsters exist and there's some buncha folks that want to play Slayer, then I'll run with it. How's that?"

Stephen nodded once. Some of the lines in his face smoothed out in relief, a visible relief that Jeremy could feel too. He reached out a hand. "That's fine, Jer."

They shook on it, and went back to breakfast in companionable silence.

CHAPTER TWO: THE HUNTERS

THE INQUISITION

They are an army of and for God, poised to strike wherever the children of the Enemy lurk, awaiting the Parousia, the Second Coming, the End Times, when the dead shall arise from the grave and Judgment will be dispensed. They shall fight alongside the Heavenly Host in the final battle against the Antichrist's forces.

The Inquisition sees itself as humanity's last stand against the darkness. They are the new Crusaders, the final bastion against the horrors that lie in wait. The general populace, if they know of the Inquisition, probably think they are mad; dangerous religious zealots, possibly guilty of the murder of hundreds.

They carry out a holy mandate, seeking out and destroying the menace of supernatural creatures. Even lay members of the organization believe that they fight the battle between right and wrong, good and evil, and that they take on an endless task for the sake of humanity, whether the ignorant care or even know.

THE SOCIETY OF LEOPOLD

The modern Inquisition has its roots in millennia of religious cleansings, the purging of heresy and the persecution of deviants and the protection of the doctrine of the Church. During the 13th century, the dominant Christian church and the Emperor Frederick II instituted Inquisitors to weed out heretics such as the Albigensians. Eventually the powers of the Inquisitors expanded and courts were established to judge and punish heresy. Torture was ordered by the Pope to be used to extract confessions.

One of the first entrusted with the sacred duties of Inquisitor was Leopold of Murnau, an aged Bavarian Dominican known for his sanctity and ardor. Early in his new career he received direct proof of the existence of supernatural creatures; he determined that these diabolical agents of Hell — for what else could they be? — were far more important as targets than "mere heretics." Leopold estimated that the Parousia was nigh and that these creatures were the forces of the Enemy, gathering for

battle. Accordingly he assembled a cadre of Inquisitors dedicated to the elimination of the unholy horde.

With the consent of Pope Gregory IX, he founded a society in secrecy to combat the supernatural enemies of the church. The followers of Leopold operated as part of the standard Inquisition but always kept an eye open for the existence of the Enemy within their jurisdiction. Leopold fell eventually to a ghoul, and vampires have since then been particular enemies of the Society.

During the 15th century, the Society was bolstered by the secret support of Pope Innocent VIII, and was reorganized by the Dominican Inquisitors Heinrich Kramer and James Sprenger. These witch-hunters thrived through the release of the *Malleus Maleficarum*, or *Hammer of Witches*, the eventual standard in witch-hunting lore used by both the Catholics and the Protestants. When the new secret society was built, a call for new leadership was answered by Matteo Severus, a Jesuit and one of Kramer and Sprenger's less publicly known colleagues, who was given the role of the first Inquisitor-General. The conjunction of Jesuit models and the Dominican influence on the Church saw the Society grow in strength and numbers, as Inquisitors continued to work quietly throughout the Reformation. Eventually the growth of Protestantism weakened the strength of the entire Inquisition through the weakening of Catholicism as a political force. The Society slowly reduced its activities.

Changing times forced the Society to avoid scrutiny as it continued to execute its mandate, and it slowly grew to become a most potent organization with hidden bases in much of Europe and the Americas. Despite internal dissent and philosophical debate, the Inquisition is still dedicated to its original cause — the destruction of all supernatural creatures — even into the modern day. In 1908 the Society became independent of the Holy See, and took all records of the Society with them. Since then they have judiciously allowed more or less information to be revealed to each successive pope as to their true mission. It is unknown how informed the current pope is as to the Society, although it is generally believed throughout the Society that he has been at least briefed.

The last two decades have seen an upsurge in recruitment, and today the Inquisition numbers some 600 active members worldwide, predominantly located in Western Europe and North America. Debate amongst the senior members of the Society continues as to the portents of modern times, the degrading morals of the world and the position that the Society should take in regard to the Enemy. The younger, and more… enthusiastic Inquisitors insist that it's time to kick ass for the Lord.

RECRUITMENT

Becoming a member of the Society of Leopold is seen as a most sacred calling. It is no simple act; it is a declaration of a vocation, and a realization of one's sacred duty. However, it is much more complex than picking up a crucifix and a torch.

The most common way that an Inquisitor will join the society is through accidental discovery. Independent religious hunters occasionally encounter Inquisitors (or evidence of their handiwork) in the course of their investigations. The Society also keeps an eye out for members of the church who seem sympathetic to the concerns of the Society.

Retired Inquisitors often take academic, parish or community positions in order that they may monitor their locale for promising individuals, who are reported to the local Provincial. A recruiter then performs a more thorough observation of the potential recruit's background and qualifications, via discrete conversations with past associates or through the Contacts or Influences to which the Provincial or his subordinates may have access. Should the nominee prove worthy of membership to the Provincial, the recruit is invited to a clandestine meeting where he may be asked to join, although the name of the Society is never mentioned unless he accepts. Recruiters are scrupulous about security and are often drafted from the ranks of the Condotierri.

All members of the Inquisition are at least nominally members of the Roman Catholic Church. However, even partial membership is open to members of other faiths (although usually only Protestants will be considered); this partial membership allows access to Society holdings and resources, but excludes them from the hierarchy.

Beyond church affiliation, the strongest qualities sought in a new Inquisitor are zeal and loyalty. The life of a witch-hunter is not for the weak-willed, timid or unbelieving: Inquisitors are warriors for Christ and members of the armies of Heaven. They must also be loyal: to their superiors, to their comrades and to the cause. The Inquisition is one part religion, one part army.

While the original Inquisition predominantly consisted of members of the clergy, and they are certainly strongly represented even today (notably in Europe), the modern Inquisition contains a broader spectrum of people. Women are admitted, and some even hold places of power within the Society, yet they may still encounter some minor bias from the more conservative Inquisitors, but they do hold equal rank and sway should they hold position. Laypeople, those who have not taken religious or monastic vows, have recently been admitted and make up a predominance of the membership of the Society in America.

HIERARCHY

Regardless of method of recruitment or personal attributes, all Inquisitors undergo a Novitiate, or orientation period. More experienced Inquisitors mentor the novices, teaching them the history, polity and philosophy of the Society. During this time the novice learns as much of the supernatural as the Society is willing to teach them: the basic truths, as perceived by the Society, of the existence of witches, vampires, ghost and other such malefic creatures, as well as examination of the records of famous witch-hunters from the past. Recently the training of novices has been ramped up to include basic martial training at the direction of the Inquisitor-General. If the mentor is a non-combatant, whether by virtue of age or preference, members of the Condotierre may be requested to provide such training.

When the mentor decides the novice is ready, the novice takes vows of obedience and loyalty to the Society (although, strangely, not the Catholic Church) and is granted the title Tertiary. Now permitted to participate independently in hunts, although he may have rarely accompanied his mentor in the past, the Inquisitors career is ready to begin.

Tertiaries are entitled to enter any of the Society's Cenacula and have provisional access to the Society's library in Rome. Tertiaries need not be full-time hunters and are permitted to pursue whatever other interests concern them. While they may live otherwise normal lives, if they engage in any hunter activity they must abide by the Society's regulations.

If they earn great respect within the Society, experienced Inquisitors may be awarded the honorary title of Councilor. They may have been involved in many hunts or been responsible for the destruction of a powerful enemy, or shown keen insight in a variety of crises. While Councilors are more respected than Tertiaries, and may be called on by the Society to discuss items of importance to the organization, they have no specific authority over them.

The next true level of rank is Abbé — the individual responsible for the actions of a specific Cenaculum. Typically selected by the local Provincial, the Abbé may be selected by the members of the Cenaculum with the Provincial's approval of the candidate. Unless the Cenaculum is troublesome, the Provincial is unlikely to disapprove the choice, but reserves the right to choose another candidate either from within or without the Cenaculum.

The Inquisitor-General can select successful Abbés, along with other notable Inquisitors, to the regional position of Provincial. These worthies monitor and coordinate the Society's activities within their geographic jurisdictions. They meet in annual council to discuss the previous years' activities and the following year's plans. Few officials of this level or higher are actively involved in witch-hunting, their roles tending toward mentors, advisors or scholars. Provincials often have a cabinet of advisors, which may include anyone they choose.

The leader of this army is the Inquisitor-General, who has absolute lifetime authority in the Society. Candidates are chosen and voted upon by Provincials and are typically chosen from among their number. While there have now been three women elected as Inquisitor-General, there has yet to be a layperson in the position. It is not unknown for the Inquisitor-General to have a private cabinet of advisors, secret or otherwise.

CENACLES

The Society is organized in small groups called *cenacles*, which answer to the local Provincial, and ultimately to the Inquisitor-General in Rome. A cenacle consists of a local group of Inquisitors, generally operating out of a central location (the Cenaculum). Cenacles share society resources and training, operating locally to watch for supernatural activity and acting to stop it. When the Society deems it appropriate, it issues an *auto-da-fé* (act of faith), in which the cenacle gathers to undertake a mission of holy purification.

Inquisitors may opt to act as Itinerants, independent of any formal home or cenacle, but most choose to reside at their Cenaculum.

The formation of a cenacle is dependant on the approval of the local Provincial. Its members must abide by the regulations and restrictions that apply to Inquisitors. Inquisitors may act together without restriction and without notifying the Holy Office, but if they do not have the official recognition of the Provincial and the Society they may not call on the Society for resources otherwise provided to official Cenaculum. Even if the Cenaculum is approved, serious funding will not arrive unless the cenacle proves itself to be valuable to the Society.

The systems for creating Cenacula for use in game are given at the end of this section. The *Cenaculum* Background is exclusive to Inquisition characters. Other

hunters have their own methods of creating and maintaining hidey-holes, secret bases or lairs (even if it's just their basement or an old Winnebago).

INQUISITORS ARE STILL PEOPLE

Despite their membership in the Society, Inquisitors are human beings with lives. They may have families, day jobs and other concerns in their existence besides crusading after the Forces of Darkness. To ignore this factor is to ignore the character.

When creating an Inquisition character, factor in his family, his loves (past and present, places, people and pastimes) and his hates. If the character has a wife and children, do they know of his calling, or is he straining his marriage with these late-night sojourns? How does his being married and supporting a family affect the verve and with which he attacks his foes? What excuse does he give his boss when he turns up to work late, bruised and haggard, or doesn't turn up for several days with no notice?

Mortal life is a strong factor in the story of any Inquisitor, as they must lead it alongside their duties to the Society. Any factor of life can lead to an interesting story hook.

CIVIL AUTHORITIES

Many of the activities undertaken by the Inquisition are typically illegal. A medley of criminal activities, such as carrying concealed weapons, breaking and entering, "stalking", destruction of property and first-degree murder, can take place during an *auto-da-fé*. While the duty of the Society inevitably overrides the laws of man (however just and proper they may be) due to the urgency of the Society's apostate, as long as innocents are not harmed then Inquisitors will continue to break these laws, however regretfully.

The police are less likely to be so accepting. Most Inquisitors, when arrested, clam up tight, revealing no secrets. The Society has some measures in place to assist any member in legal trouble, whether it be provision of legal aid, bribery or even the Provincial pulling his *Legal* Influence (of which she no doubt has a reasonable measure). In the past, deaths have even been faked to throw off authorities, with the subject being transferred to another Province (or country). All this failing, the Inquisitor is braced for a long period of imprisonment until their release can be arranged. Incarceration certainly provides time for meditation and reflection, after all.

OFFICIAL SUBDIVISIONS

There are several subdivisions within the Society of Leopold, each espousing a different approach to combating the supernatural menace. Beyond these subdivisions, various philosophical sects represent the views of different hunters with regards to the ultimate aims of the Society. Many, though not all, Inquisitors claim membership in a particular subdivision. Membership is by no means mandatory; the Inquisitors' primary duty is the hunt, rather then any other internal function. The smaller philosophical sects rarely claim any overt membership, not being "officially recognized" by the Society.

THE CONDOTIERRI

Founded in the 15th century, this quasi-military order is more concerned with protecting the Society than with directly serving its goals. They are not Inquisitors *per*

se, but serve as Cenaculum guards and bodyguards. The group as a whole is directed by a Condotierre-General, who answers directly to the Inquisitor-General. Senior-ranking Condotierri in the field answer to the senior-ranking Inquisitor present unless he has reason to believe that the safety of the Society is at stake.

Condotierri go where they are posted and are typically assigned to protect the larger and older Cenacula.

Condotierri are generally well trained in modern combat techniques and security measures. In combat situations they typically operate in "lances" of three. They tend to be recruits from the military or police professions, and they tend to keep in touch with their prior work contacts. Typical Abilities include *Firearms*, *Investigations* and *Melee*. Condotierri rarely begin their careers with True Faith, but it is not unheard of for members to develop the Numina during the course of their career.

GLADIUS DEI

This *corps d'élite*, the "Sword of God" is the most distinguished order within the entire Society. It includes the most highly respected, and shortest lived, Inquisitors, handpicked and invited by the Inquisitor-General to perform the most sacred and dangerous missions. Members of the Gladius Dei function as ultra-loyal shock troops, on-call from their local cenacles whenever the Society calls them. The nature of such missions is typically exceedingly dangerous — dealing with a vampire elder, for example, or the rescue of a Society member from the hands of the werewolves — and a call to arms is often a call to glorious martyrdom.

Highly trained, zealous, courageous and capable, the members of the Gladius Dei usually come from older cenacles, and only gather together when called on. They are rare, due both to attrition and the rigorous training required. Not every cenacle has one on hand. Cocky and perhaps eve a tad arrogant, the members take pride in the fact that no *auto-da-fé* called by Gladius Dei has ever been a failure.

Starting characters are exceedingly unlikely to be members of this subdivision, and only their ongoing and successful efforts, as well as a demonstrated devotion to God and the Society will bring them to the attention of the Inquisitor-General. Gladius Dei members usually have a great deal of Ability in *Firearms*, *Investigation*, *Melee*, and *Security*. A significant number of them have some small degree of True Faith.

THE OFFICE OF THE CENSOR

Also handpicked and invited by the Inquisitor-General (although nominations typically arise from within the division), those worthies of the Office of the Censor are the internal watchdogs of the Inquisition. Their duty is to investigate, observe and document the operations of the Society itself. They work to ensure the purity of the Society and to stamp out any potential threats, spiritual or intellectual. They remain watchful to ensure the infernal creatures that the Society must face taint none of the members.

If the Office feels that an Inquisitor is straying dangerously close to becoming tainted by the influence of the supernatural, that Inquisitor can be placed under *certiorari* and must hand over all his records to the censor who will also interrogate his associates in the course of the investigation. If a censor is investigating an entire cenacle, she must be made privy to all records, and may interview (or interrogate) any member. The cenacle is considered to be likewise in a state of *certiorari*: they can

continue their normal routine, but the censor (or one of her colleagues) must accompany them on all excursions. Thus they root out corruption and destroy unholy influences on the Society.

It is with the censors that all practitioners of *Theurgy* must "register for future reference". The study of magic is not a reputable pastime in the Society, where all believe magic to be more or less of the Devil, and its practitioners often find themselves under close scrutiny. Refusing to comply with this request is considered at the least a severe breach of protocol and an act of insubordination, almost inevitably leading to further investigation.

The growing darkness without is perhaps reflected in the growing fears of the Office of the Censor, as they become more determined to maintain the sanctity of the Society and its mission as the End Times approach. The tightening grip of the Office is thought by some Inquisitors to be either a move for the division to gain further control over the Society (to the ends the speculator fears most, of course) or a necessary burden to be tolerated as their exposure to the Enemy grows.

Censorial monitors often learn the *Occult* Ability, so as to recognize possible corruption. *Investigation* and *Theology* are also common Abilities within the division. No censors are known to practice *Theurgy*.

THE ORDER OF SAINT JOAN

Leopold's intense drive and strength of spirit inspired a French visionary, Jeanne Roullet, to begin recruiting women to the same cause — the destruction of the forces of the Enemy of God. She and her followers battled vampires and werewolves with as much fervor as their male counterparts in the Society, yet regrettably the Church frequently overlooked them. After Jeanne's death, she was unofficially canonized — although the Church did not recognize her sainthood, the sisters simply started referring to her as "Our Saint." In the 15th century, during its formal organization, the Society approached the Order about working in unison. The offer was accepted, and thus all members of the Order are honorary members of the Inquisition.

Today, this female collective of vampire hunters is passionate, vicious in battle and entirely inspired by God. The Order is nearly autonomous, recognizing the authority of the Society but maintaining its own internal hierarchy. Members of this Order often hold membership in a Society cenacle, but they never rise to high rank, as their loyalties ultimately lie with their Order's own Abbess. They have recently been approached again by the Society, with a view to incorporation, but they have refused for unstated reasons. The Order of Saint Joan does not recruit; rather it waits for some sign to indicate a potential new member. Young women who experience divine visions, or who take up the crusade on their own, are often approached for membership; some few even discover the existence of the Order on their own and are asked to join. A large number of members have strong True Faith, and the Order considers acts of Faith signs of potential sisters.

Saint Joan devotees usually have some level of *Melee* Ability, as they often take the fight directly to vampires and their ilk. The Ability of *Performance* is also encouraged; the Order persuades its members to undertake dance, gymnastics and other activities that serve both as physical conditioning and as artistic expression in order to temper their zeal.

UNOFFICIAL SECTS

Within the Society exist several smaller sects that are separated more by their ideological differences than by any particular task within it. These sects are not officially recognized by the Society, but they espouse different means of undertaking the Society's mission. Many Inquisitors, even while not claiming membership in any given sect, remain sympathetic to the views of one sect or another.

The Brethren of Albertus

Albertus Magnus believed that magic is evil, a tool of the Devil, but that one must learn it in order to combat it best. The Albertines study and practice *Theurgy* (magic stemming from the Divine) and are required to register with the Office of the Censor. While the Society certainly recognizes the efficacy of the Brethren's methodology, they remain under a constant cloud of suspicion due to their use of magic.

Albertines typically study the *Occult* and *Theology* Abilities in order to develop their mystic skills. A few Albertines have some *Lore* knowledge as a result of their constant scrutiny of the supernatural world.

The Children of Lazarus

The largest sect within the Inquisition posits that the greatest sin possible is to violate the sanctity of Christ's miracles—notably the return from death. Therefore all creatures that claim to have done so, such as vampires, are their primary targets. Mages, they reason, will die anyway, as will werewolves, yet the undead will remain until the Parousia unless granted Final Death.

The Children usually improve their *Melee* skills, so as to combat vampires with swords, stakes, torches and other such weapons that are more effective than simple bullets against the undead. Some few Children have *Vampire Lore* as a result of their constant battle.

The Fathers of the Good Death

This assembly of fully ordained priests believes that vampires are essentially evil spirits from the time prior to the Flood who have taken possession of the bodies of the innocent to bring about the moral decay of society. It is the duty of the Fathers to track down and destroy these spirits, restoring the balance of nature. They combine the spread of faith with exorcism and witch-hunting in order to defend the innocent. While their tenets may be inaccurate, leading to limited success in their missions, their zeal is unquestioned.

Fathers of the Good Death often study the *Occult*, notably *Spirit Lore*, in order to discover further information about their enemies. *History*, typically ancient biblical studies, is another common Ability.

The Sanbenito

Depending to whom you speak, this group does not exist or is a poison in the heart of the Inquisition. Certainly membership in this sect is grounds for being declared anathema by the Society. The Sanbenito are those who follow the beliefs of the Florentine Heresy and thus are often referred to as Florentines. They believe that supernatural creatures can be redeemed in the eyes of the Lord, their souls saved, and that they should be helped rather than destroyed. Because of the extreme sanctions espoused by the Office of the Censors, members of this (very) loose sect are naturally clandestine and may not even know that a fellow member *is* a member.

Due to the necessity for secrecy, Florentines are often skilled in *Subterfuge*, both to convince others (fellow Inquisitors or the creatures they seek to help) of the rightness of their cause or to conceal their activities from discovery by the Inquisition. They also have considerable use of the *Occult* Ability, so they may better counter the Devil's arguments with their own.

The Order of Saint Peter

Saint Peter defeated Simon Magus in Rome many centuries ago. Members of this order therefore target mages, warlocks, witches and all other mortals who utilize the gifts of the Devil. They make no distinction between sorcery, true magic, psychic phenomena or any other such Numina: they all result from traffic with the Enemy. Naturally, such an attitude places them in constant contention with the Brethren of Albertus and members of this Order who reach the ranks of the Censors seem to take delight in frequent investigations of the Albertines.

Members of the Order use *Investigation* to hunt down witches, recognizing the signs of magic through their *Occult* talents. However most members refuse to study the *Occult* Ability beyond a cursory level (two Traits) as overexposure may corrupt their souls with heretical knowledge. A number of members of this order seem particularly resistant to the magics of the enemy (they may purchase the *Magic Resistance* Merit for one Trait less).

The Sisterhood of Saint Claire

A sect of poverty-sworn healers founded in the 13th century, these Inquisitors excel at accelerating the healing process. Many are trained in contemporary medicine as well as archaic chirurgery. Beyond what the Society provides them to prepare for missions, they refuse all personal possessions and material comforts.

Members of this sect commonly possess True Faith, and many study the divine healing arts of *Theurgy*. Obviously, the *Medicine* Ability is common among the Sisterhood.

The Sons of Tertullian

In many ways a throwback to the earlier days of the Inquisition, the Sons believe that anyone who speaks against the Word of God must be possessed, and therefore they have a more strident concern for orthodoxy. They pursue wraiths and other possessing entities with the same ardor that the Children of Lazarus pursue vampires. To the Sons, Faith is a natural state, and other in the intercession of misguiding spirits can cause humans to exhibit disbelief. Many of the Sons have willingly accepted the directive to allow torture in their investigations, as many of them have used it for years anyway when dealing with individuals they believe to be possessed. Regardless, they tend to be excellent exorcists.

Sons of Tertullian use the *Investigation* Ability to track down ghostly occurrences and may even develop a modicum of *Wraith Lore* through the course of their career.

The Sect of Saint James

This subsect of the Sons of Tertullian combats wraiths on their own turf – that of the Shadowlands. Each member of this cult eventually commits a religious suicide with a weapon of his own fashioning and construction, in order to transport himself across the Shroud. Each suicide then attempts to destroy as many wraiths as possible before he is himself destroyed.

Of course, the extreme views of this subsect, combined with the natural attrition rate, make the sect quite small and well hidden.

Members of the Sect of Saint James garner Abilities similar to those of the Sons of Tertullian, as well as developing their *Melee* Abilities for use across the Shroud. It is common for them to also develop appropriate Abilities in order to forge their ceremonial weapon.

RECENT EVENTS

Ingrid Bauer is a hard-nosed, unpersonable, stubborn, ruthless, untrusting individual with little care for others' opinions of her. A highly effective Inquisitor with at least 14 confirmed vampire stakings, she has been quietly nicknamed "the Original Iron Maiden" for her incredible ruthlessness. In 1998 she was elevated to the position of Inquisitor-General, and since then has forged the Society's modern Inquisition into terrifying fanatical warriors, trained with swords and capable of using torture in their quest. She encourages a more militant stance to the hunt for the Enemy, and has overturned a previous ruling against the use of torture in this pursuit. Previously it was thought that such treatment was a descent to the level of the ones they sought, and was a sin. This abrupt swing of attitude has caused some concern amongst older members who wonder if a right choice was made in leadership, yet few choose to speak out loud against the decision, as arguing a decision of the Inquisitor-General is grounds for extreme sanctions by the Society.

Some censors are beginning to report to their superiors a general sliding of morals amongst the newer recruits of the Society, and in some cases established members, and are concerned as to the seeming lack of care being taken by the rest of the Inquisitors as to their choices of likely candidates. The Provincial of the Office of the Censor has yet to officially comment, but rumors amongst the more senior cenacles suggest that there may be more censors in the field at present than ever before.

The Condotierri have a comparatively high morale, as they have finally begun to see progress in their organization. Often almost treated like grunts by their peers, it is significant to them that Bauer has chosen to bless them with her attention. Their training has increased, they are being sent on more field operations to cenacles to ensure their security, and the chains have been loosened in regards to their options if called to fight for the cause. Senior members of the Condotierri are becoming concerned that their troops are being used more and more for external operations and are losing focus on their primary duty — the security of the Society itself — but find it hard to argue this point with their own superiors.

The Gladius Dei finds itself split to some degree over the moral implications of the use of torture. Primarily this is a personal choice for each warrior, but the fractioning is becoming apparent. At least one blade has been turned against a brother who had become a tool of evil through use of unnecessary cruelty. While the increase in a martial focus to the Society finds approval in their eyes, they were always the best warriors and it was only to be expected that the others would follow in their footsteps.

The rest of the Inquisition hovers, either undecided or decided but silent. For many, there is still the Enemy to hunt, and philosophical practicalities can wait for quieter moments than these. The Inquisition has hunted effectively, predominantly without torture, for centuries and can continue to do so if the cenacle prefers to do so

— there's no mandate that says you *must* use torture, so the option to refrain remains. For the more fervent (and vengeful) the option remains open to surreptitiously goad your prey, the service to God being more important than the risk to one's soul.

THE FLORENTINE DECREE

In the name of the holy and undivided Trinity, Father, Son and Holy Ghost.

This holy council of the Society of Leopold, lawfully assembled in the Holy Ghost, considering the great import of matters to be considered, recognizes that its wrestling is not against flesh and blood, but against the spirits of wickedness in high places. Wherefore, that this pious solicitude of the Society may work according to the Grace of God, it ordains and decrees that the following canons of faith are in accord with the sacred charge of the Society.

Canon I. If any member of the Society forsakes his duties, either through negligence or intent, let him be anathema. While the Society allows for the provision of general failure or error, it still sees the duties of Inquisitor as sacred and binding.

Canon II. If anyone disobeys the decisions of the Inquisitor-General or his Provincial, or his Abbé, or any other member of the Society of just authority, let him be anathema.

Canon III. If anyone disbelieves in the reality of the Prince of Darkness, or that his children walk the earth to torment and harass the faithful, let him be anathema. Such apostasy is contrary to the truths of the Society.

Canon IV. If anyone believes that Salvation is open to the children of the Enemy, or that they are deserving of the mercies of the Church, or the Society, or in any other way an adherent or sympathizer to the Florentine Heresy, let him be anathema. Such apostasy is contrary to the truths of the Society, and counteracts the good that the Society has done on Earth. He shall be branded traditor and will be deserving of the most severe punishments as penalties, without hopes of penance or forgiveness other than by God.

Canon V. If anyone is disloyal to the Society of Leopold, or reveals its secrets to outsiders, or sides with the enemies of the Society, let him be anathema. Such apostasy is contrary to the truths of the Society, and counteracts the good that the Society has done on Earth. He shall be branded traditor and will be deserving of the most severe punishments and penalties, without hopes of penance or forgiveness other than by God.

CLEANING HOUSE

In the mid-1600s, the Society uncovered actions that were deplorable to their code of conduct, in that a member of the Society was actively colluding with the Enemy. Rafaelle Renzi, a Franciscan Inquisitor and Abbé of the Florence Cenaculum, was found guilty of conspiring with supernatural creatures and revealing Society secrets to them. Renzi considered that these creatures were no different from other sinners and acted to try and bring them salvation. Renzi and others of his cenacle were burned for their heresy. The debates that followed the Florentine Heresy (as the episode became known) spurred the drafting of the Florentine Decree—the document that still guides the Inquisition to this day.

Within the past year, presumably to pull the Society back into line, and undoubtedly due to proof of heresy, Bauer has instituted a quick and effective operation rumored to be implemented through the Office of the Censor and the use of the resources of the Brethren of Albertus and select members of the Gladius Dei. Careful investigation and collation of information has resulted in a dramatic purge of externally based spies and influences. Virtually all of the moles that had been planted through the Society by vampires and other supernatural creatures have been in some way neutralized. Many of them are dead. Others have ceased to communicate with their contacts, have left the area or are no longer with the Society. Attempts by some of the infiltrating creatures to discover the fate of their tools or friends have often resulted in their identification and subsequent elimination.

While this drastic maneuver was certainly legitimate within the precedents set by the history of the Society and the Florentine Decree, the social impact on those who have lost what were previously allies and brothers-in-arms is still to be fully felt. More than one crisis of Faith has occurred; several Inquisitors have stepped down from active duty due to the loss of a dear friend, despite the arguments of others that by doing so, the deserters have doubly aided the Enemy and fallen to the weakness that affected the anathema.

Naturally the Office of the Censor has some interest in the ongoing activities of these potential heretics. In the rest of the Society, such departed members are considered anathema.

JURISPRUDENCE

Until the Florentine Decree, the Society didn't have a true legal code. Since the decree a number of transmutations and interpretations have been made to Society law. Apostasy (abandonment of the Faith, the Society or its goals) is still considered to be the greatest crime. This extends to contradicting or impeding any official ruling of the Inquisition. Such criminals are summoned to the Provincial center and a hearing of indeterminate length decides their innocence or their guilt and fate.

Penalties vary, but fall into four distinct categories:

Rebuke: Usually in a private meeting with the Provincial, the criminal is formally admonished and an official decree of punishment is circulated throughout the Society. The Inquisitor's cenacle will probably lose a degree of prestige over such an event.

Discommodation: The guilty is suspended from the Society for a month to a year, depending on their crime. Access to the resources of the Society is forbidden during that time.

Excommunication: Permanent dismissal from the Society. On very rare occasions the hunter may be readmitted, but only after great service to the Society. Excommunicated Inquisitors are often referred to as "anathema" or "under the ban", and rarely receive cordial treatment from their ex-fellows.

Execution: The rarest and most severe level of punishment, delivered through means mundane or bizarre. Let the punishment fit the crime.

Crimes include, but are not limited to:

Impeding an *auto-da-fé*: Discommodation to Excommunication

Disobeying a Provincial: Rebuke

Disobeying the Inquisitor-General: Discommodation (six months) or worse (the current Inquisitor-General is not known for her leniency in such matters).

Treason: The revelation of any of the Society's secrets to outsiders grants automatic Excommunication. The Office of the Censor is likely to retain an interest in the *traditor* (as such people are branded).

High Treason: It is rare, but some have "defected", choosing life among the supernaturals or assisting the Enemy. Such are automatically branded traditor and an *auto-da-fé* is called upon them.

TORTURE

Note: Need we remind you that the actual use of torture in a game is a Bad Thing? This isn't the sort of game where hurting others is fun. Games where torture systems are utilized should be held only in private location, such as someone's home, never in public venues like conventions, hotels or community centers.

The early church disapproved of torture as a way to deal with heresy (or anything else), but that did little to stem its use as part of standard Inquisitorial procedure. For many centuries the Society abjured the use of torture in its fight. Undoubtedly some Inquisitors did covertly use torture, but kept a low profile. Inquisitor-General Bauer has opened the flood-gates with her recent proclamation espousing the use of torture as a valid practice in the fight against the Enemy, and fervent, yet surreptitious, debate continues at all levels of the Society as to whether torture will save or damn them all.

The basic purpose of torture is to inflict pain and suffering on the subject until such time as their spirit and resolve is broken. Inflicting the pain is a means to an end, not the end itself…. in most cases.

TORTURE AND THE SUPERNATURAL

The Society has, for many years, faced down adversaries with incredible resilience in the face of physical damage, yet for all the vaunted restorative abilities of vampires and werewolves they still remain subject to the methods and devices of a skilled torturer. While some creatures are more resistant to pain, there are other methods of coercing a victim into submission or confession. Much of the lore held by the Society in regards to the physiology and behavioral triggers of such creatures owes no small credit to the use of coercive procedures, however concealed those origins may have been.

Vampires can be reduced to gibbering wrecks through the careful and methodical application of damage and pain whilst being kept at a near-hunger level. The risks of the vampire entering Frenzy are mollified to some degree by the intelligent torturer ensuring his victim is well bound and weakened due to lack of blood. Minimal levels of blood may be supplied — a dead cat becomes a welcome feast to the Beast, no matter how mangy — but granting too much may place the Inquisitor at serious risk.

Werewolves are equally problematic, due to their incredible innate resistance to damage and rapid healing powers. Simple silver shackles do much to reduce that risk — a homid rapidly changing to Crinos will likely find his hands and wrists amputated.

Ultimately, experiments with various silver-chased implements of torture have proven efficacious in many cases. While the various other Changing Breeds have had considerably less contact with the Inquisition, it is not impossible that a rare Inquisitor may be familiar with their particular weaknesses through study, time and practical application and experimentation.

Torturing a wraith certainly poses a challenge, but may be possible through the direct threat to any of the wraith's Fetters — indirect manipulation of the emotions of the wraith may give cause to weaken its resolve and give rise to the Shadow of the wraith. Destruction of a Fetter naturally distresses a wraith (the Harrowing that may follow can strengthen its dark side, probably eventually affirming the Inquisitor's suspicions of it being an evil spirit) but does not directly "physically" harm it per se. The application of certain aspects of *Theurgy*, however, allows more direct manipulation of the wraith and may be used to damage its Corpus. Emotional torture is more likely to work on a wraith than physical.

Changelings, mages, etc, are more or less as vulnerable as normal mortals. They may have access to powers that bolster their resistance to pain, but it is very hard to manifest those powers when bound to a rack or hung from barbed chains. Those who are familiar with ancient folk lore, who have a reliable information source, who themselves have *Lore: Changeling* at three or more levels or are diversely experimental may find that the fae are affected negatively by cold iron, but it is unlikely that people uneducated in such matters would have the material ready-to-hand.

SYSTEMS

Anything above simplistic applications of torture (arm-twisting, flogging, amputation) requires skill in the *Torture* Ability. While rough and ready methods may have some effect on the attitudes of the victim, the careful and skilled application of a variety of methods over a period of time is required to truly break the will of the unfortunate.

Prisoners bound to a torture device, or restrained for torture are generally considered to receive automatic damage whenever the torturer so desires, without the need for challenges. The only variable factor is how much damage the creature receives in any given application of the device. Some devices deliver damage over a gradual period, others deliver instantly. Typically a torture device will deliver anywhere from one level of bashing damage to three levels of lethal damage per application, depending on the nature of the device and its normal effect on the body. While certain applications of torture may cause aggravated damage, or higher levels of lethal damage, the idea here is not to kill the subject, but to break their will over time. A dead prisoner tells no secrets.

While under duress, the subject is also usually subjected to humiliation and psychological torture. The emotional aspect of torture can be far more devastating than the physical pain. Prisoners being tortured are usually also being interrogated for secrets and information. For each period of damage-causing or emotionally effective torture, the torturer may make a Mental Challenge against the victim's Willpower Traits (which are risked and lost as Attribute Traits would be in a similar case), which can be retested with the *Torture* Ability. The victim may retest by expending Willpower Traits. If the victim loses he will reveal some level of information related to the interrogation. When a prisoner has no Willpower Traits remaining, he will

usually give up, answering any questions even if he has to construct an answer from whole cloth to appease his tormentor.

Humanity	Action
5	Harsh and hurtful language.
4	Threats, minimal violence, smacking someone.
3	More systematic violence: "roughing someone up"
2	Use of torture devices; psychological torture
1	Systematic and detailed physical and psychological torture designed to inflict ultimate pain and suffering over a long time.

HUMANITY, FAITH AND TORTURE

Will someone who has Faith, following the tenets of her religion, ever torture someone? This very much depends on the cultural paradigm in question; torture was a standard feature of medieval jurisprudence, so Inquisitors in a medieval chronicle might not have to make as many *Conscience* checks. However, we are taught today that torture, no matter what the reason, is wrong, so modern Inquisitors who engage in systematic torture should expect their Humanity to drop quickly. Even simple arm-twisting counts as torture, but has nowhere near the impact of using an Iron Maiden on one's Morality, so Conscience checks should be at the Trait levels on the Path of Humanity given in the box below (note: this can include by-standers who let the torture take place). Remember that a character with the True Faith Numina who falls below 5 Humanity loses his Faith rating immediately.

NEW BACKGROUND: CENACULUM

The Society of Leopold is one of the largest formal hunter organizations and overall provides fair resources to its army of warrior-priests. Many Inquisitors choose to operate on their own, but an independent Inquisitor may have to wait some time for sparse resources to be sent her way, and will probably have to emphatically justify any reimbursement of operating expenses, as well as demonstrating results and effectiveness in their role in the war. Others, and the Society's developers, discovered strength in numbers and so bases of operation were founded around the world from which operations against the Enemy could be launched.

Inquisitor characters that wish to belong to an officially mandated Cenaculum must take this Background (exclusive to Inquisitor characters). All characters in the cenacle must take the same rating to belong to the same Cenaculum; this rating determines the overall strength of the Cenaculum and the resources available through the Society. The Storyteller, or the players collectively, should spend some time deciding the details of the sanctuary, based on the following guidelines. A Cenaculum must have at least two resident Inquisitors — independent Inquisitors are referred to as Itinerants.

The *Cenaculum* Background is rated from one to five Traits. All Inquisitors belonging to the same cenacle must maintain the same level of Background in order for the resources to be available to them. If a newly formed group of Inquisitors do have varying levels of this Background, the *Cenaculum* rating is that of the lowest rating of all those Inquisitors.

The growth and development (or decline) of a cenacle should be part of the flow of the story, rather than just due to the eventual purchase of more Traits. With success comes reward, and as it can, the Society will divert resources towards the more effective cenacles. As the strength of belief in the cenacle grows, and the work of God is performed with increasing effectiveness, the Cenaculum gradually becomes holy ground. If the performance of the cenacle is poor, or the Faith of those within is failing, the Storyteller is well within their rights to reduce the rating of the Cenaculum over a period of time as the Society withdraws its support and recalls its resources, and God's support also wanes (refer to *True Faith* regarding the rules for holy ground). These gains and losses in support are typically reflected in the ratings of this Background — as the Inquisitors gain in support through their efforts, the Storyteller may grant permission for additional Traits in this background to be purchased with Experience Traits, and if their failures cause the Society to withdraw support, the Storyteller can arbitrarily strip resources (and Traits) from them.

One Trait: Weak

These Cenacula are either new and have yet to prove themselves, or have been around a while without much effect, or may once have been prominent but has suffered a decline. *Weak* Cenacula have no inherent Faith rating. Other than covering the rent or lease for the low-value property, the Society provides only funds absolutely necessary to equip the Inquisitors for projected upcoming missions.

Two Traits: Marginal

Marginal Cenacula have been around for a while and their prominence is on the rise (or is declining but hasn't hit the bottom yet). Being holy ground, the building has an inherent Faith rating of one Trait. Every member of the Cenaculum has a $500 monthly allowance and basic maintenance of the property is paid for by the Society. One full-time or two part-time retainers are on the property most of the time, although no Society-provided retainer will participate in any *auto-da-fé* or similar hunting activities — purchase the *Retainer* Background if you want useful sidekicks. Minimal security measures like a noisy alarm/lights system and an operational computer (probably a couple of years out of date) round out the trappings. Rental of a car must be justified before the Society will authorize payment.

Three Traits: Average

Being just that — average — these Cenacula get basic respect and treatment from the Society, which isn't bad. Most Cenacula are *Average*. They have a Faith rating of two Traits. Each Inquisitor has a monthly stipend of $1000 and reasonable building needs (forget the Jacuzzi) are covered as required. A full-time administrative retainer is provided, along with part-time domestic help. In addition to the alarm system, a static camera system watches all the major entrances, viewable from a central security desk (which will have to be staffed by the Inquisitors themselves). Each Inquisitor is provided with a cheap personal computer with basic OEM-type software. A standard mid-sized vehicle is provided for the use of the Inquisitors, although they must cover its maintenance. Partial reimbursement is available for trains or planes (economy class, naturally).

Four Traits: Strong

Strong Cenacula tend to have been around a while, through a number of generations of Inquisitors. They have a Faith rating of two Traits. Each Inquisitor receives a $1500 monthly stipend and all justifiable business expenses, including basic

ammunition costs, are covered by the Society. Two full-time and three part-time retainers handle the domestic and clerical chores, and a security guard (who will monitor the property and leave the Inquisitors to deal with anything that arises) is on duty at all times. The Cenaculum is equipped with a complete LAN, a fax machine and stringently logged Internet access. Two standard vehicles (or one of better quality) are available at all times. 50 percent of justifiable travel expenses or auto repairs, when related to Society business, is covered.

Five Traits: Venerable

Venerable Cenacula are rare; they tend to be attached to very old churches, and are typically the homes of Provincials. They have a Faith rating of three Traits. Each Inquisitor has a monthly stipend of $2000 and all business, building and ammunition expenses are covered. 50 percent of unusual weapon costs (such as silver bullets) is receivable with justification. Five full-time retainers (or an equivalent number of part-timers) take care of the needs of the Cenaculum and the Inquisitors who reside within. Security is often overseen by a Condotierri and may include a metal detector or motion sensors. The computer system is bolstered with a scanner and printer, along with a plain-paper fax with its own line. One luxury car and three standard vehicles are provided and maintained at full cost. Reasonable travel expenses are covered in full.

THE ARCANUM

I imagine we can dispense with the usual banalities. I know why you're here. You think you know why I am here. We share certain uncommon interests.

I have been reviewing your prospectus, of course. You have been an Associate for almost three years now, and your work has been quite, quite impressive — other than that little mix-up in Hittite etymology, but that was a very obscure case. It bears no further mention. What is noteworthy is that you informed us of that solecism rather than trying to hide it. Refreshing. You have no idea how rare honesty has become. Or perhaps you do; you are here, after all.

It is for this reason — and for others that you will no doubt discern as time passes — that I have elected to sponsor your induction into the Arcanum. Make no mistake. This is not simply "another fraternal order with an impressive library." Joining the Arcanum represents the beginning of a spiritual journey, and one that you cannot turn back from. You have already begun on this journey, in fact. Otherwise, you would not be here. The difference is that when you have joined the Arcanum, you will no longer be journeying alone.

My apologies. Please make that "if you join." The choice is yours. Remember, though, if you are uninterested now, it is unlikely that the opportunity will arise again. Choose wisely. I hope to hear from you within the fortnight.

A BRIEF – AND MOSTLY FACTUAL – HISTORY

I am glad to see you again. I would have been surprised if you had turned down my invitation, but, to the best of my knowledge, people still exercise free will, and do so in the most baffling ways. Nevertheless, it is good to see you here. Let us begin with tonight's lesson.

When people speak of the beginning of the Arcanum, they commonly refer to the initial gathering, instigated by Benjamen Holmscroft on 21 November, 1885, or perhaps the first ritual, held on Christmas of that same year. As is the case with most of history, and as invariably is the case with occult history, this is an egregious simplification. 1885 is at best a focal point where the mysteries of the past become transfigured into new mysteries for the present.

That said, towards the end of 1885, Benjamen Holmscroft convened an assembly of disenchanted scholars of the occult at his 'family estate' in London for the proposed purpose of forming an organization for seeking and studying arcane knowledge. Many of these invitees were disaffected members of the Hermetic Order of the Rising Day, whose dabblings into ritual magic they saw as more licentious than enlightened. These students spent many days and nights debating the form and function of such an undertaking. In the end, guided by Holmscroft, they settled upon the model of a fraternal order. They even accepted Holmscroft's suggested name: The Arcanum.

Of the original invitees, eight elected to join the Arcanum. Most, like Holmscroft, were British. In addition to Holmscroft himself, the members included Jebediah Brown — an Anglican clergyman interested in the legends of the vampires — Roger Corwin — a collector of lore concerning lycanthropy — Peter Harker, Stewart Heath, Jonathan Kelvin — an American (Boston) student of thanatology and the spiritual sciences — Massimo Linarelli of Rome, Liam McPhee, — a Dubliner poet intrigued by the fae — and, Winthrop Murray — a renowned Egyptologist.

Holmscroft chose 25 December for the premiere ritual of the Arcanum, both an initiation of the founding members and a dedication of the entire venture. All the members, save Brown, attended, and were quite impressed by the character and depth of the ritual. When asked, Holmscroft stated that the rituals had descended from the Eleusinian and Orphean Mysteries and from the Cults of Isis and Osiris. Despite his candor and the power of the rituals, I can assure you that a few of the members were more than a little skeptical. After all, those rituals were entirely oral — no written version was ever allowed — and those cults have not existed for millennia.

Most of the initial members elected to take up residence in the Foundation House, Holmscroft's estate, though McPhee and Kelvin opted to return to their native lands. Additionally, Brown claimed not to like the atmosphere of the house, attributing to it "too much witchery." Those who could, contributed sizably to trust funds, providing the monetary foundation for the order's activities.

Over the next year, the reputation of the Arcanum continued to grow, and by the anniversary, the membership had more than quintupled. At the same time, Holmscroft relinquished some of the more mundane aspects of leadership to others, though he still kept a hand in matters pertaining to membership — and, naturally, still acted as a spiritual leader (in the metaphorical, as well as literal sense, in this case).

The next two decades or so saw the Arcanum's slow expansion, with Chapter Houses opening originally in Boston and later in Paris, Berlin, Prague, Budapest, Dublin and St. Petersburg. Keep in mind that these were seen as the centers of learning and civilization. While people might have dabbled with Orientalism (mostly in areas already under British control), nobody took the Middle East or Asia seriously as a center of learning. And, naturally, the only civilization in Africa that was worth even the remotest scrutiny was Egypt, and that had died millennia ago. In retrospect, it is interesting that the Arcanum was in some ways hidebound to the Victorian mindset,

yet in others was remarkably progressive. In a move that was viewed as a tad ludicrous, Holscroft allowed women to be initiated into the Arcanum, eventually granting them full privileges, even. Quite unheard of back then.

Even as the Arcanum grew, there were minor setbacks and tribulations. Three of the founding members died in the 1890s, two of natural causes, the third, mysteriously, his body found in a London alley. The Society of Leopold — the Vatican's occult warriors — attempted to infiltrate the group on at least one recorded occasion. Holmscroft managed to detect and foil that attempt, though no one is certain how he knew. Perhaps the most disturbing development of this period was the loss of the clergyman, Jebediah Brown. He had never been that active in the society, and in early 1888, he abandoned his residences suddenly and without explanation, warning, or any indication of where he was going. In fact, the Arcanum only found out about his departure a week after the fact. One of Kelvin's agents claimed to have spotted him in New York in July of that year, but in turn disappeared himself. At the time, it was quite disturbing, of course. It doesn't do to have a founding member behaving so mysteriously. Still, this was a rather optimistic and enthusiastic time for the Arcanum. With some of the greatest occult mind brought together, the shadow of ignorance could not help but part. Unfortunately, the twentieth century was not so charitable.

BEFORE THE BEGINNING

As noted, the birth of the Arcanum is commonly ascribed to the year 1885. However, many of the founders were members of the Hermetic Order of the Rising Day (as well as other Orders of the era) before that. Many of these Orders traced their learning to the Rosicrucians, who came in several different varieties, and thence to the Knights Templar, the Mystery Cults, and beyond. Many of these claims are, no doubt, spurious, but are they all? In the modern world, when ghosts from the past are so prone to returning to haunt the present, the true origin of the Arcanum may become more important than its members yet realize.

In 1910, one of the Journeymen at the Boston Chapter House — a Robert Brooks — opted to perform local research in search of support for certain of his beliefs. He was convinced that the witch trials of New England (as well as the original England) were based not so much on superstition as in reaction to the practice of actual witchcraft among some portion of the townspeople, and that there was much of this witchcraft still being practiced. Towards summer, he achieved contact with a society that claimed to be in communion with a dark deity, whom they addressed as Hecate, and who was neither Satan nor some other demonic being. In addition to the usual mutterings of blood sacrifices, was the range of supernatural powers attributed to this entity, including the ability to merge with the earth. In a typically enthusiastic fashion, he actually joined this cult in order to learn the truth; he went incommunicado in an attempt to disguise his association with the Arcanum. All was quiet — the rest of the Boston Chapter House Journeymen continued their own studies — until 15 July, when Brooks returned.

He had been successful in his attempts to join the cult. Its members called themselves the Children of Hecate and claimed to worship the great goddess of magic incarnate. They met weekly, and Brooks determined to attend four of their meetings. If they demonstrated no thaumaturgical marvels by then, he would contrive to leave the group. Though the first two meetings were quite banal, consisting of little more than ritualized debauchery in the guise of sex magic. On the third night, as he was forcing himself through the carnal rituals, an ebon-skinned woman of incomparable beauty erupted from the ground beneath him. The remainder of the group broke from their orgy to chant while the dark woman from the ground, Hecate, for wont of another name, joined Brooks and his consort. Alas, Brother Robert was too distracted to note much about the chant other than its being bastardized Greek, and that the name Hecate was repeated throughout. After this interruption, the orgy began anew with the entity moving throughout, joining the debauchery at will. She possessed the strength to lift even the most stout of the cultists. More disturbingly, he realized that her passionate bites were drawing blood, that she was suckling of this blood and that the cultists were deriving ecstatic rapture from this, begging to be chosen next. He fled — back to the Chapter House.

In our security-conscious age, it may seem absurd, but that night, when Kelvin learned of this — and when he learned that another Journeyman performing astronomical observations on the roof had seen intruders on the ground — simply thought that he might have to consider security for the chapter house in the future. It was too late. The Chapter House, and its library, were destroyed in a fire the next night. Some 600 texts are estimated to have been lost in the fire as well as three lives. Though it has yet to be publicly proven, most Journeymen believe that the Children of Hecate were behind this atrocity, probably following Brooks back as he fled.

The Boston Chapter House was to be rebuilt, and we opened Houses in Washington D.C. and San Francisco. Kelvin never fully recovered emotionally, he quit to the Washington Chapter House. In fact, the American Chapter Houses were granted autonomy from the Foundation House, with the Washington House preeminent among them. More to the point, the Boston Fire, as it is still called, served notice that there were forces in the world that did not embrace our curiosity. We knew that we would have to be more careful in the future. Additionally, the Executive Council decided that every Chapter House should have a member take the position of Warden to oversee the house' security.

That year (still 1910), after the opening of the new American Chapter Houses, Holmscroft retired as Grand Chancellor, and in 1914, he died. Or at least that is the official story. The Arcanum is a house of mysteries, and there are always those who, perhaps rightly, question events like that.

The Great War proved to be a bit of a vexation. Chapters of the Arcanum existed on both sides of the conflict, specifically, the Prague, Berlin and Vienna Houses fell within the region aligned with Kaiser Wilhelm. And while professionalism generally kept political concerns outside correspondence and operations, we were only human, and nationalism was still present. Of course, the war also interrupted out field research. Still, this was not as bad as the loss of the St. Petersburg House during the Communist Revolution in 1917. The Soviets seized the House. Only a handful of Journeymen managed to escape carrying what texts and records they could. The rest died trying. Even after the breakup of the USSR, we have not been able to determine how much was confiscated by the Soviets and how much was simply lost.

The condition of the Arcanum deteriorated even further with the Second World War. Though the Arcanum as a whole behaved rather circumspectly, and had even managed to infiltrate the *Thule Gesellschaft* — Hitler's famed nationalist mystical society — a few of the Journeymen in the Berlin Chapter House were National Socialists. They revealed our presence to the Nazis and the entire House fell under their purview. Loyal Journeymen fled, taking what they could, but without enough warning, a trove of occult scholarship was perforce left behind. As soon as word leaked forth from Germany, it was disseminated to the Prague and Vienna Chapter Houses. Books, research, *objets d'occult*, anything of value was extracted and hidden in safe houses or other concealed locales. It became a depressingly recurrent motif when we needed to secure the Paris Chapter House' treasures from the encroaching Germans. Fortuitously, the latter three Houses survived the war. A little worse for wear, they were, but far better than the Berlin House, which had been subverted, and was finally destroyed towards the end of the war. With the post-war tensions as they were — and with some seeing the Berlin Chapter as under a shroud of ill omen — it was decided not to rebuild.

An intriguing side effect of the Second World War was the collaboration of some of our Journeymen with the intelligence communities of the time. It seems that the investigative skills we hone (to say nothing of fluency in a wide array of languages and a familiarity with a number of different ciphers, both ancient and modern) are of some use. Though only a few of us took this path — the majority simply tried to continue their true vocation — the consequences of these relationships still resurface from time to time. The spy industry is notoriously difficult to extricate oneself from, after all.

Nevertheless, with the rise of the cold war, it became apparent that it was beneficial to possess a bit more facility at skullduggery. Prague lay on the other side of the Iron Curtain, and the growing global awareness made us turn our eyes towards lands beyond Europe and North America. It was at this time that the notion of Arcanum Colonies, small enclaves of Arcanum members working together, arose. Though we had long had an unofficial presence in places such as Hong Kong, Istanbul and Rome, we had not had the resources (or in some cases had not considered the regions safe enough) to establish Chapter Houses. The notion of the Colony brought some more flexibility to the Arcanum — and, to be honest, made a longstanding practice a tad more structured. Over the years, we have placed Colonies across the globe, in Africa, the Far East, South America, and even some stranger locales. Some Colonies have proved to be productive enough to be converted to full Chapter Houses. Others have fallen by the side or been abandoned for security reasons.

At present, the Arcanum counts some 300 Journeymen and women among its ranks with another 200 Associates. We have weathered the turning of the millennium (several different times as different calendars would have it), and we follow the same path originally located by Holmscroft and his co-founders, using his same rituals. The future beckons. Truth beckons. Can we do less than proceed?

THE RAISON D'ÊTRE

So why does the Arcanum study the Occult? Why not follow the route of conventional science or philosophy or psychology? Well, in time we will need to reduce that question to "Why do the Arcanum's three-hundred-odd Journeymen study the occult?" I am not so naïve as to believe that all members of the Arcanum are here seeking the same Eidolon — and if I thought you were that naïve, I would not have sponsored you. Nevertheless, before we tread that path, we should look at the philosophy of the Arcanum as a whole, since it prefigures the character of those we admit to become Journeymen.

Holmscroft and the remainder of the founders were dissatisfied with the character and verisimilitude of mystical studies in their time. They questioned the integrity of the self-proclaimed hierophants and the quality of the learning they espoused. In short, they were looking for a truth they did not find elsewhere. Why choose the esoteric realms for their study? Because the truth that could be found in science or the preeminent philosophies were inadequate for their needs. Though I am certain that the founders differed in their ideas and ideals — documents and records from that time certainly suggest that they did — they agreed that by pooling their knowledge, their experience, their resources, they would achieve a synergistic effect. Their understanding could be multiplied between them while their ignorance would be divided. But the question still remains: "Why bother?"

Early in our correspondences, I alluded to a spiritual journey. Though it is not so common a sentiment in these post-modern times, I would propose that the true reason behind the working of the Arcanum is a search for ultimate truth and personal perfection. Now, I am not proposing that we have achieved, nor come anywhere near achieving it, but it is a damn sight more satisfying than studying all this so you can curse that fellow who stood you up last week. Even the name of this order — the Arcanum — is a direct reference to the great Secret lying behind all magic, all alchemy, everything. Our mission is no less than to find that secret.

SYLLABUS

When the Arcanum was formed, the founders created a program for carrying out this mission. They called it the Syllabus. It has been revised a few times in keeping with the state of the world, and is always on the verge of being revised again. Still, the Syllabus has remained remarkably consistent, either as a tribute to the vision of Holmscroft *et alia* or as a commentary on how little we have progressed since then. The most recent revision of the Syllabus was in 1978, and bears the earmarks of that particular era of occultism. To date, no one has proposed a new revision which satisfies enough to replace the '78 revision, though.

Needless to say we do not all agree with each and every sentence of the Syllabus. The mainstream Arcanum Journeyman, if you will pardon the oxymoron, seems to hew pretty closely to it, but there are a number of other pseudo-political factions out there adding to the complexity of it all. In general, these factions are not that popular with the Executive Committee, or anyone else, for that matter, but they do make themselves heard with aggravating regularity. There are others, of course, but this trio is the most prominent.

Progressivists: The progressivists are one of the more populous factions, probably because they encapsulate the current zeitgeist fairly well. Progressivists seek to cast away the traditional trappings — "Victorian Bullshit," I believe they call it — in favor of a more contemporary, egalitarian system. While the Executive Committee has, on occasion issued some questionable decrees, cancelled some seemingly promising research programs, it is good to keep in mind that the Arcanum exists to look for the truth, not the fashionable.

41

THE SYLLABUS – 1978 REVISION

1. The Arcanum is an organization dedicated to the pursuit of knowledge for its own sake. We, the members of the Arcanum, seek our own enlightenment and the enlightenment of our Brothers and Sisters, and ultimately wish to aid in the enlightenment of all humanity.

2. The Arcanum posits that there exists another world, one in which the supernatural and mythological teachings of the Ancients bear truth. We believe that this world conjoins with our own, and that it is our duty to understand its secrets. We shall seek this knowledge in the places of mystery, through the pages of history, and in the lore of all peoples. As the Ancients understood, so, one day, shall we.

3. The Arcanum believes that only through scholarship and learning can one separate fact from fiction, and can mere superstition be shorn from the supernatural truth. Myths and folklore speak of higher truths, and it is through diligent study and investigation that these higher truths may be revealed.

4. The Arcanum exists to learn, not to manipulate. We are objective observers, and not judges. The Arcanum does not evaluate the "morality" of the supernatural simply in light of the fact of its existence, nor does it take action against the supernatural based upon any predetermined system of ethics.

5. What the Arcanum studies and learns, it does so for its own benefit. The resources of the Arcanum are not to be shared with anyone outside the Arcanum, nor shall the precious knowledge earned by our studies be spread without the consent of the Executive Committee. When it is time, we shall teach others; for now, it is our duty to safeguard this knowledge, to protect it from a humanity that is not yet ready to use it.

Seekers: Each seeker is out searching for his Holy Grail, Philosopher Stone, or whatever key to enlightenment he has fixated upon. Seekers take the 'personal perfection' and 'spiritual path' of the Arcanum as something like a religious quest. They are a bit extreme, and a bit over-focussed, but one cannot help but admire their zeal (as long as one is not trapped on a trans-oceanic flight with no escape from their monologue, that is).

Templars: The Templars are our militants. They take exception to the fourth point of the Syllabus. Specifically, they feel that there are certain supernatural forces or entities out there that *are* evil, and that it is hypocrisy for us to claim to be working towards the enlightenment of humanity while allowing these beings to exist. Honestly, they may have a point, but for some reason, they choose to conceal themselves behind anonymity. This has made no few speculate that there is some other faction behind them, or that they have some agenda beyond what they claim. To be frank, we really do not need the additional paranoia this engenders. Incidentally, they have never laid claim to any kinship with the religious order of the Crusades.

In time, you will almost certainly hear rumors of the White Monks — the secret masters who guide the Arcanum, either towards enlightenment or for their own secret agenda. As I stated, we do not need any additional paranoia. The White Monks do not exist. Save your curiosity for the myriad real mysteries that are out there.

CHAPTER AND VERSE

The Arcanum is modeled after the fraternal orders of the Victorian era. However, in keeping with its philosophy of favoring learning and growth over self-aggrandizement, it has managed to dispense with the proliferation of fanciful titles. In fact, the majority of the members fall under the same title. While matters are never as simple as one might desire, the Arcanum has managed to keep the number down to a handful of grades and a few administrative positions. Most members are simply too enmeshed in their studies to waste time on such nonsense.

HIERARCHY

While there is only a handful of titles, the Arcanum is large enough that it requires a bit of more variation in the distribution of work. For the most part, this centers around the disbursement of funds for research and upkeep and the approval of neophytes. This may not sound like much, but it means that they get to decide which Chapter Houses — or prospective Chapter Houses — get the money, and can cut off funding to investigations which they feel are "not suitably profitable." Now, before you get the picture that these are our own private Bilderberg Society, remember that they were all neophytes like you are once, and that they must have some wisdom, after all, they decided you were worthy. Anyhow, I am speaking of the Grand Chancellor and the Executive Committee. You have heard these titles before; now you know what they do. Additionally, each Chapter House has a Chancellor who performs the same functions on a local level, as well as the aforementioned Warder who sees to security.

THE INITIATION

Any person who experiences the Arcanum's initiation rites experiences firsthand the values of the Arcanum. Drawn from ancient Mysteries and Egyptian Cults — according to Holmscroft — the initiation rite reifies the aspirant's search for knowledge and the truth. Though the Neophytes have been taught and lectured, they are never told what to expect from the rite. In the initiation, the naked aspirant experiences a symbol-laden landscape: a trek through the labyrinth and a leap of faith from which only the Owl (symbol of both knowledge and the Arcanum) saves her, albeit painfully. Thereafter, she awakens sealed in a coffin, from which she is freed by the robed Brothers and Sisters of the Arcanum to find that she is on an island in a cavern. They have died and been reborn. The final stage of the initiation calls for the neophytes to cleanse themselves in the waters and be brought into the Arcanum. Significantly, there is no mention of any specific god or gods in this and all other Arcanum rites, only references to "The Creator."

Though most initiates suspect that the early portion of the initiation rite is accomplished through drugging or post-hypnotic suggestion, the effect of the ritual is quite powerful and its memory lasts a lifetime.

There are a number of other titles, but they vary from time to time. We have had Managing Editors, Head Librarians, Deans of our many Colleges, and a plethora of appellations that would sound rather appropriate in a fantastical renaissance

convocation. For the most part, these positions are created through a combination of personal aptitude and communally acknowledged need, and ratified by the Executive Committee. Perhaps one day you will hold one of these titles; perhaps you will never feel the need. We all have our own paths.

TITLES

However, even is we follow different paths, our journeys share certain stages. It is these stages that have given names to the different grades of membership within the Arcanum.

The Associate is not a full member of the Arcanum. Associate Members are often junior researchers or what have you who wish to work with the Arcanum, while remaining unfettered by its regulations. For many, but by no means all, being an Associate is a precursor to a fuller role. Associates do not receive full privileges: They are not allowed full access to the Arcanum's libraries; they do not receive any special teaching; they may not hold office; etc.

Neophytes are those who have elected to partake of the journey — to become full members of the Arcanum. As such, Neophytes are treated as people in search of enlightenment, not just knowledge. Neophytes are always assigned a mentor to guide them on this journey. They have access to the learning and resources of the Arcanum, but at the discretion of this Elder Brother only. Similarly, regardless of their true age, they are viewed as something akin to children, and until they have been initiated, are rarely given full consideration. It is sometimes disagreeable, but in order truly to learn, one must first realize that one is ignorant.

Once a Neophyte has been tested and initiated, he becomes a Journeyman — or she becomes a Journeywoman. Political correctness is making inroads even into the Arcanum. Journeymen are full members of the Arcanum, with the rights and privileges, and the obligations, thereof. Journeymen may address each other as Brother (or Sister, as the case may be). All full members of the Arcanum are Journeymen, from the freshest ex-Neophyte to the Grand Chancellor. That bears remembering.

Members who prove themselves to be of good temperament and providers of sound advice on many different topics come to be known as Elder Brothers and Sisters. It really has less to do with age than an inner wisdom, but that is the title we use.

COLLEGES

Much as Universities have different courses of study for students of differing interests, the Arcanum has instituted what we call Colleges to aid in the collaboration of members who share a common interest. Though the official term is College, each College chooses its own name, which does not necessarily have to include the word "College." While you may find yourself in a Colony, or whatever, with a couple of other Journeymen, odds are that your skills and interests will be more complementary than overlapping. Colleges serve to bring together enthusiasts in a certain field regardless of where their home base is. Thus, if you have a penchant for cryptozoology, you could be a member of the School of Cryptozoology and share your thoughts with like-minded Journeymen across the continents.

A college must have a minimum of six members, and any Journeyman can form one, provided he has the support of five peers. Each College is chaired by a Dean who takes care of administrative concerns, arranges meetings, chat-rooms, etc. The Deans meet quarterly for a Senate in which they update each other on their discoveries and the directions of their research. The Senate also meets with the Executive Committee to provide input to the budgetary disbursement program. Some of the more established Colleges even have their own stipends. There is nothing that says that you must belong to a College, but it does help with the funding.

Colleges come and go, but the following have stood the test of time: the Colleges of Thaumatology, Egyptology, Parapsychology, Shamanic Studies, Lycanthropic Studies, the Division of Extra-Terrestrial Studies, the Hermetic Studies Programme, and the School of Mythoarchaeology. I believe the College of Chant-o-Matics, back in the 1970s has the record for the shortest duration, and I am not entirely certain that it was not, in fact, a hoax all along.

Lodge: "Lodge" is not an individual title, so much as a collective noun. For reasons of safety — and to provide corroborating witnesses, in the case of some of the more likely developments — members of the Arcanum do not typically operate alone in field conditions. Chapter Houses usually consist of two or three Lodges, and most Colonies are little more than where a Lodge has established a safe house for the nonce.

Lodges rarely consist of Journeymen with the same specialized interests. This is done for two reasons: to maximize resources, and to provide a diverse set of skills at any given site. While the benefits of diversification may be self-evident, many Neophytes wonder why we don't send, for example, all our expert parapsychologists to thoroughly investigate a particular haunting and then move on to the next. Well, in matters such as these, it is rare for the experts to agree on which event is the most pressing. So each goes his own way. Since they invariably collaborate through their college, this means that they will review each other's research in time, and the Arcanum's repository of knowledge will be enlarged by understanding of two matters rather than one. On a grimmer note, we also do this so that, should something go horribly wrong, all of our experts in a certain field are not at risk at the same time, as almost happened to the entire College of Thaumatology back in Tehran.

Lodges are cooperative ventures, and while this ought not be on a strictly *quid pro quo* basis, as your lodge-sister helps you, e.g., uncover the esoterica of *feng shui*, it is only fitting that you collaborate with her as she delves into the mysteries of lycanthropy.

GEOGRAPHY

In the early years, our studies were shaped by the Victorian perception of the world — mostly concentrated around the British Empire — and those parts which had escaped it. Now, the Arcanum has at last truly become a global organization. I will not pretend that we are without prejudice, but we have diversified our curriculum, and spread ourselves out a good deal in the process.

Foundation House: At the center of the Arcanum lies the Foundation House, Holmscroft's family's London estates, though there are some questions about that, since it was originally called Vannever Estate, and there are no records of its ever belonging to a family named Holmscroft. What is known is that it was constructed by a Sir Thomas Scott around 1605. When he and his gentleman's companion disappeared on a trip to the Holy Land to study the history and languages of the ancients in 1612, it was deeded to a young gentleman named Byron Hartswicke. About Mr. Hartswicke, very little is known other than that he was a recluse and that he eventually left on a 'trip to the Orient.' There are no subsequent records of Vannever Hall until 1879, coincidentally, the same year that Benjamen Holscroft joins the Hermetic Order of the Rising Dawn. Let me assure you, those 250-odd years are a favorite topic of late-night speculation around the House.

Certain titles and positions within the Arcanum carry a degree of respect. If the Storyteller desires, these Status Traits may be incorporated into Arcanum interactions. Arcanum Status Traits almost never have any bearing outside the Arcanum.

Associates receive the Negative Status Trait *Outsider*. This Trait is removed should they join the Arcanum.

Neophytes receive the Negative Status Trait *Inexperienced*. This Trait is removed upon initiation.

Elder Brothers (or Sisters) receive the Status Trait *Distinguished*.

Deans receive the Status Trait *Respected*.

Chancellors receive the Status Trait *Esteemed*.

Members of the Executive Committee receive two additional *Distinguished* Status Traits.

The Grand Chancellor receives two additional *Esteemed* Status Traits.

And at the center of the Foundation House stands the Axis Mundi — its library. The name may seem presumptuous, but the words "Axis Mundi" in many ways epitomize the philosophy of the Arcanum: Knowledge is in fact the axis around which the world turns. In more pragmatic terms, the organization of the Axis Mundi is based on Hermetic ideals rather than the more prosaic Dewey Decimal System or any of its more modern descendents. Beyond confounding Neophytes, as you have probably already learned, this arrangement promotes mystical cognition. As one works with the physical proximity of Magic and Language within the library's geography, one begins to develop similar links in one's subjective terrain. You can learn a good deal by how people organize their libraries, and you can teach much by how you organize yours. Ours speaks many truths on many levels. Naturally, all of the Chapter House libraries, and many of our personal libraries, are organized around the same principles.

The Axis Mundi contains, according to the last estimate, over 80,000 volumes and 15,500 manuscripts. It has an old-style wooden card catalog, which has not been, and never will be, computerized, though there is a librarian on at all hours. Naturally, all personal effects are stored outside, though you are allowed pencil and notepad — or PDA or laptop, as of 1992. I wish you happy hunting.

Chapter House: The various Chapter Houses and their residents now account for most of the Arcanum's Journeymen. As you no doubt remember, each Chapter House is overseen by a Chancellor and has a Warder charged with maintaining its security. Beyond that, the Chapter Houses seem to have each evolved their own organizational model. Every member of the Arcanum is considered attached to the Chapter House closest to his residence for administrative purposes (or the Foundation House, if he is based out of London. It can provide a mail drop, an emergency layover site, high-speed Internet access, or, in some of the larger Chapter Houses, even a small number of residences. Each Chapter House has a library and a librarian, and loans between the various Arcanum libraries are not uncommon. Most Chapter Houses report directly to the Foundation House. For Historical reasons, the Chapter Houses of the United States report to the Washington House, which, in turn, reports to the Foundation House.

The political correctness I mentioned earlier has not breached the Arcanum's traditional geographical nomenclature yet. Chapter Houses are divided into two sectors, with Jerusalem, which was held to be the Holy Land at the creation of the Arcanum, as the dividing line. All Houses to the east of Jerusalem are oriental and all to the west are occidental. I assure you, we have heard the usual declamations against such a Judeo-Christian-oriented system. People have proposed other systems. Thus far, the Executive Committee has firmly chosen to stay with the old nomenclature.

Anyhow, there is a Chapter House in Jerusalem, the sole house that is neither oriental nor occidental.

In the occident, in addition to the Foundation House, there are Houses in Dublin, Vienna, Paris, Prague, Amsterdam, Barcelona, Madrid, Stockholm, and a few other prominent European cities. There is something of a debate over whether the Rome House is a Chapter House or a Colony, since it does not have any official members and is rather secretive, what, with the Society of Leopold in such close proximity. African Chapter Houses exist in Cairo, Kinshasa, and Lagos. We have been trying to expand our presence in Africa, getting away from our old reliance on Mediterranean and European civilizations, but the political climate has made things unfortunately difficult. Across the Atlantic, the Washington House oversees Chapter Houses in San Francisco and Boston. There are also Houses in Ottawa, Vancouver, Mexico City, Lima, and a few other Locales.

The so-called oriental Houses include covert Houses in Baghdad, Riyadh and Tehran, as well as more stable ones in Bombay, Tokyo, Singapore and Hong Kong, Sidney, and a few other cities scattered around.

Colony: In cases where we cannot devote the resources an entire Chapter House, for simple funding reasons, because there is not enough of interest, the area is too dangerous, or whatever reason, a Lodge may elect to create a Colony for the duration of their research. Colonies have no permanent presence, so members could remove themselves with a minimum of fuss should situations require. In certain cases, a Colony is a precursor to an actual Chapter House, in others, it is a temporary base erected to study some ephemeral phenomenon. Obviously, Colonies come and go on an irregular basis, but a registry of Colonies, both active and bygone is kept at the Foundation House.

NAVIGATING THE AXIS MUNDI

Until a character has developed familiarity with the Axis Mundi or any of its subsidiaries, any attempt at research calls for a Static Mental Challenge. Difficulty is 25 for the Foundation House, 15 for one of the Chapter Houses, and 10 for personal libraries, though the Storyteller may adjust these ratings for certain conditions. The *Occult* Trait allows a retest.

PUBLICATIONS AND OTHER RESOURCES

Beginning in 1912, the Arcanum began publishing a journal, the *Annual Proceedings of the Arcanum*. Naturally, nothing less than the highest quality research and writing are accepted. Every submitted article undergoes peer review and resource verification. In addition, per the fifth point of the Syllabus, we review each article to ensure that nothing slips out prematurely, and that our philosophies and methods are not compromised. While we do accept submissions from outside sources — and watch those sources whose work we do publish for potential recruits — we generally favor supporting our own scholarship.

Beyond the APA, we have an imprint, Arcanum Press, which publishes an average of two titles per year, all of the highest quality in scholarship and collation. We are still working on our comprehensive, multi-volume *Encyclopedia of the Occult Sciences*, and probably will be for the life of the Arcanum.

Naturally, we have a presence on the Intranet, both a public web page, and a private extranet with 1024-bit encryption. This network and the actual paper publications are all handled out of London.

While the Arcanum subscribes to very few periodicals — mostly due to spatial constraints — we have often arranged interviews with the authors of articles of interest on behalf of members. Additionally, we have acquired a wide range of professional contacts across the globe whose services have proven invaluable on many occasions. While the Arcanum cannot take care of everything (If it could, it would not need members, would it?), it is an excellent environment for the noblest of all goals: the acquisition of knowledge.

ASPIRANTS AND LUMINARIES

The quest for knowledge attracts certain sorts of people. Though it is easy to expect researchers and scientists who are willing to explore avenues scoffed at by their more conservative brethren, or historians and anthropologists who have developed interests outside the mainstream, the truth is that there is more to the quest for the truth than pure scholarship. After all, one has but to read Aristotle to see where theory without empirical confirmation can lead.

RECRUITMENT

There seem to be two routes that lead to the Arcanum. Some have called them active and passive; others have called them intentional and accidental. I prefer to think of them as direct and indirect.

The direct route to the Arcanum is that of an investigator or some other person who has a demonstrated interest in the paranormal. She may submit an exceptional article to the APA or some other publication that attracts the attention of some Journeyman, or encounter one of our researchers in the field, or ask particularly insightful questions at a seminar. Many of these people have studied magic in one form or another, and some have demonstrable psychic powers. They start out with an understanding of the occult that spans beyond pamphlets you can buy in supermarket checkout lines. When the Arcanum approaches them, there is even a good chance that they will have at least heard of us.

On the other hand, there are those who sort of stumble into the Arcanum. Some are victims of, or participants in, some paranormal incident, who, rather than wallowing in fear and incredulity, rise to the challenge of the unknown. Others possess skills that the Arcanum needs, but have no *a priori* interest in the paranormal. Obviously, we need to exercise a good amount of discretion in our initial dealings with these people, but they are often worth it. It is too easy for so-called occultists to get too enmeshed in their own peculiar paradigm; the inclusion of other with differing backgrounds has helped tame rabid monomania or suggest alternative areas of study on many occasions.

CHARACTER

It is often said you can recognize a member of the Arcanum by looking at his home. If the predominant décor is early bibliomaniac, with more thought given to bookcases than bedding, you might have one of us. This is only a slight exaggeration. Though most of us — most of us — realize that books are a source of knowledge rather than the knowledge itself, we do tend to have impressive libraries. Many of us also have an extensive array of professional contacts in areas related to our interests. If you only read Sanscrit, Tibetan, Tamil, and Bengali, and the manuscript you have unearthed is in Archaic Dravidian, it is good to know someone trustworthy to turn to.

For the most part, we research and quest rather than act — it is part of the Syllabus, after all. Nevertheless, we have learned that the rest of the world is not necessarily so genteel. Therefore, we have a tradition of initiating people whose character we trust, and who can help with the less esoteric, but by no means less vital aspects of our research. Most Chapter Houses have a Journeyman, or at least an Associate, who understands the less, umm, cerebral aspects of leading an expedition or performing covert research. The details vary from House to House; it is rare for someone in the Dublin Chapter House to need assistance in traversing a jungle, for instance. Additionally, this person is not usually the Chapter House warder — the warder needs to dedicate his time to the protection of the House, after all.

Still, such people are the exception rather than the rule. While a few of us have dabbled in fencing or aikido, for we can be a dilettantish lot, we are far more attentive to our intellectual studies. And such studies we have! Though we have long passed the time when every Journeyman spoke both Latin and Greek fluently, most of us are polyglots. Additionally, the average Journeyman possesses a minimum of one doctorate in a conventional subject such as psychology, archaeology, oceanography or particle physics. Many have three or more. But all of this is just the groundwork for our real vocations: Hermetic Alchemical Theory, Yogic Cosmology, Telepathic Linguistics…. The truth is both too complex and too simple to be contained within conventional society's perceptions, and it is our calling, our vocation, our privilege to hunt it down and codify it for human enlightenment.

Perhaps one of our greatest vexations is our knowledge that there are others out there who insist on hoarding the knowledge we so long for. The Society of Leopold, for example, is reputed to have a repository of the greatest learning of the occult in the Western Hemisphere. Sadly, we dare not share with them; their intolerance of the supernatural is well documented. And as we are loath to share with them, they refuse to allow our access to their archives. Even more frustrating, we have heard report that certain of the undead match our scholarship, but bring also their longevity. How glorious their collections must be.

I must apologize for that display of maudlin wistfulness. Those archives are mere rumor. But the knowledge we seek, the truth, *is* out there in the world. And we *will* find it.

THE ARCANUM CHARACTER

There are certain commonalties among most characters who belong to the Arcanum. To wit, unless the character was initiated into the Arcanum for her worldly skills, she probably focuses on Mental Traits; she probably has an extensive collection of knowledge-related Traits, *Occult*, and usually some form of *Academics* or *Hobby/Professional/Expert* Ability; and she stands a good chance of possessing at least some of the Library Background Trait. This exemplar merely covers the stereotypical Arcanum Scholar. Though that stereotype has evolved for a reason, the Arcanum has many different sorts of members and Associates. Other common Traits include Abilities such as *Awareness*, *Crafts*, *Enigmas*, *Investigation*, and *Linguistics*; and Backgrounds like *Allies*, *Contacts*, certain forms of *Influence*, *Mentor*, and *Resources*.

When it comes to special areas of knowledge, it is best to remember that the Arcanum lies outside the many secret cadres that populate the World of Darkness. Though a specialist in vampirism might have good evidence that vampires do, in fact, exist, and might even have some idea of their capabilities and demographics, she is still not a vampire. The Masquerade makes it unlikely that she would learn about Kindred politics in a Camarilla city, and the sheer nature of the Sabbat makes learning such material in Sabbat territory even less likely. For this reason, the Storyteller may want to restrict Arcanum characters' *Expert Ability* Traits to things such as *Vampire Lore* Traits rather than *Kindred Lore*, *Sabbat Lore* or *Gangrel Lore* Traits. This is not to say that such knowledge is necessarily incorrect, merely that it comes from an outsider's perspective.

The Arcanum numbers a few sorcerers and psychics among its ranks. In most cases, the sorcerers are free-form scholars who have managed to glean certain kernels of truth through hours of painstaking study rather than members of sorcerous cabals. Those who do belong to such societies must take great care to manage their oaths and obligations. Since psychics are less likely to form such societies, they are less likely to suffer such conflicting loyalties. True Faith is exceedingly rare within the halls of the Arcanum, for, to most people, such faith precludes the search for knowledge.

THE ARCANE OF THE ARCANUM — THOUGHTS FOR STORYTELLERS

Knowledge — its character and the quest therefor is almost always the central theme to an Arcanum-oriented chronicle. More even than the Masquerade-bound Camarilla, secrets are the driving force behind the Arcanum. This, of course, is because most of the other supernatural inhabitants of the World of Darkness are at least partly in the know. Kindred are trained in the Traditions, Garou are taught about the leaches, Changelings are taught the Escheat at their saining. The mortals of the Arcanum are outsiders to all of these, and must get by through the cautious and hazardous piecing together of what information slips through the walls of silence the active forces of the World of Darkness erect.

Of course, that's what the Arcanum is all about. Telling a story about men and women hunting for truth and knowledge at the cost of everything else would be rather anticlimactic if they were already privy to those truths. Once you get past the obvious, though, there are myriad techniques the Storyteller may employ to enhance and exploit this quest, both from the perspective of the members of the Arcanum and from that of the rest of the World of Darkness' inhabitants.

THE VIEW FROM WITHIN

Arcanum characters search for knowledge. Though it is easy to create a formulaic story for Arcanum characters — spread a rumor of some hidden knowledge, and watch them hunt it down — formulae get tired quickly. So what, beyond offering up a mystery of the week, can the Storyteller do?

THINGS HUMANITY WAS NOT MEANT TO KNOW

The human mind can be a fragile thing. Ignorance — or at least an ability to disregard certain facts — is sometimes necessary to maintain daily functionality.

What happens when a scholar learns some secret so horrible that it shatters her faith in the world? Perhaps she uncovers an ancient Tzimisce exegesis explaining the true purpose of humanity. Perhaps she finds a translated section of the Prophesy of the Phoenix. Perhaps she learns something repugnant about her ancestry.

A good understanding of the character (and often the player as well) is necessary to craft this sort of revelation for maximum effect. The information does not need to be true within the World of Darkness, merely believable to the character, to provide sessions of character development.

BEARING WITNESS

On a related note, there are times when the Arcanum's role as witnesses and not judges can be particularly difficult to maintain. Knowledge does not exist within a vacuum, moral or otherwise.

Many cultic practices are abhorrent to Western ideals of freedom and personal determinism. Few believe vampirism to be a wholesome form of existence. What should an Arcanum scholar do if she noticed that lycanthropes were kidnapping

troubled teenagers? What should she do if she has reason to believe she can predict the next victim? Can she simply observe and record the degradation some vampires seem to inflict upon their mortal companions?

Many events enacted in chronicles could be perceived as evil by outsiders, and the members of the Arcanum are, in many ways, the outsiders of the World of Darkness. It should take a Storyteller little effort to depict whomever else is out there as evil forces to test the non-judgmental role of the local Lodge. The Templar faction may seek sympathetic characters into its fold, drawing the characters into the hidden reaches of Arcanum politics.

THE HUMAN ELEMENT

For all their delving into supernatural matters, the members of the Arcanum are still all too human. They have weaknesses and frailties like enough to keep the action going even when the Statuette of K'daai proves to be a cheap 19th century forgery.

Most members have lives outside the Arcanum, relatives who get ill, significant others who have trouble with their jobs, the whole gamut of human experience. Sometimes, these problems can throw the entire search for knowledge into perspective. Other times, they drive the scholar further into her work.

Unfortunately, the life of a scholar has its own pitfalls — especially manifest in those who have no social life beyond the Arcanum. Rival theories, forged documents, petty politicking and plagiarism all taint the life of a researcher, even those who search for enlightenment can fall prey to self-deception.

MYSTERIES OF THE ARCANUM

As is befitting any organization that delves into the unknown, the Arcanum possesses no shortage of mysteries of its own. Call it symmetry. Chronicles that involve the Arcanum usually derive much of their drama from the quest for knowledge, and there are several different techniques that may be employed towards this end.

The first, and most straightforward, takes the Arcanum at face value: a refuge of curious scholars intent on wresting the truth from the World of Darkness. With the massive corpus of source material already published and a modicum of back-story creation, this perspective can keep players entertained for years as they unearth new secrets, falsified data, forgeries, and who knows what else against the backdrop of the Final Nights.

In this situation, the Storyteller may begin the chronicle, or at least the Arcanum portion, by making its foundation knowledge uncertain from the start — or the Storyteller may start it out on an apparently even keel and subtly pull the rug from under her players' feet.

There are many mysteries about the Arcanum, not the least of which is "Whom does it serve?" Those who are aware of it have hypothesized at various times that it is secretly the front for a Master Magus of the Order of Hermes, some powerful vampire, emissaries from the spirit courts, or some other powerful occult force. There are rumors that a secret group called the White Monks are actually in charge, not the Executive Committee and the Grand Chancellor — and that there is another group, the Red Monks, who work to thwart them. With the powerful forces lurking behind the scenes, it would appear to be inconceivable that it has not fallen under someone's sway yet.... There are other mysteries, of course: Prior to his membership in the Hermetic Order of the Rising Day, there are no records of Benjamen Holmscroft or his family, and no

few have conjectured that he faked his death in 1914, and that he is still around today. Of the rest of the founders, rumor claims that Winthrop Murray at one point managed to recreate the ancient Egyptian formula for immortality. It is also reported that Jebediah Brown has turned to science in his fight against the undead, and yet lives, thanks to the biochemical technology of his company, Crucible Genetics Amalgamated. One of Holmscroft's other invitees did not opt to join the Arcanum:Etienne DuLac founded a competing order called Les Frères de la Rose Croix; it is smaller and far less scrupulous, but no one knows what its true mission is. What happened to Vannever Hall between the seventeenth and nineteenth centuries? What happened to the books plundered from the Berlin and St. Petersburg Chapter Houses? Who was the Hecate that Robert Brooks discovered in Boston, possibly precipitating the burning of that Chapter House? There is no shortage of ready questions surrounding the Arcanum and its history, and any Storyteller can craft more for her chronicle. Or she can just keep working inwards from those, for behind each mystery, there is almost always another, deeper mystery.

GOD / THE DEVIL IS IN THE DETAILS

Papyrus fragments from a dig in Alexandria, a grimoire found in the attic of an old silversmith near the Schwarzwald, a heretical edition of the Diamond Sutra smuggled out of the Tibetan Autonomous District by an underground practitioner of *bon* — esoteric knowledge comes in many forms, each with its own special romance. The knowledge that the Arcanum seeks should exude this romance. Every location on the globe has its own mythology, its own magical history. Even *The Blair Witch Project*, which took place in backwater Maryland created a historical context for their story.

Building mythical history of this nature is almost required for chronicles featuring the Arcanum, for several different reasons. The first is pure mood: It is far more interesting, and realistic, to have the characters researching "the third through sixteenth pages of a manuscript apparently written in 15th century High German, with annotations in a 3rd century Persian dialect" than "that book you found in the Old Book Shop last week." Some players can spend hours joyfully dissecting this sort of material. Beyond mood, the Storyteller can use the historical bits as hints and foreshadowing for the direction she wants the characters to explore. Cryptic references to family lineages and foreign travels are often good for this, and a clever Storyteller can easily come up with more. Finally, a Storyteller who is strapped for ideas can often find them by simply making up or re-reading this sort of history. Did the players forget to research a certain line? Were their studies, perhaps, incomplete? Fit the established facts with a new face and *voila*, suddenly the puzzle looks different and the characters have another month's worth of work ahead of them.

THE VIEW FROM WITHOUT

Like knowledge, the Arcanum does not exist in a vacuum. Arcanum characters make excellent additions to other MET chronicles, especially those where violence is not the solution to every problem.

THOSE "MEDDLING KIDS"

Chronicles that involve a degree of secrecy — most Camarilla chronicles, for example — can always benefit from the addition of people who must be kept in the dark.

Maintaining the Masquerade is a simple matter if all the characters are Kindred. The addition of a group of Arcanum Scholars who, for the most part, pursue their own, separate arcane investigations, but are immediately attracted the instant reports of occult activity surface, can force the paranoia level up a notch. They are members of an international organization, so someone is bound to come looking if members of the local Lodge happen to start disappearing. Worse, some of them exhibit paranormal powers of their own, and they have at least half a clue about the occult world, so the usual tricks probably won't be enough to get rid of them.

Some characters will want to use the scholars to inconvenience their rivals, or perhaps to study something they don't want to poke their noses into personally. Others will insist on complete separation, keeping as far away from them as possible. Others will slip up, inadvertently drawing their scrutiny, and there will always be those who end up competing with them for their esoteric resources.

IGNORANCE IS THE SOURCE OF ALL EVIL

Arcanum characters need not direct their attentions at the other players to disrupt their machinations. Their research may have unwanted or unknown side effects that distress, confuse, or otherwise affect the supernatural population of the chronicle.

In their travels through the world, members of the Arcanum may acquire inexplicable artifacts or be compelled to enact certain magics without having adequate time or resources to determine all side effects. Worse, like a dog whistle, these effects may not be immediately perceivable by the mortal residents of the chronicle's territory, or may have different effects on different types of characters. Perhaps all Malkavians are immune to the emanations of the bas-relief from the hidden temple under the ruins outside Shabwa. Perhaps the ritual on the Urumchi manuscript deprives Kuei-Jin of rest during the day. Or, perhaps everyone within three miles dreams of Sobk, the crocodile god who moves beneath Cairo. This sort of thing can stir up all sorts of paranoia before it gets sorted out. It can also lead to new alliances and enmities as different people are drawn together to undo, or to make permanent, these bizarre effects.

And after the mess itself is cleaned up, there comes the cover-up, lest the Masquerade or the Delirium or the Mists, or whatever form of secrecy needs to be enforced be irreparably damaged. Can the Arcanum members escape with their hard-won information, or will they be 'fixed' to make certain that the wrong secrets are not revealed?

Those hunters who manage to learn of the elusive fae often wonder why anyone would bother hunting such relatively harmless creatures when horrors like vampires, werewolves and ghosts stalk the night. Such hunters obviously don't remember the old folktales where faeries kidnapped children, killed intruders, stole mortals away for centuries on a whim and otherwise used humans as their pets and playthings. Naturally, such clueless souls would be even more surprised to learn that an entire class of beings exist who are devoted to the annihilation of all things fae — the Dauntain.

Dauntain work to destroy all traces of changelings and the creativity that surrounds them wherever they might be found. Their means can be as direct as pistols and cold iron blades, or more subtle and insidious methods such as foreclosing on freeholds, institutionalizing influential changelings or transferring childlings and wilders to "special" schools away from their friends and motleys. Indeed, when one considers the natural affinity of the Dauntain for such banal things as tax forms, police reports, school bureaucracy and the like, such subtle means are more likely to be their style than a direct frontal assault. Regardless of their methods, however, the end goal is the same — the destruction of the fae and everything they hold dear.

Recent events in Concordia haven't helped matters — the destruction of the war has sent a number of changelings into the Forgetting, and many changelings have turned against each other in the conflict. The faces of this phenomenon are legion, each of them horrible: sidhe awakening for the first time to find themselves surrounded by angry commoners eager to take out their frustration on any noble they find, innocent or not; commoners who shed their mortal skin, only to find themselves pressed into military service or run to ground by sidhe huntsmen; fae who recall their true nature, only to discover their freehold burned, motley slain or other tragedies. Each fae so treated has a chance to turn their back on her true nature, and each one who does strengthens the cause of Banality, a warning even the most battle-crazed warrior would do well to remember.

What's more, mortal authorities have taken notice of a rising tide of seemingly motiveless crimes committed by young adults and juveniles as changelings on both sides get down to the business of war in Concordia. Currently the authorities suspect some sort of cult involvement, and the Banality of jail time has driven more than one young fae to the arms of the Dauntain. Chief among the proponents of the cult theory is Dr. Anton Stark, an influential psychologist and infamous Dauntain who has been responsible for the institutionalization and "deprogramming" of scores of changelings over the past decade. Police who fear that this cult is involved in a crime have started turning over suspects to his tender care, and frightened whispers from the few survivors tell of meeting an emerging generation of Dauntain — the hand-picked students and "reformed" patients of the dread Dr. Stark himself. All of them are well-schooled in faerie lore as well as the tactics for restraining changelings, and what's worse they typically work through entirely legal channels, allowing them to pit extensive mundane resources against those who oppose their "help." Indeed, if Dr. Stark and his students are permitted to draw in new recruits much longer, the toll on the Kithain will rapidly be nothing less than catastrophic. It is a dark time to battle the Dauntain, but no less necessary because of it.

HUNTERS OF IMAGINATION

Dauntain Character Creation

Step One: Character Concept

Choose concept, court, Legacies, house (if applicable), seeming, kith and Doom

Step Two: Attributes

Prioritize the three categories: Physical, Social, Mental (7/5/3)

Choose Physical Traits

Choose Social Traits

Choose Mental Traits

Step Three: Select Advantages

Choose Abilities (5), Backgrounds (5), Arts/Agendas (3), Realms (5)

Step Four: Finishing Touches

Record beginning Glamour, Willpower and Banality as determined by seeming

Add two (2) additional permanent Banality Traits

Choose Negative Traits, if any

Purchase Merits/Flaws, if any

Note: Permanent Banality Traits may be purchased at this stage, at a cost of two Traits each. Most Dauntain should begin play with at least six permanent Banality Traits, and often. more

Step Five: Spark of Life

Dauntain are a bit different from other hunters covered in this book, however, because they are not actually human (though they may of course employ human pawns and partners), but rather they are changelings who have been twisted into hunting their own kind. As such, their character creation mechanics are a bit different, as are their motivations, and players should construct their characters accordingly.

SUGGESTED READING MATERIAL

While you don't need to use any other books to create or run Dauntain characters in live-action, players and Storytellers alike can find a wealth of information on their hated changeling foes in **The Shining Host** and **The Shining Host Player's Guide**, which in turn can be used to add depth to both the hunters and the hunted in a Dauntain game. In addition, the tabletop book **The Autumn People** for **Changeling: The Dreaming** offers an in-depth look at Dauntain existence, as well as additional information on Heavy Sleepers and Autumn Fae, any of which can easily be converted for use in live-action play.

TRULY DEADLY, OR JUST DEADLY BORING?

Although they can and do overlap, and in truth many fae use them somewhat interchangeably in casual conversation, in actuality the terms "Dauntain" and "Autumn People" aren't quite the same. "Autumn People" is actually a blanket term for three categories of banal beings: Heavy Sleepers, Autumn Fae and Dauntain. **Heavy Sleepers** are "mere" mortals whose extremely narrow minds and high natural Banality make them a threat to the fae around them, though most such mortals have no idea of the existence of the Kithain (nor believe it if it's brought to their attention). **Autumn Fae** are fae who have succumbed to the Forgetting, usually due to high Banality levels, and who occasionally trouble their former cousins due to mistaken beliefs or manifestation of their buried magical powers. Lastly, while some Kithain use the name to describe any beings who hunt the fae, in truth the term **Dauntain** refers *only* to those malicious or misguided faeries who actively turn on their own kind and attempt to destroy them.

This chapter focuses almost exclusively on faeries turned Dauntain, since they are the most direct and immediate threat out of the three. Those interested in playing Heavy Sleepers should create regular mortals, except that they can have no supernatural Abilities, powers, Merits or lineage whatsoever, and are considered to have zero Glamour and 8-10 permanent Banality when dealing with the fae. Those who wish to play Autumn Fae should create them according to the rules for changelings in **The Shining Host**, save that they begin play in the Forgetting (unaware of the enchanted world) and that they must purchase a starting Banality of at least 7. Autumn Fae may also purchase Agendas as well as Arts, though all powers they use manifest unconsciously — they are not aware they are using magic.

DOOMS

Although the reasons that Dauntain choose their dark path are as varied as the individuals themselves, those brave Kithain scholars who have studied the Dauntain phenomenon have identified a number of definite patterns in the way these Autumn People come to serve Banality, general paths which they have termed Dooms. Contained within each Doom is a description of the motives, strategies and appearance of those Dauntain who fall under its auspices, as well as the seeds of what arguments or ideas might be able to bring the Dauntain back from the bitter road they travel. While Kithain are cautioned that these are broad categories and should not be trusted to blindly predict a particular Dauntain's behavior, knowing what has motivated others like one in the past can be the difference between resolving a situation gracefully and ending up with blood on one's hands. It's not much, but it's better than the nothing that is left in a Dauntain's wake.

Specific knowledge of Dauntain generally requires that a character have at least *Gremayre* or *Gremayre* x 2; of Dooms and how to deal with them, *Gremayre* x 3; and lastly of Stigmas and Agendas, *Gremayre* x 4. (Naturally, Dauntain receive all but the finer points of this lore free of charge.) These requirements may be adjusted if the Storyteller desires. Keeping Dauntain at least somewhat mysterious is recommended, unless the Storyteller wishes to have the characters lightheartedly teaming up *Buffy*-style to whomp some banal butt, rather than truly fearing the Autumn People as they should.

Note: Dauntain retain their normal kith Birthrights and Frailties, though any Birthrights that require Glamour to activate cost an additional Glamour Trait due to the draining pull of Banality on the Dauntain's soul.

THE LOST

Sad as it may be, the Chrysalis is not always a time of wonder and discovery. Some rare fae, without the guidance of a mentor to help them or perhaps a little too much attachment to the world they know, reject their new existence and everything it entails. Many of these souls fall to the Forgetting, permanently cutting off their access to Glamour, but a few cannot shake their new existence entirely, and spend their days trying to convince others that anything related to the enchanted world is nothing more than fantasy. Some even actively seek out other changelings in order to "cure" them of the "madness" they have come to resent within themselves.

It should be noted that the Lost are different from other Banality-stricken fae in a very important way. While other fae fade into the mortal world and essentially turn their backs on Glamour, the Lost one not only turns his back on Glamour, he actively embraces Banality as a means of destroying all traces of what he sees as a dangerous and chaotic element at work in the world. Some of the Lost can be brought back by showing them the truth of their new existence, that it is not some form of insanity. As most of the Lost have spent a considerable amount of time constructing intricate "theories" to avoid realizing just that, it's a difficult battle at best.

The Lost do not consciously invoke magic — that would be giving in to madness! — but may unconsciously use their powers, particularly Agendas, to combat the chimerical world when it threatens their narrow world view. Others have no powers to speak of, or no control over the ones they do have. To their fellow fae, the Lost appear sickly and gaunt, growing increasingly moreso as their distance from the Dreaming grows.

THE CURSED

Revenge can drive anyone to extremes, and none know this better than those poor (but very dangerous) Doomed souls known as the Cursed. Nearly all of them have sworn the *Oath of the Undoing* (**The Shining Host**, p. 188), and those who have not often do soon after beginning their fall. Some of them started out to avenge true injustice, while others have been pursuing petty feuds. Regardless of their original motive, they have all come to embrace hatred and revenge over any notion of honor or justice, and as a result are slowly being consumed by it.

The Cursed differ from most Dauntain in that most do not seek to harm any Kithain other than their chosen target (at least at first…), but anyone who even remotely stands in their way is dealt with as quickly and brutally as they know how. One crime leads to another, and before long they're leaving a trail of innocent blood behind them. Worse, even those who successfully manage to take their revenge find that pursuing it has changed them deeply — their former friends no longer accept them, and that the passions they once enjoyed now leave them cold and unfulfilled. Some are sickened by this realization, and take their own lives or fade into mundane jobs in shame; others, embittered and enraged by this knowledge, seek to obscure their personal tragedy in the blood of others until they are finally brought down.

Cursed are perhaps the most tragic of all the Doomed, and as such most can only be saved by epic quests of one kind or another. Since they are held in their state by an oath, they cannot break it without gaining Banality, but upholding it only brings more down on their heads. Only by realizing the folly of their quest and doing their best to

reverse the damage they've done can the Cursed turn back from destruction, and few are strong enough to admit such a wrong, much less work to see its restoration through.

The Cursed retain full control of their cantrips on their quests, although many find themselves turning more to banal uses of their powers as they attempt to wipe their hated foe from the earth. Cursed are relatively easy to spot, for Dauntain — their fae seemings become charged with hatred and malevolence, seemingly ready to explode in violence at any moment, and their eyes are full of malice. Some even manifest pointed teeth or clawlike nails as they descend further into Banality — these have no game effect, but are chilling reminders of what the Dauntain is becoming.

BLACK MAGICIANS

Not all Dauntain follow the path of Banality out of ignorance or spite; some few fae do so in an effort to master the very force that can so easily destroy them. Black Magicians are perhaps the least numerous and recognized of all Dauntain, but potentially the most dangerous as well; most master many Arts and Agendas as part of their mad experimentation with all forms of Glamour and Banality, making them devious manipulators and peerless foes in enchanted combat.

Most Black Magicians start out innocently enough — perhaps they invoke Banality to block a particularly nasty cantrip, or hide in their mortal seemings to avoid a Kithain search party. Intrigued by the results, they begin playing with Banality in an attempt to understand why it works the way it does, and before long they're performing all manner of twisted experiments to satisfy their craving for the "power" they've uncovered. What makes them even more dangerous is the fact that so few of them can be brought back from the brink of Doom, since doing so would require them to recognize and renounce their lust for power, and it's precisely that character flaw which led them to become something as twisted as a Black Magician in the first place.

Like the Cursed, the Black Magicians retain full control of their cantrips, and many even experiment with strange new combinations of Arts and Agendas as they get further along in their plans, making them unpredictable enemies. They can sometimes be identified by their voices, which take on a hollow and ominous tone, and a subtle chill in the air around their fae miens, regardless of the actual weather conditions.

NIHILISTS

Some Dauntain simply give up, seeing nothing worth living for in a life of pain and suffering… and become more dangerous in the process. Such Nihilists are like the Lost in many ways, except where the Lost have taken up the "crusade" of order and rationality to give their lives meaning, Nihilists see no point in action or emotion of any kind. They do as little as they can to survive, though surprisingly few of them are truly suicidal — that would imply a serious decision-action sequence, for one thing, and besides, deep down the Nihilist is afraid whatever lies beyond isn't any better than this. Besides, why fight anything when Banality eventually wins anyway?

The only thing that comforts these poor Kithain is Glamour, and they will do their best to seek out a steady source of it as inconspicuously as possible. Perhaps they move in next door to a struggling young writer, who slowly finds himself losing his gift, or they visit a beautiful park, which gradually seems to become less and less attractive. Destroying other Kithain or chimera is not a Nihilist's main concern, though it eventually is as she seeks to fill the void within with the Glamour that eases her aching,

and it doesn't bother her in the slightest when it happens. Not much does, after all. Only by restoring some measure of real hope to her life can a Kithain hope to turn a Nihilist away from certain Doom, a delicate thing to do without also accidentally pushing her to suicide or worse.

Nihilists seldom consciously use their cantrips — to do so costs precious Glamour, and so the only time they typically do is to avoid being noticed by others or to finish stealing some source of Glamour. To the eyes of the other fae, a Nihilist seems to shrink inside her seeming, growing smaller and fading more as she retreats from the world and its troublesome emotions.

APOSTATES

Dauntain on this heretical path believe that the salvation of the fae somehow lies in embracing Banality and inflicting it on others in hopes of "purging" them and releasing them from this painful, awkward world. Faced with some great personal tragedy involving Banality (such as the loss of a loved one to the Undoing), or perhaps just overwhelmed by contemplation of the immense Banality of the mortal world, their minds snap, seeking instead to turn this great threat into a positive thing, if only in their shattered minds. Most Apostates develop intricate theories to support this abominable position, and while no two of them fully agree with each other, in the end most concur on a few key points: that Banality is actually the ally of the fae; that all Glamour on Earth must be destroyed (usually to "send it back to Arcadia"); and that the Undoing is not the end of the fae soul, but a rebirth in Arcadia or some other paradise.

Like twisted evangelists, most Apostates seek to convert other Kithain to their cause, beginning with almost-reasonable arguments ("Hey, Banality occasionally has its uses, right?"), but almost always rapidly rising into frightening claims even the most debased Unseelie shy away from. When confronted by those who deny their "truth," Apostates become fanatic crusaders, slaying all who oppose them in the name of saving their souls. Although their fanaticism makes it unlikely, Apostates can be saved from their Doom if one can convince them that Glamour has a place on Earth as well as in Arcadia, and to recognize the dreams around them.

Apostates have a certain flair for cantrip use, especially those they feel will help convert others to their cause, although they do not hesitate to use their most deadly powers on those who oppose them. If they get Banality doing so, then so be it. They are martyrs for their fellow fae, after all. Stereotypical Apostates sometimes dress in the ragged clothes of a ranting street prophet, but they can always be recognizd by the lunatic shine in their eyes, full of pain and madness.

TYPHOIDS

Some Dauntain can't help being what they are; Typhoids spread Banality almost against their will, infected by some form of Banality that is largely or entirely beyond their control. Some develop a strange illness after being fed blood by a vampire, or after visiting the wrong haunted house at the wrong time of night, or even just by living/working with Autumn People for too long. Still more find themselves turning deadly banal after being forced to adopt a mortal job and lifestyle, though this is far from the rule (or nearly all fae would eventually become Typhoids). Others have no idea what caused their condition, or at least claim not to, but regardless of the source of the infection, the Typhoid now spreads Banality and sorrow wherever he goes, as his soul is slowly poisoned and his perspective gradually shifts to that of an Autumn Person. (The Storyteller has final say on what creates a Typhoid, and is encouraged to be highly creative and mysterious when doing so.)

As they are generally totally unaware of their condition, sometimes to the point of believing themselves to be normal mortals even while their fae seemings are still active, Typhoids present a puzzling problem to would-be Kithain heroes. None can argue with the harm they do, whether they mean to or not, but destroying them doesn't exactly seem to be justice. Rather, saving Typhoids from their Doom involves identifying and severing the connection they have to Banality. This is easier said than done, however, for not only do many Typhoids suffer from an illness without an obvious source, most are also addicted to the habits surrounding the infection (consciously or not), and actively resist attempts to sever those ties.

As unwitting agents of Banality, Typhoids often do not remember they have access to cantrips of any kind, though they may manifest them to defend themselves or their infection. The appearance of Typhoids varies widely: one whose infection stems from vampiric contact might take on a pale cast and reddish eyes, while another whose taint comes from ghostly nightmares might have a faint aura of spectral faces swirling around him.

GLAMOUR SYSTEMS

THE FORGETTING

Dealing as they do with inflicting and receiving so much Banality, it only makes sense to use the Dauntain space to detail the many ways that a Kithain — Dauntain or otherwise — can fall into the crippling state of amnesia known as the Forgetting. While in this state, a fae is considered nothing more than a normal mortal, who has only the faintest glimmer of Birthrights and cannot use Arts, fae Abilities such as *Kenning* or *Gremayre*, or many *Treasures*.

Remember that Forgetting is just as much of a threat for the Dauntain as it is for their fae opponents. Any Dauntain who wishes to retain her full powers and knowledge of the enemy must balance the need to destroy things of Glamour with moderation, else she becomes little more than a blind mortals again. Of course, some of the Doomed simply don't care and gain Banality heedlessly, preferring to blaze brightly rather than to slowly fade away, but that's another story....

Voluntary Retreat

A character can choose to "duck into" her mortal seeming to avoid things of the Dreaming, though doing so is risky at best. While hiding in her seeming, the character is effectively mortal and cannot interact with things of the Dreaming, be they friend or foe. This would seem to be an ideal way of dodging cantrips and other enchanted dangers, except that there is always a risk of getting caught in the seeming and forgetting one's fae nature.

System: To retreat, the character must spend an action and make a test of her permanent Glamour versus her permanent Banality (Willpower may be spent to win this test automatically). If she succeeds, she immediately gains a temporary Banality Trait and retreat into her seeming. If possible, she should adopt a costume or posture

which makes this change evident to other players. Those who retreat get one chance to return to the enchanted world on their own — which must be made by the end of the same scene when they retreated — by making a test of permanent Willpower or Glamour (whichever is higher) against permanent Banality; success means they assume their fae mien again. Failure means they have gone too far and forgotten their fae nature; such unfortunates are trapped in their seeming until exposed to a sufficient amount of Glamour, or spend an amount of time in it as determined by their Banality — see the Mists chart in **The Shining Host**, p. 178.

Chimerical Death

Those slain by chimerical weapons or attacks automatically gain a Trait of temporary Banality, revert to their mortal seemings and fall into a comatose state for an amount of time determined by the Mists chart. Upon awakening, they remain entirely within their mortal seemings until they gain a Glamour Trait of their own, whether through Reverie, another Kithain's help or other means such as time spent by a balefire.

Banality Higher Than Glamour

A Kithain whose permanent Banality is higher than her permanent Glamour is in danger, but only in a gradual sense. In between stories (not sessions), those fae in this condition must make a test of their permanent Glamour versus their permanent Banality for each week — or day, if the chronicle is on a tight timeline — that they are not often directly touched by Glamour. Failure means they forget their fae nature for an amount of time as dictated by the Mists chart, or until another Kithain uses Glamour to draw them out. Alternately, the Storyteller may inflict a Trait or two of temporary Banality for each failed test, if she does not wish to deal with the problem of amnesiac fae at the start of the new story.

Banality Higher Than Glamour and Willpower Combined

Kithain in this situation, whose permanent Banality is greater than their permanent Willpower and Glamour Traits combined, are in more serious trouble. In between all *sessions*, they must make a test of their permanent Glamour versus their permanent Banality for each week (or day, as above) that they do not directly interact with Glamour, with failure bringing the same penalties as described immediately above. In addition, particularly strict Storytellers may require them to spend a number of days in a freehold equal to the difference between their Glamour and their Banality every week — for each day the changeling misses, she gains one temporary Banality Trait. This last can be waived if the character is attempting to quest to reduce her permanent Banality or under an oath which prevents her from spending the right time in a freehold, though those solutions have dangers of their own.

Banality of Ten

A Kithain with 10 permanent Banality Traits is almost certainly about to be Undone — as soon as his Banality reaches this level, he has a number of days (or sessions, if the Storyteller is feeling generous) equal to his combined Glamour and Willpower ratings to find a way to reduce their Banality below 10, and must make a test of permanent Glamour versus permanent Banality every day he spends away from a freehold to avoid gaining another temporary Banality Trait. Only the most legendary and heroic feats will suffice to save a character at this level.

COLD IRON

All fae fear weapons made of cold iron, and even the most wicked Dauntain handle them with respect, since their destructive capabilities work just as well against the Dauntain as they do on their prey. Still, any game with even a few Dauntain is bound to involve cold iron sooner or later, either as the Dauntain seek to take their mad revenge, or as the hunted fae themselves make a devil's bargain to rid themselves of their tormentors once and for all.

Fortunately for the fae as a whole, cold iron weapons are quite rare, not to mention heavy and unwieldy compared to their regular counterparts. One cannot simply walk into a weapon store and expect to pick one up; cold iron weapons typically must be custom-made, and many smiths are bound to be a little curious about why a customer would want something made from such an inferior metal when much better alloys exist, not to mention that the extra effort required to forge them will likely translate to an additional expense! Finally, while arrowheads and the like are certainly possible, cold iron ammunition is all but out of the question for modern firearms more advanced than muskets — while it *can* be done, it requires a highly skilled craftsman (*Crafts* x4 or better) and no small amount of time to make bullets that will fly correctly, and they can never be used as *High Caliber* ammunition. The exception is shotguns that use iron pellet shot, which can be made normally.

Otherwise, the rules and ratings for cold iron weapons are identical for their regular counterparts, with a few changes as follows:

Bonus Traits: Normal for the weapon type, although the Storyteller may rule that some weapons such as swords or knives have one less Trait than normal, since the balance of cold iron weapons is usually considerably off compared to their normal counterparts.

Negative Traits: *Heavy* (melee weapons) or *Clumsy* (when used as ammunition in ranged weapons), in addition to any such Traits the weapon normally has.

Damage: Whatever damage the weapon normally does, only this is considered aggravated damage for any fae or chimera. In addition, each successful hit from a cold iron weapon destroys one of the target's temporary Glamour Traits, as well as gives her a temporary Banality Trait. This ruling supersedes the one in **The Shining Host**.

Proximity: All fae are one Trait down on all Physical Challenges when within a pace of cold iron (whether in weapon form or not), and at a one-Trait penalty to all tests when in direct contact with the hated metal. The presence of cold iron should be announced out-of-character as soon as any fae enter this radius, as it is impossible for them to mistake the uncomfortable feeling iron creates for anything else. Fae forced to remain in contact for any length of time (such as being shackled with cold iron manacles) suffer a level of aggravated damage every hour or so, and gain a temporary Banality Trait every 10 minutes. This rate may be changed to fit the Storyteller's needs — if a faster rate is necessary for drama, or a slower rate to prepare a brave rescue tale, then by all means adjust accordingly — but should always remain a threat, else the horrifying destructive power of cold iron is lost.

Special Note: All fae are considered to have half their normal Traits (round down, minimum one) when resolving ties against cold iron weapons. Note that unless the Dauntain has a Stigma or other power that protects him from the effects of cold iron, he is subject to the same penalties for carrying and using cold iron as any other fae. Consequently, even Dauntain prefer to keep such weapons stashed away and only retrieve them when they're certain a confrontation is imminent.

RENDING

Dauntain cannot gain Glamour like other changelings do. While they can gather Glamour from artists and Dreamers, they do so only through a peculiar and highly specific form of Ravaging known as Rending. After identifying a potential target as an aspiring artist of some type, the Dauntain talks to her in such a way as to destroy her confidence in herself and her work, deriving a sense of dark satisfaction from the shattered dreams of his target, effectively stealing her Glamour. Survivors are left shaken, exhausted and uncertain of their gift or their purpose in life, and more sensitive souls have been driven to madness or suicide by the harsh scrutiny of the Dauntain's criticism. It also bears noting that Rending is just as effective on Kithain, and more than one fae has felt her Glamour slip away in this fashion just moments before the Dauntain launched a devastating attack.

System: To identify a potential Dreamer or Kithain target, the Dauntain must make a *Kenning* test. He must then roleplay the criticism as fully as possible, preferably even encouraging the artist to disparage her own work in the process, and when he feels enough harm has been done, the real fun begins. The Dauntain may then make a test of his permanent Banality against a difficulty of the number of Glamour Traits he wishes to gain; if he succeeds, he gains the Traits he seeks and the target loses a corresponding amount. In addition, the target gains a temporary Banality Trait for every two Traits the Dauntain gains (round down), though she may spend a Willpower Trait to cancel this effect.

TEDIUM

Dauntain may also attempt to gain temporary Banality by instilling a kind of a reverse Reverie in a target through a process known as Tedium. By convincing another to perform a mindlessly menial task instead of pursuing her dreams, or by making another give up her faith in the world (such as by telling depressing anecdotes or discussing wars, plagues, poverty and the like), the Dauntain may feed on the coldly analytical reasoning that develops in a target as he shuts off his emotional ties to the world. Though less dramatic than Rending, Tedium and effects like it are responsible for much of the bleak state of the world the Dauntain symbolize.

System: Identical to Rending, above, including the effects on the hapless victim of Tedium, save that the Dauntain gains temporary Banality Traits rather than Glamour.

HAZE OF LETHARGY

Autumn People, especially Dauntain, are so deeply entrenched in Banality that their mundanity has a physical impact on others around them, especially the fae. Faint but persistent headaches, mild stomach upset, general lethargy, a dry taste in the mouth and difficulty focusing on anything but the most mundane tasks are all symptoms that occur in the presence of these drab individuals. The effect on the chimerical world is even more dramatic — sentient chimera shy away from the banal person, inanimate chimera seem to flicker or fade as they pass, and the surrounding area appears to have all the color and vibrancy leeched out of it, like a faded painting. Even mortals often feel drained around these folk, although not to the same degree as the fae — for an idea of the impact Autumn People have on the mortals around them, players should think of how it felt to be trapped in a class or meeting with the most boring teacher or manager they ever knew. Other Autumn People are seemingly immune to this effect, and indeed many feel more energized around others of their kind, as they recognize someone else "who knows what it's all about."

Note: If an Autumn Person is somehow enchanted, all of these conditions are immediately lifted, and do not return until the enchantment has passed. Such a feat is quite difficult, given the resistance Autumn People have to all things of Glamour, but it does a great deal toward leveling the playing field. Dauntain actually *do not* normally give off the *Haze of Lethargy*, since they try to keep themselves in touch with the chimerical world, though Heavy Sleepers and Autumn Fae usually exhibit it strongly. It should be noted that this effect also applies to Prodigals with exceptionally strong Banality levels, which explains why Kithain tend to avoid vampires and other such beings of death as much as possible.

System: All changelings or other creatures of Glamour are uncomfortable when in the same room as any kind of unenchanted Autumn Person (use common sense for particularly large rooms or open spaces), and should roleplay the discomfort as well; use the symptoms listed above as a guideline. Narrators should affix appropriate description cards to rooms where Autumn People are found in order to notify fae of their presence; alternately, an Autumn Person entering a room can make an out-of-game announcement to that effect, thereby alerting any fae in the vicinity. Additionally, all fae are considered one Trait down on all tests related to doing anything deviant or creative (cantrips not included) while within three paces of an Autumn Person, as the presence of such Banality makes it hard to concentrate on anything besides the mundane world. This penalty is *not* cumulative, so having six Autumn People standing next to you doesn't put you down six Traits on all tests, although your evening is certainly off to a terrible start by any other faerie standards!

WHAT THE NUMBERS MEAN: BANALITY

It's one thing to *say* a character has so much Banality, but it's another thing altogether to realize exactly what that means. Here's a brief rundown of the common beliefs and quirks of each level of permanent Banality.

Banality 1-2: Only the smallest children have Banality this low. At one Banality, the child understands there are some constants in the world, but everything else is up for grabs — monsters, magic and fantastic technology are as real as anything else, and amazing adventures can happen to anyone, anywhere. Two Banality is more like a late grade-schooler or a particularly open-minded junior high student — while Santa Claus and the Easter Bunny may be gone, the world is still wide open with possibilities, and more than a few of them are quite fantastic.

Banality 3-4: Some maturity is starting to set in at this point — three Banality is the average for most junior high students or very creative high school kids. The world has definite limits, and more dramatic magic might be out of the question, but most believe that a true love and perfect job are waiting for them, and if things happen just right they might be the next big movie star or rock sensation. Four Banality is typically late high-schoolers or college students — okay, so a career in the working world is probably inevitable but still a ways off, and who knows, with a lucky break or two they just might be able to retire at 30 or be a big artistic success.

Banality 5: Though incredibly heavy with Banality by fae standards, only extremely open-minded grumps or mortal drunks and lunatics regularly remain at this level for long. This is the border of insanity for adults or true maturity for children. Those at this level might believe in elaborate conspiracy theories, harbor delusions or suffer from paranoia about the "secret societies" they're sure exist all around them.

Banality 6: For mortals, this is the level of a creative artist. Considered off-beat by regular society, she nonetheless tries to balance the demands of the world of the creative with the needs of the mundane as well as possible. For many fae, it's typically the last stop before the Forgetting, unless they try hard to hold onto their faerie natures and gather Glamour as often as possible.

Banality 7: This is the average Banality of most mortals — sensible and cautious, they are not without the occasional burst of inspiration, but as a whole prefer the comfortable and familiar to the new and exciting. Any call to adventure seems a little silly, and even if they agree to go, they do their best to plan and prepare beforehand. Fae who retain their mien at this level often immerse themselves in the local court as much as possible in an effort to keep the mundane world from dragging them under, but still suffer from some hesitation toward that which they would've gladly embraced before.

Banality 8: This is the average level for a moderate Autumn Person or weak Dauntain. Mortals at this level resist their own innate despair and mistrust by becoming obsessive about various things, and dislike those who aren't like them in this respect. Fae at this level find it increasingly difficult to embrace their passions or just go out and live like they once did — it's easier to stay home and let someone else be the hero. This is made worse by the fact that most are aware of what they used to be compared to what they are now, which only deepens the despair. All Reverie attempts are one Trait down.

Banality 9: This is the average state of a strong Autumn Person or average Dauntain. They are so banal that their mere presence can actually be painful to the fae (see "Haze of Lethargy"), and their disbelief makes it hard for chimera to exist near them. Fae at this level almost exactly resemble their mortal seemings, tend to forget details like kith names or freehold locations, and are two Traits down on all *Kenning* and *Gremayre* tests.

Banality 10: The most severe Autumn People and the strongest Dauntain reach this level, where positive emotions all but vanish, childhood and true love is forgotten, and only the tedious holds any interest for the character. Fae at this level will almost certainly be Undone, and sadly even those that hold on tend to be shunned by their fellows due to the high Banality they carry with them.

THE GOVERNMENT

From time to time, the federal government has encountered things it cannot explain. Evidence of supernatural activity, its evidence or even its creatures has crossed the path of unwary investigators. Should a federal or civil servant take up the cause of investigating or hunting, it is most likely because the target has been breaking the law, not because the agent is interested in eliminating hellspawn.

As a matter of policy, most government agencies do not admit belief in the supernatural. The various supernatural creatures and their societies have worked diligently to ensure this, and their efforts over the centuries have paid off. Fellow agents often treat those who have encountered evidence of the supernatural in the course of routine investigations with skepticism or even hostility. This remains true even if the agent is recruited into one of the small number of "special branches" of her service that specializes in investigating, documenting and eliminating supernatural threats. Such operations work in secrecy, and insist that their agents do likewise. After all, the government is supposed to be grounded in reality — claiming to hunt vampires for the federal government sounds like a movie premise — not to mention the taxpayers might get a little irritated to think that their tax dollars are funding such nonsense.

Recent events in the supernatural world have conspired to bring greater and greater attention to it, however, especially from the government. As much as some people might find the notion of vampire-hunting for the FBI to be too fantastic, the media has given it some unexpected credibility with "The X-Files" and "The Invisible Man."

BUT WHAT ABOUT THE MASQUERADE?

Some players or Storytellers may feel that this system is giving away too much, since if handled strictly by the numbers it would mean players with vampiric, Technocratic or otherwise deeply banal characters would have to announce their banal nature upon entering a room and thus "give themselves away" to any fae in the area. (See the "Average Banality Ratings" Chart in **The Shining Host**, p. 156, for an idea of who is classified as banal for these purposes.) However, those with ruffled feathers should remember that this is a reflection of the sensitivity all Kithain have to high Banality, whatever form it might take, and not anything the fae can control. Such is the price of crossover gaming, after all. Of course, for their part, players should remember that while their seasoned characters can sense a high amount of Banality in this mysterious new character, most fae know *very* little about Prodigals. Combine this with the fact that most supernatural creatures easily pass for human, and changelings are more likely to assume that the newcomer is nothing more than a "mere" Autumn Person, until given good cause to think otherwise. Banality is everywhere in the World of Darkness — just sensing a higher amount on one person isn't enough to immediately assume he's a vampire!

If this still seems overly demanding, Storytellers may rule that deeply banal supernatural creatures need only announce their high Banality when within conversational distance with a changeling. Perhaps the strange supernatural energies flowing through the Prodigals somehow partially mask the Banality in their hearts, or maybe centuries of hiding from mortals have somewhat suppressed their banal "signature". Whatever the reason might be, not only does this rule simplify play a bit for both parties, but it also serves to give the fae as many nasty surprises as it does advance warnings, and so should satisfy players on both sides. Mixed **Mind's Eye Theatre** games can be a lot of fun, but only so long as all sides understand that no one group is receiving particular preference.

THE FEDERAL GOVERNMENT

The national government does have inroads to investigate supernatural activity, but remains extremely tight-lipped about its involvement. The directors of such efforts keep their information on a need-to-know basis, and as far as they're concerned, the public doesn't need to know. The reasons for this are varied, but range from keeping the public calm to lack of hard evidence to greed.

FEDERAL BUREAU OF INVESTIGATION

Within the FBI, there exists a division known as the SAD, or Special Affairs Department, that is charged with the official mission of investigating "bizarre, occult-style crimes." Unofficially, the SAD is aware of the existence of vampires, werewolves, ghosts, witches and faeries, although they do not necessarily know much about them beyond what can be researched in folk tales or gleaned from field encounters. Most FBI cases that involve the supernatural are referred to SAD, but the division is poorly funded, and it does not boast many agents. Many times, an agent out in the field is on his own. He can attempt to link up with the local branch of the FBI, but some branches do not treat SAD agents particularly well. There is a tendency among the bureau at large to see SAD as a sort of last stop for agents who have been reporting too many "crazy things" or as a holding pen for those who couldn't cut it. Neither story holds any water, but SAD does not have the option of marketing itself differently.

FBI agents automatically gain one free Ability Trait each in *Investigation* and *Firearms*, as a reflection of their agency training. Most agents continue to improve these skills, and many also have levels in *Drive* and *Melee* as well.

THE MEN IN BLACK

While most modern readers imagine the movie about secret agents pursuing an agenda of keeping Earth safe from galactic crises, the term has earlier orgins. During the rash of UFO sightings in the '50s and '60s, many people claimed those who reported a sighting or other close encounter with a UFO were visited by federal agents who "persuaded" them to recant their stories. They were nicknamed "men in black", because they usually wore black suits and drove black cars. The story has become urban legend in many subcultures, and has usually been discredited by the government as just another facet of the lunatic fringe. However, a few crafty agents who pursue supernatural agendas have resurrected the legend, finding it not unhelpful in their line of work. The result has been a new addition to the slang of mortals in the supernatural community — "Man in Black" now refers to any government agent who is hunting or studying the paranormal.

NATIONAL SECURITY AGENCY

As far as the public is concerned, the NSA is simply an enormous agency designed to acquire and sift through tremendous amounts of information, ostensibly seeking threats to national security. From time to time, the NSA discovers information that indicates the existence of events that might be caused by supernatural activity. In most such cases, the NSA merely notes the incident and shelves the information. If an

incident might threaten national security, however, it's referred to an NSA agent for action. The agents assigned to such cases generally work with the same goal they would have for any other security threat: Elimination of the target. Whether they know what they're hunting down is another matter. A few NSA agents have gone on to become hunters, but they keep such efforts very close secrets. After all, it wouldn't do to risk being labeled a threat oneself. Such agents soon earn a reputation for being good with strange or difficult cases.

NSA agents automatically gain one free Ability Trait each in *Computer* and *Investigation* as a result of their expertise in these fields.

CENTER FOR DISEASE CONTROL

During the course of its research into the cause and effects of AIDS and other blood-borne ailments, the CDC has made some remarkable discoveries. A small faction of CDC researches used this information to formulate a theory: That vampires do exist, and are a most unusual vector by which such diseases are spread. This faction of medical personnel represents a dire threat to the vampires' Masquerade. Some researchers may seek to capture vampiric specimens for testing and research, while others may wish to gather a preponderance of evidence about vampire activity so that other government agencies will be forced to acknowledge the creatures' existence… and eliminate their threat to national health and safety.

The CDC boasts a sort of strike-force team that is ready to pick up and travel to investigate a mysterious outbreak of disease within days. They occasionally leave one or two members behind to continue work if the team is called elsewhere. Outbreaks of ebola, hemorrhagic fever or West Nile virus will pull them in immediately, as will outbreaks of unknown sicknesses.

CDC researchers automatically gain one free Ability Trait of *Investigation* and *Medicine* as a reflection of their education and training.

DRUG ENFORCEMENT ADMINISTRATION

Certain drug busts have resulted in DEA reports that contain facts the agency is reluctant to reveal. The DEA works to prevent and regulate the traffic in narcotics, and during the course of its investigations it has encountered drug smuggling and distribution operations run by several different types of supernatural creatures. The DEA as an institution isn't necessarily aware of the true nature of these beings, but individual agents might become convinced that such things are out there and must be stopped.

DEA agents automatically gain one free Ability Trait each of *Firearms* and *Streetwise* as part of their training.

UNCONVENTIONAL GOVERNMENT

While the agencies listed above are the most commonly involved in supernatural investigation, they are not the only ones. The federal government has literally dozens of agencies, bureaus and departments that could get curious about unusual activity that happens to fall under their balliwick. Many of these agencies are underfunded and overworked, resulting in little attention being paid to *everything* that's going on. An agent who grows suspicious about possible supernatural activity often must investigate such things on his own time and finances, as the bureau has little time to devote to such wild goose chases. Some savvy lone hunters occasionally attach themselves to such departments, hoping to avoid the scrutiny they might normally be under at a more well-funded agency, but this can backfire — lack of money often means every penny is that much more carefully tracked, or the shiny high-tech toys are out of reach. These places are more often clearinghouses of suspicious incidents, leading the way for more well-equipped hunters to follow.

The Bureau of Alcohol, Tobacco and Firearms is typically called in to investigate reports of drug smuggling, weapons dealing or domestic terrorism. A city that seems to have a lot of explosions will draw their attention, as will reports of major drug busts and gun-running. Vampires in the middle of sect warfare often end up hosting these agents if the war becomes too public. They have also become very interested in the unusual amount of seemingly motiveless youth gang violence that has been marking the war in Concordia.

The Department of Indian Affairs manages federal efforts on Native American reservations, from distributing funds to managing clinics or schools. While most tribes are allowed to govern their internal matters by traditional means, the agency is likely to take notice if supernatural influence becomes too open or leaves too much residue. Shapeshifters and shamanic mages, both with blood ties to the native peoples, most often come under the radar of Indian Affairs agents.

The Internal Revenue Service seems like a strange choice for a potential hunter, but few things are as dogged as Uncle Sam coming after his due. Many supernaturals have discovered the hard way that nothing gets in the way of the taxman, and an audit is one of the most potent, untapped weapons in a hunter's arsenal. Remember — Al Capone was sent to prison for tax evasion!

CITY GOVERNMENT

Most supernatural communities encounter the government locally, through City Hall and its surrounding environs. Influence in the local government and its doings is highly prized, largely because it ensures that things get done according to So-and-so's liking. For those city agents who encounter the supernatural and choose to work against it, the experience can be an eye-opener about who can be corrupted and how. It can also be extremely demoralizing to discover how deeply the corruption's roots run.

Unlike federal government agents or the police, many city-level civil servants must worry about re-election, whether for themselves or their bosses. This has hamstrung some would-be investigators when they must choose between their jobs or the truth.

All city government agents receive one free Trait in *Investigation* to reflect their training and on the job experience.

LOCAL POLICE

The title covers a broad spectrum, from the beat cops on the street, to the desk jockeys who take down reports, to the guys in the lock-up, to detectives and vice squad, to the sergeants and captains.

Police departments cross paths with the supernatural far more than they realize, and those cops who do realize soon find themselves looking over old cases with fresh eyes. Missing persons reports, homicides involving extreme blood loss, attacks by "wild animals", strange groups meeting in parks — what might have been open and shut before may take on new meaning to police hunters.

Influence among the police is highly prized in many supernatural communities — a vampire may keep a finger on a homicide detective to help her cover up any "mistakes" in feeding, or a werewolf's sibling might be one of the regulars. Hunters soon learn to recognize a cop who might be "on the take", and learn to work around these. While it's difficult to report to Internal Affairs that a fellow officer is taking under-the-table bribes from a faerie lord regarding certain juvenile delinquents, it's not quite as difficult to conceal case files or other information. However, police hunters may find their worst enemy is not the vampire prince but the sergeant who's part of the prince's network. A great deal of emphasis is placed on procedure as means of keeping things on track and ensuring that no one gets out of line. Should a police investigator need to work around a balky sergeant by going outside normal procedure, he often discovers just how deep the corruption runs as his name is dragged through the mud as a "rogue."

Police officers automatically gain one free Ability Trait each of *Firearms* and *Investigation* to reflect their training.

INTERNATIONAL GOVERNMENT

If the governments of other countries have started hunting the supernatural, they are not sharing their information with their American counterparts — at least, not yet. Each country has its own priorities, and in many poor countries, investigating things that go bump in the night is certainly down at the bottom of the list. In the Far East and Third World, the supernatural is often an accepted part of life; many incidents that would have US agents arriving in short order are ignored by a government that is too poor or corrupt to pay attention.

The trends of globalization have brought about an increased cooperation between some countries with regard to criminals or crossing borders to investigate those who attempt to flee justice. It may be as simple as a disease researcher asking a foreign peer to look up something, or as complex as a request for an order of extradition. Some government hunters have been discovering that their quarries can have some rather cosmopolitan pedigrees, making it necessary to hunt abroad; most keep their travel papers in order. As often as governments cooperate, however, they are twice as likely to balk at handing over citizens or working with these groups.

Certain crimes, such as genocide and human rights abuses, have been deemed by the international community to be too heinous to go unpunished. Such criminals are usually hunted by special global agencies, often with the cooperation of many governments, including the US. Interpol—the international police—is one of the most recognized. Most Nazi hunting agencies are slowly reducing their activity as their targets die, but they have not quite given up the fight, and a recent photograph of a former death-camp doctor who doesn't apear to have aged a day in 60 years would be cause for great excitement indeed. Their appearance of such agencies on the supernatural hunting scene is extremely rare, but their reputation ensures cooperation from other hunters, or at least non-interference.

"Hey, Steve, I'm doing laundry," Jeremy yelled. "Howzabout I take your stinky ole shirts° while I'm at it?"

"Thanks," came Stephen's reply, somewhat muffled by the distance between them. He emerged from the outer room a few moments later, carrying an armload of jeans and T-shirts. He had removed his sweater, and Jeremy noticed a little green Celtic cross on a silver chain around his neck. Jeremy nodded to the necklace. "Jenny gave you that — for your ordination."

"Connemara marble, straight from the Auld Sod." Stephen smiled, but it didn't quite reach his eyes. "It's about the only thing they let me keep."

"Them? Oh, yeah — them," Jeremy remembered. Privately he was still not sure about this monster-hunting business, but no sense in pissing on the peace between him and Stephen.

He loaded the basket and said, "Gimme the one you're wearing — it's looking pretty raunchy."

Steve actually looked nervous at that. "It's not too bad—"

"Steve, I can smell it from here. You can borrow one of mine. *Gimme.*"

Reluctantly, Stephen pulled the shirt off and added it to the basket. Jeremy started out, then felt the basket slide from his hands as he stared at his brother and couldn't stop staring. Scars that Jeremy knew Stephen never had growing up marked his chest — a bullet hole, long pale lines like cat-scratches, gouges, dusky purple marks. Stephen turned away, searching for a shirt, and his back was a roadmap of more of the same.

"Jesus, Steve...," Jeremy whispered, feeling cold. "Who did this?"

Stephen pulled on the T-shirt and did not reply for many moments. Finally, his back still to Jeremy, he replied quietly, "It happens. It's part of the risk. Just don't ask me, please."

He retreated to the front room without another word, and Jeremy could only stare after him. The room seemed to shrink in his wake. Jeremy grabbed the laundry, and threw it in the washer, wishing he could do the same with his memories.

CHAPTER THREE: THE GIFTED

MEDIUMS

Unless you're playing in a **Mind's Eye Theatre** game that involves absolutely no supernatural aspects whatsoever — and that's possible, just very unlikely—your mortal character will eventually deduce the existence of a variety of otherworldly creatures: vampires, werewolves, wizards, faeries and ghosts. It's this last group, the ghosts, that are arguably the most misunderstood and least frequently encountered in most stories. The Kindred and the Garou are practically commonplace in many **Mind's Eye Theatre** chronicles, and a respectable number of stories focus on interactions between the mortal world and the mages or changelings, but it's uncommon to see the Restless Dead making more than a one-shot appearance in most games. And the reason for this scarcity in ghostly game manifestations is a simple one: There's often no way for the living (or the undead) to interact with the ghosts unless there's a medium present.

A medium is someone who, just as the word implies, provides a communications link between two groups, in this case the living and the dead (or the Quick and the Dead, if you prefer). Wraiths have absolutely no difficulty seeing and hearing what is happening in the land of the living. But only those most rare and unusual of persons — mediums — can accomplish the opposite. The Shroud that separates the living lands from the dead lands makes perception and communication between the two locales exceptionally difficult, except in a few isolated instances. And one of those instances is when a medium is available.

WHO ARE MEDIUMS?

Trying to answer this question with any hope of precision is pointless. Mediums encompass a diverse and disparate group, from carnival hucksters who tell fortunes with crystal balls to the ghost-stalking Benandanti. About the only commonalities between mediums is that they are both mortals who can see and hear ghosts, usually without any extra or special effort on the ghosts' part. Some mediums have to work hard to see and

hear the Dead, while for some the ability comes easily. Some mediums must concentrate and focus their will just to hear even the strongest of ghostly voices, while others cannot ever shut out the constant babble of spectral voices that follow them everywhere they go. Mediums can be from any walk of life, any gender, any age category, any culture and any social standing. There appears to be absolutely no logical pattern that determines who manifests such powers and who does not. Sometimes a person can live almost her entire life without seeing or hearing a single ghost and then something — an accident, a trauma or an unfortunate incident — happens and they can't stop seeing the things.

Most mediums who have had their talent for a while are able to glean some knowledge of existence beyond the Shroud. That doesn't necessarily mean that they are happy knowing this stuff: On the contrary, more than a few mediums see their talent as more of a curse than a blessing, and it's a dead certainty that none of them asked for this power. The majority of mediums who grasp some of the basic facts about the Restless Dead usually have incomplete information, however, and much of what they know is probably diluted by their own perceptions and prejudices. Regardless, most mediums have at best a very incomplete picture of what's going on, and so like most people they fill in the gaps by arriving at conclusions based solely on their limited observations or cherished beliefs.

CHARACTER CREATION

Mediums are created with exactly the same process that is used for all other mortal characters (see pages 100-157), but they normally have Traits that distinguish them from other human beings. The most obvious difference between a medium and a non-medium is the Merit *Medium* (see p.150). Beyond that, mediums tend to have Traits that reflect their particular style and manner of dealing with the Dead.

CHOOSING TRAITS FOR MEDIUMS

The Benandanti

See Chapter Five for details on the mystical ability that allows the Benandanti to separate their souls from their bodies and walk in the Shadowlands. All Benandanti must choose at least one level of the *Melee* Ability in order to wield their fennel swords effectively, and most also take some Ability in *Brawl* as well. Physical and Mental Traits tend to be primary and secondary (which is which depends on the individual member of the organization). Most Benandanti have at least one level of *Wraith Lore*, and those who have made successive journeys across the Shroud often have additional levels (which must be acquired through experience).

The Boardwalk Mediums

Boardwalk mediums must have very good social skills: Social Traits are primary, and they tend toward beguiling, charismatic, empathetic and persuasive Natures. They frequently have a level or two of *Occult* Ability, but they almost never have anything as concrete as *Wraith Lore* on which to rely. They eschew Influences (mostly because they are rarely in one place long enough to make solid contacts) in favor of Abilities and Backgrounds, particularly *Contacts*.

The Dannati

All of the Damnation Theorists are mediums, but they are first and foremost scholastic busybodies rather than crusading knights. Mental Traits are primary for most Dannati, and they often choose Abilities such as *Academics*, *History*, *Theology*, and *Science* to reflect their studies.

The Orphic Circle

Mortal members of the Orphics always possess at least one level of *Occult* Ability, and many garner *Occult* Influence as a means of increasing their knowledge about the nature of life and death. The more experienced members of the association also possess several levels of *Wraith Lore*.

The Paranormal Research Wing

A medium who joins this organization is invariably a scientist and must have the Abilities to reflect that sort of higher education — *Academics* and *Science*. Some also possess a few levels of *Occult* Ability, and a level of *Wraith Lore*.

The Redentori

The members of this association rarely possess any knowledge greater than a few levels of *Occult* Ability and, at the most, one Trait of *Wraith Lore*. The Redentori are largely misinformed or mistaken about the true nature of wraiths.

MEDIUM ORGANIZATIONS

There exist in various places and for various purposes organizations of people who can see and hear the Dead. Some of these associations, like the Benandanti, have a formal purpose that may work for or against the ghosts with whom they come into contact. Other groups, such as the shamans of the Native American tribes, are little more than loose affiliations in which each member has his own personal agenda.

THE BENANDANTI

Children born with intact cauls, the Benandanti are those few souls capable of seeing and even traveling across the Shroud and into the Underworld while yet living. These children are trained by a sponsor Benandante, which gives them the ability to see spirits, and ultimately to leave their bodies and affect wraiths on their home ground. The Benandanti is thus an organization that targets wraiths, whom they regard as hapless spirits unable to move on after death. By discovering and destroying those things that hold wraiths back, the Benandanti believe that they allow the poor ghosts release, when instead they are condemning wraiths to Oblivion. Worse still, some Benandanti believe that ghosts are malevolent and dangerous spirits, and they go out of their way to destroy wraiths.

It is believed that the Benandanti trace their roots back to a certain Roma family, but today the group is a loosely connected society. A Benandante will watch he friends and family for infants born with their cauls intact, and then remove the caul in a ceremony that ensure their potential to see across the Shroud. After a strict and demanding 20-year apprenticeship, the child is considered to be a full-fledged member of the association. Few know of one another outside this master-apprentice relationship, since the organization has adopted a policy of secrecy to protect themselves (they were persecuted as witches and heretics during the Inquisition). This disassociated structure fragments the authority and power of the organization, making it little more than a group of individuals who share a common talent.

Nonetheless, the Benandanti share some common practices and rituals. *Novizio* (novices) receive instruction from *sapienza* (mentors) in the perils of the Underworld. Using their cauls, which are preserved since birth, the Benandanti can perform mystical feats that bring them power while in the lands of the dead. The members of this group wield the legendary fennel swords, precious artifacts of unique magical

power that have spiritual as well as material components. The Benandanti carry these weapons into the Underworld, and for this they are feared all the more by wraiths, for a ghost struck by a fennel sword can be sent to Oblivion.

THE BOARDWALK MEDIUMS

Loners and wanderers, these mediums capitalize on their metaphysical skills by traveling from city to city and selling their talents to those who are either desperate or foolish enough to pay for their services. Many of these mediums have only a bare modicum of talent, just enough to single out a few ghostly voices. They supplement their poor skills with practiced banter and manipulative ability, glossing over their lack of detailed knowledge with clever parlor tricks and snappy patter. It's this kind of charlatan that gives mediums a bad name. They frequent crowded places where the Shroud is thin — the sidewalk art shows of New York, the French Quarter in New Orleans and the boardwalks along the Jersey shore. Most "serious" mediums shun these vagabonds, and vice versa.

THE DANNATI

The Damnation Theorists believe that wraiths are incorrigibly evil spirits of the damned who must be destroyed, not only for their own sakes but for the sake of the living. Swayed by the acts of Spectres and perhaps by personal experiences with ghosts, the Dannati actively engage in spiritual manipulation with the intent of destroying wraiths. Most members of this group are smart enough to understand that a direct campaign against the Shadowlands would be both foolish and perhaps suicidal, so they arrange instead for events to destroy Fetters, spread erroneous information that leads wraiths to Oblivion, and otherwise plague the Underworld in a variety of minor ways. Some Dannati are members of the Arcanum, and a few have managed to get themselves recruited into the Inquisition. From inside these organizations, the Dannati are able to access data and resources that contribute to their principle goal of eliminating as many wraiths as possibly.

THE ORPHIC CIRCLE

This group is unique among those organizations that focus on wraiths because its membership includes a number of supernatural individuals. Formed to study the true nature of death and the afterlife, the association has gained the participation of such creatures as necromantic vampires, death mages and even some wraiths. The bulk of the membership is still comprised of ordinary mortals, however, most of them possessing specialized knowledge of the Underworld or some ability as mediums. All of the members of the Circle share one trait in common: They seek knowledge. Their tradition draws on the myth of Orpheus, who supposedly returned from the Underworld with a set of scrolls containing necromantic secrets and lore. Members of the circle seek an understanding of life and death so as to gain power over life itself.

The Orphic Circle is, both to those without and within, very much like a cult. Its structure is similar to that of the ancient mystery cults of Dionysus, and its members engage in some of the same practices. The Circle holds annual orgiastic rites, and conducts both formal and informal study groups focusing on the Underworld and the Shadowlands. Most of the members belong to the group's Outer Circle, which is in turn led by an Inner Circle (also called the Ebon Bench), consisting of nine priests and priestesses who guide the organization. At any given time, the Orphics boast around 300 members, and membership is for life. Vacant positions are filled by appointment from the Kerberos, a 10-member council that screens potential applicants.

Upon joining the Orphics, each member must swear a mystically binding oath of secrecy. Naturally, its members target those who betray the Circle for death (the Circle has no qualms about creating more wraiths to serve its ends). Not surprisingly, the supernatural members of the association wield considerable influence among the Orphics, and more than one novice of the Outer Circle has grown envious of the powers these individuals display.

THE PARANORMAL RESEARCH WING, ALTERNATE ENERGY GROUP

The PRW, a splinter group of the AEG, consists of radical scientists who study the industrial uses of psychic energy and other supernatural phenomena. Ostensibly, these scientists embarked on this highly unusual effort in order to solve the world's energy crisis, but whether this lofty goal constitutes their true agenda remains to be seen. The PRW has discovered "ectoplasmic converter engines" that are capable of liquidating spiritual matter into inert energy, but they have not yet found any practical applications for this achievement, nor have they been able to harness the resulting energy. They continue to try, however, and many unfortunate wraiths have been liquidated as the PRW continues its experiments and projects.

The PRW's most promising experiments are conducted with as much secrecy as it can muster. Much of the group's funding comes from multinational corporate conglomerates that would not take kindly to its efforts being bandied about in the media. Though the AEG publicly denounces the efforts of the PRW, considerable sums of taxpayer money still make their way into the PRW's coffers, and the group has managed to produce some interesting pieces of equipment as a result. One of its more useful discoveries is the chaoscopic scanner.

Members of this group are scientists who apply the scientific method to their investigations. Unbeknownst to the PRW at large, several mediums have been able to join its ranks, most of them with the intent of using the PRW's work to further their own plans of identifying and destroying wraiths.

THE REDENTORI

The Redentori believe that wraiths are merely souls who do not understand that they are dead, and they maintain that the role of the Benandanti is to encourage them to move on to their final reward. The Redentori do so by destroying the material attachments (Fetters) of the wraiths. The members of this association are still cautious when dealing with the Restless Dead, however, because they realize that not all wraiths are peaceful or friendly. Nonetheless, they are more likely to assist individual ghosts as a matter of course, but their lack of understanding about the true nature of the wraiths' condition has led to some potentially dangerous situations. More than one Redentori has found himself the target of angry wraiths after trying to help them, only to discover that his actions jeopardized the wraiths' fight to carry on the pursuit of some goal or uphold some passion after death.

SHAMANS

Ghosts roamed across the wilds of the North American continent long before the coming of the first European settlers. For hundreds of years, Native Americans have passed down stories of life after death, and of the places where the soul goes when the body dies. Many legends tell of ghosts returning to family members, to warn of imminent catastrophes or to punish deserving sinners. Other stories warn of enemies

who return from beyond the grave to exact vengeance, to curse entire generations of families, and even to cause diseases that destroy crops or wipe out entire tribes.

Native Americans have long had their own methods of communicating with the Restless Dead. The exact techniques and even perceptions of ghosts vary from tribe to tribe. Native American wraiths are exceedingly rare, however, because of the geographic arrangement of that area of the Shadowlands where such spirits dwell. However, Native American mediums—shamans—are somewhat less rare than their ghostly counterparts.

Most people labor under serious misconceptions about just what a shaman is, thanks in large part to the mass media. While many shamans are in fact healers exactly as portrayed in popular culture, they are far more than just "medicine men." True shamans contact spirits and ghosts for any number of reasons, and undergo lifelong training in the methods of dealing with these creatures. Shamans are also protectors, responsible for appeasing the spirits and thus ensuring good fortune for their tribe. The current situation of the Native Americans requires much less appeasement of spirits than in former days, but the shaman still plays a vital role in tribal society even on the reservations. Most shamans have a particular spirit guide with whom they prefer to work, and many do not care to step beyond the boundaries of that relationship. Others deal with a broader range of ghosts.

GENERAL BELIEFS AND CUSTOMS

Everything in the shaman's world — human, animal, rock or tree — has a spirit. Weather, the sky, even the Earth itself are considered spirits. The spirits that populate the world take many roles in tribal life: Some are guides, protectors, advisors or watchers, for example. A spirit is capable of taking any form, and most of these forms are not human. A wraith can pass itself off as one of these spirits, but most know better than to try: The consequences of discovery are too dangerous. There are better, safer methods of contacting shamans, such as during a vision.

Wraiths get little respect from Native Americans, most likely because tribes generally believe that a ghost is trapped between worlds, usually because its body was not buried properly or died improperly. The shamans do not encourage sympathy for anyone who did not choose to heed the teachings of the living spirits of earth and water either, and thus have failed to observe the ritual aspects of death. Many tribes do believe, however, that death is just a door into another life, an existence much like the one they live while alive. Members of these tribes feel sympathy for wraiths, or fear them because of their legendary power to cause illness or disease.

CONTACT BETWEEN SHAMANS AND WRAITHS

Wraiths who contact Native American shamans have something of an advantage over those who contact mediums from other cultures. A shaman already has a pretty good idea of what is beyond the Shroud, and he is unlikely to require any convincing that he is indeed communicating with a wraith. However, the wraith should be prepared to be the recipient of considerable suspicion and mistrust from the shaman, who is unlikely to believe everything he's told about the wraith's motivations for asking for assistance. The smart wraith does a little research before contacting a shaman, to make sure that he understands the beliefs and customs upheld by the shaman's tribe.

Geographical Distinctions

Not all shamans are essentially the same. The beliefs and customs of each tribe are distinct, and so it is among shamans as well.

Shamans of the Southeast

The notable tribes of the Southeast are the Catawba, Cherokee, Chickasaw, Choctaw, Creek, Natchez, Shawnee and Shoshone. Most of these tribes share a generalized dread of ghosts, but they are especially concerned about dead enemies who may come back from the grave to exact vengeance. Shamans from these tribes often call on help from any "friendly" spirits in the vicinity if they have any reason to be suspicious of a visiting wraith. Wraiths seeking the favor of these shamans can sometimes gain it by responding to their calls for aid and driving away or destroying ghosts of which the shamans are afraid.

Among the southeastern tribes, the Cherokee are probably the most likely to receive wraiths with anything approaching hospitality. Ghosts play a more important role in their tribal beliefs than in the others of the region, and Cherokee shamans often offer visiting wraiths gifts such as tobacco or herbs in order to appease them. The Shoshone, on the other hand, are famous exorcists. They are extraordinarily adept at finding and destroying Fetters, thus freeing anyone who is possessed by a wraith.

Shamans of the Northeast

The northeastern tribes — among them the Delaware, Iroquois, Mohawk and Ojibwa — are not known for welcoming or tolerating visits from the Restless Dead. Shamans of these tribes often prepare themselves for the rigors of dealing with the spirit world through fasting and mental exercises, and after days of this hard work the wraith of a dead person is not a welcome sight. Only the weak or inexperienced shamans of the Northeast are fooled by a wraith and convinced to help it. Veteran shamans invariably call upon their spirit guides and protectors to deal with any wraiths that may appear to them. Members of these tribes simply do not pay attention to the human dead, considering them to be beneath their notice. They prefer to deal only with the spirits of the natural world (and so some clever wraiths impersonate such spirits in the hope of gaining a northeastern shaman's aid).

Shamans of the Southwest

Among the tribes of the southwestern deserts — the Hopi, Navaho and Zuni among them — ghosts, mediums, visions and spirit conversations are forbidden topics of conversation. These tribes fear the Dead, and many don't want mediums anywhere near them because they fear that ghosts might be attracted to such people.

There are some shamans among these tribes who will, however, deal with wraiths in return for something they particularly want: information. These mediums desire to know where the souls of the deceased are and what they are doing. In exchange, the shaman uses his powers to fulfill the wraith's requests, assuming the information is valuable. The southwestern tribes ostracize and even hunt individuals they believe to be trafficking with the Dead. In fact, these tribes call such people "witches," to identify them as evil dealers with the Dead. For a shaman of these tribes to assist a wraith, he must stand to gain knowledge of considerable value.

The Navaho tribe has three types of mediums: crystal gazers, skinwalkers and *yatali* ("those who walk with beauty"). Crystal gazers are not avoided because they are not considered to be very powerful or threatening. These shamans exercise their powers by looking into a bowl of water and allowing visions of trouble to appear to them. The skinwalkers, on the other hand, are witches. They deal with Spectres, and

with the help of the Shadow-eaten they cause a particular type of illness — the Ghost Sickness — among members of their tribe, and the Spectres feed from the pain and suffering of the victim as she wastes away. Naturally, the Navaho avoid the skinwalkers whenever possible, and when they cannot be avoided the tribe sends for a *yatali*, sometimes called a singer. The *yatali* are famous healers who use ceremonies and rituals to cure many different types of illnesses, including Ghost Sickness. They sometimes deal with wraiths, but they demand gifts from the Restless Dead that benefit their entire tribe.

Shamans of the Northwest

The shaman of tribes of the northwestern region — the Aleuts, Chinook, Coos, Inuit, Kwakiutl, Lumni, Tlingit, Thimshian and Yakima—are well known for their willingness to help wraiths. They expect some service from the Dead in return for this aid, however, usually in the form of information or work. Ghosts are common in the traditions and mythologies of these tribes, and perhaps for this reason mediums are likewise more common among them. This is especially true among the Inuit and the Yakima, of whom it is sometimes said that every member of these tribes sees ghosts.

Naturally, this situation creates something of a backlog of wraiths waiting to speak to the shamans of these tribes. The mediums of this region have numerous contacts among the ghosts, many of whom were legendary hunters in life and continue this profession after death. The shaman often passes on a specific wraithly request (such as a wraith's search for a particular ghost, person or object) on to one of his hunter friends, rather than undertaking the task himself.

Shamans of the Plains

The Great Plains tribes — the Apache, Arikara, Blackfoot, Crow, Hidatsa, Mandan, Osage and Sioux — represent the best place to trade souls for goods, or to find hired killers among the Dead. It is also one of the most dangerous territories for wraiths because the shamans here are so often very powerful individuals who have contingents of their own wraiths to do their bidding. Plains shamans deal with wraiths regularly and have no fear of ghosts. They believe that wraiths are very useful entities. These shamans are quite prepared to bargain with the Dead who come calling. Ghosts that show proper respect to a Plains shaman can usually expect to at least be heard; those that display arrogance, impatience or rudeness can expect to be ignored or obliterated, depending on the particular shaman and his present mood.

SPECTRE CULTS

Since the beginning of human history, desperate and the disenfranchised mortals have called upon the supernatural to aid them and advance their position in society. The story of Doctor Faustus is more than just an evil fairy tale: It is an object lesson to those who would traffic with that which they do not understand. Organized religions have made their vast fortunes by giving ear to the pleas of the downtrodden and the wretched, who contribute money they cannot afford to give to the church coffers. Even so, most religions of the world see themselves as benevolent institutions. This is not the case with those that venerate Spectres.

Most mortals don't understand the difference between demons, devils and Spectres. Because they are drawn by strong negative emotion, many of the rituals and practices designed to attract and capture the infernal also serve as beacons for the Shadow-eaten. These malevolent wraiths are capable of identifying these banquets of greed and misery, and they are quick to take advantage. Posing as the "demon" that

the mortal supplicants wishes to contact, the Spectre strikes the unholy bargain with the willing ritualists. In exchange for whatever rewards and powers the "demon" promises, the mortals give themselves over to this creature's service. A Spectre is usually more than happy to satisfy his followers' requests, which are often easy to accomplish and produce magnificent smorgasbords of negative emotional energies on which the Shadow-eaten may feast. The mortals who strike these bargains make "offerings" to their "devil," not realizing that the creature doesn't care about the sacrifices or murders or tortures themselves, but rather lusts after the buffet of terror and anguish these actions produce.

Sometimes the Spectres that create these cults aren't involved just for the sake of the easy and frequent meals they produce (though that is an important side benefit). Sometimes the "demon" is preparing for all of his followers to eventually cross the Shroud as wraiths, who are then harvested or otherwise made useful. Such agendas have been the impetus for the infamous mass suicides linked to apocalyptic cults: The negative energy produced by so many simultaneous deaths allows a Spectre to gorge himself and gain a number of wraiths for later amusement.

DEALING WITH THE DEAD

For a few mediums, those born to their power and trained since birth, dealing with the Dead is — while not exactly a mundane occurrence — something that they handle with considerable aplomb. A handful of other mediums who come to their talent later in life, but have either a cast-iron stomach or a very good mentor also seem able to take their interactions with wraiths in stride. For the rest — that is to say, the vast majority — dealing with Dead is often a terrifying experience. Consider how your character will cope with seeing the horrors of the Underworld revealed to her even as the mundane world whirls on around her, blissfully unaware of what she is seeing and experiencing. How will she handle the friends and relatives who do not believe her when she claims in a hushed and confiding tone, "I see dead people"?

Even mediums who have been aware of their special talent for a while and have dealt with some wraiths are often frightened of the things that they encounter. Consider the awful situation of a college student who, without apparent cause, begins seeing and hearing the Restless Dead around campus. One day she's having lunch with her friends in the university cafeteria, the next day she's seeing the ghost of a student who shattered his skull when he dove from the high board and hit the side of the pool instead of the water. Imagine how her friends react to her confusion and terror. They aren't going to believe a word that she says about seeing ghosts, and they (like most right-minded folks) will conclude that she is either delusional or trying to gain attention. If she continues to talk about what she sees, she's probably going to end up in the office of the school's student counselor, who may contact her parents when he realizes that he's dealing with a young person who is clearly suffering from mental illness. Think about the despair she feels when her parents don't believe her, and the deep sense of betrayal she experiences as they lock her away for "observation" in some unspeakable asylum or mental hospital. And even there, among the antiseptic corridors and drugs and doctors and orderlies, she won't be safe. The Dead will find her even there, appearing before her and demanding that she help them with a bewildering array of nonsensical requests.

Is it any wonder, then, that some mediums actually take their own lives rather than live with their condition? The only hope for our poor college student is that

someone who understands what she's experiencing will find and help her. Maybe a physician in the mental clinic where she is involuntarily incarcerated recognizes her symptoms as something indicating supernatural power. Maybe a fellow student has a great-uncle who knows about these sorts of things, and brings the old man to help her friend. Or perhaps she is lucky enough to mask her fear long enough to convince the authorities that whatever was wrong with her is over now, and get herself out of the hospital to start finding some answers on her own.

MOTIVATING MEDIUMS

What makes mediums tick? If you asked a wraith, it would surely tell you that mediums exist for the sole purpose of being a two-legged telephone for the Restless Dead. But if you ask a medium, you'll get as many answers to this question as there are individual mediums. The character's motivation for dealing with the Dead should be something more sophisticated than "Because he can." His background history should provide some idea of how and why the character interacts with the entities from beyond the grave. When and how did he first start seeing and hearing the Dead? Was it right after the bicycling accident that left him with a concussion, or has he been able to interact with ghosts since he was just a boy? And how, exactly, does he go about dealing with this situation? Some mediums hang out a painted shingle and try to make a modest living by helping other people contact their deceased relatives. Others try to help put the Dead to rest, and some even try to hunt down and destroy the ghosts that they can sense. Here, then, are some of the common motivations that lie behind the mediums' activities.

Putting the Dead to Rest

Some mediums believe that they were given their special gift in order to help the Dead find some kind of peace or transcendence. These mediums usually believe that the Dead are some kind of higher being, and that they require the mediums' aid in "getting to where they are supposed to be." That usually means Heaven, Nirvana or some other equally happy destination where the medium presumes the Dead will conclude its existence in harmony with whatever religious belief system she happens to espouse. These mediums are often fanatics about their work, eschewing other goals or hopes in favor of doing all they can to "help those poor souls find rest." Some of these mediums believe that by helping the Dead to rest they are actually helping themselves, perhaps by securing their own places in the afterlife.

Mortal Connections

A few mediums would rather converse with the Dead than with the living. This attitude is not uncommon in mediums whose talent manifested early, and who were subsequently ignored, shunned or penalized for being different from normal children. It is often the case that these mediums came to terms with their ability early on and grew quite comfortable with it ever since. Such mortals are not nearly as useful to wraiths as other kinds of mediums, because they find that these mediums are prone to using the Dead for their own petty purposes. Frequently, these mediums utilize their powers and roles to form connections with other mortals, hoping that by rendering aid to others they will be themselves accepted and appreciated in turn. These mediums tend to move around a lot, because what they do rarely turns out for the better.

The Lost

Some mediums never accept what they are and spend most of their waking lives trying to deny or fight it. They cannot shut out the pleas for aid shouted at them ceaselessly by desperate ghosts, and the voices they hear often drive them into a state of near-madness. Sometimes these half-crazed mortals end up in protective custody or asylums because they attempt to injure themselves to make the voices stop. Occasionally these unfortunates manage to live a half life among their fellow mortals by choosing one voice — sometimes the loudest, sometimes the most insistent — and they listen to it to the exclusion of all the others. These mediums spend a great deal of their time trying to help that single speaker in the hope that it will, eventually, go away. These sorts of mediums are among the most pathetic and disturbing because their grip on sanity is so tenuous.

Gold Diggers

In this age wherein worship of money is as acceptable as any other religion, is it any wonder that some mediums try to transform what they can do into monetary reward? Many of these people start out as boardwalk mediums and move on to become private consultants. Those with enough hustle and *savoir-faire* end up on late-night television, urging viewers to phone them for help with their troubles, while others become the supernatural equivalent of televangelists, bilking millions of dollars from a gullible audience. Some aspire to even greater heights of fortune and fame. Occasionally, one of these glory hounds becomes the private advisor to some powerful figure, such as an eccentric financier who is convinced that his deceased sister-in-law is giving him stock tips from beyond the grave, or a politician who believes more firmly in the stars than in the polls. These modern-day Rasputins relish their role as the power behind the throne, and they are capable of using and manipulating anyone to get what they want.

For the Good of the People

Some mediums speak fondly of "those on the spiritual plane" or "those on a plane of higher learning." They think of the Dead as relatively benign entities who desire the mediums' help in assisting the living, and that is exactly what these go-betweens set out to do with a sincerity that is both touching and frightening. These are the mediums who are most likely to show up at police headquarters with information about an unsolved murder case, or who go out of their way to protect objects that are important to the Dead voices she hears. These mediums believe wholeheartedly that they are on a mission to help others, and they take great comfort from their ability to aid the living by dint of their work with the Dead.

Vindication

Then there are those mediums who are on an endless quest for recognition of their talent. Their primary goal is to be believed, by anyone and everyone. This fanaticism makes them dangerous. Capable of going to extreme lengths in order to prove themselves skilled and authoritative, mediums seeking vindication sometimes cast themselves in the role of a modern-day Cassandra (who foretold the fall of Troy but was not believed by anyone in the entire city), wandering from place to place pronouncing dooms and dire predictions with the help of their connections among the Dead.

SORCERERS

As Shakespeare once wrote, "Some men are born great, some achieve greatness and some have greatness thrust upon 'em." Many of the powers of the World of Darkness can be described as born to greatness: the Garou and the other Changing Breeds, changelings, even the Awakened mages with their Avatars and their intuitive

mastery of magic. Others have greatness — or at least power — thrust upon them through the Embrace, or, in the case of wraiths, death. But there are those who carefully, assiduously build arcane power through research, study, experimentation and no small amount of luck. These are sorcerers — women and men (and occasionally other things) who do not have the innate ability to twist the universe to their desires, but who have deciphered ancient secrets or managed to puzzle out new tricks and methods for doing what the average person does not believe can be done.

Magic — as practiced by humans in the World of Darkness — has two distinct forms. Awakened mages perform what they call dynamic magic. Under the guidance of their avatars, they bend the laws of reality into accordance with their own will. Sorcery, also called static magic by Awakened mages, is a part of that reality, but a part that most people do not know how to tap into. Anyone can perform sorcery. At least, anyone who has the perseverance, skill, understanding, will and luck to master the arcana that comprises the different rules, conditions and spells can do sorcery.

In the past, sorcerers have often been marginalized and patronized by their fully Awakened comrades, but with the disappearance of the Master mages, they have begun to claim the honor due to them. While it is true that they are not as versatile as Awakened mages and must rely on rote study rather than intuitive, off-the-cuff castings, sorcerers have certain advantages as well. Sorcerers can achieve remarkable power in the specific areas of their study. They have a less antagonistic relationship with Paradox than true mages, with simple failure being the usual result from an attempt at vulgar displays, rather than the nightmarish events that Paradox unleashes. Also, most sorcerous groups have not made quite the array of enemies that most Tradition mages tend to accumulate. In most cases, they simply fall below the big threats' occult radar.

TOWARD A NEW TAXONOMY

As part of an attempt to gain more respect for sorcerers and other unawakened mages, Practicus Hurai of House Bonisagus has put forward a new paradigm for looking at sorcerers and Awakened mages. Hurai proposes that the reproducibility of sorcerous magic counterbalances its limited versatility; that sorcerous mages are better described as 'linear' than 'static,' since progress in those studies procedes along a linear path. According to Hurai's thesis, Awakened mages would be better described as 'affinitive' since the mages in question display 'affinities' for certain aspects of reality rather than following steadily progressing paths.

Though his thesis has been well received by many sorcerers and some Awakened mages, its nomenclature is nowhere near universally recognized, let alone accepted.

WHERE THE SORCERERS ARE

Sorcerers can be anywhere there is a source of ancient teachings and people dedicated enough to make use of them. This is not to say that they are everywhere, just that they might be anywhere. The family on the outskirts of town that is always going on nature walks together, the fraternity whose pledges seem to always go on to bigger and better things, the woman from the Old Country who has started teaching the neighborhood girls the secrets of cooking could all be covers for sorcerous groups. But

Laws of the Hunt

they probably aren't. Even if they are more common than Awakened mages, there are not that many sorcerers out there, just enough to make things interesting. See **Laws of Ascension**, pp. 28-71, for more information on the Traditions.

THE TRADITIONS

Most Traditions have sorcerers operating alongside their fully Awakened counterparts. In some cases, it has even been argued that the sorcerers are the true heart of the Traditions. After all, sorcerers are more bound to tradition than mages who can shape a new effect on a whim, so they are more closely tied to a Tradition's core teachings. Sorcerers can often be more politically powerful than mages, as well. Since sorcerous aptitude comes from intense study, often with one's peers, many sorcerers spend more time within Tradition Chantries than the less hide-bound mages. Sadly, this influence must often be exercised subtly, for mages are prone to hubris and can be quick to anger when "lesser" magicians tell them what to do.

The magic of sorcerers who follow a Tradition has the same foci, rituals and flavors as the magic of a dynamic mage of the same Tradition. Thus, an Akashic sorcerer's magic will take the form of deep meditation, ritualized martial arts strikes, chanting, etc., while a Son of Ether sorcerer will construct devices and formulae to enact her magic.

TRADITION ADVANTAGES AND DISADVANTAGES

Laws of Ascension pp. 34-70 describes Advantages and Disadvantages specific to the Traditions. In chronicles that feature both sorcerers and Awakened mages, both experience the same effects — a Dreamspeaker benefits from Heart Whispers and suffers from Dying ways whether she employs static or dynamic magic. Sorcerers in chronicles that do not involve Awakened mages may or may not include these Advantages and Disadvantages depending on the decision of the Storyteller.

Celestial Chorus — Song of the One

Since sorcerers do not study the Prime Sphere or manipulate Quintessence as such, the second facet of the Tradition Advantage for the Celestial Chorus, *Song of the One*, results in their regaining an additional Mana Trait per session rather than a Quintessence Trait.

AKASHIC BROTHERHOOD

The Akashic Brotherhood has had a long tradition of enlightenment through repetition, in which the actor becomes the action. A few Awaken under this discipline, but many others discover that orderly practice brings orderly power. With discipline, mind and body unify. With concentration, internal power grows. With proper form, internal power is brought to the outside world. The focus on prolonged meditation, the committing of the Drahma Sutra and the constant repetition of katas provide an excellent framework for Akashic sorcery, and Akashic sorcerers use those elements as foci and rituals.

Un-Awakened members of the Akashic Brotherhood may benefit from the traditional master-disciple relationship even more than their Awakened companions. Lacking the advantage of an Avatar's direction, un-Awakened Akashics must embrace the lessons and wisdom of their teachers, a situation that builds their relationships and status within their strongholds. Akashic sorcerers may belong to any of the factions, but they are most common among the Kannagara and Vajrapani, thanks to these factions' linear teachings.

For the most part, Akashic sorcerers learn the meditative and physical Paths which effectively mirror certain psychic powers, especially *Biocontrol*, *Mind Shield*, *Psychic Invisibility*, and *Synergy* as sorcerous Paths. Some Brothers take the time to learn the Paths of *Divination* and *Healing*. Within their own ranks, Akashics refer to powers that rely on meditation and mental focus as the Internal Do Path while they refer to those which act through mastery of the body and martial arts as the External Do Path.

CELESTIAL CHORUS

Though perhaps lacking the overarching sense of unity that their Awakened brethren possess, the myriad rituals and incantations of religion's many faces can be a potent source of power for the acolyte who dares to call upon the powers of her god and its servitors. From formulaic invocations of the true names of God to constructions embodying sacred geometry, from chanting sutras to invoking the presence of the Kami, sorcerers of the Celestial Chorus have techniques for calling upon divine power that have been handed from generation to generation.

Of course, Celestial sorcerers are unlikely to choose such an eclectic array of techniques. All but a very few see their religion as the single true course. Many of them view Celestial Choristers of other faiths as dangerously misguided.

Celestial sorcerers may follow any faith, but they are more often found among the more traditional adherents. Even if one is accepting of other faiths on a philosophical level, most sorcerers usually find it too disjunctive to try incorporating their practices into one's personal repertoire of magic. Celestial sorcerers are most drawn to the Anchorites and the Children of Albi; they are also surprisingly common among the Knights Templar, and many were a part of that group before it joined the Chorus. Because of their often fundamentalist views, Celestial sorcerers often serve as a divisive force within the Chorus.

Celestial sorcerers most often study the Paths of *Divination*, *Fortune*, *Healing*, and *Hellfire* (though they would insist that this is *divine* wrath). Those who truck with angels and demons — Theurgists — also study *Summoning*, *Binding* and *Warding*.

CULT OF ECSTASY

The Cult of Ecstasy is not an accommodating Tradition for sorcerers. With its emphasis on extreme experiences and transcending old ways, only those with the greatest mental and physical fortitude can hope to progress without losing their minds or simply burning out. Those who are capable of thriving in the bacchanalia of the Cult of Ecstasy are often viewed with a mixture of pity and admiration. On the one hand, they seem destined to fall just short of reaching the pinnacle to which Ecstatics aspire; on the other, you have to admire their drive and style.

Ecstatic sorcerers are unlikely to find the structure they need in the more chaotic factions, but there is plenty of material for them to sink their minds into among the Aghoris, the Hagalaz and the K'an Lu. Additionally, it is not uncommon for sorcerers with some amount of fae blood to find that the Fellowship of Pan provides a route for development.

Ecstatic sorcerers seem to favor the Paths of *Divination*, *Fascination* and *Onieromancy*. *Alchemy* is also popular for the creation of formidable potions — and the occasional hangover cure. Also, those who are of the Fellowship of Pan often learn *Shapeshifting*.

DREAMSPEAKERS

To refer to the Dreamspeakers as a homogenous crowd is to commit a massive error. Even more than the other Traditions, the Dreamspeakers are a collection of wildly different people who have been grouped together by the forces of political desperation. Even with that diversity taken into account, certain commonalties appear. A Dreamspeaker's relationship with the spirit world is the key to his power and to the respect that is due him. Since most of the societies from which Dreamspeakers arise have a longstanding traditional body of lore and ritual surrounding interactions with the spirit world, it is not immediately apparent whether a sorcerer is Awakened or "merely" a sorcerer. All power actually comes from the spirits, and it is the Dreamspeaker's ability to cajole, intimidate or manipulate the spirits is more important than the versatility of his personal magic.

As Western culture and technology continues to erode the old ways and marginalize the societies from which Dreamspeakers arise, the political climate within the Tradition has shifted, with old members threatening to leave and traditionally separate groups such as the Balamob and Uzoma moving back into the fold. In a group as loose as the Dreamspeakers, it is unlikely that this flux will stabilize any time soon.

A Dreamspeaker's place in his native society — whether outsider, tribal mentor or something completely different — is often the key to his status. That, force of will, and an understanding of the local spiritual politics are the makings of a Dreamspeaker of any flavor.

Dreamspeaker sorcerers study *Summoning*, *Binding* and *Warding* perforce. They also study such diverse Paths as *Alchemy* (in the guise of *Herbalism*), *Divination*, the *Enchantment* of fetishes, *Fortune*, *Healing*, *Onieromancy*, *Shapeshifting* and even *Weather Control*, depending on the needs of their native society.

EUTHANATOS

The Euthanatos view sorcerer members as being on a different karmic cycle than their Awakened brethren. At different points, different people need to learn different lessons. Such is the way of the world. At least, that is the party line. Though the Tradition offers a massive array of traditional technique and dogma to empower its sorcerers, it cannot be denied that they sometimes lack a certain inherent awareness of their role in the greater scheme of things.

Thanatoic sorcerers may come from any faction, but they tend to find the Lhakmist sect less conducive to sorcerous growth.

Most Euthanatos sorcerers are very cautious about the Path of *Hellfire* — it is too easy to fall from the Wheel. Still, it is not uncommon for a Thanatoic sorcerer to study it. *Divination* and *Fortune* are the favored Paths, with *Healing* as a close third.

ORDER OF HERMES

The Order of Hermes has both the best and worst to offer its sorcerers. Though sorcerers have historically played second fiddle to the Order's Awakened members, the structured nature of Hermetic magic combined with the Order's vast corpus of lore make an appealing combination. All initiates of the Order of Hermes start with sorcerous training, but those who stay at that level are often looked upon as inferior to those who Awaken. Many of the Order's sorcerers have become accustomed to the magelier-than-thou attitude of their cohorts and being relegated to support roles.

With the fall of Doissetep and the loss of most of the Masters, however, the Hermetic sorcerers are trying to claim their rightful role as a power in and of themselves.

Sorcerers are found in all branches and factions of the Order of Hermes, and each faction has a different core curriculum (e.g., *Alchemy* for the newly rejoined Solificati and the *Path of Fortune* for House Fortunae). Though there was almost certainly extensive material on each of the Paths somewhere in the Order's many libraries, much of it has been lost, hidden or destroyed in the recent cataclysms that have shaken this Tradition. Most Hermetic Initiates are trained in the spiritual Paths — invariably beginning with *Binding* and *Warding* before moving on to *Summoning* — and the Paths of *Conjuration* and *Enchantment*.

SONS OF ETHER

Most Etherites would scoff at the idea of an Etherite sorcerer. After all, the Sons of Ether are about science, not magic. Nevertheless, it is obvious that some Sons of Ether are differently gifted than others. Whereas certain Etherite scientists hop from project to project, others slowly develop their work in one or two focused, monomaniacal directions. And as long as the scientist in question produces results, who is to claim that she is less gifted than another (other than the fact that almost all Sons of Ether consider almost all other Sons of Ether to be blind fools).

Etherite sorcerers can be found in all factions, though they do not often possess the breadth of skill to act as Ethernauts — at least not in a solitary capacity.

The Paths used by Son of Ether sorcerers are all given the special techno-magical slant that colors all Etherite magic. Nevertheless, they tend to favor their own special interpretation of the Paths of *Alchemy, Conveyance, Enchantment, Hellfire* (a.k.a. High Energy Ether Physics) and *Weather Control*.

VERBENA

For the Verbena, wisdom and an understanding of the ways of blood and earth have always been the highest virtues. Those Verbena who philosophize about such things often claim that the different forms of magic — Awakened and sorcerous — are simply another aspect of the world's inherent duality. In this way, sorcerers are seen as a healthy part of the greater Verbena community. However, there is, as with the Celestial Chorus, a sort of political gap between the two groups. Sorcerers perforce adhere to and embrace the old ways, handed down mother to daughter for generations, while the Awakened mages seek newer ways of revering the world. For this reason, Verbena sorcerers tend to gravitate toward the Twisters of Fate and the Gardeners of the Tree, though no few have managed to glean viable magic from the studies of the Moon-Seekers.

Verbena sorcerers are most likely to be adept at *Alchemy* (in the form of *Herbalism*), *Divination, Fortune* and *Shapeshifting*. Less common, though still occasionally practiced, are the Paths of *Conveyance, Enchantment, Fascination, Healing* and *Onieromancy*.

VIRTUAL ADEPTS

Almost too new to have developed the historical momentum that seems to be required of sorcerous magic, the Virtual Adepts nevertheless have a number of un-Awakened techno-magicians on their turf. Whether they come from the human need to create magic everywhere — in conflict with the loss of the Ascension War — or there is just something inherently magical in talking to people on the other side of the

world via little boxes with keyboards is a matter of debate. They are out there. Of course, being magical and being elite are two very different things. Few Awakened Virtual Adepts consider their un-Awakened comrades to be consequential. Still, they are not bad — for lamers.

For the most part, sorcerer Adepts have minimal magical effect on the physical world. Some may be able to trick machines into being their friends or hack security codes and financial databases, but their real home turf is the Digital Web. On the Web, a well prepared, powerful sorcerer can take on an Awakened Adept and stand a decent chance of emerging victorious.

Most Virtual sorcery is only effective on the Digital Web, but their use of the *Path of Divination* and Paths based on *Cyberempathy* and *Cyberkinesis* can affect the real world. Digital-only Paths include almost all regular Paths except *Fascination*, *Onieromancy* and *Shadowcasting*.

ORPHANS AND THE HOLLOW ONES

What can be said about sorcerers among the Hollow Ones and Orphans other than the fact that most cannot tell the difference between a static mage and a dynamic one? Their traditions are a curious — and usually morbid — hodgepodge. Their internal politics are haphazard at best. This is not to say that they are ineffective, only that they do not have an established body of lore. Other sorcerers are often baffled at what Hollow One sorcerers are able to do without a coherent and internally consistent framework. Most Orphans are too busy doing what they do to worry about such philosophical niceties.

Hollow One and Orphan sorcerers may follow any Paths, so long as the player can provide a rationale that the Storyteller accepts.

SORCEROUS ORGANIZATIONS

Beyond the Traditions, the World of Darkness is home to myriad mystical organizations, and, as sorcerers are far more common than Awakened mages, most of these organizations are composed of sorcerers. Of course, much as there are sorcerers in the Traditions, it is possible for an organization that is otherwise comprised of sorcerers to spawn an Awakened mage or two. The biggest problem with this is that the arrival of an Awakened mage changes the playing field enough that it can be quite dangerous for her more limited comrades. An Awakening can draw a lot of attention, attention that many sorcerous societies are not prepared to handle.

These organizations are by no means as universal as the Traditions. The largest, the Bata'a, may have a significant constituency, but its members still represent only a relatively small geographical area. The organizations listed here are representative of the sorcerous groups scattered across the globe. There are many more, though, and the Storyteller and players are certainly welcome to tailor such a group for their chronicle. For more information on these organizations, see **Sorcerer, Revised Edition**, pp. 31-41.

THE ANCIENT ORDER OF THE AEON RITES

Seeking nothing less than bringing the world to perfection, the Ancient Order of the Aeon Rites (AOAR) distills the arcane truths contained within millennia of mystical thought from across the globe into Enochian, the language of the angels.

The Order as it is known now dates back to 1837, when Magister Johannes Agrippa gathered a cadre of compassionate, determined mystics, and bestowed upon them the rites and manuscripts that made up the Order's teachings. Since then, the AOAR has worked behind the scenes to bring humanity to enlightenment. The AOAR may mysteriously help someone whose work they see as moving humanity in the right direction, or they may reprimand one whom they perceive as working against this goal. They are particularly conscious of the activities of sorcerers, since the AOAR believes they should all use their power to work toward the same exalted goal.

The order features a nine-tiered structure. The outer level — the first three degrees — are new pupils who perform mundane work for the AOAR while they work to unlock the Order's esoteric secrets. The Inner Level — the fourth through sixth degrees — is populated by "frateres" and "sorores" who have mastered some degree of the Order's teachings, and who maintain the Order's financial, political and administrative situation, as well as training the Outer Level. The seventh through ninth degrees further the AOAR's mystical studies. Beyond these mortal ranks are said to be certain ascended masters, including Magister Agrippa, who have left the corporeal realm and guide the order from beyond. Lately, they have not been offering much guidance, though, so the Order's members have concluded that they have been kept busy by their other ethereal duties. The AOAR is centered in Amsterdam, where Magister Agrippa's original texts are still kept.

Order magic is ritualistic to the highest degree. Each implement, each gesture, each sound has ritual significance in multiple dimensions. Physical foci must be constructed according exact specifications — and those specifications vary depending on the user's numerological correspondences. Movements must be choreographed. To bring about perfection requires nothing less than perfection from those who make it.

The libraries of the AOAR contain careful, ritualized information on almost all sorcerous Paths, and possibly the seeds of dozens of others, but the most commonly studied Paths remain *Hellfire*, *Weather Control*, *Summoning*, *Binding* and *Warding*.

BATA'A

Formed in the syncretic confusion of the colonial Caribbean, the Bata'a represent one of the largest still extant magical traditions in the world. The history of the Bata'a begins before the European Age of Exploration with the Qua'ra people of the Caribbean and their spiritual magics. The native religions of the African slaves and Christianity were added to these foundations till they took the form of Bata'a.

Bata'a is built around communal relationships, both social and spiritual. A Bata'a, or any member of the community, can expect to give and receive aid as the case demands. In much the same way, Bata'a offer sacrifices of food, livestock and its own practitioners to gain the favor of Les Invisibles — the ancestor spirits of their people, some of whom predate the arrival of the Europeans — and loa, or Les Mystères — godlike spirits. In fact, the main role of the Bata'a is to ensure favorable relations between their living community and their spiritual one. The ultimate form of this communion is for the Bata'a to act as the spirits' "Horses," allowing Les Invisibles and Les Mystères who wish to hold a physical form to "ride" or possess them. Seeking possession is always a risky proposition. Beyond the malevolent baka who have always sought to sneak into an open Bata'a, the arrival of the Sixth Maelstrom has confused and angered even traditionally benevolent spirits.

The spirits most commonly called upon by the Bata'a are the Rada — spirits of healing and wisdom — and the Petro — spirits of conflict and elemental powers. The Rada include Ayida-Wedo, who governs the feminine principles of healing and protection; Erzulie, who offers love, lust and beauty; Ghede, who watches over the dead; Legba, the guardian of the crossroads and all journeys, whether physical or spiritual; and Loco, who commands herbs, healing and visions. The Petro include Chango, who controls the weather, guns and explosives; Damballah, the sky serpent and consort to Ayida-Wedo; Baron Samedi, who offers necromantic powers or the death of enemies; Ogoun the Chainbreaker, who controls fire, wrath and liberation; and Simbi, who incarnates the elements of air and water, and grants freedom or knowledge of magical powders and potions.

All Bata'a power comes from these spirits, and, in fact, they believe that an Awakened mage's Avatar is but another spirit who has dedicated itself to its mage. A person does not need to be a sorcerer (or a mage) to be ridden by a loa or one of Les Invisibles; sorcerers are merely those people who learn charms and spells from them. A wise Bata'a keeps the source of his knowledge in mind, for misusing it without the permission of the spirits is a transgression that is not easily forgiven.

Bata'a may learn *Alchemy* (in the form of *Herbalism*), *Conjuration*, *Conveyance*, *Fascination*, *Fortune*, *Healing*, *Hellfire*, *Summoning*, *Binding*, *Warding* and *Weather Control*. They may also consult Les Invisibles with results much like *Divination*, and learn the secret of making zombies by using the spiritual Paths.

THE CHILDREN OF OSIRIS

Founded by descendants of the Egyptian god-king Osiris after he succumbed to the vampiric Embrace, the Children of Osiris have recently seen the disappearance of its vampiric constituency and the dissolution of its mortal forces. Those who attempt to follow the twists of the Jyhad proclaim that the Setites are responsible for this downfall, having finally removed the oldest thorn from their undead sides. Others are less certain, whispering that the Children may instead have returned to their ancient holy sites for some secret reason. For millennia, the Children organized themselves into temples lead by vampires who practiced the austere Discipline of *Bardo*. *Bardo* sought to incorporate the principle of Ma'at — truth, balance and order — within the vampiric body, denying the undead nature and pointing toward a resurrection into a living form. Though the powers of *Bardo* have been mighty, none have ever spoken of this promise being fulfilled, and now the vampiric Children of Osiris are all gone.

With the loss of their unnatural leaders, it is as if a new life has been breathed into the mortal adherents of the Children of Osiris. Their studies into the principles of eternal life are more energetic. Their vision is clear. They have returned home, and though their ancient god-king does not appear to have been resurrected, it looks as if the cult has.

The Children of Osiris perform magic based around ancient Egyptian funerary practices, and study the Paths of *Alchemy*, *Summoning*, *Binding* and *Warding* with an eye toward necromantic concerns.

THE CULT OF ISIS

There is no single Cult of Isis — her followers have such a long and convoluted history that there are elements who do her work scattered in other groups such as the Verbena, the Hermetic Order's Houses Shaea and Solificati, the Followers of Set, the

retinues of several mummies, the Cult of Ecstasy and even an Alexandrian branch of the Celestial Chorus, to say nothing of the numerous cults devoted solely to her.

The mythic-historical origins of the Cult of Isis feature people in service to the goddess herself and the principle of Ma'at which she in turn studied under Thoth. When Isis became entrapped in the battle between her brother/husband Osiris and his brother Set, the previously peaceful mystical community transformed into a group of military sorcerers. After the death of Isis herself, her followers fell under the influence of many different forces, until they were diluted into hundreds of fertility cults around the Mediterranean and beyond. Horus the Avenger, son of Isis, has acted as a haughty, demanding patron throughout much of history, but his obvious lack of respect and tendency to treat Isis' cultists as pawns has brought many groups to the verge of rebellion.

The last few millennia have taken the magical forms of the Cult of Isis in many different directions, but ritual sensuality and sex have always been a part of its style, as have the usual trappings of Egyptian mysticism such as hieroglyphs and demotic writing, the ankh and sacred geometry. Members of the Cult of Isis commonly study *Alchemy*, *Divination* (in the form of *Astrology*), *Healing* and the *Enchantment* of talismans and statues.

MAISON LIBAN

Amid the chaos of the 11th century, House Tremere experienced the destruction of House Diedne, the schism with Goratrix, and the flight of Magister Mathieu de Calice, a Master specializing in Parma Magica — protective magic. Though the Goratrix/Tremere schism has had very visible consequences for the World of Darkness, it is unlikely that anyone other than Magister de Calice and his apprentices and their heirs — and Tremere himself, perhaps — remember this betrayal. Less than a month after de Calice's flight, the move to vampirism commenced, an event that was to keep the new clan busy long enough for the Magister to go to ground.

De Calice fled to northern France and hid himself and his group, both magically and socially. One of the magical techniques used was the changing of the group's name, since names have great power in Hermetic magic. De Calice chose the word "Liban" because it meant to live, leave and survive in the tongue of the Visigoths — and few of the Tremere were still truly alive.

In modern times, this tradition of discretion is still scrupulously observed. Students are taught to keep their magical and regular lives well apart. Though they may aid friends and those whom they find deserving, Liban sorcerers are not crusaders. Discretion has served them well thus far, and they have yet to see a good reason to leave it behind. Within their chantry walls, members are titled Initiate until they are deemed ready to teach, at which point they are called Prater or Mater. The greatest teacher within Maison Liban is referred to as the Pontifex.

The members of Maison Liban perform magic that is Hermetic in nature and appearance, but they specialize in the *Path of Divination* and the spiritual Paths. House Liban members are also well versed in *Countermagic*.

NEBUU-AFEF (THE ORDER OF THE GOLDEN FLY)

According to Order legend, the Nebuu-Afef were formed by warrior-mystics because of the happenings during the reign of the Pharaoh Ramses and the divine plagues that struck Egypt immediately prior to the great exodus of Moses and his people. Having each lost their first-born, the mystics set to summoning and controlling

Mastema — the angel who had visited that curse upon them in the first place. Taking their name from the piece of jewelry granted to warriors in honor of their courage — a golden fly — the members of Nebuu-Afef found themselves learning the darkest of sorceries from their new servitor.

Driven from Egypt by the forbears of the Celestial Chorus during the reign of Ikhnaton, and facing many enemies due to its ideology, the Order of the Golden Fly has spent much of its time underground in Turkey, Greece and, at the beginning of the 20th century, Austria-Hungary. After the Order tried to offer mystical aid to Hitler during the Second World War, its meeting house was destroyed by an explosion and the Order went underground again. Most recently, evidence of Nebuu-Afef has cropped up in Boston and Lebanon.

There are not many Nebuu-Afef sorcerers since Mastema does not like serving a large group, but they are strong-willed people who are unafraid of death and violence. New initiates endure torture and humiliation as they are taught the arts of pain, fear, murder and dealing with Mastema. In time, they master a bloody form of sorcery that mirrors the monsters they have become. Golden Fly sorcerers study Paths such as *Enchantment* (of weapons), *Fortune* (curses), *Hellfire*, *Shadowcasting* and *Summoning* Mastema.

Caveat Invoker

Any order who depends upon the teachings of a single otherworldly being runs the risk of being deceived. The teacher may easily claim to be instructing them in mystic secrets while actually feeding them mere folderol. Some believe that this is the case with the Nebu-Afef, that Mastema has never been controlled by them, but has fallen of its own accord and is using the Nebuu-Afef towards its own ends. If the Storyteller decides that this is the case in her chronicle, Golden Fly sorcerers do not, in fact, know any sorcery beyond a variety of rites that attract the attention of the malignant angel and let it know their desires. What actually happens is at the whim of the angel.

THE SILVER PORTAL

A true rarity among static magicians, sorcerers of the Silver Portal manage to tap into the same chaotic energies as Marauders. Owing to the chaotic nature of Silver Portal sorcery, there is very little in the way of organization within its ranks. Initiates are given the *Zolondrodere* to read — an 18th-century translation of a 14th-century Byzantine-Greek adaptation of a fifth-century Persian scroll that claimed to be a copy of an earlier document. Most of the secrets of the Silver Portal are contained within this work, though they mostly defy conventional sanity and often require drugs or self-hypnosis to unlock.

Sorcerers of the Silver Portal engage in exercises to raise the strength of their unconscious minds. Foci commonly include mirrors, chants from the *Zolondrodere* and other tools to subvert the conscious mind, but the most powerful theatre of Silver Portal magic is Maya, the Dream Realms. Storytellers may have Silver Portal sorcerers living double lives, interacting with the waking world and the Oniera, the fantastical and powerful Umbrood who inhabit the Maya in their dreams. For obvious reasons, sorcerers of the Silver Portal often attract the attention of the local changeling community, sometimes for good, sometimes for ill.

Silver Portal sorcerers may learn any Paths — the realm of Maya is without limit, after all. The Silver Portal's sorcerous knowledge is ever mutable, however. Though

it exists both within and without his dreams, the nature of the sorcerer's powers is altered each time he enters the Maya.

System: The Storyteller and narrators should keep track of the number of Path Traits the character possesses. Upon going to sleep, the player should state which Paths he wishes those Traits to represent. For each Trait, he engages in a Simple Test. Unless he loses the test, he gets the Trait until he next sleeps; if he loses, that power is locked in the chaos of the Maya. For rituals, the player follows the same procedure, but must actually win the test — the focused nature of rituals defies the wild formlessness of the Maya. Storytellers and narrators are encouraged to work these tests into a narrative that begins that night's dream if they have the resources to do so.

THE STAR COUNCIL

Spawned in the UFO craze and paranoia of the 1950s and '60s, the group called the Star Council was formed by a group of paranormal investigators who, believing that the government was hiding the truth about UFOs from them, broke into a hangar at a high-security USAF installation in 1969 and made away with some artifacts. They are still not certain what they are, but they look alien.

A small group of disparate people with an interest in the unexplained and a belief in alien visitation, the Star Council had managed to earn the enmity and attention of people from government officials to complete crackpots thanks to its controversial theories. One group within the Star Council, called the Thal'hun, claimed to be in touch with an immortal being of light called Khuvon. Since the Thal'hun seemed to better understand the artifact from the hangar, the Star Council allowed them to lead the Council on an expedition to the Middle East where violence broke out, almost destroying the Council and attracting the attention of the authorities. Since then, the Star Council has pared itself down to a trusted few and taken a more circumspect approach to their studies. Members have been the subject of numerous suspicious events, from trailings by mysterious men to unexplained time loss. At present, the mood within the group is one of paranoia and excitement. They are certain that they have almost discovered the truth, but fear they may be too late.

The Star Council is dependent upon the artifacts they stole from the government for all their powers — which they consider to be alien science rather than magic — but through experimentation, they have learned how to evoke effects that mirror *Conveyance*, *Hellfire* and *Weather Control*. Additionally, many Star Council members possess psychic powers.

AND THE REST

There are many other sorcerous orders throughout the World of Darkness. Most are tiny cabals, some are pawns of other forces, and others are only the matter of speculation and legend. Storytellers may want to incorporate groups such as these into their campaigns as back-story, offstage forces, or for whatever roles they might need. The Cult of Mercury is a ritual society dedicated to the prosperity and wealth of its members. The Mogen Ha Chav is a group of Qabbalistic mystics who protect 'the 36 Good Men' who protect the world. The Priests of the Pythian Order were a small divinatory cabal that was taken over by the being that took control of the Delphic Oracle. The 7 Thunders were a group of sorcerers who believed that they were the forces of an ancient prophecy; they have discovered that this is not the case, but are still active.

CRAFTING YOUR OWN SORCEROUS ORDER

Like all other groups, sorcerous orders rise and fall, dependent upon the forces of environment and fortune. The Storyteller may want to create (or encourage her players to create) sorcerous orders for her chronicle using the above as guidelines or inspiration.

WHAT MAKES A SORCERER

Who can study sorcery? Anybody. The knowledge and technique are out there for anybody who can find the prerequisite moldy tomes or mentor. Anybody can study sorcery, but not everybody can use it. Sorcery has evolved to use the mystic signatures of the World of Darkness' most common inhabitants — humans.

Most characters in World of Darkness chronicles are not human, and they have developed their own sets of powers. Unless it is specifically mentioned that a supernatural being can use sorcery — like the Bubasti — it is safe to assume that the powers that make it other-than-human interfere with its use of sorcery. In the case of partially supernatural creatures such as ghouls, kinain or Kinfolk, the change to their mystical presence has usually not progressed to the point where it interferes with sorcery. They may not be as powerful as vampires, changelings and Garou, but learning sorcery can help even the odds a little.

What about mages? They are still mortal, but the Awakening of the Avatar usually changes a mage's magical presence enough that the rules of sorcery no longer apply. Fortunately, for those such as Order of Hermes mages who are trained in sorcery before they Awaken, the principles learned (Experience Traits) readily transfer to Sphere magic. Others who studied less organized systems may find that it takes longer to utilize their training (non-Hermetic sorcerers may convert their Path Experience Traits at a rate of two per session).

As is always the case, the Storyteller may change the rules. She may decide that she needs all shapeshifters to have the extra edge of sorcery available for them, or that the presence of the Blood in ghouls is enough to stop the flow of magic, or Path magic and Sphere magic might both be available to Awakened mages. After all, Experience Traits going toward Path magic are not going toward the character's other powers, so it should even out. A Storyteller who decides to take this route should be prepared for the player who wants to add *Conveyance* to *Celerity* to surpass his sire in speed. She should have a ruling prepared on whether the abilities work together in an additive fashion, interfere with each other or act in some other manner entirely, and make sure that the Narrators know how it all works — even if the characters have to experiment to discover the details.

ABILITIES

More so than many other inhabitants of the World of Darkness, the sorcerer is dependent on his Abilities. Most supernatural creatures have essential forces that empower them, but a sorcerer has only what he has learned.

Progression along the different sorcerous Paths requires study, practice and experimentation. Additionally, sorcerers need to master many of the mundane aspects of reality before they can hope to master the eldritch. An AOAR sorcerer who wishes to craft a dagger that strikes spirits needs to know how to forge a dagger of the proper dimensions and materials. A Cult of Isis herbalist needs an encyclopedic understanding of herbs. Sorcerers from all walks of life need the linguistic training to

make sense of sources written in languages that have not been spoken for centuries — or to ensure they are not agreeing to something unwise when they bargain with spirits that refuse to speak in anything other than Hittite.

This spread of experience ensures that sorcerers are often able to solve problems through non-magical means, and most sorcerers try to choose mundane jobs that complement their sorcerous studies (although there are precious few modern career paths that call for a thorough understanding of the Hittites).

BACKGROUNDS

Lacking the benefits of the fully supernatural occupants of the World of Darkness, sorcerers must depend upon their own resources to further their studies. Without an Avatar to act as guide or a Totem to offer gifts, most static mages require either *Library* or *Mentor* Backgrounds, though a few (like the Star Council) manage to get by with only *Contacts* or *Allies*. Of course, *Influence* and *Resources* are as useful to sorcerers as they are to anyone else.

In addition to the usual Backgrounds, there are several that are unique to sorcerers.

Mana

Mana, called by one name or another, is common to almost all forms of sorcery. It is that extra something that some people have that allows them to do more than even other sorcerers. Sorcerers with the *Mana* Background are likely to be more in tune with their mystic heritage. They get a bit more out of meditation or have a slightly more intuitive grasp of the rituals. Some theorists believe that sorcerers who can handle Mana in this way are on the verge of Awakening, but there is no empirical evidence to back this up.

Guide

Many magical lineages hold the notion of a mystical tutor in an animal form in high regard. Sorcerers who feel the need for a nonhuman ally, or who have strong ties with nature, often choose to consort with *Guides*. In modern times, *Guides* can take forms well beyond those traditionally attributed to familiars. Etherite sorcerers may construct the bodies of their *Guides* from spare parts, and computer-oriented static mages may receive counsel from screen pals or other digital creatures — though it would be a pretty wretched *Guide* who would take the form of an animated paperclip. Perhaps the most frightening of *Guides* are those brought back from the Maya by sorcerers of the Silver Portal. For as long as they last, they can be almost anything the Storyteller allows.

Cholé

Rare, but not unheard of, among other sorcerous groups, *Cholé* is a great boon — and occasional bane — to the aspiring Bata'a. Les Invisibles and even Les Mystères vie for the chance to ride a mortal with a high *Cholé* rating, so the sorcerer may find bargaining with such beings far easier than her less blessed counterparts. The downside of this is the same as it is for all who allow themselves to be possessed: A baka or any number of malevolent Invisibles may partake of the sorcerer's gifts to wreak havoc in the physical world.

Traits like these are meant to reflect the character concept rather than limit it. If a player sees a Background or other Trait as having different advantages and limitations than those described here, and the Storyteller believes it is viable for her chronicle, he should feel free to modify them to match his vision.

Jeremy crossed campus as usual, barely noticing the damp evening this time. Stephen was back at the apartment, doing some work that he had not quite explained to Jeremy. Something about "tracing the enemy's steps," whatever that meant. Still, he'd asked Jeremy to look up a few things for him, and at this point, Jeremy was happy to do anything to keep him occupied. Now he returned, the conquering hero hoping this would shed light on whatever mystery Stephen claimed had Jenny.

As he waited for the light to cross the street, he gave the intersection an appraisal. Marco's Pizza sounded busy inside, and the campus bookstore beside it was dark. There was a nice-looking black car sitting outside Marco's — maybe townies, but Jeremy wondered why a townie who drove a Lincoln would hang out at a joint like Marco's.

He crossed the street and paused at the long, dim corridor of the sidewalk where it passed under the trees. The leaves had been making their way out, which only shaded the sidewalk even more. In the gloomy evening, the familiar stretch looked positively haunted. Jeremy shivered, and considered taking another route home — one that would not send him through the haunted forest — then he shook his head in disgust. Stephen's stories about vampires and witches were getting to him. Christ, he was going to be a basket case by the time Steve left. He squared his shoulders, told himself firmly there was nothing to be afraid of, and started down the sidewalk (muttering a Hail Mary or two).

It was on the fifth block of his eight-block hike that he realized a car was somewhere behind him. Whoever it was, they were taking their time, not passing him but prowling in the distance. Jeremy, with a well-honed gut instinct from walking at late hours, didn't like the situation, made a quick calculation of how far it would be to run back — too far, and he wasn't built for it like Stephen. He remembered there was a half-street, half-alley up on the left that he sometimes used a short cut. A few more steps and he casually turned and started to pick up the pace. He cut through a few yards, vaulting a fence when he thought he heard a car cruise past. Startled dogs barked in his wake, sentries awakened on the watch. The backpack felt like a deadweight, and he thought about ditching it when his building loomed before him.

Stephen, sitting on the couch, glanced up, startled, when Jeremy burst through the door and locked it behind him. "Everything okay?" he asked.

Jeremy thought briefly about telling him about being followed, promptly discarded it. He was getting frickin' paranoid in his old age. "Yup. Just felt like jogging."

CHAPTER FOUR: CHARACTER CREATION

Creating a mortal character resembles building a new person from the ground up. By choosing Traits to describe your character, you'll help define the role that you will play.

- **Step One: Inspiration**
— Choose Concept, Nature, Demeanor, and Association (if any)
- **Step Two: Attributes**
— Prioritize the three categories — Physical, Social, Mental (6/4/3)
— Choose Physical Traits
— Choose Social Traits
— Choose Mental Traits
- **Step Three: Advantages**
— Choose three Abilities (5)
— Assign Traits from Association (if any)
— Choose Backgrounds (3)
- **Step Four: Finishing Touches**
— Choose Humanity Traits (4)
— Choose Willpower (3)
— Choose Negative Traits (if any)
— Purchase Merits and Flaws (if any)
— Spend Free Traits (10)
- **Step Five: Spark of Life**

STEP ONE: INSPIRATION

The first step in creating your character is to decide on a basic concept. Who, at her most basic level, is your character? Almost all types of media — movies, television, novels, comic books, music, etc. — offer countless examples of good character concepts. Maybe you want to play a thoughtful scholarly person who hunts the supernatural for knowledge (and dangerous thrills). Maybe you want to play a novice sorcerer who learns the hard way that she shares the night with terrible creatures, a stockbroker with a very strange clientele, or an elderly psychic looking for her missing granddaughter. Your character could be a wealthy debutante whose social life is rudely interrupted by the decidedly inhuman gatecrashers at her latest charity ball. Maybe you're a mobster, the owner of a New Age bookstore or a cub reporter looking for your big break. Regardless, your character begins with a simple concept that serves as a touchstone as you build her.

Don't feel that you have to limit yourself to stereotypes when you think about a character concept: It's okay to think outside the box. And not everybody wants to play a character who is aware of or actively hunts the supernatural; the majority of the inhabitants of the World of Darkness are normal human beings, and their stories are no less interesting and meaningful. Just make sure that your concept can be relayed simply and easily in one or two brief sentences — if you can do that, you're well on the way to creating a fun character.

NATURE AND DEMEANOR

Think of these Traits as "personality archetypes," models of behavior to which we refer when deciding how we think and act. Remember that these descriptors are personalities painted with a broad brush: They aren't completely inclusive, and they aren't totally rigid. Most people are not limited to just one element of personality. They are usually complex amalgams of several different types. People change, too, as they have new experiences. So while archetypes aren't absolutes, they are very handy guides when thinking about who you want your character to be.

Your Nature is the most dominant aspect of your personality, the core concept, belief or behavior that drives your character at her deepest level. A character who is a Bully, for example, is above all else driven by the need to harass and torment weaker individuals. A Martyr, on the other hand, spends his entire life looking for new opportunities for self-sacrifice. The character's Nature should inform and affect all his actions and activities, though often in subtle ways. Nature also defines what your character would and would not do to get what he wants.

Your Demeanor is the mask your character wears in public, the face he presents to the world. Most people don't want everyone to know the person that they really are, so they adopt one or more public façades to conceal and protect their deepest, most fundamental selves. Sometimes your Demeanor is reflexive, as you adopt a set of behaviors that come naturally to you or are easy to emulate when you're around other people. Sometimes you carefully cultivate a particular Demeanor, reinforcing it consciously whenever you're in a situation in which your Nature might otherwise shine through. It's the interaction between Nature and Demeanor — sometimes obvious, but more often very subtle — that help make these archetypes work.

GAME EFFECTS OF NATURE AND DEMEANOR

Whenever your character demonstrates a strong example of her Nature (a Fanatic refuses to betray his pet cause even in the face of what seems like certain death), your Storyteller may choose to reward you by refreshing a Willpower Trait or Humanity Trait that was expended previously. However, when other characters glimpse your true self — your Nature — they may be able to use it against you by trying to manipulate your convictions. If you know someone's Nature, you may employ it as a bid exactly as if it were a Negative Trait, as long as the situation is appropriate to the action (ask a Storyteller when in doubt). For example, you might be able to use a Director's Nature against him if you're trying to convince him to help you stage a *coup* in your organization — you might appeal to his sense of order, for example, pointing out how much better things would be if he would step in and take charge.

ARCHITECT

You want to build something lasting, something that will endure after you are gone, and gain satisfaction from activities that will have an impact on the future.

BULLY

You know that are only two types of people in the world: The kind you can push around, and the kind you can't. Life is tough, but you are tougher, and you want to make sure everybody knows that.

CAREGIVER

The only things that can stave off the darkness that threatens to engulf the world are people who care. You are one of those — you want to help other people, to alleviate suffering and to make a real difference.

COMPETITOR

Life itself is a contest, and you intend to win. You devote all your energies into constantly proving that you are the best at what you do.

CONFORMIST

You adapt to any situation by following someone else's lead. Some would call you unimaginative or spineless, but in fact you're as creative and brave as any other. You're simply at your best when you're carrying out orders or trying to fit into a group.

CONNIVER

Why do all the work (or any work, for that matter) when you can get someone else to do it for you? You prefer to create subtle plans that get you what you want, usually by manipulating others.

CURMUDGEON

Everything sucks, and you want to make sure that everybody else knows it. No flaw or shortcoming is too minor to escape your notice and immediate complaint.

DEVIANT

Commonly accepted social norms mean little to you. Maybe you follow a personal code of morality that just doesn't mesh well with the status quo, or maybe you're always

looking at things from the other end of the telescope. For whatever reason, you simply don't fit in.

DIRECTOR

There are only two ways: Your way and the highway. You live for the challenges of bringing order from chaos, and you're damn good at it, too.

EXPLORER

You gain satisfaction from blazing new trails. Whether the *terra incognita* you're mapping is a new supernatural creature or a new theory, you shine when events take you into uncharted territory.

FANATIC

The cause is everything. Whether you are on a personal quest for vengeance against the vampire that sucked your brother dry or you just want to get to work on time, you're a person with a mission — and woe to anyone who gets in your way.

GALLANT

A life without style just isn't worth living. Your main goal is to be in the spotlight — no stunt is too wild or dangerous for you if it gets you the attention and enjoyment you crave.

HEDONIST

Life's a bitch and then you die, but there's no reason to be uncomfortable in the meanwhile. You enjoy life's pleasures and seek them out when you can.

JESTER

Your sense of humor is your shield against the pain and suffering that suffuses the world around you. You strive to find something humorous in every situation, no matter how tense or depressing, because you know that if you can't laugh you might as well be dead.

JUDGE

You want to discover the truth and see that justice is done. You seek to expose the guilty, resolve arguments and punish the wicked through any means possible, from diplomacy to fisticuffs.

LONER

You're always alone, even in a crowd. Maybe you don't understand other people, or maybe you understand them all too well. Regardless, you avoid contact when you can, and you accomplish your goals without letting anybody inside.

MARTYR

Satisfaction comes from giving of yourself, even if that means making the ultimate sacrifice. Someone must suffer for the greater good, after all, and that someone might as well be you.

PENITENT

Nobody can forgive the things you've done, so you spend your life trying to atone for your sins. You hope that by pursuing and destroying evil the scales will somehow balance.

REBEL

You're too independent and free-willed to tolerate authority, even when it's well meaning. Anyone who tries to tell you what to do, even if it's obviously for your own good, really irritates you.

SAGE

Everyone can benefit from a little advice, especially yours. You're the scholar and the counselor, the one who has seen and done it all. If everyone around you would only listen to you, life would be perfect.

SURVIVOR

The word "quit" is not in your vocabulary. No matter how dangerous or ugly the situation, you are determined to make it through alive, and you're willing to make sacrifices as necessary.

TRADITIONALIST

Sometimes the best way of doing things is the old way. Technology and innovation have their place, but people ignore the tried and true at their peril.

VISIONARY

You have a vision of the future, anything from personal gain to global change. Regardless, your vision gives you the will to carry on even when the odds are stacked against you. Your personal insight and wisdom gives you access to ideas that others just can't envision.

ASSOCIATION

The night is not a safe or friendly place. If you're playing a character who investigates or hunts the supernatural, facing the night and the creatures that inhabit it alone is even less safe (particularly when you know secrets that might get you killed). Though rogue hunters do exist, many mortals who stalk the supernatural are members of an organization, and they work together with fellow members in the pursuit of the supernatural. Many organizations do not, however, advertise the fact that they maintain an interest in inhuman creatures believed to exist only in folklore. Most would not even admit that such things existed, let alone that they bankroll individuals (sometimes at the taxpayer's expense!) whose primary task it is to track down these things and destroy or study them. In fact, the agents who hunt the supernatural are often required to conceal the true nature of their work from other members of their own organization who are not members of their "special division." The necessity of maintaining this constant level of secrecy can, of course, lead to complications in the field.

Characters who are not hunters may also find it beneficial to join the membership rolls of an organization. Many professions, such as teaching, law enforcement and transportation, are supported by labor or trade unions that provide their members with

a communications network, information about careers and job opportunities, expert legal advice and a voice in the community and political system, all in exchange for nominal annual dues. Some people belong to community service and fraternal organizations, each of which has a particular set of goals (improving living conditions for minorities, sharing political power or raising money for charities) and membership benefits. Other people belong to less formal organizations that focus on and promote hobbies or common interests, whether it's a love of cats or conspiracy theories. The most important benefits of such hobby and interests groups are a network of like-minded individuals and access to detailed information about that field. It's also possible for your character to belong to an organization that she creates herself — the Midtown Association of Psychic Friends, the UFO Spotter's Convocation or a cabal of three benevolent sorcerers are examples of such groups.

HUNTER ORGANIZATIONS

Membership, as they say, has its privileges, and seldom is this truer than when an organization is providing the support, money and materials needed to take on nocturnal marauders. Organizations provide their members with invaluable specialized knowledge about the supernatural, as well as essential equipment that can't be improvised from the local home-improvement store. That's not to say that your organization will make available to you every high-tech gizmo or lethal weapon that your heart desires — on the contrary, organizations maintain individual policies and customs that govern their members' behavior, and those agents who cannot abide by these strictures usually find themselves unemployed (or worse) very quickly. An FBI agent who requisitions thousands of rounds of silver-tipped bullets, for example, or the parish priest who asks his bishop if it's okay to "borrow" a few hundred gallons of holy water, invariably becomes the subject of organizational scrutiny, even if killing werewolves or stalking vampires is the first item in his official job description.

That said, it's undeniable that the single most valuable benefit of being a member of an organization is the fact that you'll be working closely with individuals who share your goal. Together, you stand a much better chance of surviving the terrible risks involved in taking on the creatures of the night. And never underestimate the value of having teammates who can lend moral support during a crisis of faith. Naturally, the type of organization to which you belong will dictate some aspects of how you go about fulfilling your mission.

Here are examples of hunter associations, some well known and others quite obscure. Following a brief description of each are notes about what sorts of things a member of the association might know or learn.

THE INQUISITION

Perhaps the best known of all hunter organizations, the Inquisition traces its roots back to the dark ages. Most people in modern society know, or think they know, something about the Inquisition: The word conjures images of witches burning at the stake, exorcisms and brutal torture. These people believe that the Inquisition either no longer exists, since the infernal beings it was intended to ferret out clearly don't either, or that it has taken on some less functional and more ceremonial role in the Catholic Church. They could not be more wrong. The Inquisition of today still operates under its original mandate: Seek out and destroy the supernatural creatures that are the enemies of both God and man.

Advantage: Inquisitors must always maintain the strength of their convictions, for it is this that keeps them going and gives them hope in times when their faith is challenged. Inquisitor characters may improve their True Faith by expending earned Experience Traits, rather than relying solely on Storyteller discretion. Inquisitors also gain one bonus Trait in *Church* Influence. Inquisitors who are members of an order or sect within the larger organization also gain the Advantages of that sect.

Disadvantage: Inquisitors are under closer scrutiny now than in times past, thanks to the institutional reinvigoration brought about by the latest Inquisitor-General. If an Inquisitor makes a habit of committing acts that are in violation of church doctrine, she risks becoming the target of an investigation at the discretion of the Storyteller. Inquisitors who are also members of an order or sect within the larger organization also suffer the Disadvantages of that sect.

True Faith is more common in the Inquisition than in any other hunter associations. Some study *Theurgy* (under the watchful eye of the Church). Social Traits are primary for many Inquisitors, and common Abilities include *Leadership*, *Meditation* (through prayer) and *Melee*.

GOVERNMENT AGENCIES

Unbeknownst to the rest of the population, law enforcement groups and government agencies have from time to time stumbled across supernatural creatures or their influence. If an agent takes up the cause of hunting or investigating the supernatural, he does so because one of these creatures is breaking the law or threatening national security, not because the creature in question is some sort of evil hellspawn.

Advantage: Members of government agencies are usually well trained. They are often better equipped to deal with the unexpected than the average person. Also, agents are able to call on assistance with a minimum of fuss by virtue of their affiliation. To reflect this, government agents need spend only one Experience Trait for every Influence Trait they wish to purchase, instead of the usual three.

Disadvantage: Paperwork is the bane of the agent's life. Hunters who are government agents are expected to follow agency protocols, report regularly to their superiors and be accountable for their actions. Agents who fail to follow their agency's rules may be brought up on charges, stripped of their badges or even assassinated if their superiors feel that they pose a security leak.

SCHOLARLY INSTITUTIONS

Hunters who merely seek knowledge about, rather than the destruction of, the supernatural often have the potential to inflict more damage on those creatures than all the Inquisitors and witch-hunters combined. As scholarly institutions slowly and painstakingly amass and sift a myriad of seemingly conflicting facts about their quarry, they begin to develop something that is often more valuable than anything else in hunting the creatures of the night — knowledge.

The pursuit of supernatural knowledge is sometimes a lonely quest: More than a few respectable academics have been laughed out of their colleges and companies after stating a belief in the supernatural. These types of hunters also gather in groups, the better to pool their knowledge and resources. Academic societies are dangerous to vampires, werewolves and other supernatural beings precisely for this reason: Such associations have the potential to amass a vast body of knowledge that would, if ever

presented to and believed by the public or government, prove catastrophic to the continued existence of those creatures.

Advantage: Members of scholarly groups are generally well informed about their prey. The Storyteller may decide that scholarly hunters begin play with one or more free Traits of *Vampire Lore*, *Werewolf Lore*, *Mage Lore*, *Wraith Lore* or *Faerie Lore*. Additional Traits in these Abilities must still be acquired normally by expending Experience or Free Traits.

Disadvantage: A scholarly hunter who fails to add to his association's store of knowledge loses the support of his fellows. Like those academics who live by the axiom of "publish or perish," scholarly hunters must produce some tangible results to remain in good standing with their groups.

INDEPENDENTS

There are always those who choose to follow their own path. A ghoul whose vampire domitor dies might start to hunt vampires to acquire the vitae she needs to remain a ghoul. A police officer who responds to an emergency call only to witness the horrific murder of an innocent by a rampaging werewolf may decide to dedicate his life to exterminating such creatures. A grandmother who is visited by the spirit of her deceased granddaughter might embark on a quest to put the girl's soul to rest. These, as well as any sort of hunter who doesn't belong to one of the previously mentioned groups, can be identified as an independent.

Some hunters work solo not by choice, but because they don't know that anyone else shares their experiences or goals. An independent might well join up with the Arcanum or the Society of Leopold if she knew about them.

Advantage: Independent hunters gain 12 Free Traits (instead of 10) to reflect their eclectic experience.

Disadvantage: Independents don't have anyone to call when things get rough. A hunter who finds himself facing not one but three vampires has nobody to back him up. Worse, independents must be extra careful to conceal their activities or risk being incarcerated (either for committing illegal acts or because they appear to be insane).

THE DAUNTAIN

The Kithain fear these mortals above all others. Many Dauntain were once changelings themselves, but have utterly rejected their heritage in favor of hunting and destroying the Glamour that is the essence of the fae. These hunters are the most dangerous enemies that any changeling could have, because they often possess a great deal of knowledge about the kiths and their ways. The Dauntain actively seek out and destroy fae, for reasons that vary from hunter to hunter. Some believe that changelings are merely ordinary people who suffer from delusions and are therefore in need of assistance. Others are convinced that the fae are demons, servants of the infernal sent to earth to tempt and seduce humans into acts of sin, evil and corruption in an effort to harvest their souls. The most terrifying sort of Dauntain, however, are those who are perfectly aware of who and what the changelings are, but hate and fear them for possessing what they themselves have lost.

Regardless of their motivations, the Dauntain are relentless trackers of the fae, employing weapons crafted from cold iron that they use to cleanse the world of Glamour. Dauntain who were once changelings are very difficult to distinguish from

other fae, until they reveal their true agenda (almost always at a time when their target is at a disadvantage). Mortals who take up the pursuit of changelings in the course of their human lifetime are likewise often hard to spot, because their ordinary appearance gives them a kind of protective camouflage in the eyes of the dream-preoccupied fae.

See pages 55-66 for more information about the Dauntain.

STEP TWO: ATTRIBUTES

The Traits that describe your character's capabilities are called Attributes. Your character uses these Traits during the game to perform actions and overcome obstacles. These Traits are divided into three distinct categories: Physical, Social and Mental. If you're trying to shove somebody out of your way, it's a Physical Challenge, and you might bid the Physical Trait *Brawny* as you try to use your strength to push your opponent over. Bidding a Mental Trait, such as *Clever*, would not be appropriate to the challenge in this example because shoving someone requires muscle power, not brainpower. Likewise, you probably wouldn't bid a Social Trait, such as *Ingratiating*, because chances are slim that you could charm your opponent into falling over. Only if you and your opponent agree should you bid a Trait that isn't from the category that is appropriate to the challenge.

When you bid a Trait in a challenge, you're also risking that Trait. If you fail the challenge you may temporarily lose the use of the Trait, as failure exhausts both your resources and your self-confidence. Some situations require that you bid more than one Trait in a single challenge — any time that you are considered "bids down," you must risk additional Traits. If you're considered "Traits up" or "Traits down," you modify your current number of Traits when comparing for overbids and ties. Of course, if your Storyteller permits it, you can ignore these categories entirely. This speeds up the game, although it does tend to reduce the potential for drama and tension during challenges. However, newer players may find it much easier to bid generic Traits from the appropriate category until they become more comfortable with the bidding system.

CATEGORIES OF ATTRIBUTE TRAITS

Physical Attributes describe your character's physical strength, dexterity and stamina — in essence, all the capabilities of her body.

Social Attributes describe your character's charisma, manipulative skill and appearance — the force of her personality.

Mental Attributes describe your character's intelligence, perceptions and wits — the capabilities of her mind.

CHOOSING ATTRIBUTE TRAITS

Choose which category — Physical, Social, or Mental — is primary to your character, then select which categories are secondary and tertiary. When prioritizing Attribute categories, try to keep your character's concept firmly in mind. A sales manager is likely to be stronger in Social Traits than in Physical, and a learned Arcanum scholar is likely to excel in the Mental arena. After you've chosen their priority, select specific Traits from each category to flesh out your character.

PHYSICAL TRAITS

Strength-related: *Brawny, Ferocious, Stalwart, Tough, Wiry*

Dexterity-related: *Dexterous, Graceful, Lithe, Nimble, Quick*

Stamina-related: *Enduring, Resilient, Robust, Rugged, Tireless*

Miscellaneous Physical: *Agile, Brutal, Energetic, Steady, Tenacious, Vigorous*

Agile: You have conditioned yourself to respond well in full-body movements, especially in competitive events. You're also good at scaling walls and swinging a tire iron.

Uses: Competitions, duels, jumping, running and wrestling.

Brawny: You're bulky and muscular, and built a football linebacker.

Uses: Punching, kicking or grappling in combat when your goal is to inflict damage. All feats of strength.

Brutal: You are capable of taking nearly any action to survive, and you're cruelly inventive when your safety is at stake.

Uses: Fighting an obviously superior foe.

Dexterous: You're generally adept and skillful when using your hands. The sword is mightier than the pen.

Uses: Wielding weapons in melee combat, picking pockets, acrobatics.

Enduring: You are persistent and sturdy, capable of taking a lot of punishment without giving up.

Uses: When your survival is on the line, this is a good Trait to risk as a second, or successive, bid.

Energetic: Your powerful force of spirit gives you a strong internal drive that doesn't flag. When exerting yourself physically, you can draw on a deep reservoir of enthusiasm and zeal.

Uses: Fighting, running or staying up all night to track down vampires.

Ferocious: You possess incredible physical intensity. In terms of sheer physical determination, the werewolves have nothing on you.

Uses: Inflicting serious harm, especially when you are angry or frightened.

Graceful: You are skilled at controlling your balance and coordination when using your entire body.

Uses: Dancing, keeping your balance on ice, running along the top of a narrow fence.

Lithe: Your body is flexible and supple.

Uses: Acrobatics, dodging blows in combat, escaping from handcuffs or ropes.

Nimble: Capable of making agile movements, your body responds swiftly and surely when you must sidestep danger or evade the clutches of your enemies.

Uses: Dodging, jumping, rolling or otherwise avoiding injury.

Quick: You're so fast that you can almost reload your crossbow before your first bolt hits its target.

Uses: Attacking, dodging, leaping or defending yourself from surprise attacks.

Resilient: You recover quickly from injuries, and you remain undaunted by physical dangers.

Uses: Enduring hostile environments like storms and blizzards. Resisting the pain of injuries in combat.

Robust: Highly resistant to damage and injury, your body is capable of performing extended feats of strength or endurance.

Uses: Long-distance hiking, swimming in rough seas or resisting damage in combat.

Rugged: Healthy and hardy, you shrug off injury and pain to continue struggling toward your goal.

Uses: This is a good Trait to risk after you have suffered damage in combat.

Stalwart: You're physically strong and don't compromise in the face of opposition.

Uses: Resisting damage or when holding your ground against a superior foe.

Steady: Controlled and unfaltering, you can keep yourself poised for action even over long periods of time.

Uses: Fighting in dangerous locations, flying a plane through the entire night.

Tenacious: Physically resolute through sheer force of will. You consider pain your friend and sometimes prolong physical confrontations even when it's not wise to do so.

Uses: This is a good Trait to risk in a second or successive challenge, especially when you've been injured.

Tireless: You have incredible stamina. Physical efforts aren't as taxing for you as they are for other people.

Uses: Any endurance-related challenge.

Tough: A harsh, aggressive attitude allows you to resist the temptation to submit, even when the odds are against you.

Uses: Whenever you are wounded or tired.

Vigorous: You're resistant to harm and retain your physical intensity well. Injuries don't slow you down.

Uses: Fighting, running, swimming or any challenge when you're on the defensive.

Wiry: Your body is tight and streamlined, and yet still quite muscular. You have the build of a dancer, gymnast or long-distance swimmer.

Uses: Punching or grappling in combat. Also good for acrobatics or endurance lifting.

NEGATIVE PHYSICAL TRAITS

Clumsy: Lacking physical coordination, balance and grace. You are prone to stumbling when walking down stairs and dropping objects.

Cowardly: You prefer to save your own skin rather than risk physical confrontation. You might even flee when you have the upper hand, just out of habit.

Decrepit: You move and act as if you are old and infirm, even if you aren't. You can't apply your full muscular strength, and you tire easily. It takes you a long time to recover from injuries.

Delicate: Frail and weak in body structure, you are easily damaged by physical harm.

Docile: You prefer to submit rather than fight long battles or perform extended physical acts.

Flabby: Your muscles are underdeveloped, and you can't apply your strength well against resistance.

Lame: One or more of your limbs is disabled. The handicap is as obvious as a missing leg or as subtle as an old war injury.

Lethargic: Slow and drowsy, you suffer from a serious lack of energy or motivation.

Puny: You are physically weak, perhaps because you are small or young, or because you have substandard muscles.

Sickly: Weak and feeble, your body responds to physical stress as if in the throes of a debilitating illness.

Slow: You lack muscular coordination and are always a beat behind everyone else.

Soft: You lack the physical strength for arduous tasks.

SOCIAL TRAITS

Charisma-related: *Charismatic, Charming, Dignified, Eloquent, Genial*

Manipulation-related: *Beguiling, Commanding, Expressive, Ingratiating, Persuasive*

Appearance-related: *Alluring, Elegant, Gorgeous, Magnetic, Seductive*

Miscellaneous Social: *Diplomatic, Empathetic, Friendly, Intimidating, Witty*

Alluring: You have an attractive and appealing presence that inspires others.

Uses: Convincing or seducing people to do what you want.

Beguiling: Your skill at deception is infamous. You can twist meanings and perceptions with ease. People believe what you say, even when it's nonsense.

Uses: Tricking others, lying under duress, sustaining an aura of mystery, selling used cars.

Charismatic: You have a talent for inspiring and motivating people.

Uses: Leading others or attempting to gain a position of leadership, such as running for elected office.

Charming: Your speech and actions appeal to and inspire others.

Uses: Convincing or persuading others, making a good first impression.

Commanding: You deliver suggestions and orders forcefully and convincingly.

Uses: Whenever you are fulfilling a leadership role.

Dignified: Something about you suggests honor and rectitude. You carry yourself well in social situations.

Uses: Defending against Social Challenges, or when someone tries to make you look foolish.

Diplomatic: You are thoughtful and tactful in your speech and actions. You know how to defuse tense situations and broker compromises.

Uses: Intrigue, leadership, negotiating an important deal or a truce.

Elegant: You are the epitome of good taste and refinement. You exude an air of wealth and grace, even if you aren't wealthy or a member of high society.

Uses: High society celebrations, formal events or defending against Social Challenges.

Eloquent: Listeners find you an interesting and convincing speaker. You are capable of giving inspiring speeches, stirring toasts or appropriate blessings.

Uses: Convincing or persuading others, influencing emotions or public speaking.

Empathetic: You can identify and understand the emotions and moods of others when you interact with them. You're able to sense passion and measure truth.

Uses: Detecting lies, gauging the feelings of others. Not useful in defending against Social Challenges.

Expressive: You're able to express yourself clearly, and can impart significant, interesting or detailed information even under stress.

Uses: Acting, performing or making your friends understand that werewolves are real and that if they don't get out of the house right now one is going to kill them momentarily.

Friendly: People find it difficult to dislike you after a short conversation. You're able to fit in easily with various different types of people.

Uses: Convincing others.

Genial: Cordial and warm, people find your company pleasing.

Uses: Breaking the ice, mingling at social gatherings or as a second or supporting bid in a Social Challenge.

Gorgeous: You are beautiful or handsome. You were born with a face and body that most people find very good-looking. Many people are either attracted to or jealous of your appearance.

Uses: Attracting attention. Seduction.

Ingratiating: Able to gain the favor and good will of those who know you.

Uses: Dealing with your superiors, defending against emotional powers.

Intimidating: Your presence is awesome and frightening, and you know how to use it to cow others.

Uses: Inspiring fear, bullying or ordering others.

Magnetic: People feel drawn to you and find themselves interested in your speech and actions.

Uses: Keeping someone near you, seducing others.

Persuasive: You are able to propose believable and convincing arguments and requests.

Uses: Debating, convincing others and making the implausible seem reasonable.

Seductive: You are skilled at using your good looks and body to get what you want from others.

Uses: Subterfuge, enticing, tempting and seducing.

Witty: People think of you as intelligent and humorous. You've always got a good joke or one-liner, even in the middle of a serious or desperate situation.

Uses: Entertaining or insulting someone, relieving stress in tense situations.

NEGATIVE SOCIAL TRAITS

Bestial: Maybe you have heavy body hair, a feral gleam in your eyes or a lack of timidity about your bodily functions. There is certainly something inhuman about you.

Callous: You are unfeeling, uncaring and insensitive to the suffering of others. Your heart is a frozen stone.

Condescending; Your contempt for others is impossible to hide.

Dull: People find you boring and uninteresting. Conversation with you is a chore, and you make a poor first impression.

Meek: It is difficult for you to make your presence known, so you're often overlooked. Your mild nature makes it difficult for you to enter combat, and you often hesitate before acting.

Naïve: You lack the air of worldliness, sophistication or maturity that most people carry.

Obnoxious: You are annoying and unappealing in your speech, action or appearance.

Repugnant: Whether you're disfigured or slovenly, your appearance disgusts everyone around you.

Shy: You are timid, bashful and socially hesitant. It's hard for you to meet new people or take the initiative in social situations.

Tactless: You are unable to do or say things that others find appropriate.

Untrustworthy: People believe you to be unreliable (whether you are or not).

MENTAL TRAITS

Perception-related: *Attentive, Discerning, Insightful, Observant, Vigilant*

Intelligence-related: *Cunning, Disciplined, Knowledgeable, Rational, Reflective*

Wits-Related: *Alert, Creative, Intuitive, Shrewd, Wily*

Miscellaneous Mental: *Calm, Clever, Dedicated, Determined, Flexible, Patient, Wise*

Alert: You are mentally prepared for danger and able to react quickly when it occurs. The instant a supernatural threat appears, you notice it.

Uses: Avoiding ambushes and surprise attacks. Defending against Mental Challenges.

Attentive: You note the details of what happens around you. When something unusual occurs, you are ready for it.

Uses: Preventing surprise attacks, noticing hidden foes and defeating attempts to control your mind by noticing the threat before your adversary can act.

Calm: You can withstand an unusually high degree of disturbance without losing your composure or becoming upset.

Uses: Resisting commands that provoke violence or defending against a mental power that might upset you.

Clever: You are quick-witted and resourceful. You think well on your feet.

Uses: Tricking others, using magic powers, thinking fast in stressful situations.

Creative: Your ideas are original and imaginative, and you can produce novel solutions to difficulties. You can create artistic pieces.

Uses: Creating anything or solving puzzles.

Cunning: Crafty and sly, possessing a great deal of ingenuity.

Uses: Tricking others.

Dedicated: You devotion to a cause is unswerving because you give yourself over totally to your beliefs.

Uses: Defending against any Mental Challenge that may jeopardize your beliefs or defending against memory-altering powers.

Determined: Once you start a mental endeavor, you don't stop. Whether you are researching an obscure supernatural curse or hunting for the resting place of a vampire, you are fully committed.

Uses: Staredowns, most Mental Challenges and persevering against long odds.

Discerning: Able to pick out details and subtleties, you are good at noting what others may miss. You are discriminating in your tastes and possess a remarkable clarity of vision.

Uses: Noticing the unusual, including the supernatural and psychic phenomena.

Disciplined: Your mind is structured and controlled. This rigidity gives you an edge in battles of will.

Uses: Staredowns, sorcery, defending against mental powers.

Flexible: You can change your thinking to accommodate the situation at hand. It's difficult to catch you by surprise.

Uses: Defending against ambushes or surprise.

Insightful: You need only look at a situation or think about a problem to gain an understanding of it.

Uses: Investigating (but not defending against investigation), psychic phenomena.

Intuitive: Answers seem to come to you without conscious effort on your part. Your gut gives you an instinct about what is right or wrong.

Uses: Understanding people and their motives, psychic phenomena.

Knowledgeable: You know copious and detailed information about a wide variety of topics, usually from extensive reading or experience.

Uses: Remembering important details, knowing obscure facts, sorcery.

Observant: Your depth of vision grants you the ability to look at things and notice their most important aspects.

Uses: Picking up on subtleties that others might overlook.

Patient: Tolerant, persevering and steadfast, you have no trouble waiting out your enemies even in difficult situations.

Uses: This is a good second or successive Trait to bid in a Mental Challenge.

Rational: Logic, reason, sanity and sobriety are your watchwords. You are capable of thinking coherently even about the most blatantly supernatural events.

Uses: Defending against emotion-oriented mental attacks.

Reflective: You posses an internal wellspring of knowledge that allows you to analyze and consider many aspects of a problem or mystery.

Uses: Meditating, remembering information, defending against Mental Challenges.

Shrewd: Astute and artful in your thinking, you keep your wits about you and accomplish mental feats with ease, even under stress.

Uses: Defending against mental powers, solving puzzles and mysteries.

Vigilant: Ever watchful, your attention seldom wanders. You don't miss much.

Uses: Defending against investigation attempts or mental powers that alter memories or control actions. Best used for defense rather than attack.

Wily: Sly and full of guile, you can deceive and trick others with ease.

Uses: Lying under duress, tricking others, sorting through confusion.

Wise: You are possessed of a deep and overall understanding of exactly how the world works.

Uses: Giving advice, defending against Mental Challenges.

NEGATIVE MENTAL TRAITS

Deceitful: Occasional white lies, minor adjustments to the facts and misleading others are all second nature to you.

Forgetful: You have trouble remembering even important things.

Gullible: Easily deceived, duped or fooled, you are an easy mark for con artists and tricksters.

Ignorant: You are uneducated and misinformed. You seem to know little.

Impatient: You are restless and intolerant of delays. You want everything to go your way immediately.

Oblivious: Unaware and unmindful, you would be lucky to notice a bomb if it went off under your chair.

Predictable: Because you lack originality or intelligence, even strangers can easily figure out what you intend to do next.

Shortsighted: You rarely look beyond the superficial and have trouble picking out details or making long-range plans.

Squeamish: You have difficulty coping when things become foul, dirty or uncomfortable.

Submissive: You relent and surrender at any cost, doing as you are told rather than standing up for yourself.

Violent: You have an extreme lack of self-control, flying into rages at the slightest provocation. This is a Mental Trait because it represents mental instability.

Witless: Lacking the ability to process information quickly. Foolish and slow to act when threatened.

Trait Maximums

Experience allows a character to expand her capabilities, but there are definite limits to human achievement. The maximum number of Traits that a human character may possess is affected by her age: As people get older, their uppermost capacity in some characteristics diminishes. Mortals over the age of 65 rarely retain the physical conditioning they possessed at 25, for example. And regardless of how egalitarian society may believe itself to be, it's a hard truth that as humans age they gradually become less physically appealing to the average person.

That is not to say that older or younger characters cannot be successful or effective in their chosen fields and endeavors. On the contrary, older people often possess stores of considerable experience or wisdom that help them avoid mistakes that younger people might make. The sorcerer who has lived long enough to understand how best to avoid unwanted scrutiny will be around long after the young hothead who can't resist showing off her powers is killed by a rival or thrown in jail. The street urchin who is blessed with an unshakable True Faith, is far more dangerous to unwary vampires than a middle-aged parish priest.

Some people are also capable of improving themselves somewhat beyond normal human limitations. Any partially Awakened hunters (ghouls, kinain, Kinfolk and hunters with an Intermediate level of any Numina) have Trait capacities that are slightly higher than normal humans.

The following chart illustrates the Trait Maximums for mortals:

Attribute Traits

Young (13-19 years old) 9/10

Peak (20-65 years old) 12/13

Old (65 and over) 6/7

The number before the slash indicates the maximum number of Attribute Traits that a normal mortal character can possess. The number after the slash is the maximum for a partially Awakened character.

Note: Mortal characters who fall into the Old category may not take appearance-based Social Traits (*Alluring*, *Gorgeous*, etc.).

Willpower Traits

Young (13-19 years old) 6/8

Peak (20-65 years old) 8/9

Old (65 and over) 9/10

The number before the slash indicates the maximum number of Willpower Traits that a normal mortal character can possess. The number after the slash is the maximum for a partially Awakened character.

Humanity Traits

Young (13-19 years old) 4/4

Peak (20-65 years old) 5/4

Old (65 and over) 5/4

The number before the slash indicates the maximum number of Humanity Traits that a normal mortal character can possess. The number after the slash is the maximum for a partially Awakened character.

Influence Traits

Young (13-19 years old) Half of the total of the character's Physical, Social and Mental Traits (round down)

Peak (20-65 years old) The total of the character's Physical, Social and Mental Traits

Old (65 and over) Two-thirds of the total of the character's Physical, Social and Mental Traits (round down)

As a general rule, no mortal character should be younger than 13 or older than 80. This is particularly true for hunters. While it is certainly possible to concoct backgrounds that explain why an elementary school student or a nonagenarian might be out hunting supernatural beasties, these types of characters are more often than not unviable because of their obvious limitations. Children under the age of 13 normally lack the sophistication, resources and wherewithal necessary to deal with the world as they go about tracking down werewolves and witches. The perils of ageism notwithstanding, people who reach the ripe old age of 80 are, while often still possessed of nearly their full mental faculties, usually simply not physically capable of enduring the extended, tiring activity that is the hallmark of supernatural investigation. Naturally, there are exceptions to every rule, and Storytellers should feel free to make what alterations to these rules seem to best fit their chronicles.

STEP THREE: ADVANTAGES

Advantages describe what and who you know. Sometimes it's better to know people than to be skilled with a sword. Other times, it's better to be able to swing a sword than to be able to trace a phone bill. Perhaps your character is highly skilled with firearms, or maybe she has an ear to the street. All benefits of this type are covered herein.

CHOOSING ABILITIES

The specific knowledge and skills that your character learns as she grows up and experiences life are all represented by Ability Traits. A character's Ability Traits represent special training or developed talent, and therefore they allow your character

to perform tasks that might otherwise be impossible. Even with relatively mundane tasks, such as using a personal computer or driving a car, Ability Traits improve your character's chances of success.

When your character attempts a risky or difficult task, Ability Traits can aid in the outcome. If you try any task and fail, you can temporarily expend one of your Ability Traits that is related to the situation and gain an immediate retest. You lose this Ability Trait, as well as the initial Attribute Trait that you bid to attempt the task because you lost the initial test, but you get a second chance to try to overcome this obstacle. Ability Traits used in this fashion are recovered at the start of the next game session.

A character with multiple Traits in a given Ability is more experienced and accomplished in this field than an individual with fewer Traits. Most characters will possess from one to three Traits in any given Ability: Possessing more than three Traits in Ability is quite rare. Some tasks, however, are simply too difficult or require too much skill to be attempted by a character that does not possess the appropriate Ability Trait. The Storyteller may sometimes require that your character have the proper Ability Trait in order to even attempt a particularly difficult task. Trying to sing an operatic solo without any Traits in *Performance: Singing* would result in an embarrassing disaster, while attempting to defuse a bomb without possessing at least one Trait in the *Demolition* Ability will almost certainly end in failure.

Number of Traits	Level of Accomplishment
One Trait	**Competent**: Able to earn a living
Two Traits	**Professional**: Licensed, capable of supervision
Three Traits	**Journeyman**: Bachelor's degree or instructor
Four Traits	**Expert**: Master's degree or researcher
Five Traits	**Master**: Doctorate or innovator

ABILITY SPECIALIZATIONS

Within a given area of expertise, some practitioners further hone their knowledge to a razor's edge. By choosing a specialization in an Ability, you hone your skills with a particular facet of that talent.

Ability specializations are a wholly optional rule. Remember to ask your Storyteller before taking a specialization.

Taking a specialization requires that you spend one Experience Trait or Free Trait on an Ability that you already have. Whenever you perform a task with that specialization — even if you do not expend the Ability — you gain a one-Trait bonus on resolution of challenges, as long as you have at least one level of the Ability left. You may have only one specialization in any given Ability; you cannot take *Firearms: Pistols* and *Firearms: Rifles* together, for instance. You also can never gain more than one Bonus Trait at a time from specializations, even if more than one would be appropriate to a given challenge. That is, even if you have *Medicine: Physiology* and *Science: Biology Research*, you get only a one-Trait bonus on a test of biochemistry, despite your multiple specializations.

A specialization is a fairly narrow area of research or practice. You cannot, for instance, take a *Firearms* specialization in "guns," nor could you have an *Occult* specialization of "writing." An appropriate specialization refers to one small class of

items or to one type of practice within the Ability, such as *Firearms: Antique Pistols* or *Occult: Superstitions*.

You may take a specialization in an Ability with an area of study. In such a case, you concentrate your research in one particular facet of that sub-Ability, or in one application of it. Thus, you could have *Crafts: Woodworking* with a specialization in *Hidden Panels*, or *Science: Botany* with a specialization in *Exotic Flora*.

Note that the Bonus Trait from a specialization does not have an adjective, and it is not bid or used like other Traits. You simply are "one Trait up" on challenges within the specialization.

FOCUSING ABILITIES

A few Abilities specifically require a concentrated area of study. One cannot simply study all *Crafts* at once, after all. These Abilities are specifically noted in the descriptions. When you take such an Ability, you must choose an area of study, a specific topic that you have concentrated on. Each area is considered a separate Ability, so *Science: Biology* counts as a completely separate Ability from *Science: Metallurgy*, for instance.

Academics

You possess a level of education and general knowledge beyond rudimentary schooling. With *Academics*, you can express artistic criticism, debate the classics of literature, consider philosophy and indulge in studies of culture. This broad Ability covers all sorts of humanities in learning. Academics allows you to recognize historical, artistic and cultural references. You can use *Academics* when working in such fields, when developing a critique or in researching. Calling on the *Academics* Ability may require a Mental or Social Challenge to determine your exact level of competence.

You may further direct your studies by choosing a specific field, such as *Art Criticism*, *Classical Studies*, *History* or anything else that could be studied with higher education.

Animal Ken

You have practiced long and hard to develop the ability to interact and cooperate with animals. Given time and access to an animal, you may train it to perform simple tasks (i.e., fetch, guard, attack, etc.). When the command is given, the animal must make a Mental Challenge to understand and carry out the order. The difficulty of the test is based on the level of domestication of the animal as well as the complexity of the task required. You may also use *Animal Ken* to attempt to calm an injured, attacking or frightened animal by defeating it in a Social Challenge.

Athletics

Whether due to a background in sports or just personal talent, you can engage in all manner of athletic activities — running, jumping, throwing a ball and swimming. Athletics applies to retests on most forms of raw physical activity, including swimming, acrobatics, jumping, climbing and running. You may choose to focus on one particular sport or activity. Use *Athletics* in conjunction with thrown or hand-propelled weapons like bows or thrown knives.

Awareness

You have a talent for knowing when things are not as they should be, whether by a strange feeling in the pit of your stomach or through tested observation. This is particularly useful for sensing when supernatural creatures or phenomena are in the

area, detecting evidence of strange occurrences or getting the feeling that the laws of nature are about to take a hard left. *Awareness* requires a Mental Challenge to use.

Blindfighting

You've trained yourself to fight in low-light conditions, or maybe you just naturally have great night vision. Regardless, you can compensate for darkened conditions through the use of your other senses. This Ability allows you to reduce the standard penalty for taking actions in darkness: Each level of *Blindfighting* you possess decreases the penalty by one Trait (the standard penalty is two Traits). Additionally, you can expend a level of *Blindfighting* when in total darkness to avoid having to make a retest after a successful challenge.

Brawl

You are adept at using your body as a weapon: You don't need a gun or a knife to be dangerous to your opponents. This Ability includes any form of unarmed combat, from dirty fighting to bar brawls to highly stylized martial arts. You may use *Brawl* in coordination with fists, teeth and other forms of natural weaponry.

Computer

You have learned to use computers to your advantage. You know how to infiltrate systems, swap data, access records and otherwise negotiate the information superhighway. A Mental Challenge is required to accomplish these and other acts, with the difficulty based on the system security and accessibility, time and rarity of the information. Failure can lead to investigation by normal and sometimes supernatural agencies that share this Ability.

Crafts

This Ability imparts knowledge of master artisan techniques — woodworking, leatherworking, pottery, glassblowing, gem cutting, etc. You must take a separate Ability Trait for each different trade you practice. You can make functional objects from various substances. The quality of your products depends on time devoted to their creation, materials available and the difficulty of the task in question.

Dodge

You know how to anticipate danger and use cover to your advantage. When you're attacked, you duck, weave and evade blows that would normally strike home. You may use your *Dodge* Ability only as a retest against any attempt to grab, strike or injure you physically.

Drive

Most adults have some familiarity with modern vehicles, but your experience goes beyond the basics. You are an adept driver capable of tailing and shaking tails, avoiding collisions and using your vehicle as a weapon. Using *Drive* successfully often requires a Physical or Mental Challenge. Factors influencing the difficulty could include vehicle type, road conditions and the sort of stunt attempted.

Empathy

You are sensitive to the emotions and moods of others. Your natural ability to read others gives you some insight into their motives and behavior. Though you cannot read minds or auras, you can usually make a good determination of someone's general state of mind. *Empathy* can be used with a Social Test to determine an individual's particular mood (angry, happy, sad, introspective, etc.), although *Subterfuge* may counter this capability. You may also use *Empathy* for retests with the psychic phenomenon of *Telepathy*.

119

Enigmas

Riddles, puzzles and problems are your hobby and passion. Whether you're working on the morning crossword or translating an old text, you have a penchant for coming up with unusual solutions and solving all manner of brainteasers.

You use *Enigmas* most often with a Mental Challenge to help figure out a puzzle of some sort. Obviously this Ability shouldn't substitute for all the roleplaying involved in working out the puzzle. However, when you're trying to work out a riddle or a similar challenge, you can expend a Trait to make another guess or to double your time limit.

Etiquette

With this Ability, you know how to interact politely with those around you. You know when to rise, how to make introductions, and the difference between a salad fork and a dinner fork. You can hold a toast with the best of them, and keep your cool in any situation, from high tea to a gang rally.

The *Etiquette* Ability can supplement Social Tests to blend in or impress at parties. If you make a social *faux pas*, you can immediately expend an *Etiquette* Trait to negate the gaffe — your character knew better than to make the mistake.

Expression

Words and feelings flow freely from you. When the muse strikes, you put pen to paper or fingers to instrument and pour out a torrent of emotion and stirring imagery. You can convey message and meaning in your art, from symphonies to poetry, and whatever you produce is both clear and moving.

Finance

Money talks, and you speak its language. You understand compound interest, CDs, stock market transactions, currency exchanges and macroeconomic trends. You can follow money trails, verify accounting procedures, and invest wisely. The difficulty of the Mental Challenge required to perform these tasks depends on the precautions the subject takes, the amount of money in question and your access to information. You can raise $250 per level of *Finance* you possess between game sessions.

Firearms

You are familiar with a range of guns and projectile weapons. The most common use of this Ability is to use firearms in combat, but your Storyteller may allow you to attempt a Mental Challenge to perform other gun-related functions. You understand how firearms function, how to care for them and possibly how to make minor repairs or alterations. With the *Firearms* ability, you may choose to use Mental Traits instead of Physical Traits during a challenge in which you are using a gun.

Hobby/Professional/Expert Ability

In a certain area of expertise not covered by another Ability, you have achieved some level of skill. You may have a small grasp of a trade due to some work on the side, or maybe you have devoted hours of study to the topic. *Hobby/Professional/Expert Ability* is a catchall category for unusual Abilities like *Vampire Lore*, *Thanatology* and the like. Any Ability of this type must be specifically approved and have its capabilities defined by your Storyteller.

Intimidation

You scare people. Maybe you know how to crack your knuckles in order to make your enemies quake with fear, or perhaps you know how to make threats that terrify people. When all else fails, you can use your *Intimidation* technique to convince the

uncooperative to see things your way. Note that this Ability is not the same as *Torture* — *Intimidation* involves threats (expressed or implied), not inflicting actual harm.

Investigation

You know how to locate evidence, perform basic analysis and, with sufficient expertise, you can conduct a proper criminal investigation or even reconstruct a crime scene. By succeeding in a Mental Challenge, you can tell if a person is carrying a concealed weapon or object. When dealing with plots, you may also request a Mental Challenge against the Storyteller to see if you have overlooked any clues. The Storyteller should not allow this Ability to be used as a substitute for a player's own thinking but can offer clues when you are stumped.

Law

This Ability reflects how well you understand the legal system in which you are entangled. You can use this Ability to write up binding contracts, defend clients in court and know the rights of all parties involved in a dispute. Accomplishing these tasks usually requires a Mental Challenge, with the difficulty affected by such considerations as the precedents for and severity of the crime, not to mention the legal complexity of the subject or legal action desired.

Leadership

You have a gift for influencing and inspiring others. This is a function of confidence, bearing and a profound understanding of what motivates people and institutions. By winning a Social Challenge, you can use *Leadership* to cause your target to perform a reasonable task for you. Subjects must first be under your command or serving as your subordinates. Examples include a departmental manager and his employees, a teacher and her students, and a chief of police and his officers. These requests may not endanger the subject or violate the subject's Nature.

Linguistics

You are conversant and literate in one or more languages beyond your native tongue. You must specify the language when you choose this Ability, and you may not change it. Each level you take in this Ability can represent an individual language, or greater fluency in the same language. The language need not be spoken — American Sign Language or Egyptian hieroglyphics are equally valid fields of study. This skill allows you and anyone who also knows the language to speak relatively privately. Furthermore, you can translate written texts in any of the languages you know. Translation may or may not require a Mental Challenge, depending on the clarity of the text.

Lore

You have gained some inside knowledge about a type of supernatural creature, such as vampires, werewolves, wraiths or changelings. You know what is true and what is folklore concerning their strengths and weaknesses. You may even have some knowledge of their society. You must specify what type of creature this *Lore* applies to when you choose it, and you may not change it. Having multiple levels of this Ability allows knowledge of more than one type of creature, or more detailed knowledge of a particular creature type. Specific types of *Lore* include, but are not limited to, *Vampire Lore*, *Werewolf Lore*, *Wraith Lore*, *Faerie Lore*, *Spirit Lore* and *Infernal Lore*.

Note that a character may come across some of the more common truths, myths and misconceptions about one or more supernatural creature types through personal capabilities or roleplaying. This is not an excuse come up with reasons why your character should have *Lore* Abilities for free; it simply indicates that vampires,

121

werewolves and the like have no need to study these kinds of *Lore* relating to their own creature types. Mortals generally have to come by this information the hard way.

Medicine

You are skilled at treating injuries, diseases and various other ailments of the body and mind. With a Mental Challenge, you can aid a patient to a more certain recovery from a wound, ease his pain or diagnose his mental state. The severity and nature of the patient's condition, equipment at your disposal, and any assistance or distractions that may be present can influence the difficulty of this challenge. Of course, a knowledge of healing also implies a knowledge of what is harmful to the human body and mind as well.

Meditation

By centering your thoughts, you may calm your emotions, focus your mind and relax your body. This is a very personal Ability for which you develop your own technique. It is useful for reaching the state of mind necessary for using psychic phenomena or regaining True Faith Traits. Your Storyteller may allow a character to regain Willpower or True Faith Traits by expending *Meditation* Traits and meditating out of play during a game session for some time (generally an hour) and making a Simple Test for each level of *Meditation* she possesses. Each success or tie returns one Willpower or Faith Trait (not to exceed the character's normal level or Trait Maximum).

Melee

You are skilled at armed combat and are able to use a variety of weapons, from broken bottles to swords. You are also able to care for weapons properly, preventing rust or damage. You may use this Ability for retests in conjunction with armed combat and to defend against hand-to-hand or thrown weapon attacks when you are armed.

Occult

This ability is a catchall dealing with local folklore, arcane texts, ancient legends and most other forms of supernatural fact and hearsay. This understanding of the more sinister side of the world includes knowledge of curses, rituals, voodoo, fortunetelling, magic and mysticism. Much of this knowledge is mere speculation or fantasy, and may not have useful applications outside the realm of conjecture. This Ability is most often used with retests for sorcery, and a skilled occultist can cast spells and rituals with a greater degree of success.

Performance

You can make your own original creations and express those creations to your peers. When you take this Ability, you must specify a creative specialty, such as dancing, painting, poetry, composing music, singing, or playing a single type of instrument. A Mental Challenge determines the genius of your creativity, and a Social Challenge determines the power with which you convey it.

Repair

With time, tools and supplies, you can fix or slightly alter most of the physical trappings of modern society. Because you know what makes things tick, you possess a working understanding of everything from advanced electronics to shoring up a sagging beam. This Ability also allows you to excel at sabotage. Using *Repair* usually requires a Mental Challenge, the difficulty depending on factors like the item's complexity, tools and supplies available, time pressures, extent of damage, and so on.

Science

You have a degree of factual and practical expertise in a single field of the true ("hard") sciences, such as biology, chemistry or physics. This Ability allows you to

identify properties of your field, perform experiments, fabricate items, bring about results and access information a player could not normally utilize. All but the most trivial uses of this Ability require a Mental Challenge. The difficulty depends on the resources available (equipment, data, etc.), complexity of the task and time allocated to finish it. You must choose a specific field of study. Each level of this Ability represents either a discrete field of study or greater expertise in a single field.

Scrounge

This Ability allows you to obtain and produce items through connections, wits and sheer ingenuity. This Ability is especially helpful to those who lack the financial means to purchase what they desire. Materials acquired through use of *Scrounge* aren't always brand new, are rarely exactly right and often require some time to locate, but this Ability can sometimes succeed where *Finance* and outright theft fail. A Mental or Social Challenge is usually required to use *Scrounge* successfully; the difficulty is influenced by such considerations as the rarity of the items desired, and local supply and demand.

Security

You have experience with the variety of ways in which people safeguard themselves and their possessions. Not only can you counter existing security, such as locks, alarms and guards, but you can also determine the best way to secure items and areas. Other uses of this Ability include breaking and entering, infiltration, safecracking and lock picking. Almost all uses of *Security* require a Mental Challenge with a difficulty determined by the thoroughness of the defenses, the complexity of the task and the time allotted.

Stealth

You are very sneaky, able to hide and move about without being seen or heard. With appropriate cover and care, you can conceal yourself from detection if you move only when nobody can see you or remain unmoving behind partial cover while within someone's visual range. A Mental Challenge is required to remain unnoticed by another person. Hunters use this Ability to approach their prey without being noticed or to escape when things go awry.

Streetwise

You can survive on the streets, and moreover you know how to interact with others who do so as well. This Ability allows you to deal with gangs, question the homeless and get by without an income (though not with any frills). Some uses of this Ability require a Social Challenge with a difficulty influenced by such things as the composition of the local street community and the prevailing environment among the street denizens.

Subterfuge

This is the art of deception and intrigue in the social setting. A successful use of this Ability can reveal information such as a subject's name, nationality, Negative Traits, friends and enemies. The first requirement is that you engage the target in conversation and get him to say something related to the desired knowledge (for example, you might talk together about the topic of foreign culture in order to determine his nationality). If you can accomplish this, you may then propose your true question and initiate a Social Challenge. If you win, your target must forfeit the information. To use this Ability again, you must once again lure your target into a conversation. *Subterfuge* may not reveal more than one Negative Trait per session, and it may be used to defend against others with *Subterfuge*. Conversely, you may also use the *Subterfuge* Ability to conceal information or lie without detection, and if you defend with it successfully you could even plant false information.

Survival

You have the knowledge and training necessary to find food, water and shelter in a variety of wilderness settings. Each Mental or Physical Challenge allows you to provide yourself or another living creature with the bare necessities for one day. You can also use this Ability to track someone in a wilderness setting; the Storyteller sets the difficulty and nature of this challenge. Important factors in a survival situation are abundance or scarcity of resources, adverse weather conditions, available equipment, time of the year and the type of environment.

Theology

The texts and works of various religions are well known to you, and you recognize rituals and observances from a variety of faiths. With a successful Mental Challenge, you can recognize the trappings and dogma of a given religion and recognize the faith in question. You may be able to discern the purpose of a specific ritual if you are able to observe it. Theology is also useful for retests with Theurgy, but it cannot be used in conjunction with True Faith.

Torture

You know how to inflict pain, usually with the goal of extracting information from a subject. With some tools and some time, you can force cooperation from a properly restrained subject, all without doing permanent harm (should you so desire). You can make a Social Challenge against your victim's Physical Traits in order to gain valuable information or secrets, given sufficient time. You may choose whether you wish to inflict actual damage with your ministrations; characters without this Ability who engage in torture invariably injure the victim during the course of the questioning. Use of this Ability generally takes about half an hour to elicit the answers to any one question in any detail (or to make the attempt), though individuals with a high degree of Willpower may resist longer — spending a Willpower Trait allows the victim to automatically win one of the *Torture* Challenges. The use of this Ability is a very good way for hunters to lose Humanity with extreme rapidity.

BACKGROUNDS

Your character's Backgrounds flesh out ties with mortal agencies, roles in society and beneficial resources available. Each Background is used differently. In general, having multiple Traits in a given Background allows for better or more common use of that benefit. Some Backgrounds directly affect your character's creation and development; others are called into play later during the game.

ALLIES

A few friends help you out in your endeavors. You can make a few calls and cut a few deals to get assistance in a wide range of activities. Your Storyteller will probably require you to define how you keep your allies and their relations to you.

Each *Allies* Trait possessed represents one person that you can call on for aid. Unlike Influence, your allies have special talents that make them better than the average person on the street. Though your allies may not be aware of your vampire nature, they can be quite useful if directed properly.

In general, your allies do not show up in play directly. Instead, you can use them for certain services between play sessions by notifying your Storyteller:

• An ally can be directed to follow up on research or activities that you have started. If you undertook a specific task previously, like tailing someone, researching a project or building a device, your allies can continue the work, doing so with one Ability Trait's worth of expertise. As long as they work on the project, your *Allies* Trait for the individual is tied up.

• If you need a particularly competent ally, you can expend multiple Traits to gain access to an ally with multiple levels of an Ability or Influence. Each *Allies* Trait that you spend after the first gives an extra level of expertise to your allies. They may use this expertise on your behalf, though rarely with your own skill, and they help only as long as you tie up your *Allies* Background Traits in this manner.

Be wary of calling on your allies too often. An ally may call on you for mutual aid or refuse to help if pressed into dangerous or illegal activities.

CONTACTS

With the right contacts in all walks of life, you can get a line on all sorts of useful information. Although having an "ear to the wall" doesn't necessarily provide you with good help or loyal servants, it does mean that you know who to ask when looking for the movers and shakers behind the scenes.

In game terms, your rating in *Contacts* allows you to discern rumors and information. When you call on your contacts, you make a few phone calls, check with likely snitches and grease a few palms. In return, you get rumors and information as if possessed of a certain amount of Influence. Doing so lets you find out exactly what's going on in the city within a particular area. You can get information of a level equal to however many contacts you use. If you use *Contacts* x 3 on *Industry*, for instance, you get information as if digging up dirt with an *Industry* x 3 Influence. The advantage of the *Contacts* Background is that contacts can be switched from place to place each game, getting information in different areas at your demand.

Using *Contacts* for especially dangerous or secret information may require you to spend some money or perform a few favors, at the discretion of a Storyteller. On occasion, accidents can cause contacts in one area to dry up, such as a strike that affects your *Industry* contacts, or a particularly unlucky astronomical conjunction sends your *Occult* contacts running for the hills. Your contacts do not generally function as aides or lackeys; that is the purview of the *Allies* and *Retainers* Backgrounds.

FAME

Some people become known by dint of their talent, connections or just good marketing. While many hunters and scholars shun *Fame* as the equivalent of painting a target on their foreheads, others find that *Fame's* connections open a few more doors for them than their cautious peers.

Fame allows you to exercise your connections over a longer distance than usual. Certainly, if you've got the right Influence, you can push things around on an interstate or even national scale, but with *Fame*, you can just make a few calls and get your *Contacts*, Influence or *Resources* exerted over a greater range without any impediment. This is not to say you must have *Fame* to get anything done, only that it may help. Your total *Fame* determines your maximum range for unimpeded use of your *Contacts*, Influence and *Resources*.

When you make an effort to exert your *Contacts*, Influence or *Resources* over a long range, you lean on your popularity and image, thus expending your *Fame* Traits until the

125

next game session. *Fame* is most often used in the downtime between sessions to facilitate long-range plans.

In a less mechanical fashion, your *Fame* also dictates how recognizable you are to mortals, for one reason or another. The Storyteller will certainly make the effects of your *Fame* apparent, and mortals may take notice of you at bothersome times. Being profiled on "America's Most Wanted" or spotted at the Academy Awards does things to one's reputation, after all.

Fame does have its limitations. It makes little sense for you to have this Background if you're known to be dead. Also, *Fame* does not always indicate widespread instant name recognition; you may only be known to a subset of a particular group, or to recognized experts in a certain field.

FAME RANGES

Fame Traits	Maximum Range for Backgrounds
Fame x 1	Local scene
Fame x 2	City
Fame x 3	State
Fame x 4	Adjoining states
Fame x 5	Entire country

INFLUENCE

Society builds on institutions. If you have Influence, you can sway the direction of some areas of society, pushing cities to grow as you direct. Your Influence can be used to strike indirectly at your foes while protecting your own assets, or to gain information and special resources.

Influence comes in many different areas. You must allocate Traits separately to each Influence; thus, if you have *Legal* x 4, you could still have *Police* x 3 independently but you would have to spend the Traits for each.

You cannot manage more Influence than the sum of your permanent Physical, Social and Mental Traits combined. This limit counts against all of your total Influence — your combined levels cannot exceed this total. After all, there are only so many things you can do in a night.

When you exercise Influence, you expend temporary Influence Traits. The tables for various Influence areas detail what you can do with a specific number of Traits. Performing an action requires a number of Traits equal to the level of the action; you must use three Traits to perform an action listed at the third level of an Influence chart, for instance. Thus, with high levels of Influence, you can perform many small actions, or a few significant ones.

Certain levels of Influence gift you with items, money or aides. Unlike the *Resources* Background, money and equipment garnered with Influence does not come automatically each month. If you want a steady income from Influence, you must direct your Influence in that direction continually, and this income does not come with any associated trappings of wealth (you'd have to buy a house and car separately, for instance). Aides garnered with Influence generally help only for one specific task, and they usually only have the equivalent of one level of Ability in their area of skill — for more competent and readily available help, take *Allies*.

Most cities have only a set amount of Influence in various areas. For instance, Atlanta has a great deal of *Transportation* Influence, because it is a hub of travel, while Hollywood would have a lot of *High Society* and *Media* Influence. A rust-belt city where manufacturing and heavy industry has all but disappeared would have very little to no *Industry* Influence.

Storytellers should map out the total amount of each type of Influence to be had in the city. Once all of the Influence of a given type is used up, the only way to get more is to use Influence to grow that area of society (making new projects or sponsoring investment), to destroy someone else's Influence and thus free up those resources, or to acquire an adversary's Influence in an area. Also, each city may have different reflections of the Influences listed here. A city with a thriving independent film community is going to have a different picture of *Media* or *High Society* than a city where the arts are being literally starved out due to budget cuts.

Influence effects marked with an asterisk (*) can usually be accomplished without spending an Influence Trait.

BUREAUCRACY

You can manage various government agencies and bureaus. By dealing with social programs and public servants, you can spin red tape, bypass rules and regulations or twist bureaucratic regimentation to your advantage. *Bureaucracy* is useful in operating or shutting down businesses, faking or acquiring permits and identification papers and manipulating public utilities and facilities. Government clerks at the city and county level, utility workers, road crews, surveyors and other civil servants are potential contacts or allies.

Cost	Effect
1	Trace utility bills*
2	Fake a birth certificate or driver's license
	Disconnect a residence's utilities
	Close a small road or park
	Get public aid ($250)
3	Fake a death certificate, passport or green card
	Close a public school for a single day
	Turn a single utility on a block on or off
	Shut down a minor business on a violation
4	Initiate a phone tap
	Initiate a department-wide investigation
5	Start, stop or alter a citywide program or policy
	Shut down a big business on a violation
	Rezone areas
	Obliterate records of a person on a city and county level

CHURCH

Though the modern church has arguably less control over temporal society than it did in the Middle Ages, its policies still exert considerable influence over the direction of politics and communities. Knowing the appropriate people allows insight into many mainstream religions, such as Christianity, Judaism, Islam, Hinduism, Shinto or Buddhism (fringe or alternative groups, such as Scientology, are considered *Occult*).

When you exercise *Church* Influence, you can change religious policy, affect the assignment of clergy and access a variety of lore and resources. Contacts and allies affected by *Church* Influence would include ministers, priests, bishops, Church-sponsored witch-hunters, holy orders and various attendees and assistants. Obviously, this Influence is of great use in tracking down faithful allies for a supernatural hunt.

Cost	Effect
1	Identify most secular members of a given faith in a local area
	Pass as a member of the clergy*
	Peruse general church records (baptism, marriage, burial, etc.)
2	Identify higher church members
	Track regular members
	Suspend lay members
3	Open or close a single church
	Find the average church-associated hunter
	Dip into the collection plate ($250)
4	Discredit or suspend high-level members
5	Organize major protests
	Access ancient church lore and knowledge

ESPIONAGE

The shadow world of intelligence teems with secrets, and you are versed in navigating the covert community. This Influence can be used to gain spying data, access detailed information about people or gain training in restricted abilities. Contacts and allies in the undercover world include intelligence agents, analysts, political liaisons, covert operatives, classified researchers and counterintelligence experts.

Cost	Effect
1	Know about various agencies*
	Arrange a tour of a low-security facility
	Know the names of some public intelligence employees*
2	Get a copy of someone's police record
	Arrange a "black mark" on someone's federal records
	Know some of the less-than-public intelligence employees*
3	Get copies of an investigation report
	Access minor espionage equipment (a short-range transceiver, a miniature camera or tape recorder, etc.), obtain a firearm, or soak up taxpayer funding ($250)
	Perform minor alternations to federal records
4	Obtain minor intelligence secrets
	Know some of the secret intelligence employees*
	Access more sophisticated intelligence equipments (a long-range transceiver, a reliable listening device, decoder books, etc.)
	Clean up federal records or arrange to put someone on a local or county Wanted list
5	Arrange a "sanctioned hit"
	Know rumors about Top Secret projects*

A Word about the Espionage Influence

Regardless of what level of *Espionage* Influence your character may possess, you cannot simply take for granted her ability to gain the type of gear or secrets she wants, and certainly not without considerable risk. The intelligence community is rife with traps and oversight procedures designed specifically to monitor unauthorized use of facilities and equipment, and the Storyteller may require you to engage in various challenges in order to avoid or diminish the effects of these safeguards. Even agents who are authorized to use equipment cannot access it without completing a staggering amount of paperwork, and even when they are granted use of it they are obliged to return it to their agency in good working order. Intelligence community allies who routinely "lose" equipment or report it as "destroyed" may well become the focus of internal investigations that could lead to arrest and imprisonment (and a loss of the character's Influence thereby).

Storytellers who wish to include this Influence category in their chronicle should remember that they, not character or players, control all access to sensitive information and gear. They must exercise great care not to permit its abuse, and must be willing to monitor very carefully the effect of it on their games. Some Storytellers may prefer to simply deny characters access to this category, or to strictly limit the sorts of effects that can be achieved through its use.

FINANCE

The world brims with the trappings of affluence and stories of the wealthy. Those with *Finance* Influence speak the language of money and know where to find capital. They also have a degree of access to banks, megacorporations and the truly wealthy citizens of the world. Those who fall within this sphere include CEOs, bankers, corporate bootlickers, financiers, stockbrokers, bank tellers and loan agents.

Cost	Effect
1	Earn money through a steady source of income
	Learn about major transactions and financial events
	Raise capital ($1,000)
	Learn about general economic trends*
2	Trace an unsecured small amount
	Raise capital to purchase a small business (such as a single, small retail store)
3	Purchase a large business (a few small branches or a single large retail store or service)
4	Manipulate local banking (delay deposits, alter some credit ratings)
	Ruin a small business
5	Control an aspect of citywide banking (shut off ATMs for a day, arrange a bank "holiday")
	Ruin a large business
	Purchase a large company

HEALTH

In our modern world, a myriad of organizations and resources exist to deal with every ache and ill, at least in theory. The network of health agencies, hospitals, asylums and clinics is subject to exploitation by someone with *Health* Influence. Access to this sphere of Influence can be very helpful when a hunter needs medical care with as few probing questions as possible, or to track a vampire through his victims. Nurses, doctors, lab workers, therapists, counselors and pharmacists are just a few of the workers in this field.

Cost	Effect
1	Access someone's health records
	Fake vaccination or health records
	Use public functions of health centers at your leisure
2	Access some medical research records
	Have minor lab work done
	Get a copy of a coroner's report
3	Instigate minor quarantines
	Alter medical records
4	Acquire a cadaver
	Completely rewrite medical records
	Abuse grants for personal use ($250)
	Institute large-scale quarantines
	Shut down a business for "health code violations"
5	Have special research projects performed
	Have people institutionalized or released

HIGH SOCIETY

An elite clique holds itself above the great unwashed masses by virtue of birth, possessions, talent or quirks of fate. *High Society* allows the character to direct and use the energies and actions of this exceptional demographic. Among the ranks of the elite, one can find dilettantes, the old rich, movie and rock stars, artists of all sorts, wannabes, sycophantic yes men, fashion models and trend setters.

Cost	Effect
1	Learn what is trendy*
	Obtain "hard to get" tickets for shows
	Learn about concerts, shows or plays well before they are made public
2	Track most celebrities and luminaries
	Be a voice in the local entertainment community
	"Borrow" idle cash from rich friends ($1000)
3	Crush promising careers
	Hobnob well above your station*
4	Minor celebrity status
5	Get a brief appearance on a talk show that's not about to be canceled
	Ruin a new club, gallery or other posh gathering

INDUSTRY

The grinding wheels of labor fuel the economies and markets of the world. Machines, factories and blue-collar workers line up in endless drudgery, churning out the staples of everyday living. Control over *Industry* Influence sways the formation of unions, the movements of work projects, locations for factories and the products of manufacturing concerns. Union workers, foremen, engineers, construction workers, manual laborers and all manner of blue-collar workers exist among these ranks.

Cost	Effect
1	Learn about industrial projects and movements*
2	Have minor projects performed
	Dip into union funds or embezzle petty cash ($500)
	Arrange minor accidents or sabotage
3	Organize minor strikes
	Appropriate machinery for a short time
4	Close down or revitalize a small plant
5	Manipulate a large local industry

LEGAL

There are those who know how to quietly tip the scales of justice, even in the courts, laws schools, law firms and justice bureaus. This Influence can be invaluable for harassing an enemy's assets or ensuring that a hunter's more questionable activities result as little punishment as possible. Inhabiting these halls are lawyers, judges, bailiffs, clerks, district attorneys and ambulance chasers. Uses of *Legal* Influence include issuing subpoenas against enemies and harassing targets with lawsuits.

Cost	Effect
1	Get free representation for minor cases
2	Avoid bail for some charges
	Have minor charges dropped
3	Manipulate minor legal procedures (court dates, wills, contracts)
	Access public or court funds ($250)
	Get representation in most court cases
4	Issue subpoenas
	Tie up court cases in paperwork and red tape
	Have most legal charges dropped
	Cancel or arrange parole
5	Close down all but the most serious investigations
	Have deportation proceedings held against someone

MEDIA

The media serves as the eyes and ears of the world. While few in this day and age doubt that the news is not corrupted, many would be surprised at who closes these eyes and covers these ears from time to time. Characters with *Media* Influence can gain access to station managers, editors, reporters, news anchors, camera operators, photographers and radio personalities. At Storyteller discretion, this may also include the more technical aspects of the film industry, such as sound effects, makeup artists or special effects people (actors, screenwriters and directors are the province of *High Society*).

Cost	Effect
1	Learn about breaking stories early*
	Submit small articles (within reason)
2	Suppress (but not stop) small articles or reports
	Get hold of investigative reporting information
3	Initiate news investigations and reports
	Get project funding and waste it ($250)
	Access media production resources
	Ground stories and projects
4	Broadcast fake stories in the local media
5	Kill small local articles or reports completely

MILITARY

Nations and organizations around the world make use of force as a final and ultimate resort. This Influence gives the character some minor insight into the movements of armies, rebel factions and terrorist organizations, and a few well-placed contacts on the inside. Contacts and allies within this sphere include survivalists, gun nuts, supply officers, military engineers and researchers, enlisted flunkies and actual soldiers of various ranks.

Cost	Effect
1	Know about local military operations*
	Dig up minor weapons on the gray market (knives, pistols)
	Meet some local paramilitary individuals (militia members, survivalists, publishers, psychopaths)
2	Know about special military hardware*
	Figure out which suppliers have reliable equipment (and gain access to rifles and shotguns)
	Arrange for a reprimand of a local military individual
3	Get information about military operations that are not public knowledge
	Figure out who really runs things in local military or paramilitary groups
	Access minor military equipment (communication headsets, extra ammunition) or petty cash ($250)
4	Alter or create a military service record
	"Borrow" a military weapon or piece of squad gear (assault rifle, submachine gun, sniper rifle, body armor, Humvee)
5	Learn about secret military squads in the local area
	Arrange or clear a court martial
	"Borrow" military equipment (machine gun, combat engineering explosives, flamethrower)

A Word about Military Influence

The uncontrolled or incautious use of *Military* Influence can have an unbalancing and debilitating effect on a game. Storytellers should not hesitate to restrict or prohibit the use of this Influence. Note that while some levels of this Influence category permit characters to gain access to military equipment, each piece of gear must be returned at the end of the session or during downtime. Failure to return the gear will certainly draw the attention of the military quartermaster responsible for it, and the ire of the military organization. The character may lose his Military Influence and become the target of an investigation, or, worse, the target of a special task force or squad charged with apprehending or killing the thief.

OCCULT

Most people are somewhat curious about the supernatural world and the various groups and beliefs that make up the occult subculture. Few consider it anything more serious than a hoax or harmless nonsense, or at most a curiosity. This conception is far from accurate, however, as those characters with *Occult* Influence know so well. Hard knowledge is a function of Abilities, but with this Influence, you can get connected to start learning more. Within the occult community, one finds cult leaders, alternative religious groups, charlatans, would-be occultists, New Agers, occult bookstore and supply shop owners, authors and a few more dangerous elements.

Cost	Effect
1	Contact and make use of common occult groups and practices
	Know some of the more visible local occult figures*
2	Know and contact some of the more obscure occult figures*
	Access resources for most rituals and rites
3	Know the general vicinity of certain supernatural entities (Kindred, Garou, Wraiths, etc.)
	Access rare occult components or ingredients
	Milk impressionable wannabes for bucks ($250)
	Access minor occult tomes and writings
	Research a Basic sorcery ritual
4	Research an Intermediate sorcery ritual
5	Access minor magic items
	Unearth an Advanced sorcery ritual
	Study means of developing new Numinae

POLICE

"To protect and serve" is the motto among police forces, but these days everyone can have reason to wonder who exactly is being served and protected. The *Police* Influence encompasses the likes of beat cops, desk jockeys, prison guards, special divisions (such as SWAT, homicide and vice squads), detectives and various clerical staffers.

Cost	Effect
1	Learn police procedures*
	Hear police information and rumors
	Avoid traffic tickets
2	Have license plates checked
	Avoid minor violations (first conviction)
	Get "inside information"
3	Get copies of a police investigative report
	Have police hassle, detain or harass someone
	Find bureau secrets
4	Access confiscated weapons or contraband or tamper with physical evidence
	Have some serious charges dropped
	Start an investigation
	Get money, either from the evidence room or as an appropriation ($1,000)
5	Institute major investigations
	Arrange setups
	Instigate bureau investigations
	Have officers fired

POLITICS

Nothing ever gets done for a straightforward reason anymore. It's all about who knows who and what favors can get paid off in the process. In other words, it's politics as usual. Altering party platforms, controlling local elections, changing appointed offices and calling in favors all falls under the purview of the *Politics* Influence. Well-timed blackmail, bribery, spin-doctoring or any sundry tricks are stock in trade on both sides of this fence. Some of the likely contacts and allies include pollsters, lobbyists, activists, party members, spin-doctors and politicians from rural zoning committees to the mayors of major cities or Congressional representatives.

Cost	Effect
1	Minor lobbying
	Identify real platforms of politicians and parties*
	Be in the know*
2	Meet smalltime politicians
	Garner inside information on processes and laws
	Use a slush fund or fund-raiser ($1,000)
3	Sway or alter political projects (local parks, small construction, renovations)
4	Enact minor legislation
	Dash careers or minor politicians
5	Get your candidate in a minor office
	Enact encompassing local legislature

STREET

Disenchanted, disenfranchised and ignored by their "betters," a whole collective of humanity has made its own culture and lifestyle to deal with the harsh lot that life has dealt them. Gang members, the homeless, street performers, prostitutes, petty criminals and the forgotten dregs of humanity reside in the dark alleys and slums. *Street* Influence gives you an "ear to the ground" and access to some unusual resources.

Cost	Effect
1	Have an ear open for word on the street
	Identify most gangs and know their turfs and habits
2	Live mostly without fear on the underside of society
	Keep a contact or two in most aspects of street life
	Access smalltime contraband
3	Get insight on other areas of Influence
	Arrange some services from street people or gangs
	Get pistols or other common melee weapons (saps, knives)
4	Mobilize groups of homeless
	Panhandle or hold a "collection" ($250)
	Have a word in almost all aspects of gang operations
5	Control a single medium-sized gang
	Arrange impressive protests by street people

TRANSPORTATION

The world doesn't stand still. Everything is in constant motion, and the prosperity of most nations and people relies heavily on this fact. Without the means to perform the monumental task of transporting people and goods from place to place, things would quickly grind to a halt. The forces that bridge these vast expanses include cab and bus drivers, pilots, teamsters, air traffic controllers, dock laborers, ship captains, travel firms, train engineers, conductors and untold others.

Cost	Effect
1	Know what goes where, when and why
	Travel locally quickly and freely*
2	Track an unwary target if he uses public transportation
	Arrange safe (or at least concealed) passage from mundane threats (robbery, terrorism, etc.)
3	Seriously hamper an individual's ability to travel
	Avoid most supernatural dangers when traveling
4	Temporarily shut down one form of transportation (bus lines, ships, planes, trains, etc.)
	Route money your way ($1,000)
5	Reroute major modes of travel
	Smuggle with impunity

UNDERWORLD

Even in this most sophisticated and cosmopolitan of ages, society has found certain needs and services too questionable to accept. In every age, this one included, someone has made an organized effort to provide for this demand, regardless of the risks. Among this dangerous crowd one finds mobsters, bookies, fences, money launderers, smugglers, forgers, the Mafia, the Yakuza, tongs and hit men.

Cost	Effect
1	Locate minor contraband (knives, smalltime drugs, petty gambling, scalped tickets)
2	Obtain pistols, serious drugs, stolen cars
	Hire muscle to rough someone up
	Fence minor loot
	Prove that crime pays (and score $1,000)
3	Obtain a rifle, shotgun or submachine gun
	Arrange a minor "hit"
	Know someone in "the Family"
4	Make white-collar crime connections
5	Arrange gangland assassinations
	Hire a demolition man or arsonist
	Supply local drug needs

UNIVERSITY

In an age when the quest for learning and knowledge begins in schools, colleges and universities, information becomes currency. This Influence represents a certain degree of control and perhaps involvement in these institutions. Here one finds teachers, professors, students of all ages and aptitudes, deans, fraternities, sororities, and many young and impressionable minds.

Cost	Effect
1	Know layout and policy of local schools*
	Have access to low-level university resources
	Get records up to the high school level
2	Know a contact or two with useful knowledge or skills
	Have minor access to facilities
	Fake high school records
	Obtain college records
3	Call in faculty favors
	Cancel a college class
	Fix grades
	Discredit a student
4	Organize student protests or rallies
	Discredit faculty members
	Acquire money through a grant ($1,000)
5	Falsify an undergraduate degree

MENTOR

An older or more experienced hunter/scholar looks after you and comes to your aid occasionally. Whatever the case, you can get assistance from your mentor, though his favor may be fickle.

When you call on your mentor, you risk a certain number of Traits to achieve a given effect. A lowly one-Trait mentor probably knows only little more than you, while a five-Trait mentor may well have luminous standing within your sect and a wide range of potent powers. Regardless, taking up your mentor's valuable time is costly. You must engage in a Simple Test when you call on your mentor. If you succeed, your mentor deigns to aid you. If you tie, your mentor grants you assistance, but then requires something in return. If you fail, your mentor demands the favor first before helping. In any case, your mentor can be called on only once in any given game session, and only if you have an appropriate way to contact him or her.

The level of aid that your mentor can give depends on the number of Traits in this Background (and Storyteller approval, of course):

• For one Trait, your mentor is privy to a single piece of specialized information at a level above your own. If you have *Vampire Lore* x 2, for instance, your mentor can be called on to gift you with one piece of information from *Vampire Lore* x 3.

• For two Traits, you can borrow one level of *Contacts*, Influence or *Resources* from your mentor for the duration of the session. If your mentor is very powerful (four or five Traits), you can borrow two levels.

• At a cost of three Traits, your mentor can train you in the ways of a special *Hobby/ Professional/ Expert Ability* that is outside your normal ken, such as *Wraith Lore*.

• For four Traits, if he has such abilities, your Mentor may tutor you in Advanced sorcery skills or Theurgy, or assist you in improving your psychic phenomena.

Since *Mentors* can prove unbalancing by providing too many different powers over the course of a long game, the Storyteller may lower your total *Mentor* Traits as you call on his knowledge. This decrease represents the fact that as your character learns the mentor's secrets, the mentor has less left to teach.

RESOURCES

You have access to liquid capital and spending money. You also have some solid resources that you can use when times are tight. Unlike the use of *Finance*, these resources are always readily available, and they come to you automatically due to your investments, jobs and holdings.

Your number of *Resources* Traits determines the amount of money and capital that you can secure. By expending temporary *Resources* Traits (which return at the next game session), you can draw on your regular income, as shown in the accompanying table. If you expend permanent *Resources*, you can divest yourself of holdings, allowing access to 10 times the amount shown on the table. However, the limits of what you can buy are always adjudicated by the Storyteller. Truly powerful uses of *Resources* are best left to downtimes and moderation between game sessions.

RESOURCE ALLOCATION

No Traits: Poverty. Income $200. Get roommates. Bus pass.

One Trait: Small savings and holdings; income $500. Have apartment, cheap means of transportation.

Two Traits: Modest savings and holdings; income $1,000. Have condo and motorcycle or modest car.

Three Traits: Significant savings and holdings; income $3,000. Own house, car.

Four Traits: Large savings and holdings. Income $10,000. Own large house or some small properties, two vehicles, some luxuries and unusual items.

Five Traits: Rich. Income $30,000. Own estate and grounds, multiple small properties, several vehicles, arts and treasures, luxury items.

RETAINERS

Every hero had a loyal servant or sidekick who took care of the little things while the hero was out on business. Unlike the *Allies* Background, your retainers are nearly always around, overseeing your personal effects, defending your property and furthering your goals. They may not have the specialized knowledge of allies, but they are mostly loyal to your cause, and they serve your needs first.

You should work with your Storyteller to determine how you managed to secure a loyal retainer. Your retainer's exact capabilities are up to the Storyteller; a retainer may be skillful but unmotivated, or loyal but inept. No retainer is ever perfect, but they all can be a great help.

• A retainer can be assigned to watch over a particular location. Generally, if someone attempts to break into your house, the retainers there will attempt to stop the intruder. In this case, they are treated as normal humans, run by Narrators.

• A retainer can be used to manage your assets and perform tasks. Retainers tied up in this fashion allow you to manage more Influence than normal; they add to the number of Attribute Traits that you possess for purposes of counting your total Influences. Each retainer directed in this fashion adds one to your maximum Influence Traits. If retainers are later lost, killed or reassigned, the excess Influence Traits are lost, starting with the highest levels of Influence held.

• A retainer can perform other menial functions, as allowed by the Storyteller. You can get someone else to pick up your character's dry cleaning.

STEP FOUR: FINISHING TOUCHES

The following are the final pieces of the character creation process: Humanity, Willpower, derangements, Numinae, Merits and Flaws.

HUMANITY

Humanity is a measure of your character's inner and exterior moral strength. It separates mortals from the rest of the supernatural world, and it is a reflection of the mortal's connection to the fundamental forces of life. Characters with many Humanity Traits are very much in tune with themselves and their human nature; individuals with few Humanity Traits are cold and distant.

When your character commits acts that society considers to be wrong, unethical, or evil, she may find that such acts erode her Humanity. The fewer Humanity Traits your character possesses, the more inhuman she becomes.

Losing Humanity

Humanity is often all that keeps a hunter going in the face of nightly terrors and confrontations with evil, and so it is a precious thing. Whenever a mortal commits an inhumane deed, he jeopardizes his Humanity. Whether he kills an innocent person accidentally while pursuing a warlock, or tortures a vampire to discover the location of its associates, the immoral act can lead to a permanent erosion of the mortal's Humanity.

Mortal characters possess from one to five Humanity Traits, and can jeopardize them according to the following stratification of immoral acts:

Humanity Hierarchy of Sins

Traits	Violation
5	Selfish thoughts and actions
4	Theft; causing injury
3	Accidental killing; intentionally causing property damage
2	Killing with premeditation
1	Casual killing or acts of great evil (as defined by your culture)

When characters commit an act that corresponds to, or is rated lower than, their current Humanity, they must make a Humanity Test. This is a Static Challenge against a number of Traits equal to the deed in question as per the Hierarchy of Sins. If you win the test, you do not suffer a loss of Humanity. If you tie the test, you may expend a Willpower Trait to gain an immediate retest. If you lose the test, you suffer the loss of a Humanity Trait and may suffer other ill effects as well.

Five Humanity: People often perceive you as being "holier than thou." Your piety and morality are strong and pronounced. You maintain excruciatingly high standards for your behavior and for the behavior of others, and your concepts of right and wrong are rigidly defined.

Four Humanity: Theft is wrong, and so is murder, naturally. But sometimes the speed limit is just too damn slow. You are concerned with the natural rights of others, but a degree of selfishness creeps into your everyday behavior. This rating approximates that of most "normal" humans.

Three Humanity: People die. Stuff breaks. And most supernatural creatures are evil monsters that probably deserve to die. You would never willingly kill another mortal, but vampires, werewolves, and the like don't have any right to exist. Other people might not notice anything genuinely different about you, but particularly sensitive individuals can sense that you are unusual.

Two Humanity: You're on a mission, and nobody is going to get in your way. Some "collateral damage" in the pursuit of the supernatural is regrettable, but acceptable. Theft, injury, torture and destruction are appropriate tools when dealing with monsters. At this state, your Storyteller may impose penalties when you attempt to use such powers as *Animal Ken*: Normal animals are reluctant to approach you when your connection to your own Humanity is so tenuous. Children also tend to react negatively to you, because their young minds can sense that you are something less than human, and therefore dangerous.

One Humanity: You're as bad as the monsters you hunt. The lives and property of others means nothing to you. You're hanging onto your Humanity by a twisted thread. Cold-

blooded murder is merely one more weapon in your arsenal. You find it difficult to interact with other people in a positive manner (you may not take Attribute Traits related to positive social interactions, such as *Genial* and *Friendly*). Any use of your Numinae may have nasty results, at the discretion of your Storyteller.

WILLPOWER

Willpower Traits measure the strength of your character's resolve and sense of self. By exerting your Willpower, you can withstand otherwise untenable conditions, renew your commitment to a course of action and empower certain difficult Numinae.

Willpower Traits are not described with adjectives. You simply have permanent Willpower — your normal limit of Willpower Traits — and temporary Willpower, your expendable Traits. Hunters begin play with a permanent Willpower of three Traits. When you expend temporary Willpower Traits or raise your permanent Willpower, you regain temporary Traits at a rate of one per game session (though your Storyteller may vary this pace to suit the needs of her game or to simplify bookkeeping).

Expending a Willpower Trait allows for one of any number of effects. Generally, Willpower Traits allow you to keep self-determination and to empower extremely difficult or complex actions. Using Willpower is almost always a reflexive action and does not count as your turn.

• A Willpower Trait can be spent to refresh all of your lost Traits in one Attribute category — Physical, Social or Mental. You may do so once per category per game session.

• Expenditure of a Willpower Trait allows you to gain a retest when defending against a Mental or Social Challenge. Trait loss works as normal for such retests. Note that certain supernatural powers may override this stipulation.

• Spending one Willpower Trait enables you to enter a challenge for which you lack an appropriate Ability. Thus, you can make a test even if you would normally require a specific Ability that you don't have or have used up.

• You can expend a Willpower Trait to ignore all wound penalties, up to and including Incapacitated, for the duration of one full turn.

• Spending a Willpower Trait lets you suppress a derangement temporarily. If you spend enough Willpower Traits on suppressing a derangement, you may overcome it eventually. (See "Derangements," pp. 267-270.)

• Certain powers require the expenditure of Willpower.

NUMINAE

Numinae are the rare sorcerous and psychic powers that some mortals can wield. Hunters sometimes possess such powers. Numinae cannot be acquired during character creation except through the expenditure of Free Traits. See Chapter Five for more about Numinae powers.

NEGATIVE TRAITS

By specifying certain weaknesses, you can gain extra Traits to strengthen your character in other areas. But beware: These Negative Traits can also be used against you during challenges, as they represent your character's shortcomings. Each Negative Trait

you take grants you one positive Trait that you can assign elsewhere, provided that you don't exceed your character's Trait Maximums.

MERITS AND FLAWS

Merits and Flaws represent unusual advantages and disadvantages that supercede your character's ordinary capabilities. Taking Merits and Flaws helps you make your character unique and assures that she will possess characteristics that set her apart from the ruck and run of humanity. Merits grant special benefits, and they can be taken only by expending Free or Negative Traits. Flaws represent hindrances that make your character's life more difficult, and give you additional Traits you can use to give your character more depth.

CHOOSING MERITS AND FLAWS

Taking Merits and Flaws isn't a mandatory step in character creation: You can skip it if you prefer. Your Storyteller may also choose to limit the effects of certain Merits or Flaws, or prohibit some of them altogether. But selecting a few appropriate Merits and Flaws can help flesh out your character by emphasizing the reasons for her specialization in particular Abilities or her facility with certain Numinae. Try not to choose Merits just to gain cool bonuses that you think will give your character an advantage. Don't take Flaws just to get the Free Traits they give you. Try to take Merits and Flaws as tools for better roleplaying and for making your character more interesting.

You may select up to five Traits worth of Merits or Flaws, and you may gain them only during the character creation process. When you choose a Flaw, you gain additional Free Traits equal to the Trait value of the Flaw (so if you choose a three Trait Flaw, you gain three Free Traits to use elsewhere on your character). When you choose a Merit, you must pay for it with Free Traits totaling the value of the Merit (so choosing a three-Trait Merit requires you to expend three Free Traits in acquiring it). During the course of play, a character may experience circumstances that give her the opportunity to overcome a Flaw, or to lose the advantage of a Merit, with your Storyteller's approval. To do so requires that you expend Experience Traits equal to double the normal Trait value of the Merit or Flaw.

PHYSICAL MERITS AND FLAWS

Acute Sense (1 Trait Merit)

You have an exceptionally sharp sense. Choose from hearing, vision, smell or taste. You are two Traits up on all perception challenges related to that sense.

Ambidextrous (1 Trait Merit)

Most people favor one hand over the other, but you have no penalty for doing things with your "off" hand. You can fight with two weapons, simply risking one additional Trait with each attack (normally, someone attacking with two weapons risks on additional Trait with his primary hand, and two additional Traits with his off hand). Furthermore, you suffer no penalties when performing tasks with either hand.

Double-Jointed (1 Trait Merit)

You are unusually supple. You are one Trait up on all Physical Challenges that require body flexibility, such as escaping from handcuffs or climbing up a wall to escape pursuing zombies.

Light Sleeper (2 Trait Merit)

You awaken instantly at the first hint of trouble or danger, and you do so without any sleepiness or hesitation. Most mortals are two Traits down in all tests for one turn after awakening, but you do not suffer this penalty. Furthermore your body is well rested after only four hours of sleep — an advantage to the nocturnal hunter who must also hold down a day job.

Resemble Vampire (2 Trait Merit)

You are naturally pale and slender, and your physical features resemble those of a vampire to some degree. While you obviously do not have fangs, and you still have a heartbeat, your basic physical appearance is undistinguishable from one of the undead without careful scrutiny. You can move easily among vampires without too much fear of recognition, though you should be prepared for suspicion or hostility from other hunters.

Daredevil (3 Trait Merit)

You excel at taking risks and coming through with minimal injury. You are one Trait up on any challenge in which you try something particularly dangerous. This Merit applies to combat only if you are obviously outmatched but decide to fight anyway.

Poisonous Blood (3 Trait Merit)

For reasons that might be unknown to you, your blood is toxic to vampires. Although you suffer injury and the other effects of the vampire's Kiss when a vampire drinks your blood, the vampire gains no nourishment from the fluid and suffers one health level of lethal damage for each Trait of your blood she consumes. Unfortunately, vampires can't tell that your blood is poisonous until they taste it, which means that while this Merit won't protect you from initial attack, it may well discourage the same vampire from trying to feed on you later.

Huge Size (4 Trait Merit)

You are abnormally tall or large in size, possibly standing over seven feet in height and weighing in at over 400 pounds. You have one extra Bruised health level. If you are not yourself unnaturally large, you should represent this Merit by wearing some bulky padding and heavy boots when playing your character.

Deep Sleeper (1 Trait Flaw)

It is very difficult for you to awaken from sleep. If you are awakened unexpectedly, you are disoriented and two Traits down for all challenges in the following hour. The Storyteller may also require you to make a Simple Test in order to awaken when danger threatens.

Hard of Hearing (1 Trait Flaw)

Your hearing is subnormal. You are two Traits down on hearing challenges, and you may not take the Merit *Acute Sense: Hearing*.

Impaired Sight (1 Trait Flaw)

You are severely nearsighted or farsighted, and you require corrective lenses. Without your glasses or contacts, you are one Trait down on sight-related challenges. You may not take the Merit *Acute Sense: Vision*.

Disfigured (2 Trait Flaw)

You are afflicted with a hideous disfigurement. This Flaw makes you ugly and easy to remember. You may never have any *Alluring*, *Gorgeous* or *Seductive* Traits. If your true

appearance is visible, you are two Traits down on any Social Challenge that you initiate (except those in which you are attempting to intimidate someone).

One Eye (2 Trait Flaw)

You are missing one of your eyes. You may choose which eye is missing, or determine randomly, and decide how it was lost. You have no peripheral vision on your blind side, and you are two Traits down on any test that requires depth perception, such as driving a car or firing a gun. You may not take the Merit *Acute Sense: Vision*.

Weak Sense (2 Trait Flaw)

One of your senses is defective, though not totally absent. You are two Traits down in all challenges relating to this sense. This deficiency is not correctable: Laser surgery or glasses will not improve weak sight, and a hearing aid will not improve weak hearing. You may not have a sense that is simultaneously acute and weak.

Deaf (3 Trait Flaw)

You cannot hear sound, and you must relent to challenges related to hearing. You should get your Storyteller's approval before choosing this Flaw, as it can be difficult to roleplay if you are not truly deaf.

Deformity (3 Trait Flaw)

You have some sort of deformity, such as a misshapen or withered limb, a hunchback or the like, that inconveniences you and hampers you physically. You are one Trait down on all Physical Challenges, and two Traits down on all challenges related to physical appearance.

Hemophiliac (3 Trait Flaw)

You do not naturally stop bleeding when you are injured. Cuts and wounds continue to bleed, and bruises worsen through internal injury. Any time you are wounded (whenever you lose a health level), you lose an additional health level every 10 minutes until someone helps you. Anyone with the *Medicine* Ability may make a Static Mental Challenge against a difficulty of six Traits to stop the bleeding. Vampires who feed from you discover that they cannot close the wound with a lick, for reasons they do not understand.

One Arm (3 Trait Flaw)

You have only one arm. You choose which arm is missing, or determine randomly, and decide how and when you lost it. You suffer no penalties when using your remaining hand. However, you are down two Traits on challenges when two hands would normally be required.

Partially Crippled (3 Trait Flaw)

Your legs are injured or otherwise defective. You are down three Traits in all challenges related to movement. You may need assistance walking, such as a cane, a pair of crutches or a wheelchair.

Potent Blood (3 Trait Flaw)

You blood is particularly nourishing and delicious to vampires. Each Trait of your blood is worth twice as many Blood Traits as a normal mortal's, so a vampire who drinks one Trait of your blood gains two instead. You still suffer only one Health Level of damage per Blood Trait lost, however. Vampires have lots of nicknames for people like you, such as "Slurpee" or "Tasty Treat." You cannot take the Merit *Lifegiver*.

Mute (4 Trait Flaw)

You cannot speak. You must depend on other forms of communication to interact with people, such as sign language or writing. You cannot use sorcery or any other power that requires speech.

Blind (5 Trait Flaw)

You have no sense of vision, and you must relent to all challenges related to sight. You should try to roleplay this Flaw to the best of your ability, but not to a point where doing so endangers the safety of yourself or anyone around you.

MENTAL MERITS AND FLAWS

Code of Honor (1 Trait Merit)

You have a personal code of ethics to which you strictly adhere. You must construct this personal code of honor, using as much detail as possible to outline the general rules by which you abide, and your Storyteller must approve it. You are two Traits up on all challenges that would result in you violating your code if you lose.

Common Sense (1 Trait Merit)

You possess an unusual amount of practicality and everyday wisdom. Whenever you are about to make a blunder that goes against your better judgment, a Narrator will alert you to your potential mistake. This Merit is excellent for novice players.

Concentration (1 Trait Merit)

You can shut out distractions and annoyances that would hinder others. Whenever penalty Traits are assigned for some outside phenomenon (harsh lighting, rain, loud noise, etc.), you suffer none of the penalty.

Higher Purpose (1 Trait Merit)

You have a goal that drives you and directs your actions in everything that you do. You must choose a specific goal, and your Storyteller must approve it. This Merit is common among hunters, since eliminating supernatural foes is frequently connected to lofty ideals, but your Storyteller may limit the use of this Merit so that it is not abused. You cannot take the Flaw *Driving Goal*.

Time Sense (1 Trait Merit)

You are always aware of the time, even when you've been sleeping or when you lack visual clues about the time of day. You can estimate the current time to within a couple of minutes, and follow the calendar in your head with exacting precision. You are two Traits up on any challenge that may threaten or obstruct your time sense. This Merit is excellent for judging sunrise and sunset, and therefore ideal for hunting vampires.

Eidetic Memory (2 Trait Merit)

You are two Traits up on all memory-related challenges, because you can remember nearly everything with perfect clarity. At any time, you may ask a Narrator for information regarding something you wish to recall, and the Narrator is obliged to inform you appropriately (you may be required to make a Simple Test to recall lengthy or complex information). Although supernatural powers can still cloud your memory, you are more likely to become suspicious of this condition simply because you are so accustomed to remembering everything.

Iron Will (4 Trait Merit)

You are extremely resistant to powers that affect your mind or emotions, such as the vampiric Discipline of *Dominate*. Whenever magical or supernatural means are used

to try to control your mind or emotions, you may expend a Willpower Trait to automatically resist (normally, expending a Willpower Trait would gain you only a retest). If you have expended all your Willpower Traits, or if you are unaware of the attempt to influence your mind, you are unable to actively resist but are still two Traits up on the challenge.

Jack-of-All-Trades (5 Trait Merit)

You possess a breadth of knowledge that covers a number of miscellaneous talents and skills, which you have acquired through your travels and experiences. You may utilize Abilities that you do not possess: The cost for doing so is risking an additional Trait appropriate to the challenge or task. For example, you could expend a Mental Trait to pick a lock with *Security* even if you don't possess that Ability — you must still make any required tests (such as a Static Challenge to actually pick the lock) as normal.

Anachronism (1 Trait Flaw)

You are an older hunter, and your attitudes and personality are influenced by the age in which you grew to adulthood. You have difficulty understanding and coping with the wonders of the modern age, particularly technology. It doesn't occur to you to use a computer as a hunting aid, nor to obtain a PCS phone or PDA. You are one Trait down on challenges involving modern technology such as computers.

Compulsion (1 Trait Flaw)

You are afflicted by a psychological compulsion. You choose the specific compulsion — a mania for cleanliness, perfection, theft, lying, gambling, whatever — and your Storyteller must approve it. You should roleplay your compulsion when appropriate, though you can temporarily resist your compulsion for one scene by expending a Willpower Trait.

Illiterate (1 Trait Flaw)

You are unable to read or write. This Flaw is a cause of endless frustration when you are trying to perform any kind of supernatural research.

Nightmares (1 Trait Flaw)

You experience horrendous nightmares every time you sleep, and memories of these terrors haunt your waking hours as well. At your Storyteller's discretion, your nightmares may sometimes be so disturbing that you are one Trait down on all your challenges for the next day.

Overconfident (1 Trait Flaw)

You have an undeservedly high opinion of yourself and your capabilities. You trust your abilities implicitly, even in situations where you risk defeat. Whenever you fail, you quickly find someone or something else to blame. Your overconfidence can be infectious if you are convincing enough, and can therefore lead you and your associates into very dangerous situations.

Phobia, Mild (1 Trait Flaw)

You suffer from an unreasoning fear of something. You choose the object of your phobia — heights, spiders, darkness, water, anything at all — subject to your Storyteller's approval. You must make a Willpower Test whenever you come in contact with the subject of your fears, and you are one Trait down on the test.

Shy (1 Trait Flaw)

You are ill at ease when dealing with other people, and you try to avoid social situations when possible. You are one Trait down on all challenges concerned with social dealings, and two Traits down whenever you are the center of attention for a large

group of people (more than 10). These two effects are cumulative, so making a speech in front of a crowd would make you three Traits down.

Soft-Hearted (1 Trait Flaw)

You can't stand to watch others suffer (perhaps not because you care about them, but maybe because you dislike the intensity of emotion). If you are the direct cause of suffering and you witness it, you experience days of nausea and nights of sleepless grief. You avoid situations in which you might have to witness suffering, and you attempt to protect others from it as well. You are one Trait down on all challenges whenever you must witness suffering, for the remainder of the scene.

Speech Impediment (1 Trait Flaw)

You are afflicted with a stutter, a stammer or some other impediment that prevents others from understanding you easily when you speak. You should roleplay this Flaw all the time, though not to the point of offensiveness or parody.

Confused (2 Trait Flaw)

You are often confused or befuddled, and the world seems to you a very disorienting place. You should roleplay this behavior at all times to a small degree, but your confusion becomes very evident whenever you are exposed to excessive stimuli (such as when a number of people are all talking at once, or when you enter a noisy nightclub). You are two Traits down on all challenges in such situations. You may spend a Willpower Trait to override the effects of your confusion, but only for a scene.

Low Self-Image (2 Trait Flaw)

You suffer from a lack of self-esteem. You are two Traits down in all situations where you don't expect to succeed (at the Narrator's discretion, though the penalty might be limited to one Trait if you help by pointing out when this Flaw might affect you). At the Narrator's option, you may be required to expend a Willpower Trait in order to attempt things that require strong self confidence.

Vengeance (2 Trait Flaw)

You have a score to settle. You are obsessed with wreaking vengeance on an individual or perhaps even an entire group. Your vengeance is your first priority. You can overcome this Flaw only temporarily, for one scene, by spending a Willpower Trait.

Absent-Minded (3 Trait Flaw)

You forget details like names, appointments, and what you ate for breakfast. You must win a Static Mental Challenge against a number of Traits determined by the Storyteller in order to remember anything other than your own name, address and phone number during stressful situations.

Addicted to Vampiric Vitae (3 Trait Flaw)

You are addicted to the rush and power you feel when you drink vampire blood. You'll do anything to get your fix and satisfy the craving — this might even be your main reason for hunting. Like any addiction, this one is powerful and subtle beyond belief, and only long therapy and support from your closest friends may cure you of the disease.

Company Man (3 Trait Flaw)

To you, your hunter association is nothing less than your family. It is your entire world, and you perceive everyone who is outside your world with a suspicious and mistrustful eye. You are down two Traits when interacting with anyone who is not a member of your particular association.

Driving Goal (3 Trait Flaw)

You have a personal goal that compels and directs your actions, sometimes in startling or unexpected ways. The goal is always limitless in depth, and you can never truly achieve it: It's the pursuit of your goal that counts. Maybe you want to rid the world of all vampires or find a cure for lycanthropy. Your single-minded devotion to your goal gets you into trouble from time to time and might jeopardize other goals. You can avoid your driving goal for one scene by expending a Mental Trait, and for one game session by expending a Willpower Trait. You cannot take the Merit *Higher Purpose*.

Phobia, Severe (3 Trait Flaw)

You suffer from an unreasoning and overpowering fear of something. When confronted with the source of your fear, you must make a Willpower Challenge; you are two Traits down on the test. If you lose, you flee the scene and do not return until the offending thing is removed or destroyed.

Weak-Willed (3 Trait Flaw)

You are two Traits down in all challenges in which you are commanded or intimidated. Because you are highly susceptible to the control of others, you can use your Willpower Traits only when your survival (or that of another) is at stake, or when it is appropriate to your Nature. Moreover, you cannot learn to use sorcery or Theurgy of any sort.

SOCIETY MERITS AND FLAWS

Arcane Heritage (1 Trait Merit)

Perhaps you have a witch somewhere in your family tree, or a relative with startlingly faerielike eyes. You decide why your particular family line is considered gifted with the touch of the supernatural by those who are familiar with that world. Although this Merit may draw negative attention from certain groups, such as the Inquisition, others such as the Arcanum may regard you with respect or interest. This heritage could be a part of your motivation for hunting.

Reputation (2 Trait Merit)

You are a well-regarded member of your particular society and are one Trait up on all Social Challenges with other members. You should decide what it is about you that your fellows respect: Maybe you defeated a mage single-handedly, or perhaps you have a flawless record in solving paranormal crimes.

Research Grant (2 Trait Merit)

A foundation or institution has given you a prestigious award that includes a grant of funding as well as access to information and facilities. A typical award gives you $1,000 per month, which you may use in any fashion you desire (though you should show some evidence of successful research; otherwise the grant could be terminated). This Merit also gives you access to special libraries and facilities, which when combined with the right Influences could make all the difference in researching Numinae or arcane lores.

Top-Secret Access (2 Trait Merit)

Whether due to your research credential or your government clearance, you have a source of highly valuable information. Your contact is both reliable and discreet, affording you access to secrets that most people do not know. You must make a Simple Test to access this information: A win indicates complete disclosure of data, a tie indicates partial information, and a loss indicates no information). You should define

the nature of your source. Remember, possession of top-secret information and contacts can be dangerous if you don't exercise caution.

Double Identity (3 Trait Merit)

You've managed to gain access to a secondary identity for yourself. Thanks to your espionage contacts, this false identity seems completely legal and perfectly normal, and is supported by all the requisite documentation it needs to withstand scrutiny. A double identity is normally utilized as a last-ditch escape if things get out of hand. This Merit is most appropriate to government agents, but just about anyone with the right contacts could forge a second identity.

Ecclesiastical Rank (3 Trait Merit)

You are an ordained priest or otherwise recognized in the Church hierarchy, with all of the implied social benefits. You may call on the Church for advice and aid, and people who respect your vocation may grant you favors. The number of Traits in this Merit determines your relative standing. A local priest would be worth one Trait, while three might indicate that you are an influential bishop.

License to Kill (4 Trait Merit)

You are sanctioned by your hunter association to eliminate those whose interests run counter to those of your government. Sometimes you are assigned to eliminate a particular target, but more often you are simply afforded a great deal of discretion in determining your targets. Most government agencies do not grant this authority (it is exceptionally rare in the FBI), and those that do are very careful to monitor its recipients for signs of abuse. The agency attempts to conceal your hits and cover your tracks to the best of its ability, but it reacts poorly to botched or sloppy jobs.

Despite the name of this Merit, you can in fact be held accountable by the legal system for your actions (executive order notwithstanding, the US government does frown on such things), though this is a rare occurrence. Only active members of government agencies can have this Merit. An Inquisitor might kill in the line of duty with his Church's approval, but he won't have the government's backing or support in covering up the deed.

Blackmailed (1 or 2 Trait Flaw)

Somebody has dug up some dirt on you and is forcing you to pay up or risk exposure. Whether the blackmailer is an individual or an organization, you're stuck with the results: Your blackmailer demands money or your cooperation, or maybe even your organization's secrets, in return for keeping your secret. For one Trait, you suffer from a rather embarrassing secret that might cost you your job and organizational position. For two Traits, you harbor a dangerous secret that could very well be the death of you if the blackmailer reveals it. Obviously, your antagonist won't make it easy for you to kill him. You'll need to roleplay cleverly to overcome this Flaw.

Dark Secret (1 Trait Flaw)

You have some sort of secret that would embarrass you immensely if anyone else knew about it. Maybe you became a hunter so that you could convince a vampire to Embrace you, or maybe you killed an innocent during one of your adventures. Your secret weighs on your mind at all times, but it should surface only occasionally during stories so that it retains its significance.

Isolated Upbringing (1 Trait Flaw)

Born and raised by peculiar parents, you rarely ventured into the outside world. Perhaps your father was an Inquisitor who hoped to shield you from the sins of mankind

and prepare you for your holy quest as God's avenger, or maybe you were raised in a Chapter House of the Arcanum where you spent your entire life among books. You should roleplay a degree of unease with the modern world, and you sometimes fail to understand the customs of everyday life. You are one Trait down on all Social Challenges with people from outside of your corner of reality.

Rebel (1 - 3 Trait Flaw)

You have a reputation as a rebel, a maverick or even a loose cannon within your society. Maybe your techniques get results, but you are scorned and hated for your methods. Because your practices are seen as questionable (at best) by your peers and superiors, it is difficult for you to get support and backing from your organization. The more Traits in the Flaw, the less likely you are to get such help.

Supernatural Enemy (1 - 5 Trait Flaw)

Your past has returned to haunt you in the form of a supernatural enemy. This could be a vampire, werewolf, mage or other supernatural creature. It won't be a constant threat, but it will appear from time to time to cause you and your associates grief. The more powerful the enemy, the more Traits in the Flaw. You should determine exactly who your enemy is, and how you became enemies.

Dangerous Secret (2 Trait Flaw)

You possess information of a highly secret nature. In fact, the information is so volatile that knowing about it puts your life in jeopardy. Perhaps you've uncovered a government conspiracy to breed humans and werewolves, or discovered that the archbishop is an infernalist. Not only will nobody believe you if you reveal the secret, but the individuals involved would probably bring the entire weight of the organization down on you. Revealing the secret might put you at risk of arrest or even execution. This Flaw might be one of the sources of your motivation to become a hunter: It's possible that only your supernatural quarry can provide you with the means to overcome this Flaw.

Notoriety (2 Trait Flaw)

Something that you have done, or not done, identifies you as a liability to other hunters. Your bad reputation in your own society makes your life difficult, and even independent hunters tend to distrust you. Maybe too many of your partners have been killed during your hunts, or perhaps your attitude is so zealous that you annoy everyone around you. You should choose the exact nature of this Flaw, with the help and approval of your Storyteller.

Secret Friendship (2 Trait Flaw)

You maintain a secret relationship with a supernatural creature or other denizen of the World of Darkness, such as a vampire, ghoul, mage or ghost. Exposure of this relationship would not only destroy your credibility among hunters but would probably place you on their hit list along with your friend. Worse, members of the particular supernatural community involved would probably consider you a serious threat and take steps to eliminate you. You must always cover up any evidence connected to this relationship, and you are paranoid that your secret is always on the verge of discovery.

Hunted (3 Trait Flaw)

At some point in your past, you offended or crossed another hunter. Now you have become his target. You must exercise caution wherever you go, lest one of your own kind take you out.

SUPERNATURAL MERITS AND FLAWS

Faerie Blood (1 - 5 Trait Merit)

Your blood carries a strong legacy of the fae, which affords you some of their powers. For each Trait in this Merit, you may take one Merit or Flaw normally reserved for changelings. Additionally, you also possess one Trait of Glamour and have the capacity to gain more, just like a changeling. Each additional permanent Trait of Glamour costs you three Free or Experience Traits, though you can never have more permanent Traits of Glamour than the number of Traits in this Merit. Although you may use your Glamour like a fae, you can only replenish it by creating art or receiving a token from a changeling. You may learn the Basic Arts and Realms of fae magic, giving you the ability to cast minor enchantments. Arts cost six Traits to learn, and Realms cost four. You also add the number of Traits in this Merit to the number of days that an enchantment lasts on you. With one Trait in this Merit, you can be enchanted for eight days at a cost of only one Glamour Trait (seven days for being kinain, plus one extra day for one level in this Merit).

You must take the Merit *Kinain* before you take this Merit.

See **The Shining Host Players Guide** for more information about kinain.

Magical Item (1 - 3 Trait Merit)

You possess an item that contains a measure of supernatural power. It might be a holy relic, a fetish or talisman, or anything your Storyteller permits. Your Storyteller determines your item's powers (and you might not even be fully aware of them).

Loyalty (1 Trait Merit)

You are sworn and devoted so some group or cause. This Merit works just like *True Love* (see p. 153), but the object may be an organization or an ideal.

Shivers (1 Trait Merit)

Although you can't actually see or hear ghosts, you get a creepy feeling whenever they are around. Whenever a wraith enters the room or immediate area, you may automatically make a Static Mental Challenge with a difficulty of six Traits (although none of your Traits are risked). If you succeed, you are aware of the presence of ghosts.

Danger Sense (2 Trait Merit)

You have a sixth sense that warns you of danger. When you are in a potentially dangerous situation where you could possibly be surprised, you gain two extra seconds in which to react (for a total of four seconds; normal mortals get only two).

Magic Resistance (2 Trait Merit)

You have an innate resistance to the effects of all magic, including hedge magic, true magic, Garou rituals and *Thaumaturgy*. You are two Traits up on any challenges relating to resisting spells, rituals or other magical effects, whether you wish them to affect you or not. You may never learn to use any kind of magic, however.

Medium (2 Trait Merit)

You do in fact hear dead people – the whispers of wraiths reach across the Shroud to you, and you can sometimes sense them without effort. While you cannot usually see them, you can hear them and speak to them in return.

Occult Library (2 Trait Merit)

You own a collection of rare and occult books. These precious volumes contain bits of accurate knowledge concerning the supernatural. You are not necessarily familiar

with the contents of these volumes (for that you need the *Occult* Ability), but your library can be an invaluable aid in research.

Pale Aura (2 Trait Merit)

Your aura is pale an indistinct, like a vampire's, and lacks the vibrant colors of living mortals. Individuals capable of reading your aura automatically assume that you are a vampire (or that you're just plain weird, if they aren't familiar with vampiric auras) unless they succeed in an immediate Static Mental Challenge with a difficulty of 10 Traits.

Soothing Voice (2 Trait Merit)

Your voice is calm and soothing, almost entrancing. You are two Traits up on any challenge that directly involves the use of your voice, be it for singing, inciting a crowd to riot, leadership, etc.

Ghostsight (3 Trait Merit)

You can see beyond the supernatural barrier that separates the land of the living from the land of the dead, but only with effort. By winning a Static Mental Challenge against a difficulty of seven Traits, you can see wraiths and even dimly make out the lands of the Underworld for the remainder of the scene.

Kinain (3 Trait Merit)

The blood of the fae runs in your veins, literally. Though you are not a changeling, being kinain makes it easier for you walk in the Dream as if you were. While this product of your heritage may expose you to chimerical attack, it also opens up to you a new and wondrous world. You do not necessarily have access to the powers of the fae, but you are in tune with their world and they find it easier to affect you. Unlike a normal mortal, you are more likely to remember your encounters with the changelings.

Kinain have Trait maximums that are presented in the chart on page 119. You are related to one of the fae races, and you might even share some of their abilities. You are more easily accepted in fae society than ordinary humans, and you might even be able to use some of the changeling's arts if you also have the Merit *Faerie Blood*. You possess only five Banality Traits, which permits you to explore the fae's society, since your presence is less likely to afflict them negatively and because you are less susceptible to the amnesiac affects of the Mists. Similarly, you are easily enchanted: Any changeling can enchant you by simply expending a Trait of Glamour (without the need for a token), and you remain enchanted for a full week.

If you are playing a kinain in a predominately changeling game, the Storyteller may choose to waive the cost of this Merit in order to encourage play of intermediaries between human and changeling society.

See **The Shining Host Players Guide** for complete information about the kinain.

Kinfolk (3 Trait Merit)

You are, by some quirk of fate, kin to one of the Changing Breeds. The Changing Blood has not stirred in you — you cannot change your shape — but it has nonetheless left its indelible mark. You may not understand why, but you are immune to the Delirium. This does not mean that you know or recognize sensitive secrets about the Changing Breeds, or that you can wander around the shapechangers' holy sites with impunity, but you do have a certain edge among them that no normal human can match.

Kinfolk have Trait maximums as presented on the chart on page 119. All Kinfolk are considered related to one of the tribes, and they are more likely to have close ties with at least one Garou of that tribe. Kinfolk may learn Basic homid or tribe Gifts that do not

require Gnosis or Rage, at a cost of six Free or Experience Traits, or eight for Gifts of another tribe.

If you are playing a Kinfolk in a predominantly Garou game, your Storyteller may waive the cost of this Merit in order to encourage the interaction of mortal relatives with the Garou.

See **Laws of the Wild** for more information on the Garou, their powers and their society.

Luck (3 Trait Merit)

You were born lucky and have found that the odds are always slightly in your favor. You gain three retests per story that you may use on any failed tests. You cannot make more than one retest on any single challenge.

Psychic/Sorcerous Awareness (3 or 4 Trait Merit)

You are automatically aware whenever magic or psychic power is used within 10 feet of you. The use of Garou Gifts, vampiric Disciplines or even hedge magic causes a distinct tingle to run up your spine if you have *Sorcerous Awareness*. With *Psychic Awareness*, you notice various phenomena and powers that mimic psychic abilities, such as a vampire's *Auspex*. You may make a Static Mental Challenge against a difficulty of eight Traits in order to discern the source of the effect and exactly what it was (although you must have sufficient levels of the appropriate *Lore* to differentiate between a vampire Discipline and a changeling Art, for example).

Symbol Independence (3 Trait Merit)

Typically, one must present a holy symbol in order to use True Faith effectively against a supernatural opponent. You, however, are free from this restriction.

Unbondable (3 Trait Merit)

You are immune to the vampiric blood bond. No matter how much vampire blood you drink, you will never be blood bound.

Destiny (4 Trait Merit)

A great destiny lies before you, though you may not yet realize it. Your destiny becomes manifest over the course of the chronicle. The Storyteller decides the exact nature of your destiny, though you should provide her with input and suggestions. Because this Merit tends to transform a character into the central figure in the chronicle, you must have your Storyteller's approval before choosing it.

Easy Consort (4 Trait Merit)

Wraiths and other sprits find it easier to possess you than other mortals. Although this Merit can be disadvantageous at times, it means that you are a natural channel for beings from the other worlds. Thus, they may choose to approach and barter with you for the favor of borrowing your body. Wraiths and spirits are up two Traits whenever they attempt to possess you; furthermore, you retain full awareness of all events that occur during the possession.

Ecumenist (4 Trait Merit)

While you are steadfast in your own faith, you recognize the workings of the divine in other religions. Because you see the divine spark at the core of religions other than your own, you are able to make use of any religious symbol or icon when employing your True Faith (normally you would need to present a symbol or icon related specifically to your own religion).

Prophecy (4 Trait Merit)

God speaks to you in visions and signs. These visions strike you according to some greater will: You cannot make them come to you. Your Storyteller will describe to you the exact nature of each vision, but you can be sure that the meanings of most of these signs and portents will be obscure or cryptic. It's up to you to figure out if a particular vision is a warning, a command or perhaps merely symbolic. Such experiences are often accompanied by dramatic physical sensations and devastating headaches.

True Love (4 Trait Merit)

You have found (and perhaps lost) a *True Love*, a piece of comfort and companionship in an otherwise despairing world. When confronted by adversity, the thought of your *True Love* provides strength and peace of mind. You effectively gain one extra Willpower Trait each session, spent as a *True Love* Trait. (These Traits are not cumulative; you cannot save them up.) However, your *True Love* may require rescuing or assistance from time to time.

Ghoul (5 Trait Merit)

A vampire fed you some of her potent vitae, possibly blood bonding you into service. Somehow you broke free, but the blood's force has granted you some of your mistress' power. You no longer age, and you have the Basic level of one of the physical Disciplines(*Potence*, *Celerity* or *Fortitude* — see **Laws of the Night**). This Merit has a price, however: You must continue to feed on vampire blood, or you will regain your mortality and lose all the benefits of being a ghoul.

POWERFUL GHOULS

Some Storytellers may prefer not to limit Ghouls to Basic Disciplines. After all, since most troupes won't have many elder Kindred around, giving an Intermediate Discipline to a Ghoul who serves a ninth Generation vampire seems like a reasonable means of keeping the dichotomy between elders and neonates without adding more seventh or sixth generation powerhouses.

If this idea appeals to you, you may wish to use the following alternate Ghoul Discipline limitations:

Domitor of 11th or weaker generation	Basic Discipline powers
Domitor of 10th or weaker generation	Intermediate Discipline powers
Domitor of ninth or greater generation	Advanced Discipline powers

No ghoul should ever gain access to Master Discipline powers: some powers are reserved for the elders alone. And even Advanced Discipline powers should come with commensurate age and an appropriate degree of danger. Any ghoul experienced enough to have a powerful Domitor of 9th Generation or lower will almost certainly be Blood Bound. She may also be addicted to vampiric vitae or, worse, the vitae may be an absolute requirement for her survival. An aged ghoul who doesn't get his blood fix risks aging to death very quickly.

Ghouls have Trait maximums as indicated by the chart on page 119. Additionally, a ghoul may learn the vampiric Disciplines that are appropriate to her vampire mentor's clan. A ghoul begins with one Basic level of one of the physical Disciplines, and can learn the Basic levels of her domitor's clan Disciplines at a cost of six Experience Traits

each (provided her mentor is willing to teach her). Particularly powerful domitors give their ghouls the ability to learn greater Discipline powers: Ghoul servants sustained by a vampire of the Sixth or Seventh Generation may learn Intermediate Disciplines at a cost of 12 Traits each, while ghouls of vampires of lower generations may learn Advanced Disciplines at the incredible cost of 18 Experience Traits each.

Gnosis (5 - 7 Trait Merit)

You are tied to the powers of life and Gaia much like the Garou who are your kin. You possess a degree of their supernatural awareness, the strength of which is reflected by the number of Traits you have in this Merit. You have one to three Gnosis Traits: one Gnosis for five Traits in this Merit; two for six Traits and three for seven Traits. You may use your Gnosis Traits to employ werewolf Gifts and assist in Rites, just like a Garou. Having this Merit allows you to learn a greater selection of Gifts and accords you a great deal of respect among the shapechangers. Furthermore, if a vampire attempts to Embrace you, you may make on Simple Test for each Trait of Gnosis you possess. If you succeed in any of the tests, you die quickly and peacefully without becoming a vampire. If you tie any of the tests without any wins, you die slowly and painfully, but still do not become a vampire. Only if you lose all the tests do you join the ranks of the undead.

You may not raise your Gnosis with Experience Traits: Any Gnosis that you possess during character creation is the limit of your spiritual capacity forever. However, if you expend a permanent Gnosis Trait in the course of a Gift or ritual, you may use Experience Traits to regain that lost Gnosis Trait later.

You must take the Merit *Kinfolk* before taking this Merit.

Clear Sighted (5 Trait Merit)

You are unusually sensitive to the use of supernatural powers of illusion, trickery and disguise, and you can see through them to the heart of the matter. With a successful Mental Challenge, you can see through *Unseen Presence*, *Mask of 1,000 Faces*, *Blur of the Milky Eye*, *Blissful Ignorance*, *Chimerstry* and the like. When engaging multiple opponents simultaneously, you need risk only one Mental Trait to attempt to perceive all of them; make a single test against everyone simultaneously, resolving ties as normal. If you lose any of the challenges, you lose only the one Mental Trait that you bid.

Lifegiver (5 Trait Merit)

Your life force is particularly strong and resilient to harm. You heal rapidly and can even extend your regenerative powers to others. Whenever you suffer nonaggravated damage, you heal it in half the required time. Anyone under your care gains this benefit as well, provided that you are uninjured. You automatically gain the Flaw *Potent Blood*, but gain no additional Free Traits for it.

Speaker With the Dead (5 Trait Merit)

Your sight extends beyond the Shroud of the spirit world and into the lands of the dead. You see and hear the Underworld at all times. To you, life is an existence of stumbling through two half-worlds simultaneously — one world of solid, bright matter, and the other of decaying, gray detritus. You can also see and hear wraiths and other beings that inhabit the Underworld, and you are a target for such creatures that may wish to contact the living. Malevolent spectres may hound you in an attempt to drive you insane. You may gain *Wraith Lore* without the benefit of a mentor, and you are up one Trait when using sorcery or psychic phenomena to interact with the dead.

Mysterious Guardian (6 Trait Merit)

Someone or something watches over you, protecting you from harm and aiding you on random occasions. The Storyteller decides when, why and how this occurs, as well as what other effects you may experience as a result of having such a guardian.

Fist of God (7 Trait Merit)

You have developed a supernatural ability to strike and injure paranormal creatures. Perhaps you gained this power through intense training or constant devotion to your beliefs, or maybe your crossbow was once blessed by an extremely devout monk. Whatever the reason, your "Witch Hammer" strike inflicts aggravated damage against supernatural creatures. However, the Fist functions only with one particular weapon, be it your firearm, sword, body, etc. This Merit functions only if you maintain a Humanity of four or higher (though it cannot be permanently lost).

True Faith (7 Trait Merit)

Your deep-seated belief and love for some divine power grants you the ability to wield your faith against the supernatural. The effect of this power varies from person to person and from religion to religion. See the Numinae section of Chapter Five.

Cursed (1 - 5 Trait Flaw)

Someone or something with supernatural or magical powers has cursed you. You should detail the specific nature and history of the curse with your Storyteller. The curse cannot be dispelled without extreme effort and can even be life-threatening. Some examples include:

If you pass on a secret, your betrayal will harm you in some way. (1 Trait)

You stutter uncontrollably when trying to say something important. (2 Traits)

Tools break or malfunction when you attempt to use them. (3 Traits)

Anyone you love will later become your enemy. (4 Traits)

All your accomplishments will inevitably become tainted. (5 Traits)

Magic Susceptibility (2 Trait Flaw)

You are particularly vulnerable to the effects of magic, including *Thaumaturgy*, hedge magic, true magic, Garou Gifts and other forms of magic. You are two Traits down on challenges in which you resist the effects of magic. Furthermore, all spells and rituals double their effect on you. You may never learn to use magic of any kind.

Spectre Meat (3 Trait Flaw)

While most spectres (wraiths that have fallen into the clutches of darkness and insanity) cannot perceive the living lands, you stick out to their perception like a supernatural beacon. Spectres can see you, and they are likely to plague you constantly. See **Oblivion** for more details about spectres.

Wyrm-Tainted (4 Trait Flaw)

For some reason, the stink of the Wyrm clings to you. Perhaps you willingly serve the Wyrm, or perhaps the condition is hereditary. You may not even be aware of it. In any case, Garou can sense this about you, and many of them will kill you first and ask questions later if they detect your taint.

(Note: This Flaw is too pervasive and severe for a simple Rite of Cleansing to purge. This taint has permeated every aspect of your character's life, whether he realizes it or not.)

Dark Fate (5 Trait Flaw)

A terrible doom lies before you. This inevitable demise will become more and more apparent as the chronicle proceeds, and you will often have nightmares about it. Unless you overcome the Flaw before it is too late, your character will be dead within the year, though you may attempt to accomplish something of good or lasting value first. Your Storyteller will decide your fate, though you may contribute input and make suggestions. You must have your Storyteller's permission to choose this Flaw, and your Storyteller may well require you to acknowledge that your character will die when and how she sees fit.

FREE TRAITS

Mortal hunters, unlike their prey, do not automatically get any supernatural powers. However, they do receive one advantage over the creatures they pursue: Mortal characters receive 10 Free Traits with which they may improve their Traits or acquire Numinae. Your Storyteller may choose to place some restrictions or limitations on the use of these Free Traits. Numinae (the special powers of True Faith, sorcery and psychic phenomena) are described in Chapter Five.

The following chart lists the Free Trait costs for various improvements.

FREE TRAIT COSTS

Trait	Cost
Attribute Trait	1
Ability Trait	1
Willpower Trait	1
Humanity Trait	1
Merit	Merit Trait cost
Basic Numina (Sorcery or Psychic Phenomena)	3
Background or Influence Trait	1

STEP FIVE: SPARK OF LIFE

Your character is now almost complete. All that remains is for you to add some extra depth to your character, in order to help you bring her to life.

Background: Decide how your character lived and grew up before becoming aware of the world of supernatural. Your character was probably a normal person once, with ambitions and desires that didn't involve staking vampires or banishing wraiths. Think about her education, her childhood friends, and her hopes and dreams. These historical details make your character seem more real during play.

Appearance: How does your character dress, and what sorts of things does she carry? Does she wear a dozen crucifixes or carry a PCS phone? Some hunters may wear garments that denote their particular organization: A Roman Catholic priest, for instance, might choose to wear his ecumenical garb while hunting, while other hunters may prefer clothing better suited to field work.

Equipment: Hunters typically carry the tools of their trade when they are about their work. Automobiles, camping equipment, wooden stakes, a crossbow — all these

things are equipment. You should talk to your Storyteller about what kinds of things your character might own. Remember that weapons of any kind must be represented by cards, never by replicas or real versions.

Quirks: Everybody has a few idiosyncrasies and odd personal habits. Perhaps your character has a nervous habit of whistling show tunes during tense situations, or perhaps she carries a good luck charm. Note a few quirks that your character exhibits, and work them into your roleplaying.

EXPERIENCE

Humans have a remarkable capacity for self-improvement based on experience. We learn to improve our existing capabilities, and to acquire new ones, through observation and practice. Hunters, whose safety and very lives must all too frequently rely on their native skills and inherent powers, must maintain a high degree of competence if they wish to avoid death (or its many unpleasant alternatives). But when one's life work is tracking down and confronting the supernatural horrors that lurk in the dark places of the world, simple competence is not enough: The hunter must continuously strive to exceed her current limitations and acquire new skills and knowledge to combat her chosen enemies.

When you participate in **Mind's Eye Theatre** game sessions, your character gains Experience Traits. You may expend Experience Traits to improve your character's Traits. Normally, you earn one Experience Trait for each game session in which you participate. The Storyteller may choose to award additional Experience Traits in recognition of exceptional roleplaying, extraordinary courage or acquisition of vital knowledge. However, characters should never gain more than four Experience Traits from a single session of game play.

Using Experience Traits

You may expend Experience Traits to increase existing Traits or acquire new ones. Different types of Traits have different Experience Trait costs, as shown in this table:

New Attribute Trait — One Experience Trait

New Ability Trait — One Experience Trait

New Humanity Trait — Two Experience Traits

New Willpower Trait — Three Experience Traits

New Influence Trait — Three Experience Traits (except for government agents, who need spend only one Experience Trait per new Influence Trait)

New Numina, Basic — Three Experience Traits

New Numina, Intermediate — Six Experience Traits

New Numina, Advanced — Nine Experience Traits (True Faith may not be improved or acquired with Experience Traits, except by hunters who are members of the Inquisition)

New Sorcery Ritual, Basic — Two Experience Traits

New Sorcery Ritual, Intermediate — Four Experience Traits

New Sorcery Ritual, Advanced — Six Experience Traits

Remove a Negative Trait — Two Experience Traits

Acquire a Merit — Double the Merit's Trait cost*

Remove a Flaw — Double the Flaw's Trait cost*

*Requires Storyteller approval

Stephen stirred the yellow light pad, pints and scribblings — the plans of all their labors. Jeremy set down plates of spaghetti and a loaf of Italian bread, but his brother didn't look up until he had sat down and cleared his throat. "Any luck?" Jeremy inquired as he took a hunk of bread.

His brother frowned. "Something. I've tracked down the vampire that Jenny was supposedly seen with. He moved out here recently. I spent the afternoon arranging a meeting."

Jeremy swallowed a bigger bite than he intended and choked, "Jesus, Steve, I thought you told me these guys were bad news. What was Jenny doing with one? And what are you doing with him?"

Stephen started to fork up some spaghetti, but did not seem hungry. "I don't know. She mentioned someone she was trying to help, who wanted to get out of his bad life. This guy matches everything she described." He sighed, pushing the pasta around his plate. "I don't know why Jenny would take a chance like that — it goes against everything the organization stands for. I know she didn't like the idea of torture, but why would they bring her in if they knew what she was like?"

Jeremy started to lift his fork to his mouth, then paused. "Torture?"

His brother paused, then nodded slowly. "Yes. And no, I haven't, but I know how."

Jeremy's appetite slipped away. He put down his fork and stared down at the mess on his plate, as if seeing it for the first time. The past three days crashed into him violently, and he abruptly got up, the words tumbling out: "Jesus, Steve, I don't know what's more crazy — the ones who pretend to be monsters, or the ones who pretend to be monster-hunters." With that, he retreated to his room, leaving Steve and supper at the table, and slammed the door. Once, Stephen knocking was key enough for him to enter, but now Jeremy ignored his brother's knocking, putting a pillow over his head to block out Steve's voice, until Steve finally gave up.

• • •

Around midnight, Jeremy slipped back to the kitchen, his stomach practically announcing his arrival. He noticed that Stephen had cleaned up the kitchen in the meanwhile, and there was no sign of the earlier, awkward meal. He started to step into the kitchen proper, when he realized that Stephen was at the kitchen table. Jeremy paused — what would Steve say after what happened earlier?

Stephen gave no sign that he had heard Jeremy's entrance. He seemed to be deeply absorbed in reading Jeremy's old Bible (which, the owner admitted, hadn't seen much use here). He looked unwell, underslept and above all, sad. In front of him was a picture that Jeremy kept on the fridge — "This way, I see it every day," he had told Mom — showing all five siblings about three Christmases ago, the last time they had all been together. He picked it up and studied it quietly. Then, he turned his face into his hand, and there was a long sick silence, and Jeremy heard the deep shuddering breaths of a man trying desperately not to cry.

CHAPTER FIVE: NUMINAE AND POWERS

PSYCHIC PHENOMENA

Inexplicable and unique to mortals, psychic powers are a subconscious ability to effect the surrounding world simply through thought. In the World of Darkness, few possess these exceptional abilities.

Psychic abilities are separated into different phenomena. If a mortal character is so lucky as to have psychic powers, she probably possesses Traits only in a single phenomenon. It is a rare individual with more than one phenomenon. Though it is possible to develop multiple areas of psychic aptitude with exceptional study and practice, most individuals are incapable of more than the most rudimentary psychic abilities. Improvement in one area comes at the expense of others, so a multidisciplinary psychic rarely achieves levels of significant ability in any area.

Developing psychic abilities is exhausting and frustrating. Most folks who wish to develop their "sixth sense" in any way have to do so consciously, through constant practice and insight. Trial and error forces those who practice such skills to question their faith in themselves and in the paranormal. Psychic abilities typically develop instinctively during childhood and must somehow survive the turmoil of adolescence. Younger individuals actually have an easier time developing their psychic abilities; children and adolescents are more likely to externalize their failures, keeping the necessary self-confidence to continue improving their powers. Failure and disappointment are injurious to the delicate growth of psychic power, since a psychic must have consummate self-assurance to use her abilities.

Psychic powers are selected during character creation. If you have other Numinae on your sheet, you can select psychic phenomena only with Storyteller approval. The reverse also applies. It is exceedingly uncommon for a psychic to exhibit both phenomena and, say, True Faith, as the belief of power from within and divine power from without can clash. Likewise, the degree of intensity of purpose and dedication to the development of the mind generally distracts the psychic from undertaking additional occult study to explore sorcery as an option. Most of the time, the psychic

doesn't realize the other powers exist and if he does know of them, he considers them to be similar forces to the ones he uses. Why bother with all the fidgety gadgets, 11 different herbs and spices or magic wands when you can do what you do just by thinking hard?

Improvement in psychic abilities also comes only with the Storyteller's approval, since the character must have a great deal of practical experience, practice and confidence to develop. At a *minimum*, development of a new level of skill should take one month per Trait level that the character is attempting to reach, involving exclusive study of that power. No other Trait purchases are possible during that time due to the dedication required in expanding one's mind, and naturally the study and discipline must be evident in the character's actions during play.

Purchasing completely new powers should come only as a part of a story, and an instructor or key awakening events should be required. Even then, new powers should not suddenly spring into existence in the middle of play; a character may find a tutor or undergo an experience that unlocks her latent potential, but actually developing that potential into a useful form takes time and practice, often years. Expanding one's mind is neither quick nor easy.

THE POWER WITHIN

Psychic phenomena are not instant-access powers. Unless otherwise specified, all psychic phenomena require a turn of concentration, followed in the next turn by the expenditure of a Willpower Trait (as the psychic delves into the wellsprings of her being for strength) and the appropriate challenge. Some effects may require a challenge against a target's Mental Traits.

Concentration is required for the duration of the effect (or extended maintenance, if permitted), and some sort of focus may be needed as well (hand gestures, eye contact). It is possible to activate multiple psychic powers or to perform other tasks while concentrating, but each psychic power active causes the user to suffer a cumulative two-Trait penalty on *all* other challenges.

Significant distraction — injury, emotional turbulence or confusion, for example — may cause a power to fail utterly (Narrator's call). In such cases, an additional no-risk challenge is required to maintain the power. This challenge is identical to the challenge required to activate the power in question, and is taken with the additional two-Trait (or more) concentration penalty as above. If such a challenge is lost, all powers currently active are ended.

FAST-CASTING

A psychic may circumvent the initial turn of concentration required by expending an additional Willpower Trait and suffering a three-Trait penalty to the difficulties of any challenge involving that power use and its maintenance, as well as further concentration checks (cumulative with other penalties). Psychics can never completely abandon the focus of concentration, and this is essentially a lashing out of energy rather than a directed effort.

ANIMAL PSYCHICS

Some psychics are capable of communicating with animals on their own level. Whether through growling or snarling, horse whispering, commanding whistles or

gestures, the animal understands the psychic, and in some cases may be understood in turn.

These psychics may use their power on any (nonhuman) mammal, lizard or bird that can hear them (or see them, if gestures are used). Highly intelligent creatures (chimpanzees, dolphins, gorillas) or well-trained domestic animals (dogs, horses, circus or show animals) are certainly easier to communicate with, and the Narrator may wish to lower the difficulty of the test based on the relative intelligence of the animal and the degree of involvement the psychic has had with the animal's upbringing and training. Fish are harder to control and give the psychic a two-Trait penalty. Insect minds are not affected by this phenomenon.

Challenge Type: Social (retest with *Animal Ken*)

BASIC

Communication

You can "speak" with a single animal, allowing two-way communication with the beast for a few minutes (five at most). This does not give you any form of control over the creature, although it does allow for miscommunications to be clarified.

Command

You can command the animal to perform for you, as long as you can adequately describe the trick or task, and it does not endanger the animal. The animal may be commanded to attack if it has a proclivity to do so — a police dog may be prepared to bring someone to ground, but a sheep will have second thoughts. Modifiers to the difficulty of the challenge depend on the complexity of the command and the proclivity of the animal to the action — add one Trait for a rather complex command or one to which the animal is ambivalent; subtract one for something it would likely do anyway.

INTERMEDIATE

Mass Communication

As *Communication*, but you can communicate with any animals within earshot. Multiple types of animals may be included simultaneously, but at an additional difficulty. Add one Trait to the difficulty for each additional species of animal in the area. For example, speaking to multiple dogs is possible at no additional difficulty, but letting the cats in on the message as well adds a one-Trait penalty.

Mind Link

With this power, you join your mind with that of a single animal. The link lasts until you drop the connection or your concentration is broken. While linked, you can perceive whatever the animal perceives. You can also communicate with the animal by using any of the lower level powers of this path, but you can do so mentally over whatever distance separates you. If the animal is injured, the mental feedback causes you one level of bashing damage for every level of lethal damage the animal suffers.

ADVANCED

Domination

This ability gives you total domination over the target animal's mind. It does whatever you wish, even at the cost of its own life. The animal explicitly follows one

command. The command may be conditional ("If someone attacks me, *then* kill him") but not conjunctional ("Follow the scent of this shirt *and* attack the wearer").

ANTI-PSYCHIC

This is the rarest talent yet observed. The psychic's very presence weakens the talents of even the most powerful psychics nearby. Any psychic with this talent may not purchase other psychic powers. Most anti-psychics remain unaware of their talent until approached or even attacked by other psychics.

This power is considered to be "always on" (it costs no Willpower and requires no challenge to activate) and affects a radius dependant on the level of the power possessed. An anti-psychic may dampen this aura by expending a Willpower Trait and succeeding in a Static Mental Challenge against six Traits. This negates the field for up to a scene or can focus the power purely on a single opponent for a turn. The aura pops back into effect if the anti-psychic wishes, or if the duration of the suppression expires. Of course, the anti-psychic must be aware of his power and how to manipulate it prior to being able to use this dampening effect.

All psychics (friend or foe) within the radius are considered to be down one Trait per level of the anti-psychic field in any psychic-related challenge. If the power is focused on one target, the target must also spend double the Trait cost of any power she uses during that turn.

Challenge Type: Mental (retest with *Meditation*)

ANTI-PSYCHIC POWER RADII

One Trait	5-yard radius
Two Traits	10-yard radius
Three Traits	15-yard radius
Four Traits	20-yard radius
Five Traits	25-yard radius

ASTRAL PROJECTION

This power allows the psychic to leave her material body and wander about the world in a spirit form. The spirit travels very quickly by crossing planes of thought, and, while able to observe the physical plane, is unable to physically affect it (although other psychic abilities may be used with a two-Trait penalty).

While away from her body, the psychic cannot perceive what happens to it unless still in the same immediate location. The body remains in a comatose state, unaware of its surroundings.

Two astrally projecting characters may interact freely, conversing or using Mental or Social powers. They may even attempt to injure each other by attacking the silver cord that connects travelers to their bodies. Psychics in *Astral Projection* use Mental Traits in place of Physical Traits, with damage causing the opponent to lose Willpower Traits. Once an astral combatant runs out of Willpower Traits, the cord snaps, leaving the spirit stranded in the spirit realms with little or no sense of location. Some spirits may never find their way back to their bodies or find themselves stranded in other realms

(such as the Shadowlands or the Penumbra), or even devoured by entities native to the spirit lands.

To release the astral form, the psychic must meditate for at least a turn and then expend a Willpower Trait. A successful Static Mental Challenge against six Traits (retest with *Meditation*) is required to successfully leave the body; if she loses, the psychic may not attempt to leave her body for the next 24 hours.

While the rate of travel in astral form is very quick, practicalities of live play preclude players actually flitting about the game site at high speed. Journeys within the scope of the game site should be limited to a brisk walk. For purposes of combat-scale movement, consider the movement to be 20 paces per turn. A Storyteller should run larger journeys "outside" of the site. Players in astral space should indicate their invisibility to other players by crossing their arms in front of their chest, or by wearing a colored armband.

Note: The plane that the astral form moves through, the Vulgate, is the periphery of the High Umbra. You cannot interact with or see wraiths in the Shadowlands or Umbral creatures (such as Banes or Garou) in the Penumbra unless you find a means to travel to or sense those other spirit realms. Similarly, you are invisible to them unless they can detect your manifestations in the physical world — you cannot manifest in these other realms as you can in the physical world. If encountered in the Vulgate, vampires use their Mental Traits in lieu of Physical Traits, and wraiths and Garou use their Physical Traits for "physical" combat.

Challenge Type: Mental (retest with *Meditation*)

BASIC

Seeker

You can perceive the astral realm using only sight, but cannot quite enter it. The astral realm appears to be overlaid on your normal environment. This effect lasts as long as you concentrate upon it. Failure in the challenge results in a short period (three turns) of visual confusion during which you are down two Traits in all challenges. Once this headache disappears, you may again attempt to view the other side.

Visitor

You can leave your body for one minute per Stamina-based Physical Trait that you currently possess. Sight is your only sense in the astral plane, and your range is limited to traveling approximately one mile from your real body.

INTERMEDIATE

Journeyman

You can leave your body for up to 10 minutes per Stamina Trait that you currently possess (as above) and may also hear within the astral plane. Your range is extended to roughly 100 miles from your body.

Traveler

You can now leave your body for up to an hour per Stamina Trait that you possess. Each hour (or part thereof) beyond the first requires the expenditure of an additional Willpower Trait. Also, you may materialize briefly (one turn) by expending a Willpower Trait, appearing to observers as a translucent, ghostly apparition, though you may not communicate verbally with the observers. This manifestation does not appear on normal recording devices.

ADVANCED

Wayfarer

You can astrally travel anywhere in the world so long as your body remains healthy (it will deteriorate naturally if you fail to eat, for example), and you may use all of your senses normally in the Vulgate. You may materialize as above and appear as a blurry, idealized version of your normal self. This manifestation can last for as many turns as you have current Stamina Traits (as above). While manifest, you may speak in a whisper. This sound will, like your appearance, not appear on normal recording devices. While materialized, you may use other Mental or Social-based phenomena at their normal difficulty level by expending a Mental Trait prior to using the power. The rules for concentration, multiple activated powers and so on are still applicable.

BIOCONTROL

Psychics with *Biocontrol* are capable of turning their attentions inward to the degree that they can regulate their autonomic systems as easily as other people tie their shoes. Proper use of this power allows the psychic to regulate his internal organs, reduce pain and even direct his circulatory and endocrinal systems at will. While some normal people exhibit the basic techniques of biofeedback, the talented psychic can far surpass the most dedicated disciple. Unless otherwise specified, any use of this phenomenon requires five minutes of meditative trance to activate. Most uses of this power last as long as concentration is maintained.

Challenge Type: Physical (retest with *Meditation*)

BASIC

Self Control

You have a basic degree of control over your body. By entering a self-hypnotic state, you can stop a small cut from bleeding, ignore small amounts of pain or hold your breath marginally longer than you would normally be able (up to three minutes). While in this trance, you can do nothing but focus on your body. You remain peripherally aware of your surroundings and can snap out of the trance at will.

Self-Healing

By maintaining internal focus for a long period, you accelerate your healing rate, as your control allows you to more efficiently knit flesh and fight off infection. You must spend your time resting comfortably (preferably under medical care) for the power to work. This power doubles your normal recovery rate from injury or illness, but any challenges made to reduce healing time suffer any penalties imposed by injury level. Success reduces the time for healing by one stage (see "Healing," p. 253).

INTERMEDIATE

Hysterical Strength

You gain control of your adrenal system, allowing brief periods of hysterical strength and speed. You gain the Physical Traits *Brawny*, *Enduring* and *Quick*, even if this takes you over your normal maximum Trait limit. You also gain an additional Healthy health level for the duration of this power. This effect lasts one scene, after which you "come down," your body recoiling from the excessive stress and pain. The exertion of this power is such that it may internally injure you. After the power expires,

perform a Simple Test. On a win, no damage is taken. On a tie, one level of bashing damage is inflicted. On a loss, you suffer two levels of bashing damage.

Ignore Pain Response

You can shut off your pain receptors for short periods of time. This heals no damage, but you can function without wound penalties (even while Incapacitated) for one scene. The penalties return at the end of the scene, and you cannot use this power again until you have healed at least one health level.

ADVANCED

Mind Over Matter

Your control is such that you can stop your own heart, suspend the need for oxygen and regulate digestive functions. In effect, you can consciously control your body's biological functions as if every cell responded individually to your mind. One of the following options can be used each time you activate this power. Normal concentration rules apply for multiple effects.

• You can nullify most toxins at will, although a sufficiently large dose at one time may override this power. The toxins pass into your waste systems.

• You can fight off just about any mundane disease, allergen or irritant, and may even be able to resist cancer and HIV (a Static Physical Challenge is required, against a difficulty of 7 for mundane problems, up to 9 for cancer or HIV).

• Alongside the use of *Ignore Pain Response*, you can contort your body into otherwise uncomfortable postures and slip out of bonds or into tight spaces.

• You can hold your breath for five minutes at a time while remaining physically active. Each turn of intense physical action (combat, running, etc.) reduces this window by a minute.

• You can prepare your body against trauma, gaining an additional Healthy health level (or temporarily healing one lost level), and making a Simple Test at the time of injury to reduce any level of bashing damage to nil, lethal to bashing or aggravated to lethal (noncumulative). These benefits expire at the end of the scene or hour, whichever comes first.

CHANNELING

Some psychics can call upon the knowledge of those who have gone before. They can briefly touch the shades of the dead, gaining skills and expertise they themselves do not possess. Some psychics develop a stable of spirits that they can call on for help and assistance. Others claim to connect with the collective unconsciousness. Those who have claimed to channel dead composers to write their music demonstrate this power.

If a channeler fails in any test of *Channeling*, she has opened herself up to the spirit planes. Malevolent creatures may steal some of her spirit (any Ability Traits are fair game, as are Mental, Social or Willpower Traits, and the theft may be temporary or permanent at the whim of the Storyteller). A spirit may even take control of the channeler for a brief time. Either attack involves a Willpower Challenge between the entity and the channeler. Meddling with the dead is not something to be taken lightly, and the Storyteller is advised to make this a part of their story.

Only one personality can be channeled at any one time (unless you have reached the Advanced level of this phenomenon). A channeler may not normally stack

additional Traits from multiple spirits into a single Ability. Traits gained through this phenomenon fade at the end of the current scene, and while memories of the use of the skills exist, no such Trait gain will permanently affect the character's sheet unless the player expends Experience Traits to purchase the Abilities in question. The channeler might be able to use her dead contacts over an extended time as a source of tutelage for esoteric or "lost" skills (if they themselves know the skill), with the approval of the Storyteller.

Challenge Type: Mental (retest with *Awareness*)

BASIC

Channeler

You can use this power only once per day. You have a vague sense of other personalities floating about and of the existence of some sort of consciousness beyond the body. You can gain up to two Traits in a single Ability that you do not already possess if you are successful in activating this power.

Seer

You can channel twice a day, with the ability to gain three Traits as above. You can also make a Static Mental Challenge against the local rating of the Shroud — the barrier between the lands of the living and the dead (see **Laws of Ascension**, p. 219) — to perceive the Shadowlands. The "typical" shroud rating is 7, although other factors may alter this. Places frequented by ghosts or vampires may have ratings as low as 4 or 5. Strong Nodes — places of strong Quintessence flow — may have ratings as low as 3, or 2 for the greatest Nodes. The maximum Shroud rating is 10.

You can communicate with the ghosts on the other side as long as you exclusively concentrate on this communication. For every minute that you are in the trance, a concentration check should be performed.

INTERMEDIATE

Medium

You can channel three times per day, with the ability to gain up to four Traits as above. Additionally, you may add gained Ability Traits to Abilities that you already possess (maximum of a one-Trait increase in any one Ability). You can also see into and communicate with the Shadowlands as above for an entire scene per successful check. Breaks in concentration and concentration penalties still apply.

Mystic

There is no limit to the number of times that you can channel per day, although the number of Traits that you can potentially gain drops by one for each successful channeling after the third (minimum of one Trait) until you get at least six hours of restful sleep. You can add a maximum of two Traits to any Ability you already possess. You can also allow wraiths skilled in the arts of possession (called *Puppetry* by wraiths) to possess your body freely and use all your skills. You retain full awareness of your actions during this time, and can eject the wraith on a successful Willpower Challenge against the wraith. Each such attempt costs a Willpower Trait to initiate and takes a full turn of concentrated mental struggling.

ADVANCED

Necromancer

You can channel two disparate entities at once (and thus can challenge twice and add the results to determine how many Ability Traits are gained). You are still limited as to how your channeling weakens over successive attempts (as per *Mystic*, above). When possessed by an entity, you often gain some memories from the ghost, beyond what the spirit may do and tell you. You can get a sense of the spirit's Nature, Demeanor and driving concerns by winning a Social Challenge against the spirit.

CLAIRVOYANCE

A clairvoyant may cast his senses away, perceiving events and places at great distances. Unlike *Astral Projection*, there is no "travel" to the site of focus, but rather a gradual shift of focus from the current locale to the intended destination. Although *Clairvoyance* technically refers to the sense of sight, some psychics can also cast forth their other senses. Extending perception in this way is taxing and difficult; normally it requires some preparation and a great deal of concentration. No matter how advanced the psychic is in this phenomenon, he remains an observer, unable to affect the events witnessed in any way short of calling on some other power such as *Telekinesis*, and then only at higher levels of this power. The character may end the trance at any stage. Doing so deactivates the power.

This is a tricky power to simulate in **Mind's Eye Theatre** as it involves using a character's senses at range. Mechanically, it is easiest if the player goes to the actual site of whatever she wishes to perceive, leaving an item card to mark where her body lies. *Clairvoyance* is magically undetectable and immune to detection by the use of the vampiric *Auspex* Discipline. While the psychic is extending her senses, she is unable to use them at the location of her body. An experienced clairvoyant can choose which senses are used and which remain with her body. If only some of the senses are extended, the others still operate normally. For example, she could be looking and hearing through *Clairvoyance*, but her body can still feel and smell its immediate environment.

The clairvoyant is limited to the abilities of his natural senses when far-sensing — if the target location is in total darkness, remote sight is of little use. Physical handicaps are no limit to *Clairvoyance* — a blind psychic can still see through his mind using this power. The focus point of *Clairvoyance* is not mobile, and while the clairvoyant may rotate his field of view, panning about a room for example, if he wishes to move the focus (say, to look under a table that is otherwise blocked from his initial line of sight), he must initiate the power again, focusing on the new area.

The difficulty of the activation challenge is based on the familiarity the character has with the locale to be viewed. Supernatural wards against scrying and other supernatural sight will block any visions.

Challenge Type: Mental (retest with *Awareness*)

BASIC

Secret Glimpses

With absolute concentration, you can briefly extend your senses a short distance to see something occurring outside your normal perceptions. The visions gained are hazy and sometimes misinterpreted, especially as you cannot actually hear what is happening.

You can see things at the target location, although the images are hazy and dreamlike. The maximum range of your psychic senses from your body is about 20 paces.

The preparation requires 10 minutes of concentration or meditation, undisturbed while sitting or lying in a dark or dimly lit space. You must also maintain complete concentration for the duration of the vision (up to two minutes) — performing any other task is impossible, and interruption immediately ruins the effect.

Whispers of the Hidden

You can expand your senses to a significant distance with some effort. This power allows you to see distant locations, and you can sometimes hear what's happening as well — you can make a Static Mental Challenge as you did to activate the power, but with no Trait risk, success resulting in muffled clairaudience. The range of your far-sensing is extended to about five miles.

Preparation time is reduced to five minutes of concentration or meditation. Again, performing other tasks is impossible and interruption will break the trance, which will still only last a couple of minutes at the most. While the visual senses are fairly clear at this level, the sound is still hazy and can easily be misheard.

INTERMEDIATE

Sense of the Beyond

You can combine the sensations of sight and sound, and can extend the duration of the visions. All of the visions include clear sight and sound, and you can sometimes feel objects at the location.

Preparatory concentration is reduced to only three minutes at this level of skill, and the difficulty for all *Clairvoyance* powers is reduced by one Trait. The duration of the vision is up to 10 minutes and the range is extended to 50 miles. By making an additional Static Mental Challenge against the same difficulty as the activation challenge (but with no Trait risk), you can "feel" objects at the target location. You cannot exert any force or influence over the objects.

At this level, you can also attempt to project other psychic abilities through your *Clairvoyance*. You cannot split your consciousness (no *Astral Projection*) but you can invoke other psychic powers while using your clairvoyant focus point as a point of reference. For example, you could use *Telekinesis* to move a vase in the distant location if you can see it using your *Clairvoyance*. These extra powers are subject to the normal Trait penalties for splitting concentration.

If disturbed while in a clairvoyant trance, you are now subject to the normal rules for breaks in concentration for psychic phenomena.

Hauntings of the Mind's Eye

You can clearly see, hear and touch normally at range. Additionally, you may be able to detect strong odors (as above for the other partial senses). The maximum range of your *Clairvoyance* is 500 miles. You now need concentrate only for a minute to use your awareness. Your visions can be maintained for up to 20 minutes.

ADVANCED

Cosmic Awareness

You have opened your mind completely to your unusual perceptions and can now enter a vision after only a few moments (one turn) of concentration. You can use all five senses clearly and can potentially perceive things anywhere within 5,000 miles.

Functionally, the Storyteller may chose to limit the use of this power due to the difficulty of describing events all around the world.

The difficulty to view locations is reduced by two Traits (replacing the bonus given with *Sense of the Beyond*). You can utilize other powers through your *Clairvoyance*, subject to normal concentration penalties. Additionally, you are one Trait up to maintain your concentration if disturbed. You can potentially maintain your concentration until the end of the scene or hour — whichever comes first.

At the Storyteller's discretion, you may receive visions without initiating them and experience a vision of something the Storyteller wishes you to see. These flashes of unexpected sight can be disturbing indeed, especially when they come in the midst of other important matters. You may become locked into these inadvertent trances, again at the Storyteller's discretion, but generally for no more than a minute before you can will yourself out of the trance. Such spontaneous trances do not require any activation expenditure or challenge, although if you wish to concentrate on them to extend the vision, you can activate your power normally.

CLAIRVOYANCE DIFFICULTIES

Familiarity	Difficulty
Very familiar	5
Known to the psychic	7
Completely unknown	9

CYBERKINESIS

A relatively new talent, *Cyberkinesis* allows one to control electronic machinery with one's mind. The cyberkinetic generates a small electromagnetic field that alters the operating system of computers, stereo systems, etc. While the cyberkinetic can control the machine, he cannot "read its mind" (that is the province of *Cyberpathy*). For all powers above *Switch*, the cyberkinetic must be able to see what he is doing (reading a screen or readout) — he can send information to the machine but must read it back normally. All these powers have a varying difficulty of activation based on the equipment involved (see individual entries for sample difficulties) but still require the normal Willpower expenditure.

This power is retested with *Computer* or *Science: Electronics* or a similar Ability, depending on the situation. Simply having this power does not instill any instinctive knowledge of the machines or electronics involved. Haphazard experimentation can produce interesting results.

Challenge Type: Social (retest with *Computer*, *Science: Electronics*)

BASIC

Switch

You can switch computers or easily operated electronic equipment off and on.

Link

You may now operate the equipment without touching it, as if by remote control. This does not give you any overrides, passwords, etc — you could enter the password

without using the keyboard, but you still need to know that password. Make a Static Mental Challenge, difficulty according to the task. Programming a VCR or entering data into a word processor is fairly simple (four Traits), while driving a car with power steering (seven Traits, more if in bad conditions, *Drive* for the retest) or running a computer-controlled factory (nine Traits) is somewhat more difficult.

INTERMEDIATE

Scramble

You can send microscale power surges through electronics, causing them to lock up or fault. Video equipment displays snow, recording devices pick up static. This effect lasts as long as you concentrate on the equipment in question (you must be aware of its presence and location). When your concentration lapses, the systems return to normal, although less robust systems may continue to crash as a result of the interruption. Make a Static Mental Challenge at seven Traits for most equipment, higher for more complicated or complex systems.

Password

You can override the operating systems of computers, essentially giving you any password you require. You force the system to do anything that it is normally capable of doing. You could erase data, forge e-mail from a local account holder, create new users, etc. The difficulty of the Static Mental Challenge depends on the level of security of the computer, starting at six Traits for a normal desktop system, and rising for higher levels of security and countermeasures.

ADVANCED

Run Hot

You have such control over the equipment that you can cause it to perform beyond its normal abilities. A computer calculates faster, a laser burns hotter, etc. The activation difficulty for this power is 8 Traits. This "overclocking" grants you an additional Trait the next time you use the machine during that scene but damages the equipment — add one Negative Trait to the equipment for each use of this power until it is repaired, and anyone using it subsequent to your meddling will be one Trait down.

Cyberpathy

While a cyberkinetic can control the electronics of a computer, the cyberpath can read its data, possibly in a similar manner to how a telepath can read the electrical impulses of the human brain. All uses of *Cyberpathy* require the psychic to be able to see the computer. The difficulty of all Static Mental Challenges (required to use each power) start at six Traits for standard desktop systems and rise to nine for heavily encrypted systems. The cyberpath can also read data off digital storage media (disconnected hard drives, CDs, etc), with difficulties as above. Generally speaking, each use of this power takes 10 to 15 minutes of concentration. This power is retested with the *Computer* Ability and requires the usual Willpower Trait expenditure to activate. Unless otherwise mentioned, these powers last as long as the psychic concentrates on its use.

The effects of computer viruses read with this power are up to the Storyteller's whim.

Challenge Type: Mental (retest with *Computer*)

BASIC

Analyze Structure

You can analyze the directory structure of the computer or media. You can see what files are stored but cannot mentally access them.

Read-Only Mode

You can travel the directory structure and read the contents of files. Simple graphics and text files are easy to comprehend. The nature of program files can be grasped. Unscrambling encryption is not yet an option.

INTERMEDIATE

Download

You can "copy" a file from a computer to your mind, writing the data in unused sections of your brain. While you can read text files, observe graphics or hear sound files and understand the nature of programs, you cannot "run" executable files in your head. With the *Cyberkinesis* power *Link*, you can upload the information into another computer. Remember the Trait penalties for multiple power use if you are attempting to copy data straight from one computer to another using your brain as a serial cable.

The cyberpath can hold roughly one file for every permanent Mental Trait he normally has. The normal temporary loss of Mental Traits does not indicate loss of data, although permanent losses of Traits lowers the capacity and results in the loss of any data stored in that Trait "slot." The Storyteller must decide how much data constitutes a single file. Multiple small text files might fit into one Trait slot, but an operating system kernel or a large movie file might take up several, if not all, slots in the cyberpath's head. The files remain stored until deleted or overwritten.

Files stored in this manner do not become some sort of *Eidetic Memory*, and you cannot store your own memories as "files" in this manner. Accessing the files already stored for self-viewing takes a moment's concentration and then normal reading or analysis time. While they may provide the basis for study for increasing Abilities through experience, simply possessing the information does not grant any level of Ability that the information may represent (e.g., *Lores*). Anyone hacking your brain using *Telepathy* will, depending on their level of skill, become aware of the presence of the files, perhaps have some idea of their contents or topic, but is unable to freely access them unless they have an equal or higher level of *Telepathy* than you have in *Cyberpathy* and succeed in their normal challenges to read the information.

Remote Access

You can connect to any computer that your local computer connects to. There are no additional powers other than to treat a remote computer as if it were sitting in front of you. For every "hop" between the computers (Storyteller discretion, possibly over a dozen hops around the globe), you are one Trait down in challenges to that computer.

ADVANCED

Decrypt

You are now capable of decrypting secured data. This data can either be on a computer (local or accessed via *Remote Access*) or stored in your head via *Download*. High encryption ratings increase the difficulty of the challenge.

ECTOPLASMIC GENERATION

The psychic is capable of coalescing the stuff of spirits into a tangible form. Most often, this ectoplasm manifests as a gelatinous mucus, though skilled psychics can disperse and concentrate it to form webs, sticky vapors and the like. All ectoplasm is opaque, generally blocking sight for those caught in it. Ectoplasm dissolves into nothingness a short while after the psychic ceases to concentrate on it.

For wraiths, all ectoplasmic creations are solid; they cannot move through them. Psychics can attack wraiths with ectoplasmic creations, although they would need some method of seeing the dead in the Shadowlands. All activations require the standard Willpower expenditure. The maximum concentration span possible for this power is 10 minutes.

Challenge Type: Social (retest with *Occult*)

BASIC

The Big Sneeze

Strands of snotty material can be called into existence. This ectoplasm pours from your orifices or follows in the wake of your touch, leaving a sticky trail. The goop is disturbing and nasty but otherwise harmless. It disappears after a few minutes.

You can also summon a thin ectoplasmic mist that boils out of your eyes, nose and mouth. The cloud is roughly spherical (conforming to walls, ceilings, etc) and has a radius of about five feet. The cloud hangs in the air and does not move, slowly dissolving over the course of a minute, leaving oily, viscous goo behind (which fades in a similar time). If a stiff wind is present, the mist disperses in half the time.

The Mists

The cloud you created with *The Big Sneeze* begins to obey you. It no longer disperses in wind and lasts as long as you concentrate on it. If kept in a sphere, the radius would be approximately 10 feet. However, you have rudimentary control over the shape of the fog. No complex shapes can be formed yet, but rough misty tentacles are possible. The cloud still appears before you but can be mentally moved about three paces per turn. The cloud dissolves about a minute after you cease to concentrate on it.

INTERMEDIATE

Pea Soup

A successful activation forms a solid cloud that feels like cotton candy and requires a Physical Challenge to pass through (movement is reduced to one pace per turn if successful). Bullets, blades and fists may shift the ectoplasm but cannot break it down completely. This form of ectoplasm does not move. The total volume is roughly a sphere with a 10-foot radius, shaped as you will it at creation. When you cease to concentrate on the fog, it softens (no movement challenges or penalties) and dissolves over the next few minutes.

Dream Shape

You can mold the ectoplasm into complex shapes, making it look like anything you wish, although it remains a dull white color. The shape appears in your immediate vicinity and can be moved at up to five paces per turn. It cannot leave your perceptions. The creation has five *Plasmic* Physical Traits that can be used for strength or dexterity-

based challenges if necessary. It also has three health levels and takes bashing damage from bullets and cutting weapons. If it receives lethal damage (counting impacts and fire) it immediately dissipates. If your concentration lapses, it immediately vanishes in a puff of smoke.

ADVANCED

Tulpa

You create an ectoplasmic extension of your will. Unlike the *Dream Shape*, the *Tulpa* possesses a rudimentary intelligence. You can choose to invest further Willpower into the *Tulpa* at the time of its creation; each additional Trait expenditure takes another consecutive turn of concentration. Each Willpower Trait (including the first) gives three points that can be expended as per the table below. Should you wish it, any retests that the *Tulpa* may make are made with your *Occult* Ability, no matter the nature of the challenge. The *Tulpa* disperses into mist, then ooze, then nothing when you cease to concentrate on its existence.

TULPA TRAIT COSTS

Physical Trait	1 point
Mental Trait	2 points (Cannot exceed the psychic's current Mental Traits)
Health Level	1 point (all count as Healthy levels)
Extra Sense	1 point (The *Tulpa* begins with one sense for free if given any Mental Traits)
Additional Speed	1 point/additional pace (The *Tulpa* flies, and can initially move five paces per turn)

MIND SHIELD

Some psychics possess mental barriers that protect their minds from mental attacks, be they psychic assaults, vampiric *Dominate*, *Mind* magic or other ensorcelment. This resistance affects only assaults on the psychic's mind — it will not keep a telekinetic from lifting her or a pyrokinetic from burning her. This power is considered to be "always on" — no Willpower expenditure or challenge is required to activate it. The psychic can lower her defenses at will to allow friends to affect her mind, but this leaves her open to assaults from other directions at the same time. Ironically, the psychic must expend Willpower to lower her mental defenses for 10 minutes, although she may return the shields at any time before that. Additionally, she gains a single free retest in defense against psychic assaults only. This power affects only mental attacks, not powers that affect the emotions.

Challenge Type: Mental (retest with *Occult*)

BASIC

Knock-Knock

You're just learning to shut others out of your mind. You have two additional Mental Traits for defending against psychic attacks and one additional Mental Trait for other mental attacks.

Locked Out

You can keep others out by thinking hard. You have four additional Traits for defending against psychic attacks, and two additional Mental Trait for other mental attacks.

INTERMEDIATE

Mental Wall

No one goes where you don't want them to. You have six additional Mental Traits for defending against psychic attacks, and three additional Traits for other mental assaults. You can also distinguish between "friendly" and "hostile" contacts to your mind.

I Hear You Knocking

Very little gets past you now. With this level, you have eight additional Mental Traits when defending against mental psychic attacks, and four additional Mental Traits when defending against other mental assaults.

ADVANCED

Deadbolt

Your mind is the mental equivalent of Fort Knox. At this level, you have 10 additional Mental Traits to use in defense against mental psychic attacks, and five additional Mental Traits to defend against other mental assaults.

PRECOGNITION

One of the rarer psychic talents is the ability to perceive potential future events. Seeing the future is difficult, as probabilities shift with every action, so no seer is 100 percent accurate. Focusing on very specific events (such as winning lottery numbers, the future of a stock, the fate of a leader) may require a Static Challenge, with a difficulty determined by the Storyteller.

Precognition requires considerable Storyteller adjudication due to the inherent unpredictability of future plots.

Challenge Type: Mental (retest with *Awareness*)

BASIC

Intuition

You have yet to develop a clear view of future events, but your perception of things yet to come begins to form. Generally speaking, the power makes you a good guesser with a bit of extra luck. You may make a Static Mental Challenge to guess the outcome of a situation, with the difficulty dependant on the situation. Predictions will rarely be 100 percent accurate.

Insight

You can experience dreamlike visions of the future, metaphoric expressions of what may be to come. The form of dream varies depending on the mindset of the dreamer — a New Age crystal-reader has different images of the same thing than a Wall Street financier. Again, accuracy is variable, and the interpretation of the dream may not be immediately clear.

INTERMEDIATE

Danger Sense

You develop an internal early-warning system, manifesting as raised hackles, tingling sensations, flashes of imagery, etc. Generally the warning is consistent for a given psychic. This ability is considered to be "always on": it does not cost Willpower Traits or require a Mental Challenge to activate. The Storyteller approaches you for a Simple Test if something is about to happen that would activate this power. On a loss, you have no clue of the impending danger. On a tie, you know you are in danger and are permitted a dodge at a one-Trait penalty against the incoming threat. On a win, you are aware of the danger and its nature and get a free turn of action prior to the event occurring.

You cannot call for a test every time you walk through a door or your paranoia gets the better of you. Indeed, those who rely too much on this power often develop false alarms. If you feel a test is appropriate, check with your Storyteller.

Show Me the Cards

You have developed an almost clear vision of the immediate future. With successful activation, you can see a full minute into the future. All other players should (quietly) inform you of their immediate plans and goals. If, by knowing the future, you then change your plans, the future changes and you must again initiate another use of this power to see what might happen next.

Alternatively, if the Storyteller finds this power disrupting to game flow, he may instead rule that you gain a retest against any challenge occurring in that minute as a result of the successful activation challenge.

This power can only be used once per game.

ADVANCED

Clear Vision

You can see far into the future, observing the lines of probability and predicting the most probable one. With a successful activation, you gain an overview of the situations surrounding you from the Storyteller, up to the end of the scene.

Alternatively, if your Storyteller finds this power disrupting to game flow, he may rule that you gain two retests that may be used at any time during that scene (representing the subconscious foresight and preparation of the psychic). You may not stack this power with *Show Me the Cards* to gain three potential retests in the same minute. This power supersedes the other.

At the Storyteller's option, you may also receive spontaneous visions of the future that can be used as story hooks or clues. Such spontaneous activations should not cost Willpower Traits or require activation challenges, at the Storyteller's discretion.

This power can only be used once per game. Spontaneous visions do not count against this limit.

PSYCHIC HEALING

Psychic Healers are a rare breed, even among the gifted. The ability to heal is both a gift and a curse. If the reputation of the psychic as a healer gets out, no end of miracle-seekers and hypochondriacs may begin tracking her down, or the medical profession may decide to investigate the psychic for practicing without a license.

Many healers have some degree of *Medicine* Ability, but it is rarely due to training. More often it comes from an inherent empathy with the human condition and a tendency to feel the pain and suffering of others.

Psychic Healing typically requires physical contact with a willing (or unconscious) subject. If the subject is unwilling, a Physical Challenge prior to activation may be required to achieve contact. A subject in shock or in panic may increase the difficulty of the activation challenge by up to two Traits. If the activation challenge fails, the psychic must make a Simple Test. If this subsequent test fails, she inflicts further injury on her subject (e.g., bones fused out of alignment, internal hemorrhaging) or may have the injury or illness reflected back onto her.

A healer cannot intentionally fail these tests to deliberately inflict injury on a target. Additionally, the healer cannot use her powers on herself. Dead (or undead) creatures are unaffected by this power. If the psychic has the appropriate Abilities (*Medicine: Veterinary Medicine*, for example), or *Animal Psychics*, this power may be used on animals.

Challenge Type: Mental (retest with *Empathy* or *Medicine*)

BASIC

Diagnosis

Though unable to heal at this stage of your development, you can instantly diagnose illness and injury within your target. This does not grant you the ability to heal the damage, but does allow you (if you have medical training) to suggest appropriate measures to cure or stabilize the patient. A psychic healer without medical training usually finds it difficult to describe more complex conditions to doctors—a broken bone is simple, but something as complex as AIDS may be seen as "the body does not want to fight the sickness any longer."

This power, if successful, may lower the difficulty of subsequent attempts to heal the target by one Trait (if unfamiliar with *Medicine*) or two Traits (if familiar).

A Good Night's Sleep

You have the ability to accelerate the body's natural healing processes with a touch. This takes approximately a minute's concentration and a psychic healer typically "lays hands" on the subject, perhaps massaging the affected area. At the end of the minute, the target has been treated by a "highly skilled physician" for purposes of determining recovery time for that injury. Further strenuous activity by the patient may undo the work of the psychic at the Storyteller's discretion.

INTERMEDIATE

Basic Healing

Your ability to treat wounds has advanced to the point that you can heal bashing damage and cure simple diseases or poisonings (three-Trait toxins or less). To use this power, you lay your hands on the target and expend a Willpower Trait. You then make a series of normal activation challenges. For each successful challenge, the target heals one level of bashing damage or the severity of a poison in the patient's system is reduced by one Trait. It takes a turn for each effect to take place. If any challenge is failed, you must completely reactivate the power to do any further healing on the target, in addition to checking for inadvertent injurious effects.

Triage

At this level, you can knit bones, close serious wounds and cure potent diseases. Use the same system as given under *Basic Healing,* but you can affect lethal wounds and diseases and poisons up to four Traits in complexity or strength. Each challenge requires 10 minutes of continued concentration — breaks in concentration result in having to start over. The healing of this power is swift and noticeable by external observers as being unusual, though in the case of a seriously injured patient, it may simply stabilize a critical wound and prevent death.

ADVANCED

Psychic Surgery

You can empathically reach your hands into the body of the target, removing cancers or infections from the body. You can heal toxins or diseases of up to five Traits in strength. This power can be used as per *Triage* to affect aggravated wounds, reducing them to lethal wounds. Use of *Psychic Surgery* takes about 10 minutes per Trait of the disease or poison, or 10 minutes per Trait of damage affected.

While this power typically takes too long to administer during combat, you can funnel your power into an offensive weapon, reaching into your opponent and pulling chunks of flesh from their anatomy. This typically requires a Physical Challenge as well as the usual activation challenge and Willpower expenditure. A successful strike results in one level of aggravated damage. This offensive capability lasts only one turn and must be reactivated again in order to have further effect. Misuse of this ability may be cause for Humanity checks.

PSYCHIC HYPNOSIS

Psychics with hypnotic powers dwarf the abilities of the best carnival hucksters or television-advertising executives. Though their abilities lack the immediacy and speed of similar vampiric powers, they can achieve much the same results with time and effort.

This power can be used only on willing subjects.

Challenge Type: Mental (retest with *Expression*)

BASIC

Trance State

You can place your subject into a deep trance, wherein the subject's memories become clearer. The subject may also display greater control of his physiology. This process takes a minute to achieve. Though you cannot command the subject, the person in the trance is relaxed and restful. At the Storyteller's discretion, the subject regains a Willpower Trait. The subject comes out of the trance if shaken or disturbed. You may also hypnotize yourself.

Sideshow Suggestion

After placing the subject in *Trance State,* you may command the subject to perform simple actions ("jump," "sing," "walk") that the subject would not object to performing. Each such command takes at least a turn to vocalize, likely in the midst of an otherwise innocuous sentence. Additionally, the subject has greater control over his autonomic responses and may be able to walk on hot coals, require less oxygen to breathe or even ignore wound penalties. The subject cannot be commanded to cause himself life-

threatening harm. You can also cause the subject to forget the events that occurred during the trance. Each command, beyond the initial one, requires a new challenge. The subject does not emerge from the trance until commanded

INTERMEDIATE

Delayed Action

Commands can be planted in the subjects mind during the trance that will be obeyed after the subject has come out of the trance. These commands are as per *Sideshow Suggestion*. One command can be that the subject falls into another trance at a later date or at a given trigger. A maximum of five commands can be given per session to one subject.

Fast Trance

At this stage you are so adept you can cause a subject to enter a trance with eye contact. Normal activation of this power is required; the time required to induce the trance is simply reduced to an action. The trance lasts for five minutes.

ADVANCED

Manchurian Candidate

With this power, you are capable of major brainwashing of your subject. The subject performs any task you command, even to the point of death. The target must be placed in a trance (which takes at least 10 minutes and may not be done with *Fast Trance*). After that, you spend an hour per command implanted programming the subject. This costs two Willpower Traits and you must succeed in Mental Challenges against the target to implant the commands. The target has an additional Mental Trait against commands that are simply against his morals, or two extra Traits against self-destructive commands. A maximum of five commands can be given per session to one subject.

PSYCHIC INVISIBILITY

This phenomenon could be considered a form of mass hypnosis. Similar to a vampire's *Obfuscate* Discipline, the psychic broadcasts to everyone nearby the simple subconscious command "don't notice me." This effect does not apply to electronic or other recording media, though people in the immediate area observing through electronic means (like a TV cameraman looking through the viewfinder, or someone wearing night-vision goggles) does not see the invisible psychic.

This is not true invisibility. If an invisible psychic stands in front of something, people in the can't see what is behind the psychic — they ignore the general direction of view. Those who expect to see something in a specific area but discover they cannot might start to notice that something is wrong — or their minds may decide to give up and pay attention to something else instead.

Animals are unaffected by the invisibility effect unless the psychic also has *Animal Psychics*. Beings with heightened perceptions actively searching for the invisible psychic may attempt a challenge to perceive the psychic with their talents.

The level of power the psychic has in this phenomenon imposes a penalty on those attempting to perceive him. At Basic level, the psychic is considered one Trait up, at Intermediate two Traits, and at Advanced three Traits. The relative level of the

perceiver's powers (such as vampiric *Auspex*) can counter this advantage. Note that *Mind Shields* do protect against this very specific form of mental control. Maintaining this power counts as concentration.

Challenge Type: Mental (retest with *Stealth*)

BASIC

Hide

The broadcast keeps you hidden so long as you remain completely still. Under normal circumstances, no challenge is required to remain hidden (although normal activation rules apply). If someone is actively searching the area, then you must make an additional activation challenge. If you succeed and the searcher has no special senses, you remain invisible. If she does have special senses, she can challenge to perceive you as normal. If you fail, you become visible again. If you move, speak or do anything to give away your position, the effect is broken and the power ends instantly.

Slow Movement

You have enough control to attempt to move while maintaining your invisibility. Maintaining the power counts as concentration for the purposes of Trait penalties for other actions. You also cannot do things that would draw attention to you without breaking the power. You could walk across a room, but you could not punch someone. The act of interacting with the rest of the world cancels the effect. Otherwise this power works as *Hide*.

INTERMEDIATE

Invisibility

At this level, your ability is such that you can walk around and behave normally, and remain unnoticed. You can even perform actions that may draw attention to you, although each such action requires a successful concentration challenge. The only limitation to this power is that you may not vanish if being directly observed. Vanishing takes only a split second (although it uses your action), so a distraction may give the opportunity for slipping into obscurity.

Selective Invisibility

You have enough control of your talent to reveal yourself selectively to others while invisible. While invisible as in the previous level of this power, you can selectively allow yourself to be seen by one person per Social Trait expended, if you succeed in then activating this power.

ADVANCED

Forget You Ever Saw Me

Your talent has progressed to the point that you can not only vanish while in plain sight, but those who saw you forget that you were there in the first place. A group Mental Challenge is made against the observers, ties going to the observers. If an individual observer wins, she continues to see you. If you win, the observer now ignores you and forgets that you had been visible or had interacted with them over the prior two turns.

PSYCHIC VAMPIRISM

Most psychic talents are tools. They can be used to help or harm, depending on the moral character of the psychic. This phenomenon is an exception to the rule. Psychic

vampires draw emotions and, potentially, living energies from their victims, converting them into energy from themselves, and get a rush doing it. The drain produces a euphoria that can become addictive to the psychic. Such highs energize the character, perhaps manifesting in frenetic pacing, quicker speech, brighter eyes or an intensity of action. It's that caffeine boost, it's that nicotine rush… it's that speed buzz… and you *like* it.

The Storyteller should consider the impact this power can have on her story and plots, and then consider the potential degradation of Humanity this power could bring to the character. Reserve the right to refuse this power if it might unbalance your game.

Any benefits gained from this power, if not used by the end of the game session, disappear. Your Willpower and health levels return to their current temporary levels. Keep track of stolen Traits separately and discard any unused Traits at the end of the game.

Many psychic vampires find that real vampires provide amazing energy, to the point of an almost hallucinatory experience. Using any *Psychic Vampire* power on a real bloodsucker grants the psychic vampire two Traits for comparing on ties. However, the undead have means of discovering who is misusing them and do not hesitate to return the favor (literally) on one who hunts them.

Challenge Type: Social (retest with *Empathy*)

BASIC

Rush

You feed off strong emotions. These can be positive or negative, although you typically find it easier to engender or encounter negative emotions. When activated, you can feed off the predominant emotions of a person in the immediate area, providing no benefit to you beyond a rush of power. Depending on your Nature and the emotions in question, this feeding may allow you to recover lost Willpower (Storyteller discretion).

You must be within 10 yards, and line of sight, of the target. You then expend a Willpower Trait and must succeed in a Social Challenge against the target. The target may feel unsettled by the attack, and the emotion being tapped is muted, but she is otherwise unaffected. The attack does not remove the emotion, and cannot be used, for instance, to calm an angry person. You only become aware of the true emotional state of the target as the rush pours in — the difference between someone's outward appearance and their true inner emotions can be startling at times.

Sapping the Will

The drain effect sharpens, and now you can tap the target's will to invigorate your own. Rather than the normal activation challenge and expenditure, you and your target undertake a Willpower Challenge. For this, the target's response is reflexive and the attack may be undetected if won by the target. If the target loses, you take a single temporary Willpower Trait from the target and add it to your own temporary Willpower Traits. This refreshes Traits previously lost, and additional drains may allow you to exceed your normal maximum Willpower cap of 10 Willpower Traits. While you have more than your normal Willpower maximum, you feel invigorated, high. The excess Willpower fades at one point per hour of play down to your normal (temporary) level. The range of this talent is 10 yards.

INTERMEDIATE

Energy Transference

You may now sap physical energy to enervate yourself and heal minor injuries with stolen life force. This requires expenditure of a Willpower Trait at the beginning of the turn following your initial concentration, then physical contact with the target for the full turn — a Physical Challenge may be required — followed by a Social Challenge against the target at the end of the turn. If you are successful, the target suffers a level of bashing damage, and you are healed a level of bashing damage. If you are fully healthy, each level of bashing damage caused grants you a Willpower Trait instead (up to your normal maximum level). Suffice to say, either effect feels delicious. If the target has some means of negating the damage (for example, by vampiric *Fortitude*) then you gain no benefit — the exchange of energy does not occur.

Life Leech

This dangerous talent allows you to leech vital life energies from your victims, giving an emotional high beyond compare. This ability is used as per *Energy Transference*, but you can continue the absorption of your victim's being by maintaining physical contact and making any necessary concentration challenges each turn. Each successful continuance does one level of lethal damage (or bashing, if desired, but lethal tastes nicer) to the target, healing you of one level of lethal damage (or bashing, as before) or changing one level of aggravated damage to lethal. If you are fully healed and absorb more energy, each level of damage (lethal or bashing) refreshes two Willpower Traits, which can go beyond your normal maximum as per Willpower Traits drained by *Sapping the Will*. If the target has some means of absorbing the damage (for example, by vampiric *Fortitude*) then you gain no benefit — the exchange of energy does not occur.

ADVANCED

Emotional Vortex

Multiple targets can be tapped at one time once you have learned this level of expertise. You must have used one of the lesser levels of this power on the target. Multiple targets within a city block can be tapped — they need not be in line of sight — via either of the Basic levels of this phenomenon. You concentrate for a turn and expend the usual Willpower. Group challenges are thrown to determine your success in draining many people at once.

PSYCHOKINESIS/TELEKINESIS

Either name is valid for this powerful and potent psychic ability. The ability to move objects without touching them has innumerable potential uses. Though few psychokinetics possess the strength or skill to do more than grossly manipulate a few small objects, a skilled psychic can remotely exert considerable force or perform feats of remarkable dexterity.

To activate these powers against inanimate objects that aren't in anyone's possession, the psychic must expend the usual Willpower Trait and make a Mental Challenge. If the object is being held by a person, the psychic must engage in a contested Mental Challenge against the other person's Physical Traits (the target may relent, of course). If a person is himself being lifted by the psychic, they may attempt to anchor themselves if they are aware of the attack, presuming anchor points are available, requiring a similar test (Mental versus Physical).

A telekinetic must be able to see the object that they wish to manipulate. An extraordinarily skilled psychic may be able to use this ability through her powers of *Astral Projection* or *Clairvoyance*. She can lift multiple objects using multiple activations of this power, but standard concentration rules for multiple uses of a power are applicable. The total weight that can be lifted or manipulated, even if multiple powers are activated, is limited to the character's normal physical lifting capacity even if the description below gives a larger figure. If you want to mentally bench press sumo wrestlers, you'd better get to the gym yourself.

Psychokinesis can be retested with Abilities appropriate to the situation, such as Archery to direct thrown objects, Melee to use an object to intervene against an incoming attack, etc.

Note that this phenomenon utilizes the manipulation of other objects — it does not imbue the telekinetic with mental bolts or Darth Vader's throat-grip niftiness.

Challenge Type: Mental (retest with *Empathy* or an appropriate Ability)

BASIC

Nudge

You can manipulate small nearby objects (eggs, drinking glasses, books, anything under three pounds) but without much skill or force. You can only accomplish minor feats such as turning a page, flicking a light switch or pressing a button. There is insufficient force involved to effectively attack, and the objects move slowly and imprecisely.

Only one item can be manipulated at a time with this ability (unless activated multiple times). At this level of skill (i.e., if you only have this ability in *Psychokinesis*), appropriate physical gestures in the fashion of the force exerted (flicking a page across, grasping a handle) are required to focus the psychic power. If an appropriate gesture is not made, you are considered two Traits down for the use of the power.

Propel

You may attract or repel objects, though with little control over the speed of the object (it ambles and is easily dodged). The object may weight up to 10 pounds and must be within the same room as you. You are disadvantaged by one Trait if physical gestures (beckoning, grasping and pulling, shoving away) are not used and you have only the Basic levels of this phenomenon.

INTERMEDIATE

Phantom Arm

A greater degree of strength and control is now available to you. Heavy items (up to 100 pounds) can be manipulated, but you have few fine motor skills. The item can be up to 20 yards away, but must still be in your line of sight. It can be moved at normal walking pace.

If the item is flung at someone (a quick push and release, ending the power), a level of bashing damage can be inflicted from the impact. If a weapon is flung, it will inflict its normal damage from the impact. To resolve this attack, you must win a Mental Challenge against the target's Physical Traits. They may retest with *Dodge*, if they know of the attack.

You still need to physically gesture (throwing a ball, breaking bread, cradling and turning) or suffer the one-Trait penalty listed if you have only up to this level in *Psychokinesis*.

Hidden Forces

You can now manipulate weights of up to 200 pounds, up to a city block away. Fine control still escapes you, but objects can be manipulated as if you were wearing heavy gloves. Heavy objects, if flung, may do up to two levels of bashing damage or one level of lethal damage, depending on the nature of the object. Flung weapons do not inflict additional damage above their normal damage rating.

With concentration, you can lift yourself off the ground and "fly" at a normal walking pace. Other people can be picked up and used as human clubs, causing a level of bashing damage to both the target and the weapon.

At this level of power, physical gestures are no longer required to activate any of these phenomena.

ADVANCED

Manipulation

You have mastered your ability to manipulate physical objects with your mind. Your control is such that you can undo zippers, load a pistol or pour champagne, although Narrators should increase the difficulty of such challenges should the task be particularly tricky.

The weight limit is increased to 300 pounds, within your line of sight. Such large objects typically cause two or more levels of bashing damage or up to two levels of lethal damage, depending on the nature of the object.

Additionally, you halve (round up) your concentration penalty for multiple uses of *Psychokinesis*. Other concentration penalties for other phenomenon that may be in use at the time still count.

PSYCHOMETRY

Psychometry, object reading, *Spirit's Touch* — all refer to the ability to detect the psychic residue or emotional resonance left on objects, people and places. Things exposed to strong emotional signatures hold flashes of information that a psychometric can "read" by touch (skin contact is required, usually hands). Particularly strong emotions may cause temporary sympathetic reactions in the psychic as the backlash of rage, dread or love hits her brain. If the character loses her activation challenge, she must undertake a Simple Test and win to avoid such an emotional reverie that wraps him up in the aura of the item and the events surrounding it (to the point that he may suffer injury or re-enact the impacting scene with others nearby) until his concentration is broken. Alternatively, the afflicted psychic may suffer a temporary derangement.

Challenge Type: Mental (retest with *Empathy*)

BASIC

Emotional Connection

You tap into the most recent activities that have occurred with or around a small item or location. The visions you get are dreamy and vague, more emotion than imagery. When imagery does appear, it is figurative or metaphoric. The context of emotions

involved may not be clear, and multiple handlings of the object by others will confuse the readings you gain.

Flashback

In addition to the information provided by *Emotional Connection*, you also receive a firm mental impression of the person most closely associated with the item in question. Historically strong emotions can be detected if the object is particularly old, but they will probably be confused with stronger, more recent impressions.

Use of *Flashback* on corpses usually gives an indication of how they died, although clear details of the situation are rare. Perform a Static Mental Challenge against eight Traits to get a clearer view.

INTERMEDIATE

Time and Place

You can get a clearer picture of the strongest emotional incident that involved the object or place being examined. You get a dreamlike vision of the incident, including the number of people involved and a description of the area. By concentrating on the object's owner, you can get a rough estimation of the person's age, emotional state, hints of personality and their feelings — all of these applicable to the moment and situation being screened through the object.

Larger objects and areas can be scanned for emotional impact, and you can receive physical sensations related to the incidents that have occurred. Feeling a knife cutting your throat or a vehicle ramming your midriff can be somewhat disconcerting, however, and may break your concentration. These impressions are emotionally intense and often disturbing, and will have lingering mental effects on the psychic for the remainder of the scene, although this provides no other distractive penalties in terms of the game rules.

Days Gone By

You can clearly visualize the event in question, as well as gathering general impressions of what the owner of the object went through during the course of the day the incident occurred. As an alternative, you can replay what happened to the object during the past day, even if there were no strong impressions left on the object that day.

If an area is being scanned, you can pick up on events up to a month in the past. All images from *Psychometry* can now involve all five senses, and you can find yourself becoming entrapped in scenes of intense emotion. Witnessing particularly horrific acts (notably if witnessed from a first-person perspective) may be cause for a Simple Test to avoid acquiring a derangement.

ADVANCED

Touch the Soul

In addition to a clear image of the event, you also receive clear emotional impressions of the other people at the event, gaining insight into what they were feeling. You get rough images of the people present and some idea of their emotional state at the time of the events in question. You can also use an object as a focus to get a general impression of the owner's location at the current time.

If you touch a person and activate this power, you could gain visions of things that emotionally concern the individual, although specifics are difficult to interpret. A

successful Mental Challenge against the target allows discovery of the person's Nature and their current emotional state.

At this level of ability, you may find yourself bombarded with spontaneous visions if you enter areas or encounter objects with strong emotional charges. Such spontaneous sensing is at the Narrator's discretion but should not involve the activation costs normally associated with the power.

PSYCHOPORTATION

Psychoportation is a remarkably powerful ability and could prove disruptive to the game. Storytellers should carefully consider the implications of allowing this ability to enter the game before allowing it to all and sundry. Of course, one would expect that of all the kewl powerz in the **Mind's Eye Theatre** range, but this one bears extra consideration. Think also about how complex it could be to represent *Psychoportation* during the course of the game.

Psychoportation is the rare ability to teleport oneself and one's immediate possessions over short distances without actually crossing the physical space in between. Let the Storyteller worry about the physics of how it works, because it probably works differently for individual psychoporters.

The teleporter can carry a small amount of personal possessions with him — up to 100 pounds of carried material. No living creatures (or other characters) can accompany the teleporter on his journey between places. If additional material is carried, the teleporter suffers psychic feedback to the effect of six levels of bashing damage and a headache that lasts the rest of the scene putting him down one Trait in all challenges. If the teleporter attempts to carry other creatures with him, the power instantly fails and both receive the damage and the headache.

If the psychic fails his activation challenge for this power, he must make a Simple Test. On a win, no additional harm occurs, the power simply fails to activate. On a tie, the psychic ends up somewhere other than where he wished to travel (Narrator's call as to where and what happens to his possessions). On a loss, the teleporter lands partially inside a solid object somewhere and is ejected forcibly, causing six levels of aggravated damage to both the psychic and the object as the matter collides explosively.

Challenge Type: Mental (retest with *Awareness*)

BASIC

Short Hop

You can move to anywhere within 10 yards per Mental Trait you currently possess. This takes one action. You may only travel to a location you could normally reach by walking (no entering locked rooms) and the destination must be within your line of sight (other psychic senses such as *Clairvoyance* are applicable).

Simple Jump

As per *Short Hop*, but you may travel up to 20 yards per current Mental Trait in a turn.

INTERMEDIATE

Long Jump

As per *Short Hop*, but you may travel up to 40 yards per current Mental Trait in a turn. You can double this distance by spending the prior turn in intense (exclusive) concentration and succeeding in an additional Mental Challenge.

Very Long Jump

As per *Long Jump*, but you may travel up to 80 yards per current Mental Trait.

ADVANCED

Blind Jump

Though the range of the hop does not increase, you can now jump to destinations that you cannot see — you may teleport to a place that you are familiar with that is within range. To memorize a location, you must spend a scene in the area examining it, and expend a Willpower Trait. Item cards for each such location should be created. The location must be typically stationary — memorizing the interior of a car will not allow you to leap into it, especially if it is mobile at the time. Such attempts almost always lead to physical mergence, as mentioned above. Messy.

PYROKINESIS

Never actually use fire to represent this power, or any other similar power. Duh.

Psychics use this power to agitate molecules to such a degree that fire results. *Pyrokinesis* can only start fires — it does not grant control over them, nor can it extinguish them. These fires are indistinguishable from normal fires and last until they burn out or are put out by normal means. Pyrokinetics are not immune to their own fires. The maximum range of this power is 10 yards in any case.

Note that for all intents and purposes of play, the fires created by *Pyrokinesis* are real fires. This means all the attendant problems for vampires (frenzy, aggravated damage, etc.) still apply.

Challenge Type: Social (retest with *Meditation*)

BASIC

Matches

You can produce small sparks of flame, generally only enough to light highly flammable items like gasoline, paper, kindling, etc. These sparks visibly leap from your fingertips (or eyes, or mouth), jumping out to within your physical reach. The sparks are not hot enough to seriously burn people, although they may certainly be startled by the spark's appearance. Flinging a spark involves a Mental Challenge against the opponent's Physical Traits, and the opponent may use *Dodge* to retest the challenge as with normal ranged combat. If the spark hits, the target must make a Simple Test (win or tie) or lose his next action from surprise — this may only happen once during a given conflict or scene (once you know someone can do it, how can you keep getting surprised?). The target can expend a Willpower Trait to avoid this reflexive action. Vampires, instead of using this system, must make a *Courage* Test.

Ignite

By concentrating, you cause nearby flammable materials to burst into flame. The difficulty for activating this power depends on the combustive qualities of the target materials. Once ignited, items continue to burn naturally. The ignition process is visible as a heat haze momentarily appearing between you and the item. The fire created is as

big as a torch, although it can easily spread. If you try to light a person (or vampire) on fire (causing one level of aggravated damage, causing a *Courage* check to a vampire or a surprise check as above for others), the target can attempt to dodge the effect. You must make a successful Mental vs. Physical challenge against the target, and the target may retest with *Dodge*. Fires lit on people or vampires extinguish at the end of the turn.

INTERMEDIATE

Fireworks

You can now create small bursts of flame out of thin air — super-excited air molecules become plasma that ignites just about anything that burns. These can be created up to 10 yards away per Willpower Trait you currently possess after activating this power.

If you wish to strike anyone in the area, you must succeed in a challenge as per *Matches*. A successful strike inflicts two levels of aggravated damage per turn that the target is exposed to the fire (which is about the size of a campfire). To extinguish the flames, the target must avoid panic (a *Courage* Test for vampires, others must make a Willpower Challenge) and then succeed in a Static Physical Challenge. Each such attempt takes one turn. (See "Stop, Drop and Roll" for rules on extinguishing fire.)

Pyrotechnics

At this level you can not only create fires, you can control the path and shape of the fire. The difficulty of this power depends on the size of the flame (four for a torch, six for a bonfire, eight for an inferno) modified by the complexity of the action (0 to shift the direction in still air, -1 to create gaps in the flames, +3 to diminish the flames). Each change in the fire counts as a separate use of this power.

This power can also be independently used to create shapes in flames (difficulty 5 for simple forms, up to 9 for complex shapes.). Your control over them lasts as long as you concentrate on the actions you wish the flames to perform, until the end of the scene or hour.

ADVANCED

Inferno

You have immense and exacting control over all forms of flame. You can create large fires at a distance. These can appear at distances of up to 15 yards per current Willpower Trait possessed after activation. While initially the size of a bonfire, the flames are about the heat of a Bunsen burner and spread rapidly, consuming as much as they can before being extinguished. People near the edge of the fire can jump out of the area (Physical Challenge, retest with *Dodge*, presuming there is somewhere to run to) but those caught within the *Inferno* take three levels of aggravated damage per turn spent in the flames.

PYROKINETIC CHALLENGE DIFFICULTIES

4 Traits	Very easily lit materials (paper, gasoline, vampires)
6 Traits	Flammable objects that normally require minor assistance to light (wood, charcoal)
8 Traits	Objects that do burn with the aid of accelerants (clothing)
9 Traits	Objects that do burn, eventually (people)

SYNERGY

One of the rarest psychic abilities is the talent to merge the skills of two or more psychics together, providing a powerful psychic gestalt with more power than the psychics using their talents individually. The psychic can interlink twice as many psychics as he has Traits in this phenomenon, up to 10 at the Advanced level. All must be in physical contact with each other. An unwilling participant in the linkages formed here drops the *Synergy* power instantly. Due to the complexity of this power, Storyteller guidance is recommended.

Challenge Type: Mental (retest with *Awareness*)

BASIC

Psychic Sense

You can sense other psychics. This triggers automatically when you touch another psychic (which may require a Physical Challenge), or you can concentrate and activate the power normally to sense other psychics in your line of sight. You also gain some minor concept as to the level of power of the target viewed (Basic, Intermediate, Advanced in whatever their highest power is rated at). This does not detect mages with the *Mind* Sphere, or other supernatural creatures who possess mental powers.

Share Will

At this level, basic links can be formed. By acting together, the group can use any psychic power of a participant in the link. The synergist (you) handles all Mental Challenges involved as normal. However, each of the participants can expend a Willpower Trait to provide spare Willpower Traits to you, which can be used by you as normal. The gestalt can only generate one shared effect at a time. If the power used is sensory (*Telepathy*, *Clairvoyance*, *Psychometry*, etc), then all people in the link receive the results of the power.

INTERMEDIATE

Group Effect

The psychic network has grown to the point that in addition to sharing Willpower Traits as above, you can more effectively combine the network's wills so that in any challenge, the highest Trait level among the group is used, even if you lack the power yourself.

For example, Andrew the Synergist, with seven Mental Traits, Intermediate Synergy, and two Awareness Traits links with Bruce, who has eight Mental Traits, Basic Telepathy and four Awareness Traits, and Deirdre, who has Intermediate Telepathy but no current Awareness Traits. Andrew can hereby use Deirdre's Intermediate Telepathy with access to eight Mental Traits and four Awareness Traits available for retests.

Share Powers

The gestalt now allows for multiple powers to be used through the link. Each member can donate two of the following to the network: a power, Attribute or Ability. All members of the link become able to use that power, Attribute or Ability as if they had it temporarily added to their character sheet. These phantom Traits (counted separately for each member of the linkage) vanish when expended or lost, or when the link fades. Willpower can be donated between any of the participants as per *Share Will*.

ADVANCED

Power Gestalt

Not only may the group now each use multiple powers at once (subject to normal concentration rules), they can freely intermingle the effects of those powers, possibly combining two or more powers into a single, shared power. For example, a clairvoyant and a telepath could combine their powers, allowing them to far-see a target and read his mind at the same time. Storytellers should supervise such scenes and ascertain whether particular permutations of synergized characters are permissible or will work.

TELEPATHY

In the simplest form, telepathy allows the psychic to read minds. The telepath must be able to sense the target (whether through her own natural senses or through supernatural senses like *Clairvoyance*) in order to be able to read the target's mind. Rather than simply reading text from the surface of the target's brain, the telepath senses impressions and, with experience, learns to interpret subtexts, streams of thought, motives and eventually the deeper thoughts of the target. Some skilled telepaths can also manipulate the mind they have entered, planting suggestions or speaking to the target in a "mental voice." *Telepathy* requires the usual Willpower expenditure, a Mental Challenge against the target, and a turn of concentration before activating.

Telepathic communication between psychics is possible on a limited basis. Two telepaths may communicate if they are both willing, neither requiring a challenge (you both relent) although Willpower expenditure is required by both parties to initiate the link. The sensing requirements still prevail. More than two cannot communicate on the same link. The level of communication is limited by the skill of the lesser of the two telepaths. A master psychic is hampered by the clumsy mental ramblings of the apprentice and so either may only be able to exchange basic emotions or words. Although a skilled (Advanced) telepath may be able to link to multiple people as long as the appropriate activations are made, he will only be able to transmit to or receive from one character at a time. Switching between channels takes a normal action. Characters in willing telepathic communication are considered to be concentrating and suffer the normal penalties. If either side loses concentration then the link is broken, no matter who initiated it (as are all other operational links, due to mental backlash). If the link is consensually dropped, other links can remain operational. A willing link lasts until concentration is dropped or broken, or until the end of the scene or an hour, whichever comes first.

To communicate thusly with a nontelepath (or an unwilling telepath), the psychic must initiate both a "read" and a "write" contact with the target. If the target is unwilling, Mental Challenges are required as normal. The level of communication that is established is still limited by the abilities as given by the Trait level of the psychic. Lesser telepaths can only transmit and receive glances of information — you need to reach Intermediate level before a true "conversation" can take place. A willing link lasts until concentration is dropped or broken, or until the end of the scene or an hour, whichever comes first. If the target is unwilling, then Mental Challenges for each "read" or "write" are required, each effectively taking an action.

Telepathy takes considerable concentration, and low-level telepaths frequently need to maintain sight with their targets. Such intense scrutiny is bound to make even a nonpsychic observer curious.

Challenge Type: Mental (retest with *Empathy*)

BASIC

Emotional Contact

At this level, you can feel basic strong emotions present in the target and sense his current mood.

• You may enquire of your target "What is your current emotional state?" and expect a truthful reply.

• You can send a simple impulse or rudimentary thought ("!Danger!" "....Cold....", "=Toleration=") to which the target is under no compulsion to react.

• A target can be induced to twitch or perform a simple or habitual gesture.

The Unspoken Heart

You can now access the surface thoughts of people, the "internal monologue" with which people think at the "top" of their thought processes. It can make you privy to the comments that people think but often leave unsaid.

• You may ask the target "What did you leave unspoken just now?" and expect a truthful answer. Typically one cannot glean useful information by using this level of power. Any thought that the target is actively concealing remains hidden.

• You can project a single defined word or a simple idea to the target.

• You can cause a target to make one short motion, such as crossing his arms and legs while seated.

INTERMEDIATE

Psychic Link

You can now read recent memories or plans for the near future from the mind of your target.

• You may ask your target one simple question, which they must answer truthfully, such as "Was the last statement you made truthful?" "What are your responses to my prior telepathic message?" or "What manner of creature are you?"

• At this level you can send full sentences, strong complex emotions or even streams of memory. The target can be made to believe false input to his senses.

• You can cause a target to take one unusual action, such as dropping a weapon, or ducking for cover rather than running away.

Mind Probe

Reaching deep into the mind of your target, you can uncover deep memories and long-term drives. Line of sight to the target is no longer required to use *Telepathy*, although nonvisual range is limited to a room or so away. You must be familiar with or have a good description of the person and his current apparent mood.

• You can ask the target to describe any one scene of a few minutes from his memory. You can notice if a memory has been covered up, either subconsciously or by external influence, but not the nature of the concealment.

• You can send several sentences of information, implant memories or cover up or alter a present memory. Revealing hidden memories through additional uses of this power can lead to unpredictable results if the memory is traumatic, and psychic backlash may affect you if the Storyteller so dictates.

• You can temporarily seize control of the target's body for one turn, but you must maintain concentration through that turn or lose such control.

ADVANCED

Secrets Revealed

• You have learned to fully read the surface thoughts of nearly anyone. You can ask the target any reasonable question about his recent and current thoughts.

• Thoughts can be read with complete clarity and understanding. Memories of any age can be analyzed, overwritten, uncovered or deleted. Each such alteration requires a challenge.

• You can completely physically control a single victim for as long as you maintain *complete* concentration. This does not empower you to use any of their special physical abilities (such as vampiric blood expenditure or shifter shape-changing), simply to control their normal physical actions. For purposes of challenges, Strength and Stamina-related Traits are used as they exist in the target, but any Dexterity-related Traits are drawn from your own Perception-related Traits. This may not boost the target over her normal Physical Traits maximum — simply replace her Dexterity Traits with your own Perception Traits until they reach that maximum. You may not use any retests on your target's behalf on actions that you cause her to take. Unless you subsequently alter her memories, your target will remember her actions.

TELEPATHIC CONTROL, PROJECTION AND SENSING (OPTIONAL RULE)

Telepathy covers a powerful range of abilities — scanning, sending and controlling abilities are included at each level of the power. Each different effect of the power requires a separate activation and using multiple *Telepathy* powers, such as using *Psychic Link* to communicate to the target and then using it again to read his response, incurs the usual concentration penalties. If a Storyteller believes this level of power to be overbalancing for the purposes of her chronicle, then we recommend that the Phenomenon be broken down into three separate Phenomena:

Telepathic Sensing: The basic ability to sense emotions or thoughts.

Telepathic Projection: The power to send ideas, emotions and thoughts into another's mind.

Telepathic Control: Directly taking control of a subject's mind and forcing him to perform an action.

The descriptions below illustrate the break points for these powers. Each bullet point would count as a complete power for the path, e.g. the first Basic power for *Telepathic Sensing* would simply be that you can possibly read a person's emotional state, but would not include the other two capacities listed. A character would have to develop each power individually in order to gain all the powers of the larger Phenomena in the main rules.

Additionally, you can read the minds of multiple targets at once (subject to concentration and activation rules as normal). You can experience information secondhand — for example, reading the mind of a clairvoyant as she views a distant location, seeing the image that she sees.

At this level of power, you can potentially rewrite the personality of your target or step them over a cliff. It is strongly suggested that a Storyteller oversee any use of this level of power to ensure fairness and smooth game play. This power has been known to backlash on the telepath occasionally, imprinting memories of the target into the psychic's mind due to the rush of personalized impressions, or passing phantom pain (even possibly sympathetic damage) back through the link if the controlled target is harmed.

SORCERY

Sorcery is the defining property of a sorcerer; without it, a sorcerer is just another mortal who knows a lot about some strange subjects. Though some argue that static and dynamic magic are different forms of the same phenomenon, there are very distinct differences in how they work. In dynamic magic, the will of the mage reshapes reality itself, while static magic uses hidden tricks within the nature of reality.

As is the case with Sphere magic, though, one of the rules of reality is that it is harder to do things that the average Joe (or Jamal or Jian Lu) on the street does not believe can be done than to do stuff that he accepts. It is even harder to do it when the average Joe is watching. Magic that defies the common concepts of reality is called vulgar magic; magic that can pass for everyday occurrence is called coincidental magic. The standards of what are coincidental depend on local beliefs. The average Jian Lu on the street may not accept what the average Joe would and vice versa.

CASTING SPELLS

When a player chooses to create a magical effect (cast a spell), the following process can be used to determine the results.

Determine the Effect: Figure out what the effect is, from flying away from the approaching patrol car, to causing a friend's firstborn to be blessed with healthy skin, to drawing fire from the heavens upon those who would defile the sacred grove.

Check the Character's Capabilities and Resources: Does the character know how to bring about such an effect? Does the character have the requisite knowledge of sorcery? Of mundane matters? If the character knows enough to accomplish the effect, he can proceed to more physical concerns. Does the character have the tools or materials necessary? Different schools of sorcery accomplish magic using different tools. A Star Council member is not going to be able to do much without the strange artifacts he uses, and a Hermetic sorcerer is pretty much out of luck if she cannot scribe the correct sigils when the stars are properly aligned.

If the character does not have the proper knowledge and tools, he cannot cast the spell.

Determine the Difficulty: The base difficulty for a magical effect is the effect's Path level in Traits, modified as listed below:

Perform the Effect: Casting the effect calls for a Static Challenge against the effect's difficulty. A player does not need to consult a Narrator when performing such an action — any convenient player suffices though it is always good form to let the player know that the challenge is for a magical effect, not against her character. If the player wins the challenge, the effect goes off as planned. If he loses the challenge, the effect

fails, whatever expendable components were used for it are lost, and the character loses the bid Trait. If the player ties, he must compare his Mental Traits against the difficulty of the effect. If he has more or equal Traits, the spell succeeds. If he has fewer, it fails.

The player may overbid with his Mental Traits if he has twice as many as the spell's difficulty. If he does this, the overbid Trait must be a Willpower Trait. On the other hand, the opponent may overbid if she believes the difficulty is over twice the character's Mental Traits.

Unless other conditions have been invoked, standard sorcerous spells require one turn per level of effect to cast. Certain sorcerous effects call for rituals; rituals require a minimum of five minutes per level of effect to cast.

Pay the Consequences: Most spells cost a Willpower Trait to cast. As soon as the challenge is completed, this Willpower Trait is marked off. This happens whether the spell worked or failed.

Also, in the case of a failure or vulgar magic, the sorcerer may find herself paying an additional price. If the Storyteller has decided that Paradox can apply to sorcerous magic, the sorcerer may find herself gaining Paradox as Sphere magicians do.

THE LAWS OF COINCIDENCE

It is the responsibility of the player to provide the rationale when she attempts to describe her magic as coincidental. This explanation should take the current environment into account. "What luck, the leader of the crazed mob got struck by a bolt of lightning!" is far more likely to be convincing outside in a storm than inside a shopping mall. Likewise, fireballs almost never qualify, though a Star Councilor might be able to present his Artifact #4 as an experimental Napalm Projector. In general:

• If the average person off the street wouldn't believe it, it's not a coincidence.

• If it takes more than a sentence to explain why it's a coincidence, it's not.

• If it takes more than a minute to come up with the sentence explaining why it's a coincidence, it's not.

If the Storyteller feels that the players can be trusted to render objective, fair callings on the matter, she may allow players who are witness to a magical effect to vote on whether it should qualify as coincidental.

VARIATIONS ON THE THEME

Magic is never that cut and dried. There are a variety of techniques that can affect the complexity of the game — and the survivability of the sorcerers.

MAGICAL STYLES

In the same way that people throughout the world have developed different forms of art, different solutions to the problem of how to convey a deeper truth, they have developed different methods for communing with the supernatural and affecting the hidden forces of reality. A member of Nebuu-Afef places a curse upon the lineage of his enemies by invoking the power of Mastena, the Angel of Slaughter, in the ancient Egyptian style with scarabs, hieroglyphs and chants in the language of the pharaohs.

Meanwhile, less than a hundred miles away, a scientist of the Star Council may re-key the command sequence on Artifact Three that inserts a genetic defect into the target family. In rules terms, both sorcerers are using the *Path of Fortune* to place a curse, but beyond the rules, the routes by which they place the "curse" are completely different. If the Nebuu-Afef or the Star Councilor were forced to rely on the techniques of the other, they would fail completely. In other words, a sorcerer is limited to her own set of tools and rites when she casts a spell. A Bata'a who knows the *Path of Conjuration* cannot opt to use a rune-inscribed wand instead of the sacrifice of a rooster because she happens to have found an AOAR wand but doesn't have a rooster.

Different paradigms may also generate certain complications in how different sorceries interact. Sorcerers who approach magic from different directions often have trouble merging their magic. In addition, if the Storyteller is willing to handle the extra complexity, she may establish house rules unique to her chronicle. For example, she may decide that AOAR sorcery and Silver Portal sorcery cancel each other out or that Maison Liban wards offer two additional Traits of protection against Bata'a magic. These extra rules should be analyzed for both playability and game balance within the chronicle, and codified for the Narrators so they can be consistent in their rulings.

MAGICAL EFFECT DIFFICULTY

Apprentice:	1
Initiate (or Basic Discipline, Gift, Sphere, etc.):	2
Disciple:	3
Adept (or Intermediate Discipline, Gift, Sphere, etc.):	4
Master (or Advanced Discipline, Gift, Sphere, etc.):	5

DIFFICULTY MODIFIERS

Fast Casting:	Double basic difficulty
The effect is vulgar:	+1
The effect is vulgar and there are unawakened witnesses:	+3
Grade of Success:	+2 per Grade of Success desired.
Teamwork:	-1 for each assistant who wins a Simple Challenge. If none of the assistants win, +2.
Spending Mana:	-1 per point of Mana so spent (up to –3)
Wounds:	As usual. Unconscious characters cannot perform sorcery — except for those like the adherents of the Silver Portal who do so in the Maya.

KNOWN SPELLS

Each path description includes sample spells representative of the powers of that Path. Upon learning a level of a Path, a sorcerer automatically learns one spell of that level. Thus, upon learning the Apprentice level of a Path, a character gains an automatic Apprentice-level spell; upon learning the Initiate level of a Path, she gains an Initiate-level spell. The player should keep a card for each spell she knows to serve as a rules reminder and as proof that she knows the spell in question. Additional spells may be learned with Experience Traits. Known spells are the easiest to cast, and use the rules as described here. Such spells may or may not include extra Grades of Success, but such details are always determined when the spell is learned.

Unless otherwise noted, all sample spell difficulty levels are the default for their level.

FREEFORM SPELLS (OPTIONAL RULE)

In certain circumstances, a sorcerer may need to craft a magical effect to fit a certain situation rather than just using one he has memorized. If the player has the appropriate mystical and mundane knowledge, he may attempt to reformulate the sorcerous rules he knows to accommodate his exact circumstances. As this involves a good deal of off-the-cuff theoretical work, it can be a dangerous and difficult process.

System: Because of the mental work involved, casting a freeform spell always has a +2 difficulty modifier. Additionally, it takes twice as long as a known spell to case (two turns per level of effect). It is possible to fastcast a freeform spell, but the +2 difficulty modifier gets doubled as well.

PARADOX (OPTIONAL RULE)

Under certain circumstances, sorcerers may acquire Paradox — bizarre effects that afflict those who defy conventional reality. In general, this will only happen to sorcerers in the case of spectacular failures or vulgar magic in front of unAwakened witnesses, and even then, since sorcery does not try to bend reality, but use its hidden rules, Paradox has a lesser effect on static mages than their dynamic counterparts. Storytellers who wish to apply Paradox to their sorcerers should consult **Laws of Ascension**, pp. 172-176. If these rules are in place, sorcerers receive one Paradox Trait any time they successfully use vulgar magic in front of unAwakened witnesses or fail in casting a vulgar spell.

RITUALS

Certain Paths lend themselves to a slower, more elaborate form of magic. Rather than turns, these rituals take a minimum of five minutes to cast for the simplest, and some can end up lasting for hours.

System: Rituals are handled the same as spells in terms of Experience — instead of learning a spell, the character learns a ritual. In order to maintain the concentration necessary for the complexity of these castings, a character also needs to possess the same level of knowledge in the necessary Path — you can't cast a ritual from a Path you haven't studied, or one that's beyond your knowledge. The sorcerer may add her *Rituals*

Ability to her bid when performing the ritual. Rituals take a minimum of five minutes per level of effect to cast. They cannot be fast-cast but are well suited to teamwork provided all the sorcerers in question have the requisite levels.

GRADES OF SUCCESS

A sorcerer may want to achieve more with a spell than the basic power of a Path allows. For example, an Isis Cultist may need to heal lethal rather than bashing damage, or an AOAR initiate may need to *Fascinate* an entire debate audience into being more tolerant of the new refugees in town. In cases such as these, the character may elect to cast a more elaborate and demanding version of the spell — a spell requiring a greater Grade of Success. If a spell fails because of the additional Grades of Success called for, it fails completely, just as if it were a regular spell. The caster does not end up with a lesser spell because she failed at a greater one.

System: When determining the difficulty of the spell, the player must declare which extra Grades of Success she desires. Each Grade of Success called for increases the difficulty of the test by two. Because of the complexity of such activities, a sorcerer may only invoke one Grade of Success per level of study in the Path in question. Thus an Initiate in the *Path of Fortune* could perform a blessing with two additional Grades of Success added on to it.

TEAMWORK

There are times when it really helps to have an extra body tending the alembics or chanting the Third Chorus to Ahura Mazda. Sorcerers who use the same style of magic and possess the proper knowledge may combine efforts to cast a more potent spell than they could on their own.

System: When using teamwork, one sorcerer — usually the most skilled — is considered the main caster; the others assist him. The main caster determines the form of the spell and how any extra levels of success are used.

Each assistant must have some knowledge of the Path that is being used and operate using the same style as the main caster (the Storyteller is the final arbiter on which styles are close enough). Also, the spell takes one turn longer to cast for each assistant who is working on it. Each assistant makes a Simple Test, and for each success, the difficulty of the effect is reduced by one. If none of the assistants succeeds, the difficulty of the spell is increased by two.

HANGING SPELLS

Sorcery is not well adapted to off-the-cuff spell casting. It requires careful preparation and performance to enact any sort of effect. Unfortunately, there are times when it is really useful for a sorcerer to be able to cast a spell in a couple of seconds rather than the minutes or hours it normally takes. For these occasions, Sorcerers have learned how to "hang" spells.

System: The sorcerer casts the spell normally and spends a single Willpower Trait that she cannot recover while the spell is hung. A narrator or Storyteller writes out an item card for the spell. Casting the spell in the future takes one turn, at which point the character must pay whatever cost the spell has. Since having a hung spell is a constant drain on the character's mental faculties, she goes into any Mental Challenge down one Trait per hung spell.

FAST-CASTING

In those cases where a sorcerer needs a spell, but did not have the foresight to hang one, he can try to fast-cast the spell.

System: A sorcerer may rush through the motions and incantations of a casting in half the time (round up). Attempting to fast-cast a spell doubles the basic difficulty of the spell in question. Thus a fast-cast Initiate-level spell takes two turns and has a base difficulty of six! Fast-casting costs a Willpower Trait in addition to any ordinary cost of casting. Sorcerers cannot team up to fast-cast a spell.

ENERGY-SAVING SHORTCUTS

As sorcerers become more skilled, they often develop tricks to reduce the effort of casting simpler spells.

System: A sorcerer who knows a Path at two levels higher than the effect she is attempting to invoke may reduce the Willpower Trait cost by one by adding two to the difficulty of the spell.

SPENDING MANA

A sorcerer who knows how to handle Mana may use it to facilitate her magic.

System: A sorcerer with a source of Mana (such as the Background, understanding of the *Mana Manipulation* Path, or some Mana-charged item) may lower the difficulty of a spell by one Trait per Mana Trait spent, up to a maximum of 3.

COUNTERMAGIC AND UNWEAVING

As they learn the ways of sorcery, most static mages gain an understanding of how to undo the effects of others of their ilk. Counterspells are defensive magics that interfere with the mystic flow of spells that another sorcerer is casting. Unweaving is the disassembly of an enchantment that that has already been cast.

System: The caster of a counterspell must be have at least Apprentice-level knowledge of the Path of the spell she is trying to disrupt; in the case of *Thaumaturgy* or Sphere magic, she must have knowledge of a Path analogous to the spell. Casting a counterspell calls for a Static Mental Challenge against a difficulty of the level of the spell. Success adds one level of difficulty to the spell per level of knowledge in the Path that the counterspell caster has.

Unweaving calls for extended work against a long-standing enchantment of some sort. The Storyteller determines the strength of the enchantment (Usually double the level to which the original caster knew the effect in question, but possibly higher for more powerful creatures). Every five turns, the sorcerer may make a Mental Challenge against a difficulty of the level of effect of the enchantment. Two should be added to the difficulty if the enchantment was formed by Sphere magic or vampiric *Thaumaturgy*, and other enchantments are entirely outside this technique unless the Storyteller rules otherwise. Each successful challenge drops the strength of the enchantment by one. The unweaving sorcerer may attempt to speed up the process by increasing the difficulty of the challenge; for each two-Trait increase in the challenge difficulty, the sorcerer reduces the enchantment strength by an additional point per successful challenge. Unweaving may benefit from fast-casting and teamwork.

For Example: Sarma is attempting to break into a vampire's library but has discovered some sort of warding magic. Wanting to be careful, she decides to unweave

the ward rather than risk triggering whatever effect it might have. Since the vampire in question was an Intermediate-level thaumaturge, the Storyteller decides that the effect was equivalent to a Disciple-level Path — difficulty three. Because the enchantment is thaumaturgical rather than sorcerous, she adds another two to the difficulty, making it difficulty five. Since the vampire actually knew some more advanced *Thaumaturgy*, she decides to raise the enchantment strength a bit more and calls it eight. With only eight Mental Traits to call upon at the moment, Sarma decides not to make things more difficult and settles in for a prolonged session of unweaving. It is a good thing that she decided to pay her visit a little before noon.

PATHS

Each Path represents a linear progression of knowledge in a different area of magic on the part of the sorcerer. As such, Paths are broken into five different levels, indicating the relative amount of knowledge the sorcerer has in that particular area.

Apprentice — One who has begun to study the particular aspect of magic. Apprentice-level spells have a default difficulty of one.

Initiate — A sorcerer who has learned the foundation of the Path's secrets and is moving into the arcane mysteries. Initiate-level spells have a default difficulty of two.

Disciple — One who has gained a general level of understanding of a particular Path. Disciple-level spells have a default difficulty of three.

Adept — A sorcerer who has advanced beyond regular study into the Path in question and probably performed some impressive research or experimentation. Adept-level spells have a default difficulty of four.

Master — A sorcerer who has progressed along a Path to the limits of modern sorcery. Master-level spells have a default difficulty of five.

For crossover purposes, the Apprentice and Initiate levels are Basic powers, the Disciple and Initiate levels are Intermediate powers, and the Master Level is an Advanced power.

Through the use of Grades of Success, it is possible that sorcerers who have been around long enough to gain Master-level understanding may create or perform spells whose powers exceed those listed in their Paths. Storytellers are advised to limit such castings to Storyteller characters and may consult Sorcerer, Revised Edition or adjudicate the extent of these powers as circumstances warrant.

Each Path also has an associated Ability. These Abilities represent the external scholarship that is required to fully master the Path. A sorcerer must have that Trait at least to the level he wishes to learn the Path. Some Paths have multiple associated Abilities. The player should choose whichever associated Ability she feels best fits her character's magical style. Additionally, the Storyteller may rule that the character needs to expand her knowledge (gain a new *Lore* or some other Ability), or gain a reliable source who has that knowledge, should the character start delving into mysteries that surpass the ordinary realms of her Path.

ALCHEMY

Alchemy is the art, or possibly science, of transmuting materials according to their spiritual properties. Depending on the perspective of the practitioner, this Path has its

origins in ancient Qabbalistic or Taoist philosophy made material, understanding of herbs and unguents passed from mother to daughter for generations, and the latest applications of quantum harmonics. *Alchemy* can take many forms in modern days, from the abstruse principles of Advanced *Chemistry* to the old lore of *Herbalism*. Though the rules structure is the same as with *Alchemy*, the feel and scope of Advanced *Chemistry* and *Herbalism* are worlds apart.

Alchemy as alchemy is essentially Hermetic in nature, with philosophical underpinnings that reach back to the Qabbala and beyond. It teaches that base substances can be purified into higher essences — as in the traditional lead into gold — culminating with the Philosophers' Stone, which is reputed to have marvelous powers including mastery over death. Some alchemists realize that this is a metaphor for personal transformation into exalted understanding, but most content themselves with more fiscal applications. There are many alchemical treatises throughout the World of Darkness, but most are couched in arcane symbolism or so riddled with disinformation that the aspiring alchemist is often forced to rely on personal experimentation instead.

Herbalism looks to the natural properties of different parts of plants and animals — from comfrey to ground tiger testicles — to enhance the human metabolic process. Different regions tend to develop their own versions of *Herbalism* to take advantage of native plants and animals, but the principles remain similar throughout the world. Herbalists are less likely to record their discoveries and procedures in text, so it is often necessary for an aspiring herbalist to get a more experienced one to act as mentor.

Advanced *Chemistry* uses principles of science that have yet to be accepted by the mainstream scientific community. From Orgone energy to the etheric world gravity grid to precise atomic lattice creation, Advanced *Chemistry* lies on the cutting edge of scientific knowledge. With nothing but theory and experimentation to guide himself, the advanced chemist is in many ways the loneliest of the alchemists, but she is also the one most likely to have her discoveries generally accepted by the public.

Apprentice: The alchemist can create substances and chemicals that appear to be more advanced versions of existing substances. Painkillers, poisons, drugs, glues and solvents are common forms.

Initiate: The alchemist can create even more advanced substances than those available at Apprentice level, including potions that allow a character to exceed his physical limitations by one Trait or experience mystical senses in a limited fashion.

Disciple: The alchemist can create substances that allow the subject to reach superhuman levels or gain limited mystical powers. She can also create materials that surpass normal limitations of strength, durability, etc.

Adept: The alchemist can create substances that can increase a person's abilities by up to two Traits for a scene, or materials that have a noteworthy effect.

Master: The alchemist can create substances that duplicate a particular power of a supernatural creature. Such concoctions often require extensive study of the creature in question, often with components derived from them as well.

It is rumored that there were alchemists who knew even more potent secrets, such as the creation of mummies and the secret of eternal life. If those secrets ever, in fact, existed, they are very well hidden now.

SYSTEMS

Alchemy's associated Trait is *Alchemy*. For sorcerers who study it in the form of *Herbalism*, the associated Trait is *Herbalism*. For those who study it as *Advanced Chemistry*, the associated Trait is *Science*. The Attribute category is Mental.

Rather than casting spells, alchemists produce potions, salves, unguents and other substances for later consumption. Each casting produces a single dose of the substance that can be recorded as an item card for later use. Because *Alchemy* relies on the steady transformation of materials, all *Alchemical* spells are handled as rituals, and each ritual (sometimes called a formula) takes one day per level of effect. Each dose lasts one turn unless otherwise noted.

Alchemy can be a very costly process calling for rare substances and expensive equipment. The Storyteller may require that an alchemist dedicate one or two *Resources* Traits to materials and laboratory upkeep or that the alchemist put some effort into obtaining the requisite ingredients for his arcane experiments.

SAMPLE SPELLS

Apprentice: *Dionysus' Forgiveness:* A foul-tasting brew that purges alcohol from the body.

Initiate: *Ointment of Maedb:* A salve that, when rubbed on the eyes, allows the subject know if a creature is inherently supernatural. This allows the character to recognize that an Awakened mage or a Bastet was magical in some way, though not how.

Lionheart Elixir: A potion that grants the character an additional *Brawny* Trait for five turns, after which it switches to *Lethargic* for the rest of the scene. The potion does not allow a character to exceed 10 Physical Traits.

Disciple: *Powdered Truth:* A fine metallic dust that reveals invisible objects and illusions when sprinkled upon them.

Anavitriol: An oil that dissolves glass but has no effect on any other substance.

Adept: *Huang Ku'n Chi:* An incense whose smoke returns two Willpower Traits to people who meditate for 10 minutes while breathing it.

Accelamine: A pill that speeds up a person's thinking so that their reflexes are twice as fast. Consuming the pill grants him three additional *Quick* Traits for a scene, even if they bring the character over his Trait maximum. At the same time, the character experiences a shorter attention span, giving him the negative Mental Trait *Impatient*.

Master: *Tempering Balm:* A lotion including ground werewolf claws that grants the subject the ability to inflict aggravated damage in hand-to-hand combat for a scene, but makes him highly allergic to silver for a week.

CONJURATION

Conjuration is the art of magically moving objects other than the sorcerer from one place to another. The moved object may simply disappear from one place and then appear in another, which scientific types call apportation, or the object may travel the intervening distance under some mystical power, which scientists call telekinesis. Awakened mages claim it is a limited application of the Sphere of *Correspondence*.

Conjuration works best when the sorcerer prepares the object ahead of time through a simple ritual that binds the object to the sorcerer. This ritual is inherent to the *Conjuration* Path; it requires no additional experience and is learned along with the

Apprentice-level spell. The ritual takes as long as it takes the sorcerer to write up a card that indicates that the item has been prepared. A conjuror may only have as many items prepared in this manner as she has Willpower Traits.

Apprentice: The conjuror can move a single object that weighs no more than an ounce a couple of feet, with almost no control.

Initiate: The conjuror can move up to two objects that weigh a couple of pounds about 20 feet, with about the level of coordination a person could get by hitting them with her elbow.

Disciple: The conjuror can move up to three objects that weigh up to 100 pounds 100 feet, with the accuracy of an off hand.

Adept: The conjuror can move up to 10 identical objects, or four totally different objects, weighing up to 1,000 pounds half a mile, with regular motor control.

Master: The conjuror can move up to 25 identical items weighing up to a couple of tons up to five miles, with almost perfect precision.

SYSTEMS

Conjuration's associated Trait is *Occult*. The Attribute category is Physical. *Conjuration* spells cost one Willpower Trait unless the object has been prepared ahead of time as described above.

A conjuror can move living creatures that weigh half as much as the nonliving mass she can move. Humans, and other sentient creatures, are easily moved only if they are hypnotized or unconscious. Conscious humans add two Traits to the difficulty of the challenge. If they are unwilling, they add four. Snatching something from the hands of someone else also adds two Traits to the difficulty.

Beginning with the Disciple level, a sorcerer can use a conjured object to strike at someone as if it were a melee weapon. This attack is resolved as a ranged weapon with Traits based upon the objects that are being used as weapons.

The sorcerer may cast a spell that uses the next level's quantity, weight limit, distance or level of precision at a cost of one Grade of Success per exceeded limit. Only one level's improvement can be gained in this fashion. For example, an Initiate-level conjuror could move three 20-pound candelabra one hundred feet with two extra Grades of Success. She could not move one of the candelabra half a mile regardless of how many Grades of Success she chose because that is an Adept-level range.

SAMPLE SPELLS

Apprentice: *Pick a Card:* The sorcerer prepares a card, shuffles it into a deck, and then has it appear in her pocket. More impressive with Tarot decks.

Initiate: *The Willful Rapier:* Originally developed when dueling was in vogue, this spell gives a weapon a sudden jog. The attacker is considered two Traits down **for** that one attack. Sorcerers often upgrade this spell to more potent versions as their studies continue.

Disciple: *Bladeswitch:* More commonly used with a loaded shotgun these days, this spell is commonly hung and then used to bring a weapon from nearby (within 100 feet) into a place where the sorcerer's opponents do not want it to be.

Instant Reload: The sorcerer can exchange the ammunition in a handgun — either a clip or up to three bullets with different ammunition. In order for this to work, both

the ammunition in the gun and the ammunition it is to be replaced with must be prepared in advance.

Adept: *Shitstorm:* This spell grabs a number of small, similar objects and whirls them around the sorcerer in a deadly whirlwind. Any character who moves to within melee range of the sorcerer receives two automatic damage Traits from the objects. The damage may be bashing or lethal depending on the type of objects. If there is nothing in the immediate vicinity for the spell to grab, the spell is wasted.

Master: *The Hidden Chapel:* Called *Instant Stonehenge* by less reverent sorcerers, this ritual is used to summon selected boulders from the nearby countryside and arrange them into a particular configuration around the caster. The proper casting of *The Hidden Chapel* can transform a clearing into an impressive megalithic site in just half an hour. Casting the ritual in reverse returns the stones to their prior location.

CONVEYANCE

The *Path of Conveyance* encompasses personal transportation from magic carpets to seven league boots to teleportation chambers.

Apprentice: The sorcerer can move herself (and usually her clothes) about 10 feet at double her normal running speed.

Initiate: The sorcerer can move herself, her clothes and about 20 pounds of paraphernalia 100 feet at about 40 mph.

Disciple: The sorcerer can move herself and up to 200 pounds of cargo about a mile at 100 mph.

Adept: The sorcerer can move herself and up to 400 pounds of cargo up to five miles at about 250 mph.

Master: The sorcerer can move herself and up to 600 pounds of cargo up to ten miles instantly.

SYSTEMS

Conveyance's associated Trait is Occult. Its Attribute category is Physical. *Conveyance* spells cost one Willpower Trait and last until the sorcerer has traveled the allotted range or reached her destination.

A human (or humanlike) passenger takes the same magical energy as 200 pounds of cargo. Carrying a resisting passenger adds two Traits to the spell's difficulty.

A creature that is the subject of a *Conveyance* spell may take two *extra* steps per combat turn per level of the spell without any ill effects. Thus, the subject of a Disciple-level *Conveyance* spell could take seven steps and still be considered moving cautiously.

A sorcerer with a hanging *Conveyance* spell of Disciple-level or better may call Fair Escape even if surrounded or in the middle of combat, but if the spell requires physical passage there must be room for her to escape. This can only be countered by other supernatural abilities that allow their users to operate at similar speeds.

The sorcerer may cast a spell that uses the next level's speed, cargo capacity or distance at a cost of one Grade of Success per exceeded limit. Only one level's improvement can be gained in this fashion.

SAMPLE SPELLS

Apprentice: *Just a Jump to the Left:* Though this spell does not actually move the sorcerer anywhere, it adds some randomness to her movements, adding two Traits to the difficulty of all attacks made upon her while she dodges, flees or dives for cover.

Initiate: *Besom:* The classic witches' broom becomes possible at this level. Many students learn this with an increased range Grade of Success. This spell is often upgraded as the sorcerer progresses in understanding.

Adept: *Nitrous Invocation:* This spell, which works on bicycles, motorcycles and some small European cars, temporarily kicks the vehicle into overdrive (about 250 mph) and improves the handling just enough to prevent immediately crashing. Unfortunately, the duration of the effect is only a minute, and the vehicle subsequently breaks down unless the sorcerer has the *Technology* Trait and can make a Static Mental Challenge at difficulty 5.

Master: *Teleportation Chamber:* This ritual is worked upon an apparatus or area the size of a shower stall. Whoever enters and activates it is instantly removed to a specified location up to ten miles away. Specifying the destination takes one turn, but activating the chamber is instantaneous and counts as Fair Escape. It is up to the Storyteller what happens to those who activate the chamber without specifying a destination. Difficulty 6.

DIVINATION

From the stock market to the prognosis for a new boyfriend, knowledge of the future has always been in demand. Unfortunately for the prospective forecaster, those warned of a less than ideal fate often take out their wrath on those who warn them. Another hazard of divination is that some supernatural creatures know when they are being scryed — and are usually displeased by the attention.

Apprentice: The sorcerer may gain a vague insight into a very simple question that looks up to a week away.

Initiate: The sorcerer may gain an accurate, but highly symbolic, insight into a specific question up to a month away.

Disciple: The sorcerer may gain only slightly confusing insight into a regular question that applies up to a year away.

Adept: The sorcerer may gain mostly comprehensible information about a general topic up to ten years away.

Master: The sorcerer may gain accurate, comprehensible information about almost any topic, even one that has been deliberately hidden or obscured or is up to five decades away.

SYSTEMS

Divination's associated Ability is *Enigmas*, and it uses Mental Traits. There is no Willpower Trait cost for using the *Path of Divination*; however, all bid Traits are lost whether the casting is successful or not.

There are no specific spells for *Divination*, but each sorcerer must choose a form of divination, such as astrology, cartomancy, palmistry or other more obscure and often less pleasant forms. A sorcerer may learn additional forms much as she would learn spells under

ordinary circumstances. The Storyteller may rule that certain forms of divination are more accurate or provide better information than others in certain circumstances.

Each casting is handled as a ritual (five minutes per level) with more time bringing more accurate and precise information as the skill of the seer allows. Only Storytellers and Narrators may resolve a *Divination* challenge, and they ought never show their hands for the challenge. Even though she does not know the result of the challenge, the player may attempt an overbid, but she will never know how successful she was.

The sorcerer may cast a spell that uses the next level's accuracy, range or area of information at a cost of one Grade of Success per exceeded limit. Only one level's improvement can be gained in this fashion.

STORYTELLING *DIVINATION*

Since few Storytellers know the future — and those who do like to keep it secret from the players — *Divination* can be one of the most frustrating Paths to handle. Unless you choose to disallow it outright, there are certain tricks to keep in mind: The future is always malleable, so what the player does in response to the casting changes the future. Symbolism and vagueness are the Storyteller's friends. "The dark man will cause you harm," is far easier to accommodate and far more likely a problem for the characters than "Hieronymous has plans to steal your grimoire" or "An Egyptian man you do not know will accidentally run into you on his way to work," though it could apply to both situations. A more symbolic reading could have been "The onyx eagle will cause the moon to be lost." Some people find it difficult to be cryptic on command, so it may help to prepare some catch phrases for different characters within the chronicle or to review likely targets of divination before each session.

ENCHANTMENT

Enchantment — the vocation of crafting (minor) magical talismans — is a Path for the patient and those whose talents are not limited to the cerebral. Not only must the enchanter spend days or weeks tending the furnaces, etching the sigils, tying the catgut with the sacred knots, she must also construct the original item to be enchanted. Only a sorcerer with such intimate knowledge of an object can hope to imbue it with magic.

Enchantment also covers the creation of techno-scientific gadgets by enlightened scientists (though they may prefer to call it "*Invention*").

While the sorcerer is crafting the talisman, she may set any special restrictions or rules (such as "only works for women" or "activates when the user says "Alcatraz") she wants upon it, so long as the rules do not increase the power of the talisman beyond her level of understanding. Such conditions add to the complexity of the enchantment and take longer to craft.

Apprentice: The enchanter can create a simple talisman that might offer a one-Trait bonus to certain situations. Most Apprentice-level talismans are mistaken for well-crafted conventional items by those who do not know what to look for.

Initiate: In addition to two-Trait talismans like apprentices can create, the enchanter can create a talisman that has a subtle but obviously magical effect.

Disciple: The enchanter can create objects with obviously magical but not very powerful effects.

Adept: The enchanter can create talismans that allow their user to surpass human abilities. Such talismans can also duplicate Basic-level supernatural abilities such as Disciplines, Gifts, etc.

Master: The enchanter can create items and devices with formidable power, including Intermediate-level supernatural powers.

SYSTEMS

Enchantment's associated Ability is *Crafts.* In the case of techno-scientific enchantment, it is *Technology.* Both use Mental Traits.

An enchantment always begins with the construction of the object to be enchanted. This may be played out, relegated to a series of *Crafts* challenges or handled in downtime. The better constructed an object is, the more potent enchantment it can accept, so most enchanters put great time and effort into the initial crafting.

Once the object to be enchanted is completed, the actual enchantment is a ritual that takes from one to three days (depending on the judgment of the Storyteller) per level of *Enchantment.* If the enchanter is kept away from his project for more than a few hours at a time, the enchantment fails.

All enchantments cost one Willpower Trait upon completion of the enchantment, whether successful or not.

The first time a sorcerer successfully crafts an enchantment, the process has a difficulty one Trait higher than usual.

Like *Alchemy, Enchantment* can be a very costly process calling for rare substances and expensive equipment. The Storyteller may require that an enchanter dedicate one or two *Resources* Traits to materials and laboratory upkeep, or that he put some effort into obtaining the requisite parts for his bizarre devices.

Sorcerous talismans are affected by un-Awakened observers much as other vulgar sorcerous magics. When a user tries to get a talisman to perform a blatantly magical act in front of un-Awakened witnesses, he must win a Simple Test. Failure means the magical effect does not occur.

SAMPLE SPELLS

Apprentice: *Cloak of Shadows:* A cape that adds one *Arcane* Trait to the wearer.

Initiate: *Bottle of Luck:* A whiskey flask that intercepts and stops the first bullet that would hit its carrier.

Disciple: *Hermetic Damascene:* Comfortable silklike material that is strong enough to absorb two health levels of lethal or bashing damage. The material lasts about a month before the process begins to degrade.

Adept: *Peter's Torc:* A solid silver torc that imbues the wearer with *Brawny* x 3. In addition, the wearer may call upon it once per day to double his natural Physical Traits in a single challenge. The torc must be kept where the moon can shine upon it whenever it is not worn — and always for the night of the full moon — or it ceases functioning.

Master: *Purse o' Plenty:* A change purse that always contains about $5 worth of coins appropriate to wherever its owner is. So long as at least a quarter is left in it and it is used no more than four times a day, it replenishes itself.

FASCINATION

For millennia, sorcerers have used the *Path of Fascination* to bend others to their will. Loyalty, love, lust, faith and other such emotions are inspired by those upon whom the sorcerer uses these powers, but the wise sorcerer knows that such artificial affection often leads to dire consequences.

Fascination usually generates positive emotions directed toward the sorcerer, though throughout the years, some have had reason to create spells that generate negative emotions, usually fear, toward themselves.

Apprentice: The sorcerer can produce a mild effect (gain one Social Trait) with respect to one person for a couple of minutes.

Initiate: The sorcerer is increasingly beguiling (gain two Social Traits) with respect to two people for one scene.

Disciple: The sorcerer can command the attention and interest (and gain three Social Traits) with respect to up to 10 people for two days.

Adept: The sorcerer becomes admired and courted (and gains four Social Traits) with respect to 50 or so people for a couple of weeks.

Master: The sorcerer becomes the inspiration (and gains up to five Social Traits) with respect to a hundred people for several months.

SYSTEMS

Fascination's associated Ability is *Occult*, and the Path uses Social Traits.

Subjects do not get automatic resistance toward spells of this Path, but supernatural creatures, people with five or more Willpower Traits, and beings who know some similar form of power increase the difficulty of spells cast upon them by two. These effects are cumulative, so spells cast upon a vampire who knows *Presence* have a difficulty four greater than normal.

Any spells that focus on negative emotions have one Trait added to their difficulty.

The *Path of Fascination* does not grant complete command over a character, and she may resist orders that go against her beliefs or desires. In these cases, the sorcerer may add Traits to his side of the challenge as listed above.

The sorcerer may cast a spell that uses the next level's potency, duration or number of targets at a cost of one Grade of Success per exceeded limit. Only one level's improvement can be gained in this fashion.

SAMPLE SPELLS

Apprentice: *Authority:* This spell grants the caster the *Commanding* Trait, usually just long enough to get past a security guard.

Initiate: *Novi Amici:* The sorcerer temporarily gains *Genial* x 2 as he becomes more likable. This spell works only on people who do not already know the sorcerer.

Disciple: *Adonis:* The caster gains *Gorgeous* x 4, but at the price of a *Callous* Trait side effect.

Adept: *Queen of the Damned:* For two weeks, the caster gains the Traits *Alluring, Intimidating, Elegant* and *Witty*. This spell works only at night.

Master: *Personal Harem:* This ritual enables a sorcerer to so dominate the thoughts of a large number of people that they tend to her with rapt adoration, offering up money,

possessions, time and other favors just to be graced with a kind word or smile. Many sorcerers have used this power to build up cults of fanatical worshipers. The sorcerer gains an automatic *Magnetic* x 5 for all members of the affected group.

Gentle Let Down: This spell slowly lowers the effects of another *Fascination* spell, lowering the intensity of the feelings over the course of weeks to a gentle camaraderie.

FORTUNE

Curses and blessings, the stuff of happenstance and coincidence, these are the provenance of the *Path of Fortune*. Sorcerers who study this Path can reshape luck and mold probability to their wills. Awakened mages like to claim that the *Path of Fortune* is a limited version of the *Entropy* Sphere, but sorcerers find that it has power enough on its own. Though the actual blessings or curses may be of limited duration, their effects can last indefinitely. For example, a parapsychologist's blessing gets her out of the haven just before the hungry vampire shows up, or a skilled broker gets a reputation as a loser thanks to a week of remarkably bad luck.

Apprentice: The sorcerer can affect a single, named target for a single event. The effect is a minor inconvenience or benefit with no rules-related effects.

Initiate: The sorcerer can affect two targets or a single, poorly defined one for a day. The effect can offer a Trait of benefit or discomfort or produce one level of wounding.

Disciple: The sorcerer can affect a small group of associated people for a week. The effect can cause serious trouble, such as a debilitating but not life-threatening illness, or good fortune that brings lasting benefits.

Adept: The sorcerer can affect around 25 loosely affiliated people for several months. Permanent trauma and bankruptcy or remarkable fortune and welfare may result.

Master: The sorcerer can affect up to 100 remotely connected people for years. Slow painful death — or the cheating thereof — may be effected at this level.

SYSTEMS

Fortune's associated Ability is *Occult*. Techno-sorcerers use *Science*. Either challenge uses Social Traits. *Fortune* spells cost one Willpower Trait.

The sorcerer may cast a spell that uses the next level's group of effect, duration or potency at a cost of one Grade of Success per exceeded limit. Only one level's improvement can be gained in this fashion.

SAMPLE SPELLS

Apprentice: *Death Curse:* In this ritual, the sorcerer *permanently* discards *all* her Willpower Traits to cast a *Fortune* spell. Each Willpower Trait reduces the difficulty of this curse by one. Additionally, she may invoke effects that are a level beyond her normal power — two levels if she forces it up a Grade of Success.

Disciple: *P'an Kuan's Blessing:* The subject of the blessing gains a two-Trait bonus on all challenges involving bureaucrats. In addition, he functions as if he has one Influence: *Bureaucracy* Trait.

Master: *Blight Upon the Campbells:* This ritual tarnishes the reputation of a family, giving each member three *Obnoxious* Traits. Worse, the effects slowly spread to all who willingly consort with the victims, poisoning their behavior at the rate of one Trait per

game session of association. Deserting the afflicted family allows the Traits to depart at the same rate, but if the character returns to them, the Traits return immediately.

HEALING

The healing touch has been valued since time immemorial. Though not the flashiest of Paths, *Healing* allows life, and hope, to continue where it would not. Still, there are no instantaneous results, no miracle cures — the healer is merely encouraging the body's own natural work, only faster. More importantly, overuse of this Path drains the caster, leading to burnout and even death. Though not necessary, many healers learn some rudiments of *Medicine*, which is not always Western — homeopathy, acupuncture or other traditional methods are also useful.

Apprentice: The healer can relieve pain, sterilize wounds and cure bruises from bashing damage.

Initiate: The healer can stabilize mortal wounds, whether lethal or bashing, negate basic poisons and cure minor diseases.

Disciple: The healer can cure wounds from bashing damage and bruises from lethal damage.

Adept: The healer can cure incapacitating bashing damage and wounds from lethal damage, negate advanced poisons and cure serious diseases.

Master: The healer can cure incapacitating lethal wounds and even undo congenital defects.

SYSTEMS

Healing's associated Ability is *Empathy*, and the Path uses Social Traits. Its effects are permanent. Casting a *Healing* spell costs one Willpower Trait.

Healing spells have their difficulty reduced by one Trait if the sorcerer knows *Medicine* to the same level as the spell.

Bashing damage is always coincidental to heal, and can usually be cured instantly. Healing lethal damage is coincidental only if done away from un-Awakened observers. Additionally, this healing is not instantaneous — it merely reduces the healing time to that of the next lower form of damage. Sorcery has no effect on aggravated damage. Negating a poison or curing a disease does not undo the damage the poison has already done, but it prevents more damage and allows the character to work on healing the existing damage. A sorcerer can only work on a given wound, illness or poison once. Subsequent spells affecting the same problem only tire the sorcerer. For obvious reasons, this Path has no effect on the dead or undead.

SAMPLE SPELLS

Apprentice: *Healing Rest:* This ritual places the subject into a deep sleep that removes two health levels of bashing wounds and restores one Willpower Trait.

Initiate: *Wakey-Wakey:* This spell revives any unconscious character, for good or ill.

Adept: *Boneweal:* This spell prevents a character from receiving a Negative Physical Trait after recovering from a mortal wound.

Master: *Look into the Light:* This ritual restores injured — and even aged — eyes to full capacity over the course of a week.

HELLFIRE

Tapping into the most destructive elemental energies, the *Path of Hellfire* is the Path of choice for those whose goal is quick destruction. As different sorcerers have discovered different elements with which to smite their foes, different versions of this Path have arisen. The powers of the *Path of Hellfire* may manifest as lightning, strange fires, arcane radiation and other destructive forces, but all can be deadly. Some believe that the powers of this Path are tainted with infernal essence; others claim that power is just power and it is the use thereof that establishes its moral nature. Note that the limitations of spellcasting make this Path of limited use in unexpected combat.

Apprentice: The sorcerer can touch a single target, inflicting one health level of damage.

Initiate: The sorcerer can cause two health levels of damage to those within a two-foot-square area up to 10 feet away.

Disciple: The sorcerer can cause three health levels of damage within 10 square feet up to 25 feet away.

Adept: The sorcerer can cause four health levels of damage within 10 square feet up to 100 feet away.

Master: The sorcerer can cause five health levels of damage to a 25-foot square up to 250 feet away.

SYSTEMS

Hellfire's associated Ability is *Occult*, and its Attribute is Social.

Casting a *Hellfire* spell costs one Willpower Trait.

Hellfire causes lethal damage by default. The character may convert a lethal wound to aggravated by increasing the difficulty of the spell by one Trait per level of aggravated damage. A spell that calls for touch requires a Physical Challenge if the target is avoiding being touched. Likewise, any ranged *Hellfire* attack calls for the sorcerer to succeed in a ranged combat challenge in order to hit the intended target. For vampires, any fires cast with Hellfire mean a *Courage* Test, and aggravated damage if they are struck by the flames.

The sorcerer may cast a spell that uses the next level's range, power or target area at a cost of one Grade of Success per exceeded limit. Only one level's improvement can be gained in this fashion.

SAMPLE SPELLS

Apprentice: *Love Tap:* The sorcerer focuses harmful arcane power in her hand; even a gentle tap does one level of lethal damage. Some combine this with a regular hand attack, adding the lethal damage to the bashing damage of the punch, but others prefer to use this subtly to pretend that there is some sort of preexisting infirmity and that the tap merely brought attention to it.

Initiate: *Hair of the Dog:* The sorcerer can offer himself limited protection from the forces of her form of *Hellfire*. This ritual allows the sorcerer to treat all lethal damage from the elemental form as bashing damage.

Hellblade: This ritual imbues a melee weapon with the powers of *Hellfire*. After performing this ritual, the character can activate the weapon by spending a Willpower Trait. For the duration of the scene, or until the sorcerer loses hold of the weapon, it does two additional levels of lethal damage.

HELLWIND, ETC.

In addition to the basic attack form of fire, *Hellfire* spells may employ a variety of different special effects such as earthquakes, poisonous smoke, whirlwinds or other elemental effects. These are different Paths, which must be studies separately. Each has its own advantages and disadvantages. Cryogenic attacks may cause surfaces to become icy; poisonous vapors may obscure vision; the possibilities are only limited by the malevolence of the players and Storyteller.

MANA MANIPULATION

Chi, Mana, Quintessence — nearly every mystical tradition recognizes the flow of mystical energy in some form. *Mana Manipulation* is the art of recognizing and shaping such flows to one's benefit

Apprentice: The sorcerer can sense Mana, determine if an object or location is charged with it, and possibly get an idea of the flavor (or Resonance) of any such Mana for one turn.

Initiate: The sorcerer can perform Apprentice-level Mana sensing on creatures. For two turns, she may discern the general power of Mana she perceives and recognize when someone else is using magic to redirect mystical flows.

Disciple: The sorcerer can briefly redirect Mana, blocking it from its normal course for three turns. While this does not prevent use of personal Mana, Gnosis, etc., it can prevent someone else from drawing it from a place of power.

Adept: The sorcerer can draw Mana at will from a place of power, cause another to lose her personal store of Mana, and redirect Mana on a local scale to change the mystical Resonance of a place for four turns.

Master: The master of Mana can use redirected Mana as a shield against hostile magic, block another sorcerer's use of Mana for five turns and even affect the long-term magical Resonance of a location.

SYSTEMS

Mana Manipulation's associated Ability is *Occult*, and its Attribute is Social. *Mana Manipulation* spells cost one Willpower Trait.

Mana Manipulation spells can affect one Mana Trait per level of effect. Related Traits, such as Gnosis and Quintessence, can be affected at double the effort, rounding down. Thus, a *Mana Manipulation* Disciple could affect one Gnosis Trait.

Mana Manipulation rituals take one hour per level of effect and last for one month per level of effect (rather than the duration listed above). Depending on the Storyteller's ruling, given enough time, the Resonance of an object or place may change permanently to conform with the workings of a skilled and patient Mana manipulator.

For more on magical Resonance, see **Laws of Ascension**, pp. 119-121.

SAMPLE SPELLS

Apprentice: *Gordian Knot:* This spell performs careful analysis of a magical field, reducing the difficulty of unweaving efforts by one Trait.

Disciple: *Angel Tear:* This small bottle can hold one Mana Trait for one night.

Adept: *Feng Shui Mirror:* The ritualized alignment of this mirror allows the sorcerer to slowly alter the character of a place of power (Node, caern, etc.). For the most part, the effects will be Storyteller-determined, but they can include changes in who can draw power, the type of spirits who frequent the area and other mystical characteristics.

Master: *Sanctum Sanctorum:* This complex ritual shapes the spiritual Resonance of an area, such as the sorcerer's library or laboratory, to favor her magic. All spells the sorcerer casts whose effects are confined to the area covered by the ritual — no more than a 20-foot square room — are considered one Trait up. This ritual takes at least one hour a night for a whole month to initiate, plus three hours a month to maintain. Failure to maintain the *Sanctum Sanctorum* calls for the sorcerer to start fresh.

ONIEROMANCY

Many have long known that there is power in dreams, and sorcerers who follow the *Path of Onieromancy* have learned to take this power for themselves. A skilled onieromancer can travel to and impose her will upon the Dream Realms, visiting nightmares upon her enemies, spying upon the dreams of her rivals and conveying messages to allies. Most denizens of the World of Darkness dream, and many supernatural creatures have powers that allow them to tap, control or enter those dreams.

Apprentice: The onieromancer can perceive the dreams of one whom she touches, perhaps learning a bit about the character's nature or history.

Initiate: The onieromancer can enter the dream of one whose true name she knows. Though her entrance and starting role is dictated by the dream, she may impose minor changes appropriate to the dream.

Disciple: The onieromancer can safely enter the dream of someone whose body parts or secretions (nail clippings, saliva, blood, etc.) she possesses. With this level of understanding, she is safe from the potential hazards of the dream and may alter the dream to a greater extent, actually changing the nature of the dream. An onieromancer may try to craft a dream that restores or removes a Willpower Trait from the dreamer if she so wishes.

Adept: The onieromancer can create entire dream sequences and control portions of dreams in minute detail, affecting anyone whose prized possession she holds.

Master: The onieromancer can move freely through the dreams of anybody whose frequently used possessions she holds, and can even meld dreams of different people together or draw a person from one dream into another.

SYSTEMS

Onieromancy's associated Ability is *Occult*, and its challenges use Mental Traits. Though *Onieromancy* spells do not cost any Willpower Traits per se, wounds received in dreams are first taken from Willpower Traits, then Mental Traits. When a character has no Mental Traits left, she can no longer interact with the Dream Realm.

The sorcerer may cast a spell that uses the next level's potency, duration or number of targets at a cost of one Grade of Success per exceeded limit. Only one level's improvement can be gained in this fashion.

Onieromancy does not have any distinct spells, just the ability to have an increasing effect on the dreams of others.

SHADOWCASTING

Despite accusations that this Path is tainted with infernal power, the sorcerous ability to shape and control shadows is arguably no more evil than any other Path. Nevertheless, some practitioners seem to revel in the unnerving effects that this branch of sorcery produces, making even those who believe that the Path is not inherently evil suspect that it may attract unsavory sorts.

Apprentice: The sorcerer can increase the deepness of shadows in a room-sized area, adding or subtracting one Trait to affected challenges — such as intimidation, stealth, disguise — for one turn.

Initiate: The sorcerer can arrange shadows and muffle sounds to conceal himself or cause confusion for two turns, adding or subtracting two Traits to affected challenges.

Disciple: The sorcerer may leach colors and sounds and cause shadows to flicker and coil, adding or subtracting three Traits to affected challenges.

Adept: The sorcerer can compel shadows to reach out for people (though they are still intangible) adding or subtracting four Traits to affected challenges. Recording devices fail automatically when brought into the darkness formed by this level of *Shadowcasting*.

Master: The sorcerer can shape shadows into truly horrifying forms adding or subtracting five Traits to affected challenges. At this level, the shadowcaster also gains the ability to see in all but the deepest supernatural darkness.

SYSTEMS

Shadowcasting's associated Ability is *Occult*. It uses Social Traits for challenges. *Shadowcasting* spells cost one Willpower Trait to cast.

If the sorcerer is attempting to scare someone, the target must make a Static Willpower Challenge against double the level of the spell or be treated as down the spell's level in Traits for the duration of the scene. These checks may be modified by the amount of ambient light — *Shadowcasting* is not that potent in full sunlight — and the susceptibility of the target to fear of unnatural darkness.

The sorcerer may cast a spell that uses the next level's potency, duration or versatility at a cost of one Grade of Success per exceeded limit. Only one level's improvement can be gained in this fashion.

SAMPLE SPELLS

Apprentice: *Aura of Menace*: The sorcerer deepens the shadows around his eyes, giving himself a disturbing mien and adding one Trait to any attempts at intimidation.

Initiate: *Stage Makeup*: The sorcerer can alter his features through the subtle rearranging of shadows. This spell cannot be used to imitate someone else, only to look different. Additionally, the effects look very unnatural up close.

Adept: *Vertigo*: The sorcerer causes the shadows in an area to sway and bob, causing people within the area to suffer a four-Trait penalty on all *Melee* challenges.

Master: *Haunting*: This ritual causes the shadows of a room or area to form ominous shapes in the peripheral vision of intruders. At first, the shapes and movements are subtle, but as minutes pass, they become more overt and threatening. Every two minutes, the victims must make a Static Willpower Challenge with the difficulty

starting at one and increasing by one each time. Failure sends them fleeing, but if they last through 10 challenges, they are immune to this particular casting. *Haunting* takes two hours to cast, but lasts until the next new moon. The entire ritual is washed away if the area is subjected to unshaded sunlight.

SHAPESHIFTING

Though there are natural shapeshifters in the World of Darkness, some sorcerers have studied how to alter their bodies through magical artistry. Sorcerers who follow this primal Path risk losing their personalities to the beasts they form themselves into. Many sorcerers see this power as a connection to the sacred animal powers of nature; others see it as a chance to do something weird.

Apprentice: The sorcerer can perform minor cosmetic changes upon himself, perhaps gaining a single Trait for certain challenges.

Initiate: The sorcerer can perform more serious changes to herself, such as growing claws or more sensitive ears, perhaps gaining two Traits for certain challenges.

Disciple: The sorcerer can replace one of her body parts with a chosen animal feature, perhaps gaining three Traits for certain challenges.

Adept: At this level, the sorcerer can affect a different person instead of himself. The sorcerer can effect a partial transformation into another creature producing something that is half-human, half-animal. This transformation can add up to four Traits for certain challenges.

Master: The sorcerer can now affect two people at a time, and can perform complete transformations into animals.

SYSTEMS

Shapeshifting's associated Ability is *Animal Ken*, and uses Physical Traits for challenges. For techno-sorcerers, the associated Ability is *Science*, and the Path uses Mental Traits. Casting a *Shapeshifting* spell costs one Willpower Trait. All *Shapeshifting* spells last for one scene. This duration may be extended to another scene through the expenditure of a Willpower Trait.

Note: Adept-level *Shapeshifting* cannot transform someone into a Garou's Crinos form. Instead it produces something like a bipedal wolf that is somewhere between a wolf and a human in size.

If the sorcerer for some reason loses all Mental Traits or all Willpower Traits while in another form, she loses her human mind and adopts the mind of the form she has taken. Sorcerers who recover from this invariably find that they have gained some sort of Negative Trait from the experience.

Upon attaining Adept level, the sorcerer can opt to include features from more than one creature at a time at a cost of one Grade of Success per additional creature.

SAMPLE SPELLS

Apprentice: *Eagle Eyes*: The sorcerer gains the eyes of an eagle and an extra *Observant* Trait for use in visual challenges.

Initiate: *Talons*: The sorcerer grows talon-like claws that add two lethal health levels to damage she causes in unarmed combat.

Disciple: *Calvinophagy*: The sorcerer can extend her digestive tract through her mouth in a manner similar to a fly, dissolving food outside her body before bringing it in. Though not suited for combat, living beings that are in contact with the extruded digestive tract for an entire turn take one health level of aggravated damage. Any injury to the extruded digestive tract inflicts one extra level of damage, and no armor prevents it.

Adept: *Bat Boy:* The sorcerer can adapt herself for operation in the dark by enlarging the eyes and developing echolocation. Growth of claws and a slight decrease in size fill out the package. In addition to the abilities listed for *Talons*, the character gains the ability to see in total darkness, and an added *Nimble* Trait for good measure.

Master: *Bast's Blessing*: The character takes the form of a black housecat.

THE SPIRITUAL PATHS: SUMMONING, BINDING AND WARDING

Sorcerers have long been known for the company that they keep. Demons, ghosts, spirits and other unfathomable beings come when the sorcerer beckons. A sorcerer is powerful enough on his own, but one who is attended by such powerful entities is even more puissant.

Such powers are naturally quite dangerous, for no being likes being confined or compelled to act against its will, and it is impossible to tell if the binding rituals were correctly performed until they are put to the test. Many extradimensional beings are difficult to bind, and worse, they are often clever enough to seed the occult community with false binding rituals. A sorcerer who succeeds in summoning Sabaroutha only to discover that his binding ritual was a ninth-century forgery is a very unhappy sorcerer.

Certain groups, such as the Bata'a, center their entire magical style around these Paths; they have vast experience with Les Invisibles and generations of practice at their techniques and rituals. Others, like the Order of Hermes, have vast archives of information and ephemeredes from which they can deduce (hopefully) the proper procedures. At the other end of the spectrum are sorcerers with little more than a musty grimoire or a suspiciously helpful spirit guide. Though the former are certainly better equipped for these Paths, it must be remembered that even now, these are imperfect sciences.

SUMMONING

A *Summoning* commands an entity to appear by the most expeditious means. *Summoned* creatures do not generally know where they are going, just a general destination that becomes more specific as they approach. *Summoning* is not the same as *Conveyance*; if the entity does not have the means to reach the summoner, it does not arrive. In this case, the subject feels a compulsion that it cannot act upon; it is probably very frustrated. The compulsion to arrive lasts until the subject reaches the designated location or the sorcerer stops performing the ritual.

Summonings may be directed against a specific being or against the nearest representatives of a class of beings (such as rats or cab drivers).

Apprentice: The sorcerer can summon a swarm of small, unintelligent animals such as bats, a single minor nature spirit or a simple device.

Initiate: The sorcerer can summon up to two creatures or swarms. He can now summon ghosts, larger animals such as wolves, or television-sized technological devices.

Disciple: The sorcerer can summon up to three creatures or swarms. He can summon normal humans, self-willed nature spirits, or computers and complex electronic equipment.

Adept: The sorcerer can summon up to four creatures or swarms. He can summon sorcerers, Kinfolk, ghouls and similar supernatural creatures, as well as automobiles or golems and techno-magical devices.

Master: The sorcerer can summon up to five creatures or swarms. He can summon supernatural beings such as vampires and werewolves, machinery on the scale of airplanes, and lesser angels and demons.

Systems

Summoning's associated Ability is *Occult*, and uses Mental Traits. Casting a *Summoning* ritual costs one Willpower Trait.

All *Summoning* spells are rituals and are handled first as a magical spell to see if they work at all, and secondarily as a Mental Challenge against the subject's Willpower Traits to see if the subject can resist. Though the initial casting takes five minutes per level, the sorcerer needs to keep the ritual going long enough for the subject to arrive. The Storyteller may require that the sorcerer sacrifice additional Willpower Traits in the case of exceptionally prolonged *Summonings*.

Summoning a specific creature is more effective if the sorcerer incorporates some aspect or possession of the creature into the ritual. For each of the following used by the summoner, the Storyteller should deduct one from the effective Willpower of the subject: true name, part of body, article of clothing, prized possession.

WARDING

Wards are magical protection against specific creatures or groups of creatures. Wards take two different forms: personal wards and magic circles. Personal wards protect a single person or item from something; when the item or person moves, so does the protective aura. Magic circles (which are not always circles) are scribed on the ground and act as barriers against their chosen subject, keeping them either within or without.

Apprentice: The sorcerer can protect herself against small, unintelligent animals, or minor nature spirits, for a turn.

Initiate: The sorcerer can protect herself against ghosts and large animals for up to a minute.

Disciple: The sorcerer can protect herself against humans, self-willed nature spirits, or complex electronics. She can construct magic circles large enough to hold a single human for up to a scene.

Adept: The sorcerer can protect herself against lesser supernatural creatures, golems and the like. She can construct magic circles large enough to hold up to hold up to five humans for up to a day.

Master: The sorcerer can protect herself against vampires, werewolves and lesser angels and demons for an entire story.

Systems

Warding's associated Ability is *Occult*, and the Path uses Mental Traits. Casting a ward costs one Willpower Trait. All *Warding* spells are rituals.

Each level of *Warding* subtracts one Trait from the target creatures in any attempts to harm (in any way) whatever or whomever is protected by the ward. Failing to breach a powerful ward can be a quite draining experience; each attempt costs the warded creature one Willpower Trait. Unlike most spells, the actual challenge to determine the ward's success does not occur until the ward is tested. The Willpower Trait is spent, but no one knows if the spell worked until the warded creature attempts to harm the subject.

BINDING

Binding rituals compel a creature to perform or not perform certain functions. It is through this Path that sorcerers are able to perform feats beyond their own abilities. They bind other beings to act for them.

A well-informed sorcerer selects the beings he binds based on their abilities and predilections. *Binding* a Djigaahehwa, an Iroquois fertility spirit, to destroy a vampire will rarely be as fruitful as binding Capabile, angelic messenger of the sun. A wise sorcerer attempts to propitiate creatures it has bound or seeks other means of getting them to do as he wishes, for spirits are long-lived and make dangerous enemies.

Apprentice: The sorcerer can bind small, unintelligent animals or minor nature spirits for a turn. The bound creature cannot act against the sorcerer.

Initiate: The sorcerer can bind ghosts and large animals for up to a minute. The bound creature must truthfully answer any single question put to it.

Disciple: The sorcerer can bind humans and self-willed nature spirits for up to a scene. The bound creature must answer any questions put to it and must perform any one service described in a single sentence — though it may twist the intent of the service.

Adept: The sorcerer can bind lesser supernatural creatures, golems and the like for up to a day. The bound creature must perform a task for the sorcerer as directed, following the orders closely.

Master: The sorcerer can bind vampires, werewolves and lesser angels and demons for up to a story. The bound creature must answer the questions and perform a task for others whom the sorcerer specifies.

In all cases, restrictions from the previous level's bindings apply, so an Adept-level binding prevents its target from attacking the sorcerer.

Systems

Binding's associated Ability is *Occult*, and the Path uses Mental Traits. Casting a *Binding* spell costs one Willpower Trait. All *Binding* spells are rituals. The bound creature can spend a Willpower Trait to resist a binding, but the sorcerer may recast the binding.

Sample Spells

Apprentice: *Call of the Asp:* The sorcerer summons the nearest poisonous snakes to slither at his feet.

Disciple: *St. Norton's Blessing:* The sorcerer places a series of warding glyphs on a computer's CPU, protecting it from all software viruses until it crashes.

Attack of the Asp: The sorcerer sends any poisonous snakes near him — usually those summoned by *Call of the Asp* — to go in a certain direction and bite anyone they encounter.

Adept: *Pressing the Blood Servant:* This ritual binding is worked upon a ghoul, forcing it to tell the sorcerer all of its master's weaknesses. One of the less obvious

drawbacks of this spell is that many ghouls are so emotionally involved with their domitors that their judgment of what constitutes a weakness is seriously deficient.

Master: *Guardian Angel:* If the sorcerer has learned the true name of an angel and can arrange for its presence (perhaps through the appropriate *Summoning* ritual), she may direct it to protect a single mortal from spiritual or physical harm for a year and a day. Occasionally, demons masquerade as angels and allow themselves to be bound by this spell so that they can torture the subject under the guise of protecting her. As always, the wise sorcerer should be extraordinarily cautious when dealing with such creatures.

WEATHER CONTROL

Whether it is a gentle wind at sea or the rain that nourishes the crops, weather has been vital to the course of human civilization. Those who can control the weather can fetch a handsome price — whether in gratitude or fear. Weather magic can be very powerful, but it is also slow and tiring.

Apprentice: The sorcerer can affect small changes (a raise or drop of five or so degrees, a change in wind velocity of 5 mph, etc.) over a 50-foot-square area for a minute.

Initiate: The sorcerer can change the temperature by ten degrees, summon fog, make the sky cloudy, create or still 10-mph winds, etc. over an area of about half a mile in diameter for a couple of minutes.

Disciple: The sorcerer can call the winds and rain, bring about 30-degree changes in temperature, calm turbulent seas, etc. over an area of two miles in diameter for half an hour.

Adept: The sorcerer can call upon storms or banish them away, command the tides, and even call lightning over a five-mile diameter for an hour.

Master: The sorcerer can bring blizzards and storms of ferocious magnitude over a 20-mile diameter for a day.

SYSTEMS

Weather Control's associated Trait is *Occult*, and the Path uses Social Traits. Apprentice-level and Initiate-level *Weather Control* spells cost one Willpower Trait. Disciple-level and Adept-level *Weather Control* spells cost two Willpower Traits. Master-level *Weather Control* spells cost three Willpower Traits.

Weather Control spells are all rituals.

Weather effects are slow to arrive. If the spell is the same level as the skill of the sorcerer, it takes up to an hour for the effect to build. If the spell is one level below the caster's level of understanding, it takes 10 minutes. Effects even further below the skill of the caster occur within one turn of the caster's completing the ritual.

Adept-level and greater weather witches can call forth lightning, hailstones and other hazardous weather conditions. Such dangers are notoriously difficult to direct — the sorcerer must succeed in a Simple Test to even try to aim the effects at a target. If she fails, they randomly affect all who occupy the area of effect, even the sorcerer. If the sorcerer can direct the weather's fury, it can be handled as a ranged attack with the target getting double benefit of any defensive Traits. These attacks inflict health levels of damage, either lethal or bashing, depending on the type of attack.

The sorcerer may cast a spell that uses the next level's potency, duration or area of effect at a cost of one Grade of Success per exceeded limit. Only one level's improvement can be gained in this fashion.

SAMPLE SPELLS

Apprentice: *Summer Breeze:* A gentle breeze arises to soothe the summer heat.

Disciple: *Up the Creek:* A current moves the sorcerer's boat along at 10 knots or adds 10 knots to the boat's speed.

Adept: *Snow Day:* the sorcerer doubles the amount of precipitation that an existing storm dumps on an area. This can make roads impassable, cause flooding, increase the difficulty of *Drive* challenges and have a host of other effects.

THEURGY

When members of the Society of Leopold possess any Numinae other than True Faith, they refer to it as *Theurgy*. For its advocates, it is merely another manner of invoking the aid of Heaven. For its detractors it is still magic and thus evil. Those who possess *Theurgy* in the Society are required to register that fact with the Office of the Censor, although undoubtedly some do not; pity them when they are discovered.

All uses of *Theurgy* involve some form of ritual or prayer invoking the power of Heaven, whether in the name of God, Jesus Christ, the Blessed Virgin or any of the various saints and angels. Theurgists have different names for each Numina, which are referred to as "ways."

Unless mentioned otherwise, all these powers take one turn per Trait level of ritual to activate, the expenditure of a Willpower Trait and success in a Mental Challenge. Any activation challenge can be retested with the *Occult* Ability unless dictated differently below.

VIA GENIORUM

The path most distrusted by critics of *Theurgy*, this Via deals with the realms of spirits and the demonic, a most unsavory occupation. Practitioners of this path argue that all creatures are of God, including the spirits and demons. Others contend that there exists a host of spiritual creatures that answers to neither God nor the Enemy, who can yet be commanded through the power of Heaven. Of course, most who use this Via keep their studies and inclinations a secret, lest a curious Censor summon them.

The powers of this Via are split into two forms — rituals and grades. Each use of power by a character involves both elements. The Inquisitor casts a ritual that is influenced by the powers granted by the grade. Summoning Archangel Michael requires knowledge of the summoning ritual for archangels and five Traits in *Via Geniorum* (and praying you get the right archangel), while dismissing a Gaffling requires only knowledge of the *Ritual of Dismissing Gafflings* and two Traits in the Via. Binding the archangel requires a specific ritual for Michael (which is unlikely to really be his true name).

Needless to say, due to the freeform nature of this power, Storyteller discretion is advised as to the spirits that turn up — such creatures may not necessarily be directly under the control of the Theurgist unless extreme precautions have been taken. More information regarding spirits can be found in **Laws of Ascension** and **Laws of the Wild**.

RITUALS

Rituals are divided into four different types: *Summoning, Binding, Dismissal* and *Protection*. Players should keep separate track of which rituals they learn for which creatures. In order to assess the Experience Trait cost for any given ritual, refer to the equivalent Grade that is required to summon such a creature — the ritual to bind an angel would be Advanced and thus cost 6 Experience Traits to learn.

Rituals of this nature typically take an hour per Grade to perform.

Summoning Rituals call a single spirit to appear in the immediate area. Summoning a spirit requires knowledge of the summoning ritual for that type of creature.

The difficulty to activate these rituals is eight Traits and a successful Social Challenge. Successfully summoning a creature does not mean that it is bound or that you are protected from it in any way.

Binding Rituals force a single *specific* summoned spirit into temporary servitude. Binding rituals vary from creature to creature. They typically rely on the accurate knowledge of the creature's true name. "Close" is not close enough — there is no room for guesswork.

The difficulty to activate these rituals is eight Traits, and you must also beat the target creature in a Social Challenge. Success results in the creature being unable to act against the Theurgist. Additional Social Challenges can then be made to force the target to answer a question truthfully or to perform a simple task within its capabilities. The target is not necessarily happy about this and can initiate a Social Challenge using their Gnosis Traits in return to cause the Theurgist to falter, releasing the binding. Otherwise, bindings last until the end of the scene.

Dismissal Rituals allow a Theurgist to force a creature to return to its native realm. These are the most common rituals known to the more pious Theurgists. Such rituals are differentiated between creature types, not specific individuals.

Activating a dismissal ritual is at a difficulty of seven Traits and also involves a contest of Willpower vs. Essence. Perform a Willpower Challenge as if it were a normal Mental Challenge, risking Willpower Traits (rather than Mental Traits) for the Theurgist and Essence Traits for the spirit — further Willpower or Power Traits can be expended by either party to retest. Success for the Theurgist results in the spirit returning to its home plane. Otherwise, it remains to do as it will.

Protection Rituals protect targets from general types of creatures. Usually these rituals involve the creation of some form of ward or sigil on the target, perhaps a small handheld object or a large stone circle. Theurgists often surround their Cenacula with an intricate network of sigils. The difficulty for activating these rituals is seven Traits. Any creature of the specified type that attempts to destroy or cross such a ward or sigil must succeed in a Static Gnosis Challenge against the Willpower of the Theurgist immediately subsequent to the creation of the ward. Create an item card or other written record for each ward so you don't forget the Trait difficulty in the future.

VIA IGNIS – THE WAY OF HOLY FIRE

The Inquisitor calls on God's Fire to punish the wicked, summoning searing flames to light the way in the darkness and burn the faithless. The *Via Ignis* is one of purgation and damnation, reminding the Infernal of that which they can never truly escape and letting the Damned experience the flames of Hell before their Final Deaths.

Via Ignis summons what appears to be normal fire, but it burns even those protected from normal flames. The Theurgist is immune to his own fire, but not to any normal flames that may result if something (or someone) nearby catches fire. Handle His wrath with care — the fire of God sometimes burns without prejudice, and wisdom in its use will preserve you as surely as the fire itself.

While this holy fire has no additional special effect on vampires other than those given herein, it still gives cause for such creatures to make *Courage* Tests (dependant on the size of flame presented, refer to **Laws of the Night**, p. 110) and causes them aggravated damage.

The maximum range for any flame generation is touch or the object being held (see below for restrictions). Unless otherwise dismissed, these powers fade at the end of the scene or if the Theurgist is rendered unconscious. When used for combat purposes, any retest takes the appropriate Ability (*Brawl*, *Athletics*, etc.).

BASIC

Burning

The light of the Lord manifests as a candle flame in your hand, glowing strongly enough to illuminate the nearby area (as a dim, flickering lantern would). This flicker can be used to ignite other materials, but the resultant flame is normal fire — only the flame in your hand is invested with God's strength. The flame can be commanded to line the edge of your hand or knuckles, granting you the additional *Burning* Physical Trait for the purposes of nonweapon combat (*Brawl*) and causing lethal damage rather than bruising. This power can cause a one-Trait *Courage* Test for a vampire facing it at close range.

Searing

Your entire hand becomes sheathed in holy flame, lighting the immediate area clearly.

The light of God may burn through shadows created by vampiric *Obtenebration* if you can beat the vampire in a Mental Challenge. If successful, you reduce the darkness penalties for *Shroud of Darkness* or similar darkened areas by one Trait. If you wish to have both hands affected by *Searing* to further reduce the darkness, you must activate the power twice and make the Mental Challenge twice.

Your flaming fist can be used to strike other creatures, and you gain the single bonus *Burning* Trait as per *Burning*. Additionally, any strike you make with your *Searing* hand causes lethal or aggravated damage, as you desire, although the damage is always aggravated to vampires. These creatures can expect a two-Trait *Courage* Test as well.

You do not gain multiple Trait or damage bonuses for having both hands alight.

INTERMEDIATE

Branding

Your power expands such that you may now enshroud handheld weapons with the limning aura of holy fire. You may begin to learn the *Branding Weapon* ritual (see below) for each separate class of weapon you wish to be able to ignite — igniting a sword requires a different ritual from igniting an axe.

While you use a *Branding* weapon as normal, you have the additional *Branding* Physical Trait. The weapon inflicts one level of aggravated damage to any supernatural creature that you strike with it, in addition to its normal damage.

VIA GENIORUM GRADES

Each level in this power allows the Theurgist access to more complex interactions with greater forces. Please note that these powers will not affect wraiths (see *Via Necromantiae*, below). The Storyteller should determine the strength of the spirit using the guidelines below.

Spirits don't have normal Traits, unless they create or possess a material body. A spirit uses its Rage instead of Physical Traits to attack, its Gnosis instead of Mental or Social Traits, and its Charms to perform psychic or magical effects (if you don't have **Laws of the Wild Revised**, select some appropriate Numina levels). Its Power Traits enhance Charms and fuel its existence. Some also have Abilities.

Via Geniorum Ratings

Rating	Spirit level
One Trait	Insignificant spirit entities only; incidental shades. 7 points among the following Traits:
Power: 1-5	**Charms:** *Airt Sense* only, no cost
Rage: 1-5	**Abilities:** 1-2
Gnosis: 1-5	
Two Traits	Minor spirits (e.g., Gafflings, minor elementals, low level Minions) but not true demons. 13 points among the following Traits:
Power: 1-6	**Charms:** 1-5
Rage: 1-6	**Abilities:** 1-5
Gnosis: 1-6	
Three Traits	Servitor-rank demons, more powerful minions, Jagglings. 25 points among the following Traits:
Power: 1-10	**Charms:** 1-5
Rage: 1-7	**Abilities:** 1-10
Gnosis: 1-7	
Four Traits	Englings, greater spirits, low-level demons. Such creatures can be very dangerous to the caster. 30 points among the following Traits:
Power: 1-15	**Charms:** 1-6
Rage: 1-8	**Abilities:** 1-15
Gnosis: 1-7	
Five Traits	Greater-level demons, minor incarna. Beware. 40 points among the following Traits:
Power: 1-20	**Charms:** 1-7
Rage: 1-8	**Abilities:** 1-15, maximum of level 6 in one Ability
Gnosis: 1-8	

Note: Attempts to summon major-level spirits such as the Celestines are likely to result in God frowning on your attempts to summon divine help from avenues other than Himself. Don't forget what might happen if the censors find out, either. Oh, and the Celestine is also unlikely to be amused.

Additionally, while using the powers of *Burning* or *Searing*, your Trait bonus is now *Burning* x 2.

Cleansing

Fire from your hands can take shape into a melee weapon of your preferred choice. Each Inquisitor often takes a personally preferred type of weapon — swords are common, although hammers, censers and staves are also popular, chainsaws less so — although they can create any form of weapon they wish. This includes batleths and other exotic weapons, but others might see this as further evidence of the occult taint of Theurgy.

Only taking the basic shape of the weapon, the flickering flames can then be wielded using the *Melee* Ability, inflicting two levels of aggravated damage per successful strike against a supernatural creature. Vampires must make a two-Trait *Courage* Test the first time they are struck by such a weapon in a given combat. If they succeed, they can stand to face the threat through the rest of that combat sequence/conflict.

You also gain two *Burning* Bonus Traits for the weapon — you do not gain the normal Bonus Traits that you would from a real item of the same sort. Sorry, no seven-Trait flaming greatsword-style lightsabers. There are no Negative Traits to the weapon, other than it shedding bright light (see *Searing* — it grants one challenge and one free retest on the illumination challenge).

If you need to use your hand for something else, you must deactivate this power. If the weapon is two-handed in nature, then you must deactivate the power to use either hand. You cannot create two one-handed weapons with this power, nor can you have two activations of this power running concurrently, and you cannot pass this weapon on to another person. Otherwise this power ends when dismissed, the wielder is Incapacitated or at the end of an hour or scene, whichever comes first.

ADVANCED

Purifying

The intense heat of God's wrath causes your aura to crack and spark with heat to those who can see it (e.g., vampiric *Auspex*). Any supernatural creature attempting to strike you in hand-to-hand combat (*Brawl*, or *Melee* using weapons with the *Short* Negative Trait) must win or tie a Simple Test or suffer a level of aggravated damage for each successful strike they make. This can cause vampires to take a two-Trait *Courage* Test.

When using the power of *Burning* or *Searing*, you now cause two levels of aggravated damage per successful strike and have a total of three additional *Burning* Physical Traits. You also gain those three Traits when using the power of *Cleansing*, but damage is increased to three levels of aggravated damage.

When using a weapon dedicated through *Branding*, you now gain a total of two additional *Branding* Physical Traits, and you inflict a total of two levels of aggravated damage in addition to the weapon's normal damage. A vampire must now make a three-Trait *Courage* Test when struck by a specific *Branding* weapon for the first time.

RITUALS

Branding Weapon (Basic)

Each of these rituals is distinct and separate, and must be learned individually. Categories of weapons include: swords (short, long and great being separate categories), knives/daggers, clubs/maces, polearms, spears, staves, stakes, axes, etc. Missile weapons

cannot carry the holy flame. Each such ritual costs three Experience Traits to learn (and takes several months to practice before it can be used) and takes about half an hour to perform.

After the ritual has been performed on a specific weapon, it may be activated with *Branding* while you hold it unsheathed. Once you complete the dedication, the weapon remains empowered until your death. Only you may use this special power with that weapon; others may use it as a normal weapon, but only you can activate *Branding* with that specific weapon. If the weapon breaks or is desecrated, it loses its power to carry the flame and must be repaired or rededicated.

VIA MEDICAMENTI, THE WAY OF REMEDY

Theurgists who practice the *Via Medicamenti* are healers, often much appreciated during a dangerous *auto-da-fé*. Theurgists require at least two Traits of the *Medicine* Ability in order to learn this Via. The path does not heal aggravated damage, nor does it heal the dead or undead. Other supernatural creatures may be affected positively by this Via, although Inquisitors still have to deal with the social implications of such actions should they be discovered.

BASIC

Ease Suffering

Your touch can grant relief and strength against all forms of physical pain. The ailment doesn't go away, but the patient feels better for a while. By laying hands on the patient in a restful situation, you can temporarily relieve the penalties for levels of damage they have taken. For each Trait you have in this Via, you can remove one wound level's equivalent of penalty. For example, if you have only one Trait in this Via, you can remove only the penalties for someone being Bruised. If you have four Traits, you can remove the pain from someone who is Incapacitated, allowing them to move about slowly and cautiously, but without pain. Excessive exertion by the patient (such as moving more than one step in a combat turn or initiating a Physical Challenge) instantly negates the effects of this power.

Heal Minor Wounds

Characters under your care heal up to 50% faster than they normally would, as long as they are only Bruised. Minor injuries such as sprains and strains or illnesses such as influenza similarly heal at an accelerated pace under your attention. Secondary infections in open wounds can be eliminated, ensuring a faster recovery from such injuries.

INTERMEDIATE

Heal Major Injuries

As per *Heal Minor Wounds*, yet you can affect injuries at the Wounded level with the right rites, accelerating their healing by 50%. Additionally, with five minutes of attention, you can bring an Incapacitated character back to consciousness and even help her hobble about, though she still suffers the normal penalties from those injuries.

Heal Chronic Condition

You can heal chronic conditions such as asthma or arthritis, but it takes time and effort (hours to weeks). Incapacitated injuries under your care heal up to 50% faster than

normal. Broken bones and severe trauma likewise benefit from your care. Your touch instantly banishes all but the worst pain.

ADVANCED

Hand of the Christ

Your healing gift is such that you can ease the suffering and heal the illnesses in the most severe cases. Deadly conditions such as AIDS and cancer can be cleansed from the body of your patient. Such miracles of healing take considerable time (sometimes months) and tire you greatly; you are at a one-Trait penalty to all actions other than those directly involved for caring for your patient until the treatment is completed. Broken bones and major trauma can be healed in one to three weeks — more serious illnesses and injuries can take three to four weeks, possibly more if the medical situation is complicated (e.g., full-blown AIDS with pneumonia or advanced cancer). The difficulty for activation of this power depends on the severity of the condition, typically 7 to 9 Traits, and the activation challenge must be made successfully every week. Failure of the first activation challenge means the power does not work on the patient in this instance, and God claims her in time. Failure of a challenge after the initial activation extends the required time for treatment by an additional week. If two such challenges are failed in a row, the power fails and the condition continues its due course, beyond your help.

Successes in such severe healing result in the condition being sent into remission, perhaps even being completely cured with time and repeat treatments.

VIA NECROMANTIAE

Contacting or banishing the dead forms the focus of this Way. These rituals resemble, in part, aspects of the *Via Geniorum*, but affect wraiths rather than spirits. As you learn levels of this path, you can also learn the rituals that the specific level mentions.

If you possess a Fetter for the specific wraith that you are summoning or attempting to control, you have two additional Traits against that specific wraith in the case of ties in any challenges while they are affected by your use of this Via.

Difficulties for the use of this Via depend on the Theurgist's skill level. If the Gauntlet in the location in which the ritual is enacted is different from this number, use the higher of the two numbers for the difficulty level. Refer to **Laws of Ascension**, p. 221, for sample Gauntlet ratings.

The required invocation time for a ritual in this Via (unless otherwise mentioned) is 10 minutes for Basic rituals, 20 minutes for Intermediate rituals and 30 minutes for Advanced rituals, whichever aspect of the power is higher. For example, using *Calling*, a Basic Ritual, on a specific wraith would take 20 minutes, as you need Intermediate-level skill to be able to specify your target.

BASIC

Séance

You can open yourself to the nearby departed and get the attention of those with which you are familiar. What they do is up to them, but you can attempt normal Social Challenges against them to sway their viewpoints. You may learn the rituals of

Forbiddance and *Calling.* You have no control over what wraiths may be called. Your difficulty for all Static Challenges using this Via is seven Traits.

Communion

You have a rudimentary capability to communicate with wraiths. You can learn the rituals of *Visualize* and *Warding.* You must still rely on social interaction to persuade the wraiths to grant you favors or perform tasks for you, but at least you can see what you're dealing with. Your difficulty for all Static Challenges using this Via stays at seven Traits.

INTERMEDIATE

Influence

Your talents at piercing the Gauntlet have improved. When you call, something almost always appears. You can now injure troublesome spirits and you can target individual wraiths for summoning. You can learn the rituals of *Dolor* and *Gossip,* and the difficulty for all Static Challenges for this Via is now 6 Traits.

Vision

Powerful in spirit, you are capable of compelling the obeisance of wraiths that you summon. You can visually pierce the Gauntlet. The inhabitants of the Shadowlands who know of you may approach you for favors or advice. You can learn the rituals of *Impression, Compulsion* and *Deny the Veil.* Your difficulty for all Static Challenges using this Via stays at 6 Traits.

ADVANCED

Pierce the Veil

No wraith is beyond the reach of your power. Although you must remain cautious when dealing with particularly powerful wraiths, you can send out messages to those far beyond mortal reach. You may now learn the *Distant Call* ritual. Your difficulty for all Static Challenges using this Via drops now to 5 Traits as you master your craft.

RITUALS

Calling (Basic)

You may summon ghosts to you. Successful activation of the power means that *something* will come in response to your call, unless you are of a high enough Trait level in this Via to specify the wraith you wish to have attend you. They are under no compulsion to remain in your area and may leave as soon as they appear if the situation is dangerous to them.

Forbiddance (Basic)

You can push wraiths out of a given area by activating this ritual and succeeding in a subsequent Social Challenge against the wraiths in the area (which may involve a mass challenge). Success indicates that the wraiths must move away from the immediate area (room, zone — consider 10 feet from the place the ritual was cast to be a reasonable distance). This power lasts until the end of the scene.

Visualize (Basic)

Normally you can't see the wraiths with which you communicate. Invoking this ritual allows you to get a brief glimpse (one turn) at the wraith with which you are dealing. Wraiths often take on unusual appearances, often stylized representations of

their own self-image, and may have been altered either by the wraith itself or by others of its kind — a person you knew in life may look significantly different in death due to the malleability of its Corpus. Casting this ritual takes only a turn.

Warding (Basic)

You can protect an area from wraiths by enacting this ritual. You must delineate the area to be protected with some sort of special material (holy water, incense, etc.) or ceremony. Once the ward is in place, no wraith may enter that area for the following week.

Compulsion (Intermediate)

You may demand service from a wraith you have successfully summoned. You must best the wraith in a Social Challenge and then must have more current Willpower Traits than the wraith. If so, you may give the wraith a single command that it is compelled to obey (until the end of the session). This does not mean that the entity is obeying willingly and may result in angry ghosts if abused. Greater wraiths may also take notice if their minions are being distracted too often.

Deny the Veil (Intermediate)

You can see beyond the curtain of the living world into the Shadowlands, the decaying reflection of reality. This ritual lasts for the remainder of the scene. You can still see the living world, just with the Shadowlands superimposed upon it.

Dolor (Intermediate)

You may inflict spiritual damage on a wraith by succeeding in a Mental Challenge against the target. Success indicates that the spirit takes one level of damage. This ritual takes only a few moments to activate, allowing it to be used once per turn in combat.

Gossip (Intermediate)

You may spread word among the local wraith community and have some assurance that your message will reach its intended destination — your target wraith. The wraiths that carry this message are under no compulsion to keep the message, its nature, origin or destination a secret, and you have no control over which wraiths may hear your words or hear that it was you who spoke them. You may send a short (one sentence) message to a wraith that you have previously summoned or for which you possess a Fetter.

Impression (Intermediate)

This specialized ritual allows you to become a focal point for your target wraith, essentially becoming a Fetter for that wraith for the following week. The wraith probably follows you and tries to protect you, although the exact nature of its reaction remains its business.

Distant Call (Advanced)

With a successful Social Challenge, you can call a wraith from the far realms of existence. Most Theurgists using this Via access only the wraiths of the Shadowlands, yet you may call to those in the Tempest and other such distant realities. There is no guarantee that the wraith will (or can) come to you. Those who have Transcended are unaffected by your power but may hear your call. Those in the Labyrinth may hear of your message, but are most likely so lost as to be unable to return.

VIA ORACULI

Through the *Via Oraculi*, a Theurgist may glimpse the unknown future or see the unseen past. The Theurgist must meditate and pray for some time (depending on how

far forward or back she wishes to see) before checking to see if the power activates as normal. As with other such powers, the level of difficulty and resultant visions must be set and supervised by a Storyteller; any attempt to see more than 100 years into the past or 50 years into the future automatically demands a difficulty of 10 Traits.

The player must specify what information the character desires. Generic information calls for a lower difficulty (six Traits), while specific information requires a higher risk. A Theurgist asking whether his Cenaculum will be attacked later tonight challenges against six Traits, while gaining information on the number or kind of attackers increases the difficulty.

The clarity and duration of the vision will generally be inversely proportional to the distance between the Theurgist and the event in terms of time. An event in the last few hours may have startling clarity and last several minutes, while events a few years in the past may be blurred and last only moments. Additionally, the future remains ever mutable, and what may be seen in the here and now may be different when the time actually arrives, possibly dependant on the actions taken by the Theurgist in reaction to his visions.

Storytellers: As with any of the divinatory powers given in this book (and others), handling visions of the future is inherently difficult given the nature of the game. Keep track of the visions that you hand out. Remember that you don't have to hand out every detail to the player who uses this Via. God moves in mysterious ways, and it's useful for you to do so also. Being vague with visions gives you plenty of "fudge factor" later should you need it to keep your story's consistency. Visions do not come attached with footnotes.

One Trait	You can see up to one month into the past or two weeks into the future. You must pray and meditate for at least 10 minutes.
Two Traits	You can see up to 1 year into the past or six months into the future. You must pray and meditate for at least half an hour.
Three Traits	You can see up to 10 years into the past or five years into the future. You must pray and meditate for at least one hour.
Four Traits	You can see up to 100 years into the past or 50 years into the future. You must pray and meditate for at least six hours.
Five Traits	You can see any point in the past or up to 1,000 years into the future. You must pray and meditate for at least one day.

STIGMAS AND AGENDAS

STIGMAS

As fearsome as their philosophy and practices make them, perhaps what truly sets the Dauntain apart as objects of fear and loathing in fae society are their insidious powers known as Stigmas. Not all Dauntain develop them, but those that do become true terrors to their faerie foes, able to channel their innate Banality to perform many frightening effects. While a number of "common" Stigmas are provided as examples, the Storyteller (and player, if the Dauntain is player-controlled) are encouraged to create Stigmas customized to the particular Dauntain's history, personality and style; they should be terrifying flourishes, not just a means of stacking effects onto a character.

Regardless of their origin, all Stigmas are governed by a basic set of rules:

•A Dauntain must have at least seven *permanent* Banality Traits before she can even hope to take a Stigma; any less and Banality hasn't sufficiently taken root in her spirit. Dauntain may only take Stigmas with explicit Storyteller permission, and in no event may any player-controlled Dauntain start with more than one Stigma. Finally, once play begins, Stigmas cannot be purchased simply with Experience Traits (although a Storyteller may demand some Experience be spent on top of any other requirements he feels are appropriate). They can only be gained if the Storyteller feels the character's personal storyline offers compelling reasons why the character should develop a new Stigma in addition to her regular powers.

• Whenever a Dauntain gains a new Stigma, whatever the source, she gains a permanent Banality Trait as well. (This is not doubled for sidhe characters turned Dauntain.) Thus, few Dauntain would ever seek to develop more than one or two Stigmas at most, for while they offer great power, they hasten the Dauntain's own Undoing as well. Should this permanent Banality ever be removed somehow — unlikely, but theoretically possible — the Stigma is lost with it.

• Stigmas strengthen a Dauntain's ties to Banality. For each Stigma he possesses, he is considered one Trait up to resist all *Kenning* tests or similar efforts to identify him as one of the fae. Dauntain with Stigmas are simply more mundane, and thus harder to detect, until they strike.

•Except where otherwise noted, activating a Stigma is a "free" action — the Dauntain may attack, cast cantrips or perform any other action she likes in the same turn she uses a Stigma, without penalty. Each Stigma may only be activated once per turn, however, again except as noted.

Conversion

This terrifying Stigma allows the Dauntain to convert a changeling's Glamour directly to Banality. To invoke this Stigma, the Dauntain makes a number of Simple Tests equal to his permanent Banality, minus the target's permanent Glamour (minimum one test). Thus if a Dauntain with nine permanent Banality is battling a changeling with six permanent Glamour, three tests are made. For each test the Dauntain wins, the fae must convert one temporary Glamour Trait to a Trait of temporary Banality. In the event of a tie, the highest permanent relevant rating wins. Each use of this Stigma earns the Dauntain one temporary Banality Trait.

Disbelief

A Dauntain with this power can cripple chimera and shrug off cantrips with little more than a cold glare. He need not even be consciously aware of what he's destroying, merely enter the area near the Glamour in question. As soon as he encounters any changelings or chimera, the Dauntain may immediately make a test of his permanent Banality versus the permanent Glamour of each nearby fae or chimera. Success means that the Dauntain receives an automatic retest on any cantrips cast against him by any fae he defeats, and furthermore he is two Traits up to defend against any Wyrd cantrips used against him by fae he's defeated with this Stigma. In the case of chimera, all defeated chimera suffer one level of chimerical damage.

The Dauntain may further augment this effect by spending a Willpower Trait, provided that he is aware of the cantrips or chimera around him and actively invokes his disbelief against them. Willpower spent in this fashion allows for an additional test against the cantrip caster or chimera in question.

Erasure

Even the slightest touch of a Dauntain with this Stigma can prove debilitating to all creatures of Glamour. This functions much the same as Ravaging but is even more destructive since the Dauntain doesn't need to know anything about his target beforehand. The Dauntain must touch the target to use this Stigma, which requires a Physical Challenge against resisting targets; if successful, the *Erasure* begins. For each Mental Trait the Dauntain spends, the target loses one Glamour Trait, up to a maximum number equal to half the Dauntain's permanent Banality (round down). A Storyteller may also be called in to adjudicate the effects of a Dauntain using this power to drain the Glamour from a place or thing. Each use of this Stigma either costs one Glamour Trait or adds one temporary Banality Trait.

Hatred

The Dauntain's hatred of the enchanted world and its inhabitants is now so strong that he may harm them with it directly. By focusing his hatred on a particular target and making a Mental Challenge, he can remove one of his target's Glamour Traits with success. Doing so requires the Dauntain's full attention for the entire turn, and cannot be performed more than once per turn.

Herd Mentality

By dispersing his hatred and disbelief into the surrounding area, the Dauntain may effectively call any Autumn People or even other Dauntain in the area to him. Autumn People do not know exactly why they are drawn to the Dauntain's location but instinctively seek him out and are naturally inclined treat him favorably when they meet. Other Dauntain sense immediately that one of their own needs them, and may make any appropriate preparations before they arrive. Since this Stigma may often require the assistance of Narrators to effectively portray, it may not be selected without Storyteller permission, and it is fully within the Storyteller's rights to declare that no appropriate targets are within range, especially if the Dauntain is in an area of high Glamour (or fails to give the Storyteller enough advance notice). If other Autumn People or Dauntain are already in the game, a Narrator should immediately alert them to this Stigma's usage and the Dauntain's description and general location.

Iron Ward

The Dauntain's denial of the world of the Kithain has increased to the point where even cold iron, traditionally anathema to all things fae, does not harm him as it once did. He suffers no discomfort (nor gains Banality) from mere contact with cold iron. Every time the Dauntain receives a wound from cold iron, he may make a Simple Test for each level of damage taken — on a win or a tie, that level is converted to regular damage of its type. Thus if a Dauntain with this Stigma is hit with a cold iron sword that inflicts two levels of aggravated damage, he may make two Simple Tests, and for each one that he wins or ties one level of damage is converted from aggravated to lethal. Note that the injury is not prevented in any way, merely reduced to a less serious form, and the Dauntain's fae soul is as destroyed as any of their victims' if they are slain with cold iron.

Numb

Dauntain with this Stigma do not consciously invoke it. Rather, it activates almost like a protective shield, warding off the powerful emotions the Dauntain himself cannot handle. Upon meeting the Dauntain, any fae character must make a

test of her Glamour against the Dauntain's Banality. Should they fail, the changeling automatically loses one Willpower Trait for that evening and is one Trait down on all Social Tests related to displaying strong emotions. Furthermore, he immediately gains a temporary Banality Trait. This power is particularly common in Nihilist Dauntain.

Ravage

This Stigma is outwardly like normal Ravaging, except that the Dauntain may Ravage *anything* with Glamour in it: Kithain, chimera, mortals, Treasures, artwork, freeholds, etc. The Dauntain uses the normal system for Ravaging (see **The Shining Host**, p. 193); Kithain and mortals defend themselves as usual, while a Storyteller provides difficulty levels for robbing Glamour from sentient chimera or inanimate objects, as well as the effects of wresting the Glamour from such sources if the Dauntain succeeds. The rewards are otherwise identical to Ravaging in every way.

Shunt

Dauntain with this talent may temporarily "short circuit" a changeling's fae mien, forcing her to revert to her mortal Seeming. With little more than a touch (Physical Challenge if the target resists) and the expenditure of a temporary Banality Trait, the Dauntain may immediately force the targeted Kithain to make a test of her permanent Glamour vs. the Dauntain's permanent Banality. If the Dauntain wins, the fae immediately reverts to her mortal Seeming, and cannot use cantrips, Wyrd Birthrights or otherwise interact with the chimerical world, though she can spend a Willpower Trait to retain her memory of it (and who the Dauntain is) for one scene. The target may not attempt to retake her fae form until the end of the scene, at which time she must spend a Glamour Trait or win a test of her permanent Glamour vs. her permanent Banality to reassume her fae Seeming. Failure means she is stuck in her mortal Seeming and immediately begins to forget the enchanted world as per her rating on the Mists chart. A fae may be targeted by this ability only once per scene.

AGENDAS

Although most are loath to think it as such, many Dauntain employ a brand of magic that is uniquely their own, which vaguely resembles Kithain cantrips but instead focuses the Dauntain's power to spread boredom and Banality in the world. These powers, called Agendas, are identical to Kithain Arts in terms of the amount of Experience Traits required to purchase them and in general how they are used, with a few prominent exceptions and additions:

• Agenda cantrips do not use Bunks — such silly requirements are anathema to the Dauntain. Instead, the Dauntain must pay a Glamour Trait for each Agenda cantrip she wishes to cast (in addition to any other costs the cantrip might have). If the Dauntain is out of Glamour, her Agendas do not function until she has Glamour to spend.

• Each time a Dauntain uses an Agenda, it costs one Trait of temporary Banality (in addition to any Banality costs it might have). By allowing magic — even boring magic — into her life, the Dauntain is recognizing the enchanted world, which eats away at her Banality a little. Such spending can *never* lower a Dauntain's permanent Banality, however; if she is out of temporary Banality, she simply cannot use her Agendas until some level of mediocrity is restored (i.e., temporary Banality is regained).

• Agenda cantrips are otherwise handled exactly like their Art counterparts, including all the requisite tests and retests. See **The Shining Host**, p. 153, for complete rules on casting cantrips.

• Before anyone gets any funny ideas, *only* Dauntain and Autumn Fae may learn Agendas. Even regular Kithain who have high permanent Banality are still assumed to be dedicated to the cause of Glamour and faerie life, and so cannot grasp the banal mindset necessary to learn the Agendas. Only by utterly turning their back on all things of Glamour or pursuing the dark path of Banality — becoming an Autumn Fae or Dauntain — can they begin to master the principles of the Agendas. Should a Dauntain or Autumn Fae somehow ever redeem herself and give up her errant ways, all levels of Agendas are lost immediately, though kind Storytellers may allow them to be exchanged for equivalent levels of Arts given time spent with a suitable mentor.

BURNOUT

The World of Darkness is a cold place, where paranoia and hatred all too often take hold where love and tolerance ought to be. Dauntain with this Agenda are adept at dulling and refocusing the emotions of others around them, quashing those passions they dislike and replacing them with others that will further the cause of Banality.

Type of Challenge: Social (retest with *Empathy*)

Art Note: Except where otherwise noted, all emotional or intellectual changes invoked by this Agenda strike the target as perfectly natural, at least at the time, and as such they will naturally resist any attempts to convince them that they ever felt differently. They may even ridicule their former state, seeing it as "melodramatic" or "unrealistic" compared to their new feelings.

Basic

Mindblock: A Dauntain with this aggravating power can inflict a temporary but highly effective mental block on his target, rendering her unable to think about one *specific* topic of the Dauntain's choice for 15 minutes. For example, a guard might be made to avoid thinking about where he's supposed to be stationed, or a sluagh could be made to forget about eavesdropping on the Dauntain's conversation. A successful cantrip test allows the Dauntain to inform the unfortunate target of her new difficulty, which she must roleplay to the best of her ability. Note that while it may make some Abilities more difficult to use, this cantrip doesn't allow the user to block an entire range of one Ability in a target, only one specific use of it. A target made to forget how to use her sword can still wield other weapons with her *Melee* Ability just fine, and a musician whose *Performance* skill with the guitar has been blocked might still be able to sing or read music. If this loss is brought to her attention, the target is perplexed but still unable to perform the blocked action or think about the blocked subject.

Type: Chimerical

Heartbind: A horrifying power to behold, *Heartbind* renders the target unable to feel one positive emotion — joy, love, friendship, humor, loyalty, compassion, etc. — of the caster's choice for 30 minutes. During that time, hot passions run utterly cold, and attempts to stir the targeted emotion fail miserably. From the target's point of view, the emotion seems distant and distasteful, and the idea that he once demonstrated it in any degree seems shameful and repulsive to him. This power may even suppress a target's *True Love* or *Immortal Passion*, although attempts to affect such powerful

emotions grant the target an automatic retest to shake off this power's effects in addition to any other defenses he might have. At the end of the duration, the emotion flows back into the target normally, but an abandoned friend or spurned lover might not be so quick to forgive what happened while it was gone....

Type: Chimerical

Intermediate

Obsession: This power instills the target with an obsessive desire to perform one dull activity in as much excruciating detail as possible, and until that task is completed he has trouble responding to any outside stimuli short of direct threats to life and limb. All actions outside of those taken to fulfill the obsession are at a one-Trait penalty, and the target will seek to get away from distractions as quickly as possible. As soon as the task is complete, the target returns to normal, although he thinks nothing odd of his behavior unless it is brought to his attention by others. This task must be one that can reasonably be completed in a scene or hour (whichever comes first) at most, and must be as routine and dull as possible. Note that the victim need not rush through the necessary steps of the activity; indeed, the target should perform them with as much deliberation as possible, in order to ensure that everything turns out perfectly. This power is often invoked by the caster incessantly badgering the target about the task in question ("Don't forget to defrost the refrigerator! Have you defrosted the refrigerator yet? When are you going to defrost the refrigerator?").

Type: Chimerical

Acquisition: A target hit with this power is immediately filled with the overpowering desire to possess as many samples of one type of thoroughly mundane object as he can get his hands on. If he actually manages to collect all the items in the area, he begins busily sorting his collection into precise types and categories. Should this be finished, he begins showing off his collection and happily extolling its virtues to everyone around him for the rest of the power's duration. This power lasts for a number of hours equal to the Dauntain's permanent Banality rating minus the target's permanent Glamour (maximum one session, minimum one hour). During that time, the target must spend a Willpower Trait to focus on anything other than collecting the chosen items. Each Willpower Trait spent this way allows for 10 minutes of peace, but after that time the target resumes hunting for the objects he craves. The Dauntain must specify the type of item to be sought after as part of the casting, and the target must be able to understand what the caster means or the cantrip fails. Note the requirement of a "mundane" item — "pencils" or "shoelaces" are fine, but asking a target to collect things like "antique banjos" or "human livers" causes the Agenda to fail automatically. Kindly players should choose something that can actually be obtained around the play area. (If you're going to divert the target's attention for the better part of an evening, at least give them something to do!)

Type: Chimerical

Advanced

Geek Out: Targets stung by this insidious power not only give up one treasured pastime, duty or relationship for the duration of a game session, but actively replace it with a new, dull hobby. ("Do you guys wanna come over and play some of my new Black Dog games? I just got Zombie: The Lurching' — it's got all kinds of *kewl powerz!*") The target will attempt to indulge/show off her new hobby as often as possible, and regular social interaction becomes so difficult for the new enthusiast that

233

she is considered two Traits down on all noncantrip Social Challenges, even those relating to her new passion, as her personality is so warped that she alienates others who would normally be sympathetic to her hobby. Furthermore, the target gains the Negative Traits *Dull* and *Obnoxious* for the duration of the cantrip's use. Fair targets for this power range from a particular duty (guarding a freehold, leading a motley, etc.), to a favorite hobby or even a personal relationship such as a friend or a lover. At the Storyteller's discretion, this might even include an entire Ability, provided it can be viewed as a hobby or duty — by this logic the Dauntain might be able to cause a talented fencer to give up his *Melee* skill for a night, for example, or maybe cause a scholar to lose interest in *Occult* or *Gremayre*, but it's hard to see Abilities such as *Dodge* or *Stealth* the same way.

Type: Chimerical

OPTIONAL RULE: BANAL BUNKS

If the Storyteller permits it, she may allow Dauntain characters to perform "banal Bunks" — also called Routines — for their Agendas, much as normal Kithain do regular Bunks when casting cantrips. Naturally, the only requirement for Routines is that the actions performed must always be exhaustingly mundane: reciting pages of the phone book, meticulously picking bits of fuzz out of the carpet, filling out stacks of forms, etc. These Routines are assigned the normal amount of Traits as a regular Bunk would be, based on either the criteria the Storyteller determines (as in **The Shining Host**) or according to the optional Jester's Rules system presented in **The Shining Host Player's Guide**, p. **202**, if the Storyteller uses that optional rule. It should be noted that while they add a new dimension to playing a Dauntain, it is recommended that Routines be used only for player characters and/or in games that feature Dauntain as their central characters (and what kind of game are you playing?!). Agendas are already quite powerful on their own, and allowing Dauntain to make them even more so may easily threaten game balance in mixed settings.

Note that unless the Storyteller uses this optional rule, Dauntain *cannot* perform Bunks or Routines of any kind for their Arts or Agendas — they must use their raw Traits when resolving their cantrip challenges. Such is the price of serving empty Banality.

STULTIFY

All too often the minds of others are filled with useless distractions and idle daydreams that keep them from becoming fully productive members of society. A Dauntain with this Agenda can change all that, sweeping aside such inefficient notions as creativity and human decency and ensuring that a target's attention remains absolutely focused on the task at hand.

Type of Challenge: Mental (retest with *Leadership*)

Basic

Rosetint: The first step toward winning others over to the cause of Order is to show them the best parts of what they once considered to be nothing more than dull routine. At the caster's direction, the target examines one topic he once despised and immediately sees the "good" in it. The target will speak favorably about the topic at

the slightest provocation and actively resists attempts to discourage or even just badmouth anything related to it ("Y'know, Jerry Springer isn't a bad guy — he provides a forum for the voiceless...."). He need not drop what he's doing to indulge his new favorite subject, but if faced with nothing else particularly pressing to do, he'll bring it up in conversation whenever possible. While little more than a minor (if irritating) effect on its own, *Rosetint* is more commonly used to "prime" a target for further uses of this Agenda; all attempts to use other *Stultify* cantrips on a target under the effects of *Rosetint* are considered two Traits up. This cantrip lasts for 30 minutes.

Type: Chimerical

Dull Impulse: A subject under the effects of this cantrip is compelled to perform a harmless but hopelessly mundane task repeatedly for 15 minutes. The caster may specify a task in particular, or she may simply leave the subject to his own devices, in which case he performs the first such task that comes to mind. Sweeping floors, organizing bookshelves, filing papers and cleaning windows are all common tasks, although any similar mind-numbing labor works just as well. Targets may defend themselves if attacked, but they cannot act offensively and return immediately to their task as soon as the danger passes. They retain their regular intelligence (and thus will not place themselves in danger for their task, such as sweeping the street in front of an oncoming bus), but enter a semi-dazed state and respond sluggishly at best to attempts at conversation or actions other than their impulse, gaining the Negative Traits *Predictable* and *Oblivious*. They resist efforts to physically prevent them from fulfilling their task with a corresponding amount of force.

Type: Chimerical

Intermediate

Proselytize: This cantrip is identical to *Dull Impulse*, with the addition that the target not only performs the action the caster desires, but actively attempts to recruit others to participate as well. If the caster remains in the area, she is considered one Trait up on all tests (including cantrips) for each additional person recruited in this fashion, up to a maximum of five Traits. Furthermore, the Dauntain gains a temporary Banality Trait for each recruit, up to her normal maximum. Finally, by spending a Willpower Trait during casting, the caster may attempt to compel the target to follow certain ideas or loyalties rather than just perform set physical activities, although if the cantrip fails the Willpower Trait is still considered spent.

Type: Chimerical

Procedural Addiction: Dauntain with this power can force a target to examine one specific action in such detail that he forgets what he's doing in favor of examining how it is done. The target will pick apart the action even as he performs it, greatly increasing the time required to finish it. In game terms, for the rest of the session the time it takes the target to perform the action specified by the Dauntain is doubled, and he must carefully recite every step aloud as he performs it. Note that while this cantrip could technically be used to force a target to analyze such actions as "swing a sword," such attempts seldom do much to curb a target's fighting capabilities beyond perhaps a moment of surprise (though trying to use an attack specified by this cantrip puts the target at half normal Traits, round up, due to the increased time it takes to perform it). This cantrip is better used on less direct actions. Imagine the ire of the sidhe ruler forced to carefully consider each step of making a pronouncement, a satyr developing

"performance anxiety" or the sheer profanity spawned by a nocker when even turning a wrench has been put under the microscope!

Type: Chimerical

Advanced

Micromanagement: This fearsome cantrip is effectively identical to *Procedural Addiction*, except that the target creates procedures for *every* action he performs, no matter how minor. Furthermore, he attempts to record these procedures and teach them to others whenever possible, and he insists that others do things his way. The target gains the Negative Traits *Predictable* and *Dull*, and most likely has a very hard time getting even the most minor things done due to the sheer amount of self-imposed "red tape" that surrounds him. A target under the influence of this cantrip gains one temporary Banality Trait per hour, and as a result the sidhe fear this cantrip greatly. This power lasts for one night/session.

Type: Chimerical

WEBCRAFT

Just as people naturally prefer the security of the familiar status quo to the uncertainty of the new and the different, so too can the Dauntain draw on the forces of stasis and solidarity to reinforce that which she holds dear, whether it's as simple as a treasured possession or as complex as a philosophy she follows. Those few Prodigal shapechangers who've witnessed this Agenda's use claim it draws on the power of an entity known as "the Weaver," who maintains the conformity of the universe. Easily the least common of Agendas, it is all the more powerful for its rarity.

Type of Challenge: Mental (retest with *Science*)

Basic

Weave Web: By concentrating on an object and spending a Mental Trait, the Dauntain is able to reinforce the mundanity inside it, making it stronger and more durable. With success, the object inflicts an additional health level of damage (if it is a weapon), or gains an additional health level to resist damage (if not) — crushing mundanity, indeed! This power can be used on bullets or arrows, but each must be reinforced separately. Activating *Weave Web* requires the Dauntain's entire attention for a full turn. This power cannot be used on the same object more than once per scene, and can only be used on objects without much beauty or originality to them; a gorgeous hand-crafted sword with a decorative hilt cannot be augmented this way, but a mass-produced replica might be. A Dauntain must be able to see the item to use this power. This power lasts for one scene or one hour, whichever ends first. Note: This Agenda does *not* work on items of cold iron; their innate magic resistance defeats even such banal powers as this.

Type: Wyrd

Overwhelming Wincing: A Dauntain with this power is capable of causing others actual physical pain with the power of her Banality, which manifests in the form of throbbing headaches for those around them. This cantrip costs one Mental Trait and lasts for one scene. Although everyone within three paces feels this power's effects descriptively (and should roleplay accordingly), by spending a Banality Trait the Dauntain may choose to focus the power on one target in particular — if she can best that target in a Mental Challenge, the target is wracked by a debilitating migraine. Such

sufferers take a level of chimerical damage and are at a one-Trait penalty to all actions for the next 10 minutes, as they can do little else except cringe in pain. The Dauntain may attempt to target several individuals with this power at once; each additional target requires another Banality Trait and is handled according to regular mob scene rules.

Type: Chimerical

Intermediate

Warp Will: To use this cantrip, the Dauntain must actually perform some highly mundane action, then spend a Banality Trait. Everyone within 10 paces must immediately make a test of their permanent Glamour or Willpower (whichever is higher) against the Dauntain's permanent Banality. Failure means that the target immediately loses one Trait of Glamour or Willpower (as specified by the Dauntain during the casting), as the Dauntain's mundanity wears away their spirits. This cantrip may only be used on a target once per session.

Type: Chimerical

Wend Your Way: By using his Banality to form a protective shield around himself, the Dauntain can overcomplicate one action to such a degree that others around him lose any hope of deciphering what he's doing and wander off to find more interesting things to do (such as watching paint dry). The Dauntain receives an automatic retest on any challenges to go unnoticed by others around him. Those who wish to initiate a challenge related to the caster's activity (or interrupting it) must first make a Mental Challenge — failure means they cannot even attempt the challenge, as the boredom around the Dauntain robs them of the desire to act. This power costs one Banality Trait, and lasts for one scene or until the Dauntain chooses to stop the action in question.

Type: Chimerical

Advanced

Cry "Woof": With this bizarre but extremely dangerous power, the Dauntain can summon a Weaver spirit to aid him in restoring stasis and order to a location. The spirit is not a mindless servant, though, and will not tolerate being treated as such. Some common spirits summoned by this power are pattern spiders or Paradox spirits of the *Mind* Sphere (see **Laws of the Wild** or **Laws of Ascension** for details on such spirits), though what actually appears depends on the Storyteller and the needs of the story itself. The Weaver-spirit has the same number of health levels as regular characters and may be harmed by physical weapons if it is fully materialized (or by chimerical weapons if it maintains a spirit form). Cantrips such as *Holly Strike* harm such spirits normally. Storytellers may feel free to give the spirit a number of Arts or Agendas (related to maintaining order and stability) to simulate its magical powers, and should assume it has extremely high levels of Banality. When this power is invoked, the Dauntain must immediately make a Simple Test; on a win or a tie, the spirit is receptive to his motives and will generally act as he desires, but on a loss the spirit rampages through the area, under no one's control, and may even attack the Dauntain.

Type: Chimerical or Wyrd (depending on the spirit and what it does)

BENANDANTI RITUALS

With special training and rituals passed down through the ages, those born with a caul may learn the Benandanti way of seeing into and even traveling in the Shadowlands. While extremely risky, many are willing to take the chance in hope of gaining knowledge. Since the Benandanti pass their knowledge through families (especially children born with cauls), any Benandanti character can possess these rituals.

UNHOODING

This ritual marks the beginning of a Benandante's life. Usually the ritual is performed by a blood relative of a child born with a caul, although a *sapienza* (an older, more experienced Benandante) may do so. The caul is removed and special magics worked on it before it dries. Once the *Unhooding* is successfully performed, the caul is used as the focus for *Ekstasis*.

An *Unhooding* takes several hours to perform once the caul is removed. While of little use during the game, it is necessary to create new Benandanti. Without *Unhooding*, a child with a caul cannot use the powers of the Benandanti. Once the ritual is performed, the effects are permanent.

EYELIDDING

By passing your caul in front of your face, you can see into the Shadowlands. It costs only one Willpower Trait, and takes a single turn. After performing *Eyelidding*, you can see into the Underworld from your position, including any wraiths present. You cannot interact with the Underworld, only look at it. The effect lasts for one scene.

EKSTASIS

Those who would learn *Ekstasis* must first be well trained in the supernatural — at least two Traits of *Occult* is necessary to begin learning this ritual. You find a quiet spot between dusk and dawn, and enter a trance, using your caul as a focus. This is followed with a Static Mental Challenge at eight Traits. With success, your spirit enters the Shadowlands while your body remains behind.

Once in the Underworld, you may travel wherever you like (including to the Labyrinth and the Tempest, if you're bold enough) and interact with wraiths. You are not actually reformed in plasm, so certain wraithly powers like *Moliate* or *Usury* do not work on you, nor do powers of the living that affect wraiths (such as *Via Necromantiae* or vampiric *Necromancy*). For all intents and purposes, you are a living spirit in the Deadlands. As the ties between the lands of the dead and living are strongest at night, you must exit before dawn. If daylight arrives at the location of your body, you must find another exit if you wish to leave, or wait until night returns (and a lot can happen between now and then).

On arriving in the Shadowlands, you must make a Static Mental Challenge (difficulty is the Shroud rating) to orient yourself. To leave, you must return to your point of origin and make the same challenge. Failure on either challenge leaves you stranded — your exit is closed to you, or you start wandering down the wrong Byway.

FORGING THE FENNEL SWORD

A fennel sword is a powerful talisman that the Benandanti use in the Underworld. Built during *Ekstasis*, fennel swords can strike and even injure wraiths, traveling with their bearers in spirit form.

Creating a fennel sword requires very specific components and procedures. First, gather the fennel, which was planted in the soil of a known wraith haunt and seeded with your caul. The fennel must be gathered on the dawn on midsummer, wrapped in the caul, and kept cold and away from sunlight. You meditate for the entire day, then return to the haunt that night. The spirit of a deceased Benandante is summoned as a guide (by a variety of means), and you enter *Ekstasis* while holding the fennel. Now in the Shadowlands, you take the caul and fennel that have followed you and go with your spirit guide to a special forge. The sword must be built with a combination of the spirit fennel and *ferro spettrale* (a spirit-iron kept at the forge). You must answer a series of questions from the guide regarding the Shadowlands and your beliefs. Failing is not recommended — the guide strips the cauls from such failures, stranding them in the Underworld. Success allows the forging to proceed.

Forging the sword is a task that requires a series of Static Physical Challenges at six Traits, retesting with an appropriate Ability (such as *Crafts*). Five successful challenges are necessary to finish the sword; failure on any challenge means the sword is flawed and useless, and you must start over (including growing new fennel). When the sword is finished, it must be named and plunged into a Nihil to cool; this empowers it for a year. Each month on the new moon after the first year, the sword must be again plunged into a Nihil to keep its powers or it must be reforged. Once the spirit weapon is built, many Benandanti forge a second, physical weapon (which requires the same challenges as for the spirit blade). The physical weapon becomes bound with the spirit one, and both are equally powerful.

A fennel sword has the following abilities:

Bonus Traits: 3

Negative Trait: Fragile

Concealability: Trench coat

Fennel swords inflict aggravated damage against Oblivion-tainted targets when used in the Underworld. Swinging the sword in the real world does nothing; you must be in *Ekstasis*. The physical sword can banish wraiths and spectres (make a Social Challenge against the target; success forces the target wraith or spectre to leave the room). These swords are mystically tied to their creators; should your sword be destroyed, you lose a permanent Willpower Trait. If the sword's name is known, its name may be used in lieu of any other special components in rituals against you. Fennel swords are not built for combat in the real world. Should you strike a physical person or object, he must immediately make a Simple Test; on a tie or failure, the sword shatters.

Jeremy shivered in his Polarfleece top, more from fear than cold. Beside him, seemingly implacable, sat Stephen. His eyes flickered across the loading dock from their hiding place in the alley, his face betraying no emotion. Jeremy had never seen him like this. When Stephen used to race cross-country, he was focused, but this intensity frightened him. Jeremy shivered again, and Stephen turned, his features relaxing somewhat.

"Are you cold? I brought coffee in the thermos."

"No thanks," Jeremy murmured. "Just nervous, I guess."

Stephen nodded, his mouth trying to fight a smile. "I know the feeling."

"I still wish you wouldn't do this, not after what you told me."

"Jer, we went over this. I don't like it either, but it's a risk I'm willing to take for Jenny."

Jeremy was about to answer when there was a sound of a car cutting its engine and a door opening. Stephen's hand cut off any other words from his brother, and he slid off his perch like a panther. Jeremy slid behind him with considerably less grace, and his brother shot a quick glare behind him. He started to follow Stephen out, but Stephen turned and pushed him back into the alley. "Jeremy, I want you stay here. This guy is dangerous." Without waiting to see if Jeremy had listened, Stephen walked out to his meeting.

Jeremy wasn't sure what to expect. Yeah, Stephen had said this guy was a vampire, but it was hard to tell. He was pale, yeah, but not white-white like the Goth kids. He wore an expensive-looking suit, with long chestnut hair neatly dressed in a colonial-style ponytail. They were too far away for Jeremy to hear the conversation in detail, just rising and falling voices. He reached for the thermos, thinking that coffee would be a good idea after all.

He heard the sound of a car door opening, but not fully closing. Then sounds scrapings, of shoes on grit and the sound of metal whispering from its hiding place. He turned behind him, and instinct launched him out of the alley, screaming, as three figures in dark clothing came charging toward him, shouting, "Deus vult, traditor!"

In front of him, Stephen and the vampire turned, and Stephen's eyes were wide with horror—

• • •

Jeremy sat in the back of the police cruiser, clenching Stephen's Connemara cross so tightly that it was starting to dig into his palm. Around him, police radios spat noisy bursts of chatter and the lights flashed silent beacons into the night. The blood on his Polarfleece top – Stephen's blood – was drying into stiff patches. He heard the sound of a heavy zipper closing, and could not repress his shudder. A coroner's bag being zipped – and Speedy was inside it. The cops had not come in time, Stephen was dead, and the three bastards who had surprised him in the alley were long gone.

He heard footsteps, and the local sheriff bent over to look at him, laying a false-fatherly hand on his shoulder. "Son, we need to ask you some questions...."

CHAPTER SIX: RULES, SYSTEMS AND DRAMA

Rules are an integral part of any game. They define what characters can and cannot do. Only when confrontation occurs are rules necessary to govern those situations. Still, the primary focus of this game is to tell a good story.

CHALLENGES

There comes a time when two or more players come into a conflict that cannot be resolved through roleplaying alone. The system detailed in this chapter allows for the resolution of conflicts efficiently and quickly. This sort of face-off is called a challenge, and it makes for a very simple system of conflict resolution. In most cases, a Narrator does not even need to be present when a challenge is played.

Roleplaying does not necessarily have to end when a challenge begins. In fact, roleplaying becomes more important than ever if players intend to enjoy a confrontation and avoid disputes. Experienced players can integrate a challenge into their roleplaying so seamlessly that outsiders don't even know that anything unusual is going on. At the players' option, special hand signals can be used to indicate when certain Traits and powers are being employed.

In order for this system to work, players need to work together. They have to educate each other on the rules and agree on what Traits can be used in a challenge. Compromise and cooperation are the bywords of the game. Arguments over whether or not a particular Trait bid is appropriate wreck both the momentum and the mood of a game.

USING TRAITS

Before you can begin to learn how challenges work, you must first understand what defines a character's capabilities. A character is created by choosing a number of adjectives that describe and define that person as an individual. These adjectives are called Traits, and they are described fully in Chapter Four. These Traits are used to declare challenges against other characters or against static forces represented by a Narrator.

INITIAL BID

A challenge begins with a player "bidding" one of her Traits against her opponent. At the same time, she must declare what the conditions of the challenge are — firing a gun, attacking with a knife, using Numinae or the like. The defender must then decide how she will respond. She can either relent immediately or bid one of her own Traits in response.

When players bid Traits against one another, they may use only Traits that could sensibly be used in that situation. Essentially, this restriction means that a player can usually use only those Traits from the same category as her opponent's Traits. Most challenges are categorized as Physical, Social or Mental, and all Traits used in a challenge must be from the same category. Experienced players may offer each other more creative leeway, but only by mutual agreement.

If the defender relents, she loses the challenge automatically. For example, if she were being attacked, she would suffer a wound. If she matches the challenger's bid, the two immediately go to a test. Those Traits bid are put at risk, as the loser of the test not only loses the challenge, but also the Trait she bid for the rest of the evening.

TESTING

Once both parties involved in a challenge have bid a Trait, they engage in a test immediately. The test itself is not what you may think — the outcome is random, but no cards or dice are used. The two players face off against one another by playing Rock-Paper-Scissors.

If you lose the test, you lose the Trait you bid for the duration of the session (usually the rest of the evening). Essentially, you have lost some confidence in your own capabilities and can't call on them for a while. You can no longer use that Trait effectively, at least until you regain confidence in your Traits.

The test works like the moment in poker when the cards are turned over and the winner is declared. The test produces one of two possible outcomes — either one player is the victor, or the result is a tie.

In the case of a tie, the players must then reveal the number of Traits that they currently have available in the category used (Physical, Social or Mental). The player with the least number of Traits loses the test and therefore loses the challenge. Note that the number of Traits you've lost in previous challenges, or lost for any other reason, reduces the maximum number of Traits you can bid in ties. You may lie about the number of Traits you possess, but only by declaring fewer Traits than you actually have — you may never say that you have more Traits than you actually do. Doing so allows you to keep the actual number of Traits you possess a secret, although doing so may be risky. The challenger is always the first to declare his number of Traits. If both players declare the same number of Traits, then the challenge is a draw, and both players lose the Traits they bid.

Example of Play: *Joe Shabbadoo, a stage magician, has been cornered by Fitz, the vampire he's been tracking. Fitz's nails sprout wolflike talons, and Joe knows card tricks won't save him now. Fitz takes a savage swipe at him ("I'll Ferociously rip your guts out!"), and Joe responds by swinging a handy steel pipe ("Only if you want a Brutal smack upside your head!"). They go to a test, and both shoot Scissors. As the challenger, Fitz reveals his Traits*

first — he has seven. Joe then shows his — nine. The test goes to Joe, and the vampire, now slightly confused by the head-bashing, realizes this mere mortal isn't so "mere."

ROCK-PAPER-SCISSORS

What we mean by Rock-Paper-Scissors is the following: You and another person face off, and, on the count of three, you show one of three hand gestures. "Rock" is a basic fist. "Paper" is just a flat hand. "Scissors" is represented by sticking out two fingers. You then compare the two gestures to determine the winner. Rock crushes Scissors. Scissors cuts Paper. Paper covers Rock. Identical signs indicate a tie. Certain advanced powers allow some characters to use gestures other than Rock, Paper and Scissors. Before players can use the gestures in a test, however, they must explain what they are and how they are used.

ADJUDICATION

If you have question about the rules or the conditions of a challenge, you need to find a Narrator to make a judgment. Try to remain in character while you look for a Narrator. Any interruption in the progress of the story should be avoided if at all possible, so work problems out with other players if you can. If you do not know the correct application of a certain rule, it's usually better to wing it rather than interrupt the flow of the game.

It should be noted that a challenger who fails on a Social or Mental Challenge must wait at least five real-time minutes before repeating the failed challenge (and not spend them arguing over the results of the previous challenge — you can't protest a ruling with a Narrator for 4:58, then drop your argument and say, "Oh look, time's up."). This rule includes supernatural powers that use Mental or Social Challenges unless they specify otherwise — a character cannot continue attempting one try at *Psychometry* after another until he finally succeeds. This stricture does *not* include trials that are failed but then redeemed through retests or overbids.

COMPLICATIONS

There are a number of ways in which a challenge can be made more complicated. The basic rules are enough to resolve most disputes, but the following rules add a few bells and whistles.

NEGATIVE TRAITS

Many characters have Negative Traits, Traits that can be used against a character by his opponent. During the initial bid of any challenge, after you have each bid one Trait, you can call out a Negative Trait that you believe your opponent possesses. If he does indeed possess the Negative Trait, your opponent is forced to bid an additional Trait, although you must still risk your one Trait as usual. If he does not possess that Negative Trait, *you* must risk an additional Trait. You may call out as many Negative Traits as you wish during the initial bid phase of a challenge, as long as you can pay the price for being wrong.

If your opponent does not have additional Traits to bid, then your Trait is not at risk during the challenge. Additionally if you guess more than one Negative Trait that your opponent cannot match, you gain that many additional Traits in the case of a tie or an overbid (see below). The same works in reverse, favoring your opponent if you do not have additional Traits remaining to match incorrect Negative Trait guesses. It is considered *very* cheap to list off which Negative Traits a player might possess, if you have no valid reason to suspect as much in-game.

Example of Play: *Undercover DEA agent John Smith is attacking Mathias, a notorious drug dealer specializing in supernatural potions. Mathias would prefer to run and live to deal another day. John begins with his initial bid ("Freeze, bastard, or you'll get a* Brawny *fist in your face!"), while Mathias attempts to escape ("I'm too* Quick *for you to catch so easily."). John then suggests that Mathias possesses the Negative Trait Lethargic ("All those illicit parties have made you too* Lethargic *to get away"). If Mathias did indeed possess that Negative Trait, he would have to bid an additional Trait to continue the challenge. However, the pusher does not possess the* Lethargic *Trait, and now John — having underestimated his opposition — is the one who has to bid an extra Trait if he wishes to continue trying to capture Mathias.*

It can be risky to bid Negative Traits, but if you're sure about what you're doing, you can raise the stakes for your opponent, possibly even to the point where she relents rather than risking additional Traits.

OVERBIDDING

Overbidding is the system by which powerful characters may prevail in a challenge, even if they lose the initial test. Joseph the bodybuilder with eight Physical Traits should be able to crush Phil the researcher who has only three. This system is designed to make that possible.

Once a test has been made, the loser has the option of calling for an "overbid." In order to call an overbid, you must risk a new Trait; the original one has already been lost. At this point, the two players must reveal the number of applicable Traits they possess in the appropriate category, starting with the player who called for the overbid. If you have double the number of Traits as your opponent in that category, you may attempt another test. As with a tie, you may state a number of Traits less than the actual number you have and keep your true power secret. Overbidding can be dangerous unless you are confident in your estimation of your opponent's abilities.

Example of Play: *Our dealer from an earlier example, Mathias, is back and leaning on one of his favorite contacts, Markus, to learn who may have squealed on him ("Markus, I'm too* Persuasive *for you to resist — come clean and I'll go easy on you."). Markus, however, is not swayed by Mathias' honeyed words ("And I'm too* Dignified *to swallow that line of bull."). They test, and Markus wins, but Mathias merely gets more determined. Believing himself more socially adept than Markus, Mathias leans with a little more force ("Markus, you know how* Intimidating *I can be if you hold out on me."), and calls for an overbid. Markus, as the defender, does not need to risk another Trait. Mathias announces his Social Trait total — a whopping 14 — while Markus has only five, and the overbid proceeds. They test again, and this time, Mathias wins. Markus loses his* Dignified *Trait, and had best start talking....*

STATIC CHALLENGES

Sometimes you may have to undergo a challenge against a Narrator rather than against another player. For example, a hacker may use a Static Mental Challenge with the *Computer* Ability to break into another computer system. In such circumstances, you bid a Trait that would be appropriate, then perform a test against the Narrator. Before the test is made, the Narrator decides on the difficulty of the task that you are attempting — this is the number of Traits you are bidding against, which is used to compare in the event of a tie. The test proceeds exactly as it would if you were testing against another character. Of course, you may attempt to overbid in a Static Challenge, but beware, because the Narrator can overbid as well. The number of Traits attached to the challenge should represent the difficulty and danger inherent in the challenge.

Sometimes Narrators may leave notes on objects, such as books, doors or even magical items. These notes indicate the type of challenges that must be won for something to occur (such as deciphering a tome or picking a lock).

SIMPLE TESTS

Simple Tests are used to determine if you can do something successfully when there is no real opposition. Simple Tests are often used when using Numinae. Most Simple Tests do not require you to risk or bid Traits, though some may.

When a Simple Test is called, a test (Rock-Paper-Scissors) is performed against a Narrator. In most cases, the player succeeds on a win or a tie, although in some cases, it may be necessary for the player to win for him to receive any benefit from the challenge.

RETESTS

Certain Traits allow a character to retest. A retest allows a character to ignore the results of the first test and test again for a new result. Retests are most commonly gained through Abilities, but other Traits may also provide them; such Traits are noted in their descriptions. Generally, expending one level of an appropriate Ability allows for one retest.

Multiple retests are possible on a single challenge, but each retest must come from a different source. A character may retest a challenge once using a level of *Brawl* and then retest again through the Merit *Luck*, but he may not gain multiple retests with the *Brawl* Ability on the same challenge.

Retests may be canceled ("blocked") by a character who is capable of matching the conditions of the retest. Thus, if a player uses *Firearms* to retest when firing a gun, the opponent may expend a level of *Dodge* to block the retest and force the attacker to accept the results of the original test.

Example of Play: *Christine, a paranormal researcher, is being held hostage by Miguel, the human leader of a spectre cult. Things are looking bleak, until Edward, an Arcanum scholar she studies with, breaks in and takes a shot at Miguel ("I'm Determined to see you dead for harming Christine!"). Miguel responds by diving for cover ("I'm Quick enough to get behind the couch and out of range.") They test, and Edward loses. The previously meek scholar seems to have found his rage, though ("I'm a better Firearms shot than you think!"), and calls for a retest. They test again, and this time Edward wins. The shot hits the cultist in the arm.*

Miguel tries to grab Christine for a human shield ("I've got you in a Brutal grip — you're coming with me!"), but Christine isn't going quietly ("This time, I'm Quicker than you!"). The two go to a test, and Miguel loses. He immediately calls for a retest with Brawl ("I'm too

good to let you best me in Brawl!*"), which Christine blocks with* Dodge *("I can't punch you, but I can* Dodge *you!") and no retest is made. Christine rushes to Edward, who is setting up for another shot.*

RELENTING

At any time before the actual test is performed, a player may choose to acquiesce and admit defeat. Characters who relent lose the challenge automatically, but they do not lose any Traits, even if they bid one before relenting. Relenting helps the game flow along more smoothly than extended Rock-Paper-Scissors matches do.

BONUS TRAITS

Certain weapons and special powers grant a character bonus Traits during a challenge. You may add these extra Traits toward a character's total when determining a tie involving that weapon or special Ability.

ORDER OF CHALLENGES

Since multiple challenges will inevitably occur simultaneously during any given fight, occasionally the Narrator needs some means of determining who acts first and who acts last. Each person involved in a given game turn checks the current number of Traits appropriate to the action he wishes to attempt. A character punching someone would use Physical Traits to determine speed, while a character casting a spell would probably use Mental Traits. If an action does not require any sort of Trait challenge, it occurs last in the turn. As with overbidding, you may declare fewer Traits than you possess if you wish. Characters with equal numbers of Traits are assumed to go "simultaneously," though for resolution purposes the Narrator may simply choose one to act first.

Sometimes a character with a high number of Traits attacks a character with fewer Traits, who decides to strike back. In this case, the character with fewer Traits resolves his action in the same test as the faster character, but in doing so, he loses the ability to take any aggressive action for the turn — he uses up his one action with the counterattack.

This rule can occasionally cause as much confusion as it tries to solve, and the Narrator may choose to apply this only when there is a debate or other critical need to establish who's going first.

Example of Play: *Edward and Christine are inching back toward the door, trying to hold the advancing Miguel at bay. Unfortunately, here comes Miguel's second, the vicious Kalem, who attempts to block their escape. Christine has five Physical Traits left, and Kalem has his full 10 Traits. Kalem looms over Edward and Christine ("I'm too* Stalwart *for you to get by me!"), but desperation makes Christine consider the unthinkable ("I may be only* Wiry, *but it's enough to kneecap you with this heavy candlestick!"). They test, and Kalem loses; he howls in pain from the blow, suffering a wound, and drops aside. The pair is not out of the woods yet, though — Miguel is taking his action for this turn to move into a better position, and Edward's not sure he's got enough Traits to press the offensive. Things are getting desperate....*

THE MOB SCENE

It's a fact of life that sooner or later a large group of characters will decide to mix it up. Group challenges can seem intimidating even to experienced Narrators and Storytellers; these rules are meant to streamline the process and make such situations easier to resolve, rather than devolving into endless matches of Rock-Paper-Scissors.

First of all, find who is challenging whom. The easiest way is to count to three and have everyone point to the person they wish to target that turn. If no one is being challenged by more than one person, then challenges are carried out normally.

If one character is challenged by several targets, or tries to challenge multiple opponents at once, resolve it in the following manner. First deal with groups in the order of largest to smallest, just for ease of play. Each attacker must bid an appropriate Trait as normal for the challenge required; logistics put a limit of up to five characters attacking another character at once.

Next, the defender character must bid enough Traits to counter every opponent in the group; if he does not have enough Traits, he must relent to the rest of his opponents (although he may choose which ones he relents to). Resolve such relented challenges first — it is very possible the defender may fall before the rest of the group can act!

Finally, the defender and any remaining attackers engage in one simultaneous test. The defender then compares his sign to each of the attacker's signs, applying the appropriate results. Thus, if the defending character throws Scissors and his attackers throw Rock, Scissors, Paper and Paper, the defender is considered to have lost to the first challenger, tied the second (resolved like any other tie) and beaten the last two. The defenders and attackers lose Traits bid in any given loss. If the defender in the previous example had bid one Trait against every attacker, he would have lost one Trait to the first attacker, and an additional Trait if he had lost the tie as well.

Once the tests have been made, they are resolved in the standard order of actions and initiative. It is possible for a defender to lose Traits to the first attackers and then lose a tie to an attacker later in the same mob challenge. That's OK — the first attackers "softened up" the defender. However, unless the defender has a special power that allows him to take multiple actions, he may only attempt to injure one of his attackers, and it must be one who lost a challenge. If none of the attackers lose, the defender simply suffers the results of their actions.

When the defender in a mob challenge uses Abilities or other powers to gain retests, each attacker's challenge is treated as a separate test. Thus, a defender would need five *Melee* Traits in order to retest against five attackers in a melee combat.

TIME

Time in **Mind's Eye Theatre** works as it does in real life. It moves forward inexorably, relentlessly. For the most part, everything is played out in real time, and players are expected to stay in character unless they have a rules question.

It is assumed that a player is always "in character" during the course of a story. A player should never drop character when interacting with other players. Doing so ruins the atmosphere for everyone involved. Challenges may be talked through, but a player is always considered to be active in the game. If a player needs to take a break, he should

inform a Narrator. That player should not interact with other players while out of character.

The only other exception to the "in-character rule" is when a Narrator calls for a "timeout." This call may be necessary to resolve a dispute or to change the scene if the story calls for it. When "Timeout!" is called, all players within hearing distance must stop whatever they are doing until the Narrator calls out, "Resume" or "Lay on!" Timeouts should be kept to a minimum, since they interrupt the flow of the story.

CHRONICLES, STORIES, SESSIONS AND SCENES

Mind's Eye Theatre time breaks down into five major allotments: chronicles, stories, sessions, scenes and turns. A chronicle is defined as a series of smaller stories that are all connected somehow, and which may take months or even years to complete. Each complete plotline within the chronicle is called a story. A session is just that: one actual night of play, although Storytellers may define a session as one night of game time if the action was left in medias res at the end of the previous game. (Since many characters regain spent Traits in between sessions, this distinction can be important.) Finally, a scene is the amount of time it takes to resolve the action in one location; once the characters shift locations, the scene has ended. If a session will be taking place entirely at one location, a scene can then be defined as roughly one hour.

TURNS

To keep everything straight when players start throwing challenges around or attempting complex actions, the time is right to start using turns. Turns are considered to last about four seconds, although this measure may vary from challenge to challenge at the Storyteller's discretion. In any given turn, a character may take one action. Some actions may take multiple turns to complete, such as hacking a sophisticated computer system. Other actions, like speaking a short sentence, do not use up a character's turn at all. Once everyone involved in a turn has taken an action, the turn ends and another turn begins.

In some instances a character may be interrupted before he can take his action, or be forced to respond to events developing around him. In such instances, a character may always defend himself, although doing so uses up his available action for the turn.

If a power affects a character for 15 seconds, it is assumed to be in effect for four turns when turn-based time is in effect. In normal roleplaying, such powers work for their allotted amount of time.

DOWNTIME

Many aspects of a character's unlife are critical to her continued existence, yet they do not make for dramatic roleplaying, or they are too intricate to take time during sessions to perform. Storytellers are encouraged to use "downtime" between sessions to allow characters to maintain their holdings, learn Numinae and see to other facets of their existence. Other actions and interactions may take place during this time, with Storyteller supervision. As long as players don't use abuse downtime privileges, the time between sessions can be a rewarding roleplaying experience in itself.

HEALTH

A character in a **Laws of the Hunt** game has different health levels that represent the amount of injury the character can endure. These levels include: Healthy, Healthy, Bruised, Bruised, Bruised, Wounded, Wounded, Incapacitated and Mortally Wounded. If a Healthy character loses two health levels from a combat challenge, he becomes Bruised. If he loses three more health levels, he becomes Wounded, and so on.

Healthy — When a character is Healthy, he is virtually or completely uninjured. He suffers no penalty aside from possibly being cosmetically scuffed up a bit.

Bruised — A Bruised character is more seriously roughed up, and his injuries have started to impair him a bit. He is considered one Trait down on all bids, so the player must risk an additional Trait to have a chance in any challenge.

Wounded — When a character is Wounded, he is seriously injured in one or more parts of his body. To reflect this injury, he must risk an additional Trait to attempt a challenge (because of the Bruised health level of damage), and his opponent wins all ties, regardless of who has more Traits. If the injured character has a power that normally allows him to win all ties, he resolves ties through comparing Traits instead. Note: a character may always attempt to overbid.

Incapacitated — An Incapacitated character is completely out of play for at least 10 minutes. Even once he regains consciousness, the character is still effectively immobile, although he may now whisper pained sentences. He may not enter into challenges, and he is essentially at the mercy of other characters until he heals at least one health level. Characters hit with bashing damage at this point are rendered unconscious for one scene or hour, whichever comes first. They're out cold, but they're not in any serious danger except from prolonged bashing attacks. Characters who are hit with lethal or aggravated damage, however, drop to Mortally Wounded. Such injuries are more than capable of finishing them off for good.

Mortally Wounded — A Mortally Wounded individual has little time left. He does not regain consciousness normally, and he loses a Physical Trait every 10 minutes from bleeding, shock or other complications. As soon as the character runs out of Physical Traits, he dies. Only the assistance of someone with the right magic or the *Medicine* Ability can halt this loss, and the character will not even begin to heal unless he is treated by magic or taken to a hospital. Those who fail to improve or stabilize in time undergo the complete and permanent cessation of all metabolic activity that's conventionally known as death.

Example of Play: *Remember Joe Shabbadoo from way back? While he managed to get some lucky shots on Fitz, the vampire still managed to land three swipes across Joe's midsection, leaving bleeding clawmarks behind and inflicting three levels of aggravated damage. Joe lost both Healthy levels and a Bruised level. While fleeing the vampire, Joe attempted to climb over a chainlink fence, lost the challenge and fell over on the other side, for a level of bashing damage that takes another Bruised level. In a great deal of pain, Joe struggles to his feet and keeps running. He suffers another bad fall, and the Narrator deems Joe receives another level of bashing damage, now reducing him to Wounded. Thankfully, Joe gets to a more populated area, where his condition attracts some concerned attention — someone calls an ambulance.*

HEALING

Laws of the Hunt characters are mortal, and they must heal at the same rate as other normal humans would unless they have access to magic, vampiric vitae, werewolves with the *Mother's Touch* Gift, weird science or other supernatural aids. Furthermore, they are susceptible to infections and diseases, and they must tend their wounds carefully to avoid such complications. This risk may not be as much of a threat for undercover government agents with insurance and extensive hospital facilities, but a street kid without insurance or ID may have serious cause to worry about the nasty cut she got in that back-alley brawl.

BASHING/LETHAL DAMAGE

Some types of damage are more dangerous than others. A punch to the jaw is less likely to kill than a knife to the throat. Bashing damage is any injury that is painful but which fades relatively quickly, such as that taken from kicks, punches or tackles. Lethal damage (which comes from bullets, swords, knives, etc.) is intended to kill, and it takes mortals a long time to heal. The Narrator is the final arbiter of what counts as bashing or lethal damage. A single person kicking someone usually does bashing damage, but a helpless character being stomped on by a gang of attackers might well start taking lethal damage to reflect the savage nature of the beating. Bashing damage doesn't usually reduce a character below Incapacitated without effort, so it is typically less likely to be fatal. However, lethal damage can drop a character to Mortally Wounded in a hurry. A character who has reached the Incapacitated health level with bashing damage subsequently takes lethal damage from further bashing attacks. The bashing damage converts to lethal damage, and it may eventually mortally wound or kill the character.

Bashing wounds heal fairly quickly. Lethal wounds take longer to heal, and aggravated wounds may leave permanent damage. If a character cannot or will not use magic to treat her injuries, she heals according to the following chart. Natural healing is a slow process, and it assumes that the character is getting plenty of bed rest and maintaining a low level of activity.

AGGRAVATED WOUNDS

Wounds that go beyond the normal bounds of even most magical healing powers are called aggravated wounds. Such wounds are caused by injury from fire, magical weapons, some magical effects, or from the teeth and claws of a supernatural creature. A Narrator can also deem any other sufficiently severe injury to be aggravated, depending on the circumstances. If a character leaves his wounds to heal normally (that is, with time and bed rest), those wounds heal at the same rate as lethal damage.

ENVIRONMENTAL AND ELEMENTAL EFFECTS

Fire, water, suffocation and electricity may all prove deadly to the average (and above-average) mortal. While the effects of environmental and elemental powers and attacks are up to storyteller, the following guidelines may be helpful.

FIRE

In game terms, all wounds directly inflicted by normal or magical fires do aggravated damage to mortals and other creatures that are affected by fire (e.g., vampires, werewolves,

etc.), and flaming weapons add an additional lethal level of damage to a weapon's normal damage. Moreover, those who are attacked directly or indirectly by fire may suffer an additional level of aggravated damage each subsequent turn until the fire is put out.

Stop, Drop and Roll

A character who is on fire must take an action to try to put herself out. This is resolved after all other actions take place. It requires a Static Physical Challenge against a number of Traits equal to three times the number of health levels of fire damage that the character was exposed to during the turn (*not* the actual amount of damage that she took). If she wins, she extinguishes the flames (though she may re-ignite if she stays in contact with open flame). Players should roleplay this appropriately, though not to the extent of causing a false alarm.

WATER, DROWNING AND SUFFOCATION

Wounds inflicted by suffocation from smoke, drowning or a lack of oxygen may cause a level of bashing damage per turn if the affected character fails a Simple Test; on a win or tie he manages to hold his breath a little longer. After one full minute (16 combat turns) the character must win, not tie, the Simple Test to avoid damage. After a character reaches Incapacitated, the damage becomes lethal damage and may subsequently kill the character.

ELECTRICAL EFFECTS

Wounds from electrical attacks inflict bashing or lethal damage on living targets at the Storyteller's discretion, while weapons that magically or technologically discharge an electrical charge normally add an additional level of bashing damage to a weapon's base damage. For the technically minded Storyteller, high amperage attacks are lethal, and low amperage, high voltage attacks are normally bashing. If the target is wet, of course, things are worse; all damage effects become lethal.

RECOVERY TIMES

Injury Level	Bashing/Lethal
Bruised to Healthy	One hour/day
Wounded to Bruised	One day/week
Incapacitated to Wounded	One week/month
Mortally Wounded*	Two months

*Unless characters at this health level go to a hospital, they heal only by magic or the Storyteller's discretion. Most will gain a Negative Physical Trait of some kind from the experience (such as *Delicate*, *Decrepit* or *Lame*).

These times are cumulative, so a character at the second Wounded level from lethal damage takes two weeks and two days to completely recover: one week per Wounded level, plus a day each to heal the Bruised levels. Likewise, a character who takes the same amount of bashing damage would take two days, two hours to heal back to normal, reflecting the less serious nature of most bashing damage.

DISEASE AND INFECTION

Mortals, frail creatures that they are, must cope with the possibilities of disease and infection. It's difficult to fight the unliving when you've got a nasty case of the flu, and as if supernatural claws weren't bad enough, there's always the possibility of those lovely suppurating wounds.

Of course, disease and infection are fairly incidental to play, but they can provide a new and looming threat for mortals. Additionally, incorporating disease and infection gives all the more reason for hunters to study *Medicine* and healing magics and provides some interesting story possibilities for hunters from the Centers for Disease Control and other health institutions.

DISEASES

Characters generally catch diseases through exposure to tainted material and unsanitary conditions. Since hunters spend a lot of their time wandering through graveyards and crawling in sewers, disease is a very real danger.

Mortal characters should worry about disease only if the Storyteller decides to make an issue of it. There are no hard-and-fast rules for getting sick. A Storyteller might have each player make a Static Physical Challenge to avoid disease after wandering through a particularly nasty and refuse-strewn location, or after coming into contact with virulent foes. (Animated rotting corpses, diseased monstrosities and leprous street dwellers are all staples of horror fiction, after all.)

Once a character is diseased, the Storyteller should determine the disease's severity. Minor diseases like colds are nothing more than a nuisance, but more serious afflictions can threaten a hunter's life.

MILD DISEASES

A mild disease is uncomfortable but not completely incapacitating. Mild diseases typically cause the character to suffer from the Negative Traits of *Sickly*, *Repugnant* and *Oblivious*. Mild diseases last for about a week, although a skilled healer can rid the character of the symptoms in a day (by using healing magics or *Medicine*). Mild diseases might include a nasty cold, a sinus infection or a mild flu.

SERIOUS DISEASES

Serious diseases carry the risk of permanent damage, but they are usually surmountable with rest and some medication. A hunter suffering from a serious disease may well be completely incapacitated by the symptoms, and he is likely to have a great deal of difficulty even with everyday activities. Serious diseases afflict a character with the same Negative Traits as mild diseases, and they cause the character to lose two health levels while suffering from the disease. Thus, a normal mortal suffering from a serious disease is automatically at least Bruised for the duration of the disease. Serious diseases generally last for a month, though a skilled healer or health practitioner can clear up the symptoms with a week of rest and care. A serious disease that is untreated — that is, if the character survives without the help of a skilled healer or health practitioner — generally leaves the character with a permanent Negative Physical Trait such as *Lame* or *Decrepit*, though some may cause scarring that makes the character

Repugnant. Furthermore, a character who suffers from a serious disease and remains untreated must win or tie a Simple Test to avoid death. Pneumonia, smallpox and malaria are examples of serious diseases.

DEADLY DISEASES

Deadly diseases are generally fatal if untreated, and they may even kill a character who has medical assistance. Deadly diseases are completely incapacitating; a hunter suffering from a deadly disease cannot enter challenges at all for the duration of the disease. Without medical assistance, characters with deadly diseases recover only at the Storyteller's discretion. Characters who are treated with magical remedies or medical assistance might recover after a full month of rest and care. In either case, a Simple Test is required for each month in which the character suffers from the disease; if the test is tied or failed, the character dies. Deadly diseases include typhoid fever, acute hepatitis and Ebola.

INFECTIONS

Hunters are in a dangerous line of work, and they are likely to suffer injury from their prey. Worse still, a hunter often can't risk going to a hospital; too many awkward questions could easily lead to arrest or commitment in a mental facility. As a result, hunters often have to rest at home and take their chances with wound recovery. Combined with the wide variety of often dangerous or dirty environments in which hunters fight, infection of wounds is a constant threat.

A hunter risks infection any time he suffers a wound in a particularly filthy environment and doesn't subsequently receive treatment. A Storyteller may (but does not have to) call for a Simple Test, with failure indicating that a wound has become infected.

An infected wound does not heal normally. Instead, at the end of any period of healing time, the player must make another Simple Test. Success indicates that the infection has cleared up and the hunter can continue to heal normally (although the wound does not actually heal at this time); failure means that the infection worsens and the character suffers another health level of damage. The infection continues, and the character must test again once the requisite time has passed. For instance, if a hunter suffers two wounds, dropping to the first Bruised health level, and subsequently receives an infection, the player must test after a day. Failure would cause the character to suffer another level of injury, dropping to the second Bruised level, while success would mean that the infection has cleared up so the character can heal normally. This system simulates the fact that a bad infection takes a while to get much worse, but that a nasty infection also takes a while to heal.

A character who does not get rest automatically suffers degradation from the infected wound. Thus, if a hunter suffers from wounds that leave her Bruised and gets infected, she automatically loses a health level and drops to the second Bruised health level after a day if she does not rest.

Proper treatment can help to clear up infections. Medical attention from a character with the *Medicine* Ability or appropriate healing powers can defeat infection without a test once the character has rested for the requisite amount of time. Thus, a hunter at the Wounded health level must rest for a week before his infection clears up, but under medical care, no test in necessary; the infection heals automatically. Other supernatural powers like the werewolves' *Mother's Touch* or the *Heather Balm* of changelings may heal a mortal much faster... but most mortals do not have access to magics like those.

Accelerated healing from healing Numinae does not speed the rate at which infections heal, it simply assures eventual healing. A Wounded character with an infection must therefore rest for a full week to clear up an infection, even if magical or skilled healing is used.

COMBAT

Combat is the usual intent behind Physical Challenges. Essentially, combat involves two characters in physical conflict. The players agree what the outcome of the challenge will be, each player bids an appropriate Trait and a test is performed to determine the victor. The following section allows for variations on those basic rules, such as situations using surprise or weapons.

The agreed outcome of a Physical Challenge is often the loser being injured. This is not the only possible result, though. The two parties can agree to nearly anything, whether it's tripping an opponent or throwing him out of a window. The results of a combat challenge may also be different for both participants; for example, if a frenzied Malkavian is trying to tear apart a fleeing mortal, the mortal might try to get away from his opponent instead of hurting her.

SURPRISE

If a player does not respond within three seconds of the declaration of a Physical Challenge, the character is considered to have been surprised — he is not fully prepared for what's coming. Sometimes a player is busy with another activity or is playing a character who just isn't prepared for the attack. But any player who sneaks around whispering challenges to get the element of surprise is cheating, plain and simple.

Surprise simply means that the outcome of the first challenge in a fight can only harm the surprised defender, not the challenger. For instance, if a player did not respond in time to an attack, but still won the challenge, the challenger would not be injured. Furthermore, if the challenger loses the test, she may call for a second challenge by risking another Trait. After this second challenge, regular challenge rules resume. Overbidding is permitted for both challenger and challenged in surprise situations.

MOVEMENT IN COMBAT

Three Step Rule

Anyone in or just entering combat is subject to the "three step rule." You may take up to three steps during any combat action and still attack. Moving one step is considered walking cautiously, two steps is moving directly (down one Trait in Physical Challenges), and three steps is running (also down a Trait in Physical Challenges). A Numina that allows for an additional action would allow you to take three additional steps, and so on.

FAIR ESCAPE

Fair Escape is a simple rule that allows players to escape from potentially dangerous situations without actually bounding over furniture or diving out of windows. This rule also allows players to avoid combat without going through cumbersome challenges to see if they can "get away."

When you use this rule, you can call "Fair Escape!" any time you see another player approaching with whom you do not wish to interact. Once you call "Fair Escape," you may leave the area without being pursued. There are several guidelines that must be followed when using this rule, however:

• You may not use the Fair Escape rule if the person approaching is nearby (within conversational distance). In such cases, you must initiate a challenge in order to flee. Use common sense in places where there is a great deal of noise and conversational distance is reduced to a minimum (e.g., a crowded nightclub).

• Situations that involve an ambush (all exits blocked or the target is surrounded) or ranged weapons can sometimes negate the use of Fair Escape. Again, use common sense.

• A character using some form of invisibility or similar powers may employ a Fair Escape at any time before a challenge has been initiated, unless someone with some form of supernaturally heightened senses counters him.

• Characters with supernatural speed such as a changeling with *Quicksilver* or a vampire with *Celerity* may gain a Fair Escape by activating their speed before a challenge is initiated. In the case of two characters using supernatural speed, whoever uses the highest level of speed wins (all ties go to the fleeing party). Thus, a ghoul using Basic *Celerity* cannot Fair Escape from a vampire who is using Advanced *Celerity*.

These rules are meant to hasten play, not complicate it. Always try to employ common sense when using Fair Escape. (As a rule of thumb, if it takes several minutes to explain why a Fair Escape would be justified, it probably isn't.)

WEAPONS

For obvious reasons, no real weapons are ever allowed in **Mind's Eye Theatre** games. Even nonfunctional props are forbidden if they can be mistaken for weapons. This system does not use props of any kind, nor are players required (or allowed) to strike one another. Instead, characters should use weapon cards, which display the Traits and pertinent details of a particular weapon.

A weapon gives its wielder extra Traits for combat or other appropriate challenges. Sometimes this advantage is offset by a disadvantage in terms of a Negative Trait. Each weapon has one to six extra Traits that may be used in any challenge in which the weapon is employed. These Traits *cannot* be used as an initial bid. Instead, they add to the user's total when she is comparing Traits. In addition, some weapons have special abilities that may be used, such as causing extra levels of damage or affecting more than one target.

Statistics for weapons are written on cards and carried along with your character sheet. Weapon cards specify the capacities of each weapon and allow other players to see that you actually possess a weapon. When you have a weapon card in your hand, you are considered to be holding the weapon.

Some weapons have Negative Traits that can be used by the wielder's opponent in precisely the same way as regular Negative Traits. The weapon's Negative Traits can only be used against the wielder of that weapon. Negative Traits for a weapon must be appropriate to the situation. For instance, if you are firing a pistol and your opponent wants to use the gun's Negative Trait *Loud* against you, that Negative Trait could be ignored if you have a silencer on the gun.

Concealability

Each weapon has a concealability rating. If the weapon is not concealable, or if you do not have the proper amount of clothing or cover to conceal it, you must have that card on display at all times. You cannot, for example, pull a broadsword out of your pocket. Instead, you must carry that card in hand at all times or, optionally, you could pin the card to your shirt, indicating that the sword is slung over your shoulder.

Availability

Serious firearms and archaic melee weapons can take some time to locate. Firearms also require permits to obtain, which involves undergoing background checks or waiting periods in some areas. A character can turn to more "colorful" channels in order to procure equipment, but the black market often means shady dealings and vastly inflated prices. Weapons that have Influence values listed under Availability indicate the level and type of Influence required in order to procure the weapon through illicit channels. Finally, of course, there's cost: A character must have some level of the *Finance* Ability or money-raising Influence to procure exotic melee weapons and nearly all firearms.

Once a character has a weapon, that doesn't mean he can keep it forever. Too often characters run about firing shotguns and large automatic weapons without facing the massive police manhunts that such battles invariably provoke. Take care that characters with powerful weapons understand the equally powerful repercussions that come from their use. These consequences not only preserve game balance but also enforce a sense of realism, keeping the game from turning into *Die Hard* with funny powers.

Those characters who have access to certain weapons due to their particular resources (as federal agents or law enforcement officers) are under even more scrutiny than usual. Just because one has a nifty weapon does not give the bearer license to go hog wild — indeed, firing indiscriminately may result in the weapon being taken away and a superior looming in from above.

The Internet makes some amazing things available to anyone who can flash the right sort of ID and a credit card — Soviet-era firearms, chain mail, even the fabled dragonsbreath rounds. However, just because it's out on the Internet does not mean the Storyteller is under any obligation to let you have it. If she does, look the gift horse very carefully in the mouth — the character's purchase may have just sounded an alarm to an alert anti-terror Web browser.

SPECIAL WEAPON CAPABILITIES

Some weapons have special abilities, allowing an attacker to inflict extra damage, ignore certain types of protection or strike multiple opponents. (Such powers are noted under the weapon descriptions.)

Armor-Piercing

Special rounds, generally Teflon-coated, are able to pierce armor with ease. Although they do not inflict extra damage, armor-piercing rounds ignore any defenses from armor. Such rounds are typically tricky to acquire, though, and legal inquiries often follow their use.

Destroy Shield

Although rare in this day and age, certain Inquisitors still use shields. A weapon capable of destroying a shield penetrates it automatically and renders it useless after a certain number of blows, no matter what the size or strength of the shield may be.

Fully Automatic

A firearm with this ability is capable of emptying dozens of rounds into a single target at close range. This attack inflicts an extra health level of damage automatically due to sheer volume of fire; however, after emptying the clip from fully automatic fire, the character must spend one action reloading the weapon before it may be fired again.

High-Caliber

Firearms of particularly high caliber can cause crippling wounds with only a few shots. When a high-caliber weapon hits a target, the attacker should make a Simple Test immediately. A win indicates that the target suffers an additional health level of damage from the shot.

Incendiary

Burning weapons cause aggravated wounds to just about anything. Some, like flamethrowers or Molotov cocktails, burn the target with streams or explosions of fire, while others such as incendiary rounds ("hot loads") burn the target with superheated ammunition. See the damage section for the effects of fire.

Mass-Trauma

Certain weapons are so powerful they inflict massive damage on a target, literally tearing away portions of flesh. Such weapons score an extra health level of damage when used appropriately.

Speed

Fast weapons can be used to "pre-empt" an opponent's attack, allowing the attacker with the speedier weapon to strike and resolve his challenge first. A character must have the *Melee* Ability to use this special ability, and he must be attacking or otherwise actively using (parrying, disarming) the weapon in order to gain this benefit. Fast weapons only gain a pre-emptive strike against opponents in hand-to-hand or melee combat.

Since many attacks are handled simultaneously for ease of play (both players testing at once and the winner scoring a hit), this ability is not always very useful. However, if the Storyteller opts to allow each attacker to test individually (attacking striking defender, then defender counterstriking), this ability puts characters with fast weapons on the offensive.

Spray

The weapon can strike several targets at once, as noted under the weapon's specific parameters. The shooter makes one test against all the targets simultaneously. Each target who fails the test suffers the weapon's damage, while each target who succeeds avoids the weapon's damage. The shooter risks only the Traits required to test against each member of the group, and he loses only those Traits if any of the defenders wins the test.

Staking

Staking weapons paralyze vampires when a successful blow penetrates one's heart. The attacker must win or tie two successive Simple Tests in order to successfully stake the vampire.

BIDDING WEAPON TRAITS

During a normal hand-to-hand fight, characters bid Physical Traits against their opponents' Physical Traits. However, if a character is using firearms, he may use Mental Traits instead. If his opponent is also using a firearm, she bids Mental Traits as well. If the opponent is not using a firearm and is merely trying to dodge, then the attacker uses

Mental Traits to attack, while the defender uses her Physical Traits to dodge. This instance is one of the few in which Traits associated with different Attributes may be used against one another.

WEAPON EXAMPLES

MELEE WEAPONS

Knife/Dagger — These easily concealed weapons are very common, lightning fast in the hands of a skilled user, and they can also be used as ranged weapons if a character uses the *Athletics* Ability properly.

Bonus Traits: 2

Negative Traits: *Short*

Concealability: Pocket

Damage: One lethal health level

Availability: Any

Special Ability: *Speed:* In close combat against any weapon that has the Negative Traits *Clumsy, Heavy* or *Slow*, the knife fighter gains the option to pre-empt the opponent's attacks and strike first in any turn, as long as he has the *Melee* Ability.

Wooden Stake — A short length of wood sharpened at one end, these humble weapons have nonetheless been the downfall of many vampires over the centuries.

Bonus Traits: 2

Negative Traits: *Short*

Concealability: Jacket

Damage: One lethal health level

Availability: Any

Special Ability: *Staking:* A wooden stake can pierce the heart of a vampire (thus paralyzing the unfortunate Lick) if the wielder wins or ties two successive Simple Tests after striking.

Club/Ax — These two common weapon types can be anything from chair legs to hand axes to billy clubs; one bludgeons while the other cuts, but the essential function is the same.

Bonus Traits: Club: 2, Ax: 3

Negative Traits: *Clumsy*

Concealability: Trench coat

Damage: Club — One bashing or lethal health level; Ax — Two lethal health levels

Availability: Any

Special Ability: Ax: *Destroy Shield*. Axes render shields useless after three blows.

Fencing Blades —Few hunters or other mortals rely on the fencing weapons of yesteryear, though exceptions exist. These thin blades rely on speed instead of strength, and they inflict most of their damage from piercing rather than slashing. Foils and rapiers just aren't as popular as symbols of magic, and the practice foils lack much real effectiveness. Those melee artists who practice combat fencing are more likely to use a heavy French foil, a Spanish or Italian rapier, or a German schlager. These weapons are thicker and more deadly than the modern sport tools with which most people are

familiar. Fencing blades also include the katana, simply because using a katana relies more on speed than on strength. Most katana are crafted by hand. While mass-produced versions exist, they are substantially inferior to their pure cousins.

Bonus Traits: 2

Negative Traits: *Fragile*

Concealability: Trench coat

Damage: One lethal health level

Availability: Any. A fencing foil tends to attract less police attention than an ornamental saber, especially if the character is wearing or carrying fencing gear. Hand-crafted katana are typically heirlooms of great value, and their owners guard them closely. In other words, you cannot simply walk into a store and buy one. If you do find someone to sell you a genuine katana, it will be expensive.

Special Ability: *Speed:* In close combat against any weapon that has the Negative Traits *Clumsy, Heavy* or *Slow*, the fencer gains the option to pre-empt the opponent's attacks and strike first in any turn, as long as he has the *Melee* Ability.

Broadsword — Perhaps the most archetypal form of Inquisitor weaponry, swords have long been the focus of holy missions and powerful magics. Even unenchanted blades can even the odds in a fight, and an Inquisitor's fiery blade can instill terror in the hearts of many unholy threats. This category of weapon covers every blade of medium length, from western broadswords to scimitars. The only exception is the katana, whose crafting practices give it a slightly different set of characteristics. The typical broadsword has a heavy, thick blade and a chisellike edge made to hack through armor and batter the opponent to death while cutting off chunks of flesh.

Bonus Traits: 3

Negative Traits: *Heavy*

Concealability: Trench coat (barely)

Damage: Two lethal health levels

Availability: Broadswords typically must be special-ordered, although cheap and not especially durable versions are sometimes available at military-supply stores or Renaissance festivals.

ARCHAIC RANGED WEAPONS

Longbow — These huge, powerful bows make mincemeat of regular armor, and a few anachronistic Inquisitors and martial artists are trained archers. Characters use the *Athletics* Ability for retests when using bows, and those without this Ability receive only a third of the usual Bonus Traits (round down) due to the difficulty of using these weapons. Modern compound bows are smaller and use pulley systems to generate powerful pull; these bows do not have the Negative Trait *Clumsy* but give the user only five Bonus Traits.

Bonus Traits: 6

Negative Traits: *Fragile, Clumsy, Heavy*

Concealability: None

Damage: Two lethal health levels

Availability: Any

Special Ability: *Armor-Piercing*: Longbows ignore chain armor. *Staking*: Arrows may be used to stake a vampire, if the archer wins or ties two Simple Tests after a successful hit. *Destroy Shield*: One shot from a longbow renders a shield useless.

Shuriken/Dart — Martial artists in particular are fond of using these small chunks of sharpened metal as emergency weapons, but other hunters sometimes use darts or other small hurled objects as well. Such a weapon is usually more a nuisance than an implement of destruction. In some rare cases, a weapon of this sort may carry poisons, but that's up to the discretion of the Storyteller to adjudicate.

Bonus Traits: 1

Negative Traits: *Clumsy* (Shuriken and darts are notoriously inaccurate beyond short range)

Concealability: Pocket

Damage: One lethal health level

Availability: Any

Special Ability: *Spray*: Shuriken and darts may be thrown in groups that can strike multiple close targets, if the thrower has enough skill (at least one level of *Athletics* Ability). Such a spray hits up to three targets that are within a pace of each other and within 20 feet of the thrower.

FIREARMS

Pistol — This designation covers nearly any sort of small- and medium-caliber handgun commonly encountered, from zip guns and holdout pieces to 9 mm's and standard police-issue sidearms.

Bonus Traits: 2

Negative Traits: *Loud*

Concealability: Pocket

Damage: Two lethal health levels

Availability: Any, if registered; *Police* 4, *Street* 3 or *Underworld* 2 otherwise.

Heavy Pistol — This designation covers the monsters of the handgun range, from the Desert Eagle to a .454 Cassull. These tremendous guns use high-caliber ammunition to punch large holes in their targets.

Bonus Traits: 2

Negative Traits: *Loud*

Concealability: Jacket

Damage: Two lethal health levels

Availability: Any, if registered; *Police* 4, *Street* 4 or *Underworld* 3 otherwise.

Special Ability: *High-Caliber*: Heavy Pistols allow a Simple Test on a successful hit. Success indicates the target takes an extra level of damage.

Rifle — Favored by many hunters and snipers.

Bonus Traits: 3

Negative Traits: *Loud*

Concealability: None.

Damage: Two lethal health levels

Availability: Any, if registered; *Police* 4, *Street* 4 or *Underworld* 3 otherwise.

Special Ability: *High-Caliber*: Rifles may be loaded with high-caliber ammunition. Note that the character must specifically acquire such ammunition to gain this benefit — it is not included automatically when using a rifle.

Shotgun — This powerful weapon fires a spray of pellets, making targets easy to hit.

Bonus Traits: 3

Negative Traits: *Loud*

Concealability: None

Damage: Two lethal health levels

Availability: Any, if registered. *Police* 4, *Street* 4 or *Underworld* 3 otherwise.

Special Ability: *Spray*: A shotgun may affect up to three targets if they are standing immediately next to each other and are farther than 20 feet from the person firing the shotgun. This effect can be gained only if the shotgun is loaded with pellets, not slugs. *Mass-Trauma*: A shotgun can cause an extra health level of damage to a single target standing within five feet.

Submachine Gun — These weapons are very powerful, and they fire a large number of bullets very quickly, making them the favorite weapons of many gangs, where accuracy isn't as important as hitting a large number of targets at the same time. The law requires these guns be sold with only semi-automatic capability, but a use of the *Repair* Ability can convert them to fully automatic fire.

Bonus Traits: 2

Negative Traits: *Loud*

Concealability: Jacket

Damage: Two lethal health levels

Availability: Any, if registered and semi-automatic. *Police* 4, *Street* 4 or *Underworld* 3 otherwise.

Special Ability: *Spray*: A submachine gun may affect up to five targets if they're standing immediately next to each other and are farther than 10 feet from the person firing the gun. *Fully Automatic*: A submachine gun inflicts an additional health level of damage if the entire clip is emptied into a target standing no more than five feet away.

ARMOR

Since it stops incoming damage, armor effectively grants a character extra health levels; these health levels are lost before the character himself suffers any damage in combat. Of course, armor does not soak all attacks — a suit of chain mail does little good for a character who is choking to death from smoke inhalation, for instance.

Different types of armor can absorb different amounts of punishment before losing their effectiveness; it should be noted that armor that has lost all its health levels is not necessarily completely destroyed, but more likely that it has been temporarily rendered useless instead. Of course, some attacks may destroy armor beyond repair. Fixing armor requires the proper tools and a Static Physical Challenge with the *Repair* Ability.

Armor has two different traits for game purposes. Health levels indicate how many levels of damage the armor can absorb before becoming useless and in need of repair. Negative Traits are the drawbacks a wearer gains for donning a particular type of armor.

Chain mail — This category covers most medium levels of metal armor, including scale and brigandine. True chain mail is quite rare in the modern age, but some mortal Inquisitors keep a suit on hand.

Health levels: 2

Negative Traits: *Heavy*

Availability: Any. Chain mail generally must be custom made, and it can cost upward of $500.

Plate mail — Extremely expensive and hard to come by, these ornate suits of interlocking metal plates provide excellent protection but sacrifice a great deal of mobility.

Health levels: 3

Negative Traits: *Heavy, Clumsy*

Availability: Any. Plate mail generally must be custom-ordered, and it can cost upward of $3000.

Ballistic vest — This basic level of protection shields the wearer from some dangers, and it doesn't attract the same kind of attention that more complicated forms of armor are bound to bring.

Health levels: 2

Negative Traits: *Heavy*

Availability: *Police* 4, or *Underworld* 3.

Reinforced (bulletproof) vest — The favored type of armor for military personnel and law enforcement officers expecting dangerous situations, these vests provide excellent protection, even stopping many types of small-arms fire.

Health levels: 3

Negative Traits: *Heavy, Clumsy*

Availability: *Police* 5, or *Underworld* 4.

RANGED COMBAT

Many weapons allow a character to stand at a distance from a target and engage him in combat. In such situations, the character must still go over to the target (after shouting "Bang!" or "Twang!") and engage in a challenge.

If a character has surprised her opponent, even if she loses the first test, she has the option of calling for a second test. Once the second challenge is called, play continues as normal with that new challenge. The target is considered to be surprised for the first attack, and if he has no ranged weapon with which to return fire, he is considered "surprised" for as long as the aggressor can attack him without facing resistance (that is, if he wins on a challenge, she doesn't take damage).

If the target is aware of the attack before it happens, and he has a ranged weapon of his own, he is not considered to be surprised for the first attack. He may shoot back right away, and challenges are resolved as stated.

After the first shot is fired (and the first challenge is resolved), the target may attempt to return fire (assuming he is armed). The loser of a firefight challenge loses a health level.

Characters using the *Athletics* Ability to throw projectiles such as knives or axes fall under the same rules for regular ranged combat, including cover. Questions of range

should not be a problem, but use common sense if it becomes an issue, and don't forget to make allowances for things like enchanted weapons.

COVER

Fighting with ranged weapons allows combatants to stand some distance apart; participants can therefore "dive for cover." When resolving each ranged combat challenge, each combatant can present one Trait of cover to add to his total number of Traits. These cover Traits may not be used for bidding, but they do add to a player's total if Traits are compared. This cover can take the form of whatever obstacles are around and within reach (*don't* actually dive for them). A Narrator might be required to describe what cover is around unless the combatants can agree on what cover is available.

If cover is extensive, it may be worth more than one Trait. The number of Traits available for cover is left for challengers to agree on, or for a Narrator to decree. Hiding behind a boulder, for example, might be worth two Traits, while hiding behind a thin wood fence might count as only one. If one combatant goes completely under cover (he cannot be seen at all *and* is thoroughly protected), he is considered impossible to hit. The attacker must change his position to get a clear shot.

MELEE AND BRAWLING

Melee fighting can occur only when two parties are within weapon's reach of each other. Characters using melee weapons often have access to special abilities if they also possess the *Melee* Ability. For example, a trained character using a fencing foil can take advantage of his weapon's speed when fighting a character wielding a battle ax.

Brawling can occur only when two characters are within arm's length of each other. Characters engaged in brawling may use unarmed combat techniques on each other, including trips, kicks, punches, wrestling holds and throws. However, regardless of the description, unless the character possesses some supernatural power or other ability that specifically allows for extra damage, all brawling tests result in one health level of bashing damage.

SPECIALIZED FIGHTING STYLES

Buying a specialized fighting style under the *Melee* or *Brawl* Abilities allows you to describe how your character moves to allow retests and permits a certain flair for your attacks and defenses, but does not allow you to do extra damage or specific injuries.

DERANGEMENTS

Psychics who overuse their powers and shamans who truck too often with malicious spirits risk developing derangements when faced with overpowering conditions of extreme terror, guilt or anxiety. The Storyteller may decide a derangement is in order after any experience that generates especially intense and unpleasant emotions, or which violates a character's beliefs or ethics severely. All derangements carry "triggers," circumstances that cause the effects of the derangement to become active. Once activated, derangements remain in effect for the rest of the scene, and players must modify their character's Traits, attitudes and behavior in accordance with the derangement description. Characters may resist a derangement by expending a Willpower Trait — this effect lasts for only one scene; if the trigger is still present at the end of that time, the character must spend another Willpower Trait. In the case of particularly intense mental stress, Narrators may rule that additional Willpower Traits or a Static Willpower Challenge is required.

It is up to the Storyteller to determine what amount of time and Willpower is required to cure a derangement, and such cures are best left to thoughtful and involved roleplaying rather than simple Trait expenditure.

Note: There is nothing funny or arbitrary about the way a "crazy" person acts. The insane character is only reacting to the stimuli that he perceives to be real — to *him*, his behavior is perfectly normal. Players should never forget the **Mind's Eye Theatre** rules of safety still apply when roleplaying derangements.

Bulimia

Bulimic characters salve their guilt and insecurity by overindulging in activities that comfort them (such as eating). Characters with this affliction will gorge themselves as much as possible under stress then purge their systems drastically. At the Narrator's discretion, the character may overindulge in other pleasurable activities — sex, dancing, even magic — but such alterations should be uncommon, and they should be justified in the character's history.

Crimson Rage

A character with this derangement experiences unprovoked fits of anger due to pent-up feelings of helplessness and inadequacy. Most such fits are triggered by failure to overcome some obstacle, or being confronted by a specific type of situation (such as pain, emotional distress or romantic failure). The player should work with the Narrator to determine what triggers his character's derangement. Whenever this derangement is active, the character gains the Negative Traits *Violent* x 2 and *Impatient*, and the player should roleplay the fury as well as possible within the **Mind's Eye Theatre** rules of safety.

Fugue

Characters suffering this affliction react to stress by adopting a specific set of behaviors. In the process, they suffer blackouts or periods of memory loss. When confronted by extreme stress, the character must win a Static Willpower Challenge. If he fails, the character blacks out and the player must roleplay the character's trancelike state. Otherwise, control of the character passes to a Narrator for a scene, who dictates the actions the character takes in order to remove the stress. At the end of the fugue, the character comes to his rightful senses with no memory of his fugue actions.

Hysteria

Characters with this derangement are unable to control their emotions properly when subjected to stress or pressure. They become vulnerable to wild mood swings and fits of intense violence against the source of their discomfort. The character must make a Willpower Test against five Traits any time such stress is present. If she fails, she is two Traits down on all Social tests due to her wildly fluctuating moods, and she gains the Negative Trait *Violent* as well. In addition, this derangement activates automatically whenever the character fails in a particularly stressful or important challenge. (Narrators have final say on what classifies as such a dramatic failure.)

Manic-Depression

This derangement causes a character to suffer devastating mood swings. Whenever the character fails to achieve a personal goal, she must win a Static Willpower Challenge or fall into a depressive state for a number of scenes determined by the Narrator. While depressed, the character's Willpower Traits are considered halved

(round down, minimum one) for purposes of Trait comparison, and she may not use any powers or Numinae to raise her Physical Traits or otherwise lighten her mood. After that, she enters a period of highly upbeat energy and excitement, in which she pursues her goals obsessively for a number of scenes equal to the time she spent in depression. During this manic time, she has the Negative Trait *Impatient* x 2.

Megalomania

These individuals have made power the focus of their existence, and they must always be the most potent individuals in their environment. Where the power stems from is irrelevant as long as they are dominant. They believe that other people are divided into two classes: lesser beings and beings elevated beyond their worth. Due to their supreme confidence, those with this derangement are considered one Trait up on all Willpower Tests while their derangement is active. However, they must also make a Willpower Test (difficulty six Traits) to resist any opportunity to put people in their place or reprimand any contentious upstarts who dare to presume beyond their station during that time. Although megalomaniacs play for keeps, the actions they take against others in this state need not be mindlessly violent. However, they are typically vicious in the extreme. Such actions are designed to humiliate the offender and exalt the character's standing in the eyes of others.

Multiple Personalities

A character with this derangement has suffered mental anguish so severe that his mind reacted by creating additional personas. Each personality is relevant to the trauma that caused it, and the player should work with the Storyteller to determine each personality's Nature and what triggers a particular one to rise to the surface. When a personality is triggered, it assumes control until the conditions it was created to deal with have passed. Characters can manifest different Abilities and even Numinae for each personality; however, all such Traits must still be purchased normally. What a personality believes it can do is often very different from what it is actually capable of. Any such arrangements must be worked out with the Storyteller.

Obsessive/Compulsive

Characters suffering from this derangement are driven to control their environment. Obsessive characters keep one aspect of their life constant, be it personal cleanliness or simply keeping things quiet. Compulsive characters perform specific actions or sets of actions, such as washing their hands constantly or always saying lengthy prayers after touching another person. Obsessive/compulsive characters are one Trait up to resist any supernatural mental coercion like vampiric *Dominate*, changeling *Chicanery*, or mage *Mind* Effects or any other attempts to coerce them to give up their set behaviors, but they attack anyone who tries to prevent them from adhering to their derangement. They need not try to kill the target, but they will inflict as much harm as is necessary to allow them to indulge in their derangement once again. If no clear individual is the source of their frustration, then the nearest person at hand will suffice. Failing that, the scenery or even the character himself is in for a world of hurt.

Paranoia

Paranoid beings believe that all their woes and suffering stem from a malicious external source. Many afflicted beings come up with intricate theories about just who is against them and why. Those they suspect of being against them are often subject to swift and brutal violence. Paranoid characters trust no one, not even family members or close friends, and they have a difficult time interacting with others. They are one

Trait down on all Social Challenges while their derangement is active, and they suffer from the Negative Traits *Violent* and *Condescending*.

Regression

Characters suffering from this affliction avoid facing responsibilities or consequences by retreating to a younger state of mind in which they feel that less will be required of them. They may alternate between times of whimsy and temper tantrums, but they will always seek to put a more powerful individual between them and whatever is plaguing them. Victims of this derangement are two Traits down on all Mental Challenges.

Schizophrenia

Individuals with this derangement have had their psyche fractured by terrible, unresolved inner conflicts. Most people conceive of this disorder when they think about insanity. Victims might imagine anything from the relatively harmless delusion that they're walking a goldfish on a leash to the more sinister conviction that they must cut out their children's eyes to keep them from being tainted by the evil on television. Even still, this disorder is anything but arbitrary. The player should work with the Storyteller to determine a general set of behaviors relevant to the original trauma. Characters with this derangement are unpredictable and dangerous. In situations where their inner conflict flares up, they must retest any kind of challenge to retain self-control that they win. (If they win that retest, they do not have to retest again, though.) Furthermore, they are two Traits down on all Willpower-related tests.

TRUE FAITH

True Faith is belief in a power, entity, consciousness — sometimes even a purpose — that is greater than oneself, and as such, it is not limited to any particular religion. Even supernatural monsters like vampires can have it, but even so, only those beings of the most pure character — the truly selfless, caring, compassionate and courageous — have a chance at possessing True Faith. Most creatures come across True Faith only when they do battle with the Inquisition or other hunters, and True Faith is often rare in those groups. Then again, vampires and werewolves and mages are not common, either.

True Faith must be purchased as a Merit, which gives a starting character one True Faith Trait. As the strong belief in a higher power gives the character with True Faith the ability to affect many supernatural creatures, characters may only improve their Faith with exceptional roleplaying and Storyteller approval. Inquisitor characters may increase their Faith by acting appropriately for their Faith and spending three Experience points for each additional True Faith Trait; other characters must work with their Storyteller in determining how to advance their belief. True Faith ratings for characters may vary from one to five True Faith Traits; a person with five True Faith Traits is a veritable saint.

Though more common in rural areas, holders of True Faith might number as few as one per 100,000 mortals in a city. Though a few individuals may have 6 or more True Faith Traits, they are the rarest saints of the World of Darkness, and probably number no more than one per billion ordinary mortals.

True Faith is normally not saccharine or wimpy. It represents a fiercely held belief, usually with ethics involving compassion, justice and helpfulness. Those who possess high ratings of True Faith may even seem unbalanced or insane to those who do not share their beliefs. While those who possess True Faith are usually selfless and caring, some take a fiercely protective role toward the innocent. These are the wielders of True

Faith most often found in the Inquisition or as hunters — while compassion may be a rule of their code, Faithful justice can be harsh indeed.

CRISES OF FAITH AND REGAINING FAITH TRAITS

Any time a character loses a challenge in which she uses True Faith, she begins to question her faith, or at least her standing with her higher power. She is down one Trait on all Social Challenges and may not invoke her Faith until a Storyteller rules that she has resolved her crisis of Faith, perhaps by meditating, praying or otherwise spending 30 minutes out of play reaffirming her Faith.

Because they are so meaningful, lost or spent True Faith Traits are difficult to regain. A storyteller should allow a character to regain True Faith Traits only when he participates in a meaningful expression of Faith; mere ritual is not enough. Storytellers would be justified in requiring characters to spend 30 minutes out of play witnessing, participating in Mass or confessional, or otherwise drawing upon the wellspring of their Faith.

HOLY SYMBOLS, BLESSED ITEMS AND RELICS

Possessors of True Faith are often able to use the symbols of their Faith in invoking their deity or combating the supernatural. Crucifixes, crosses, mandalas, icons, phylacteries and copies of scriptures are also often found. By brandishing his holy symbol, the bearer gains the Social Trait *Intimidating* when repelling undead and warding off demonic and supernatural powers. If used to strike a supernatural creature, a holy symbol grants the extra Physical Traits *Burning* and *Searing*, and it inflicts one level of aggravated damage. If a vampire or other undead or infernal foe has the Flaw *Repelled by Crosses*, he takes an additional level of aggravated damage when touched on bare skin by a cross wielded by a person with True Faith.

BLESSED ITEMS AND PEOPLE

Blessed items are created when a person with five True Faith Traits blesses an item or person, such as a worshipper, holy symbol, sword or scripture of her faith. It takes a half an hour of prayer or meditation and the expenditure of a True Faith Trait to bless an item or person. A blessed item temporarily acquires one of the following blessed bonus Traits until used: *Burning, Searing, Blinding, Branding, Purging, Cleansing* or *Purifying*. In combat, the wielder of a blessed item may bid the blessed Trait in a normal Physical Challenge. If successful, the item's touch does at least one health level of aggravated damage (more if the item's normal damage is higher; a blessed broadsword would cause two health levels of aggravated damage). Note that only the base damage becomes aggravated. If the wielder loses a challenge in which he bids the blessed bonus Trait, the item is no longer blessed. If the wielder bids a normal Physical Trait, then the blessed Trait is not risked and the item does normal damage.

Blessing another person is a very ceremonial event, and the blessing gives that person one retest that may be used in a single challenge. A person or item may only receive the benefits of one blessing; blessings cannot be "stacked."

RELICS

Found in many religions, relics are pieces of saint's bodies or possessions that have been invested with holy energy over the centuries. Though even a fake or misperceived relic can become holy if enough believers trust in it, relics are rare. They can range in size from a splinter of bone to a large altar, and are usually housed in a container called a reliquary. They may have as many Holy Traits as the Storyteller needs; the begging bowl of a venerated Buddhist saint or a Christian saint might have one or two Holy Traits, while splinters of the True Cross might have five Holy Traits. Most relics encountered in game are likely to be no greater than three Traits. A supernatural entity that touches a relic without being invited by its wielder takes one level of aggravated damage for every Holy Trait the relic possesses. Unlike blessed items, the Holy Traits are not normally lost when a challenge is lost, unless the relic is damaged or defiled.

HOLY GROUND

When congregations meet and venerate a particular site, it may sometimes become holy ground. These locations carry their own Faith Traits, which can be used to bolster the True Faith Traits of a believer for whom the ground is holy. Holy ground will normally have from one to three Faith Traits, though places of worldwide worship like the Vatican, Mecca or the Wailing Wall might have five or more Faith Traits. A grand cathedral of hypocrites would likely have no Faith Traits, while a small chapel in the woods or a pool where a dedicated group met for years might have two or three Faith traits.

A believer with True Faith can call upon her higher power to ward holy ground against uninvited supernatural intruders for a scene. Once holy ground is activated in this manner, uninvited vampires and demonic creatures cannot enter or cross it without spending a Willpower Trait or a number of Mental Traits equal to the holy ground's number of Faith Traits. Doing so allows the uninvited creature to stay for 10 minutes or travel up to 50 feet into or through the holy ground. If a vampire or demonic creature is present when the holy ground is activated, they must spend the Willpower or Mental Traits immediately or leave. Moreover, any of that holy ground's believers may add the holy ground's Faith Traits to their own when resisting supernatural powers, even if the believer does not possess True Faith.

USES OF TRUE FAITH

ONE TRAIT OF TRUE FAITH

Regaining Willpower

For every hour spent alone and meditating, praying or otherwise sincerely performing the rituals of her faith, a believer with True Faith may regain a spent Willpower Trait. If she has not spent any, she may gain a temporary Willpower Trait in excess of her normal permanent Willpower traits. This number of excess temporary Willpower Traits may not exceed the believers total True Faith Traits, and any excess Willpower Traits disappear 12 hours after they are first gained.

Faith is a powerful motivator, and True Faith Traits may also be substituted for temporary Willpower Traits when a believer has no temporary Willpower Traits left. Alas, the reverse is not true.

Repel Vampires

A character with one Trait of True Faith may attempt to repel vampires by brandishing his holy symbol, invoking his belief ("In the name of _____, I command you to be gone," etc.) and employing a Social Challenge. Success means the vampire

must flee the area immediately. Failure means the vampire must retreat a few feet and cower before taking action, and the vampire still may not initiate any attacks during the next turn, although she may defend herself normally. A vampire may resist this use of True Faith only by attempting to overbid with Willpower; if she currently possesses at least twice as many Willpower Traits as the faithful character, she remains unaffected. A character may attempt to repel multiple vampires with a group challenge, affecting as many vampires as they have Traits of True Faith.

Infernalists and servants of demonic evil suffer even worse. Such creatures of dark powers must automatically flee when a believer invokes True Faith, regardless of the result of the Social Challenge or the number of True Faith Traits possessed by the believer.

TWO TRAITS OF TRUE FAITH

Holy Resistance

A believer with at least two permanent True Faith Traits may expend a temporary True Faith Traits to resist a mind-controlling supernatural power for a scene, once it is used against him. When attacked, the believer must expend one True Faith Trait in lieu of the normal challenge. This will protect him from mind-controlling powers from that creature for one scene. This effect works against mind-controlling powers like vampiric *Dominate*, the *Puppetry* Arcanos or a Changeling's Sovereign Art of Dictum, but not against powers that influence emotions like vampiric *Presence*, wraithly *Keening*, or Changeling *Chicanery*.

Faith Healing

A believer with at least two permanent True Faith Traits may expend a temporary True Faith Trait and attempt to heal someone who is injured by laying on hands, chanting or otherwise acting appropriately for her faith. If she wins or ties a Simple Test, she can heal one health level of damage. If she fails, then she cannot, and suffers a crisis of faith (see above).

THREE TRAITS OF TRUE FAITH

Sense Unholy Presence

In a quiet or otherwise undistracted setting, a person with three True Faith Traits may sense the presence of the unholy, including vampires, infernalists and the demonic. This obviously won't work if the believer is distracted by loud noises, club lights and the like. If he wins or ties a Simple Test, he senses the unholy presence; this even penetrates powers that hide the creature, allowing the believer to sense vampires using *Obfuscate*, Black Spiral Dancer werewolves using *Blur of the Milky Eye* and similar powers.

FOUR TRAITS OF TRUE FAITH

Holy Invulnerability

A believer with at least four permanent True Faith Traits is immune to becoming a ghoul, a fomor or other base or fallen creature. Moreover, if a mind-control or emotion-swaying power like wraithly *Keening* or vampiric *Presence* is used upon the believer, she may expend a temporary True Faith Trait and become resistant to that creature's mind-control or emotion-swaying powers for the rest of the scene.

FIVE TRAITS OF TRUE FAITH

Blessing

A believer with at least five permanent True Faith Traits is able to expend a temporary True Faith Trait and bless an item or person, as described above. This normally takes 30 minutes for an item and a suitably impressive ceremony for a person (likewise taking some time).

ALTERNATIVE FAITHS

Faith is a power derived from beings beyond mortal comprehension, and the manifestation of True Faith in an individual will vary according to her belief in that religion. The powers of Faith, however, do not always depend on the type of Faith.

Generally the rules for Faith as given above apply for all religions, but the descriptive effects for storytelling purposes can vary according to the religion in question. Certainly the rituals involved will vary.

For example, *Via Medicamenti*, a *Theurgy* power (q.v.) is variously referred to in the outside world as Faith Healing, psychic surgery, or simply a "miracle." The effect is still ostensibly the same if used by a Wiccan or an Inquisitor. Similarly, the powers to expel spirits through exorcism, whether by Theurgy, psychic powers or True Faith all achieve roughly the same ends through different means. An observer is unlikely to be able to tell the difference — in fact even those who have experience with such matters may have a hard time telling which "sort of power" is being used in a given interest. An exorcism through psychic powers may just as easily involve the psychic enacting a ritual similar to one of the Faithful expelling a wraith.

When dealing with religiously powered characters in a chronicle, examine which power is perhaps most appropriate for the development of the story or the character in question. Not every Inquisitor has True Faith. Some reverend fathers may manifest psychic powers and presume them to be the power of the Lord, although those who check for spiritual purity may know the difference. A Quabbalist with the power to read computer information with his mind may consider it a faith in the mathematics of the Torah that allows him said access to the patterns on the disks before him. If the information as to the true nature of the power is revealed in the course of the game, his brethren may hunt the character for being possessed of demon-inflicted powers rather than those god-granted. On such hooks are stories hung.

THE BEATIFIC

Note: Always consider the power level and story of your chronicle before introducing characters with such powers as those given below. Don't use these rules if you just think "they're kewl."

Individuals who are particularly strong in Faith (six permanent Traits or more) are literally beacons in the World of Darkness. They are called many names: friends of God, saints, holy men; their title matters not. They are the advocates of Heaven on Earth, living vessels of faith.

The Beatific gain the Merit *Holy Aura* — their aura burns so brightly for any creature that can see the aura. Even those who cannot see auras sense something more about these people.

The Beatific no longer need to rely on holy symbols to call on the powers of their Faith when contending directly with the forces of darkness.

The Beatific may make a Static Faith Challenge (as with any other challenge, risking a Faith Trait instead of a Mental Trait, for example) against a difficulty of 7 Traits to detect the presence of any supernatural creatures within the immediate area. This will not pinpoint such creatures, just alert the Beatific to their presence. By expending a Willpower Trait, the Beatific can pinpoint the nearest supernatural creature, but they will remain ignorant of its nature.

The Beatific can automatically see through all levels of Kindred *Obfuscate*, *Chimerstry*, and other related Disciplines, Gifts or other powers on a successful Mental Challenge against the initiator of the power. This may be retested by the Beatific with the *Awareness* Ability.

Vampires, wraiths and demons cannot stand to be in the presence of the Beatific and will retreat. They cannot approach any closer than one foot per Faith Trait the Beatific possesses without beating the Beatific in a Static Willpower Challenge against the number of Faith Traits the Beatific possesses, expending a single Willpower Trait whether the challenge was successful or not. If the Beatific approaches, they are forced to back away.

Demons and other creatures recoil from the touch of the Beatific, and they refuse to touch them. Kindred touching the Beatific with malicious intent receive aggravated damage equal to the number of levels of damage that would have been inflicted on the victim. However, the Beatific can touch Kindred without any difficulty, causing no automatic damage.

TORTURE AND THE SUPERNATURAL

Note: Need we remind you that the actual use of torture in a game is a Bad Thing? This isn't the sort of game where hurting others is fun. Players of characters being "tortured" are asked nicely not to scream too loudly.

Hunters have, for many years, faced down adversaries with incredible resilience to physical damage. Yet for all the vaunted restorative abilities of vampires and werewolves, they still remain subject to the methods and devices of a skilled torturer. While some creatures are more resistant to pain, there are other methods of coercing a victim into submission or confession. Much of the lore held by hunter organizations in regards to the physiology and behavioral triggers of such creatures owes its discovery to such coercive procedures, however concealed those origins may be.

Vampires can be reduced to gibbering wrecks through the careful and methodical application of pain and starvation. An intelligent torturer can prevent even a hungry vampire from becoming frenzied, ensuring his victim remains weak from lack of blood. Minimal levels of blood may be supplied — a dead cat becomes a welcome feast to the Beast, no matter how mangy — but granting too much may place the Inquisitor at serious risk.

Werewolves are equally problematic, due to their rapid healing powers and incredible innate resistance to damage. Simple silver shackles do much to reduce the risk — a werewolf in Homid form rapidly changing to Crinos will likely find his hands and wrists amputated. While the various Changing Breeds have had considerably less contact with the Inquisition, it is not impossible that a rare Inquisitor may be familiar with their particular weaknesses through study, time and practical application.

Torturing a wraith certainly poses a challenge, but it may be possible through the direct threat to any of the wraith's Fetters — items thought to attach ghosts to the world of the living. Indirect manipulation of the emotions of the wraith may weaken its resolve and give rise to the Shadow of the wraith. Destruction of a Fetter naturally distresses a wraith (the Harrowing that may follow can strengthen its dark side, probably affirming the Inquisitor's suspicions of it being an evil spirit) but does not "physically" harm the entity. The application of certain aspects of *Theurgy*, however, allows more direct manipulation of the wraith and may be used to damage its Corpus. Emotional torture is more likely to work on a wraith than physical torture.

Changelings and mages are more or less as vulnerable as normal mortals. They may have access to powers that bolster their resistance to pain, but it is very hard to manifest those powers when bound to a rack or hung from barbed chains. Those who are familiar with ancient folk lore, who have a reliable information source, who themselves have *Changeling Lore* at three or more Traits or are naturally experimental may find that the fae are affected negatively by cold iron, but it is unlikely that people uneducated in such matters would have the material ready.

Humanity	Action
5	Harsh and hurtful language
4	Threats, minimal violence, smacking someone
3	More systematic violence: "roughing someone up"
2	Use of torture devices; psychological torture
1	Systematic and detailed physical and psychological torture designed to inflict ultimate pain and suffering over a long time

SYSTEMS

The basic purpose of torture is to inflict pain and suffering on the subject until such time as their spirit and resolve is broken. Inflicting the pain is a means to an end, not the end itself… in most cases. Anything above simplistic applications of torture (arm-twisting, flogging, amputation) requires skill in the *Torture* Ability. While rough and ready methods may have some effect on the attitudes of the victim, the careful and skilled application of a variety of methods over a period of time is required to truly break the will of the unfortunate.

Prisoners bound to a torture device or restrained for torture are generally considered to receive automatic damage whenever the torturer so desires, without the need for challenges. The only variable factor is how much damage the creature receives in any given application of a device. Some devices deliver damage gradually, others deliver instantly. Typically, a torture device delivers anywhere from one level of bashing damage to three levels of lethal damage per application, depending on the nature of the device and its normal effect on the body. While certain applications of torture may cause aggravated damage, or higher levels of lethal damage, the idea here is not to kill the subject but to break his will over time. A dead prisoner tells no secrets.

While under duress, the subject is also usually subjected to humiliation and psychological torture. The emotional aspect of torture can be far more devastating than the physical pain. Prisoners being tortured are usually also being interrogated for secrets and information. For each period of emotionally effective torture, the torturer may make a Mental Challenge against the victim's Willpower Traits (which are risked and lost as Attribute Traits would be in a similar case), which can be retested with the *Torture* Ability. The victim may retest by expending Willpower Traits. If the victim loses, he will reveal some level of information related to the interrogation. When a prisoner has no Willpower Traits remaining, he will usually give up, answering any questions even if he has to construct an answer from whole cloth to appease his tormentor.

HUMANITY, FAITH AND TORTURE

Will someone who has faith, following the tenets of her religion, ever torture someone? This very much depends on the cultural paradigm in question. Torture was a standard feature of medieval jurisprudence, so Inquisitors in a medieval chronicle might not have to make as many *Conscience* checks. However, we are taught today that torture, no matter what the reason, is wrong, so modern Inquisitors who engage in systematic torture should expect their Humanity to drop quickly. Even simple arm-twisting counts as torture but is nowhere near as vicious as using an Iron Maiden, so *Conscience* checks should be at the Trait levels on the Path of Humanity given in the box below (note: this can include by-standers who let the torture take place). Remember that a character with the True Faith Numina who falls below 5 Humanity loses his Faith rating immediately.

FROM HERE TO THERE BUT NOT BACK AGAIN: TRANSFORMATIONS

GENERAL CONCEPTS

To all appearances, the World of Darkness is heading to Hell in a handbasket. To keep the mood and feel of the Gothic-Punk world, the transformation from mortal to vampire, werewolf or changeling should be a terrifying loss, and not an elevation to a caped and furry or fanged crusader against crime. Ghosts and vampires and werewolves are monsters, not Muppets.

With this in mind, the Storyteller is the final arbiter in determining what effect the change from normal human being to supernatural creature has upon a character. Beware of the player who tries to mix and match powers to have just the right type of Gift or Discipline after a change; it is perfectly reasonable to rule that any strange transformations automatically send the confused character's soul and psyche to Oblivion or some other permanent, irreversible fate.

MORTAL TO MAGE: AWAKENING

When a mortal Awakens as a mage, they frequently put aside their past cares. The Ascension War may have been lost, but contending with one's Avatar may take time from studies, prayer or social obligations. At the Storyteller's discretion, newly Awakened mages may retain any sorcerous Praxes that they had previously, though these static arts cannot be combined with the more fluid realities of Sphere magic; this is often the case with initiates into the Order of Hermes. In like manner, a believer with True Faith might retain their Numinae if they gravitate toward an appropriate Tradition or Craft for their Faith; unfortunately, they no longer gain the benefit of any of its powers beyond the ability to use True Faith Traits in lieu of Willpower Traits. Otherwise, newly Awakened mages forget their past psychic and True Faith Numinae as their Avatars lead them toward Ascension.

MORTAL TO KINDRED: THE EMBRACE

There are several paths for mortals to become vampires in the World of Darkness. Whether your chronicle is angst-filled and tragic or more like the frenetic nights of *Near Dark*, remember that the tension between a vampire's Beast and his Humanity or other path is a core element in this genre.

Mortal Embrace

If you want to include vampires from **Laws of the Night** and the transformation from mortal to vampire in your chronicle, go for it; if not, let the attempted Embrace fail, killing the mortal. When a normal mortal is successfully Embraced, she normally becomes one generation weaker than her sire and she gains three basic powers of Cainite Disciplines from her sire's normal clan Disciplines. She may also add one Physical, Social or Mental Trait to her normal Traits. At Storyteller discretion, she may lose a Humanity Trait. She also gains rather fatal or uncomfortable allergies to sunlight, fire, wooden stakes and the lack of a good blood supply.

Most mortals will lose all psychic, sorcerous and True Faith Numinae. Only the very, very rare Cainite can reconcile True Faith with the ravenous Beast; allowing a player to let their character do so is risky at best. At the Storyteller's option, a sorcerer who is Embraced as Tremere, Giovanni or Tzimisce may use up to half of the Experience Traits she used to purchase sorcerous Numinae before her transformation to repurchase *Thaumaturgy*, *Necromancy* or *Koldunic Sorcery*. A sorcerer Embraced by an occult-minded Malkavian is *not* going to suddenly start sprouting *Thaumaturgy*!

Kinfolk with Gnosis or Rage and kinain with Glamour suffer much worse when they are Embraced; they lose all Traits of Gnosis, Rage or Glamour; the Curse of Caine is much more powerful than mere relation.

Mortal to Ghoul: Enthrallment

Cainites frequently blood bond mortals with three tastes of Cainite blood over three different nights, creating a soul-deep unnatural love for the vampire. Occasionally, though, one will feed a half liter or more of her blood to a mortal and share some of her vampiric powers. When a normal mortal is successfully made into a ghoul, he ceases aging and normally gains one basic power of the Cainite Disciplines of *Celerity (Alacrity)*, *Fortitude (Endurance)* or *Potence (Prowess)*; the default is *Prowess*. He may also add one Trait to any category of his choosing.

There are exceptions. Vampires cannot ghoul believers with four or more True Faith Traits; their faith protects them. Those thin-blooded Cainites of the 14th Generation must win or tie a Simple Test to get the ghouling to take, and 15th-generation vampires must win the test outright.

When a ghoul does not receive at least one Blood Trait a month (or more frequently, in some cases), he reverts back to a normal human of his appropriate age; this

is fatal if the ghoul is older than a century or so. He also loses his Cainite Disciplines, though he will normally retain the basic power of each of the Disciplines he had known if he becomes a ghoul again.

Ghoul and Revenant Embrace

When a ghoul (or Revenant) is Embraced, she keeps her Cainite Disciplines, except for the physical Discipline she gained as a ghoul (unless it is one of her new clan's Disciplines). Otherwise, the transition is much smoother than it is for a normal human, though she does not gain the extra Attribute Trait (she received it when she was ghouled).

MORTAL TO GAROU: THE FIRST CHANGE

When Gaia touches a mortal and the First Change occurs, all psychic, sorcerous and True Faith Numinae are swept away as the new Garou or Bête revels in the transformation. Even the insidious takeover of the Ananasi has this effect. As a very rare option, the Storyteller might elect to allow a new-changed shifter with True Faith in Gaia to retain her faith enough to use True Faith Traits in lieu of Willpower Traits as allowed for mortals.

MORTAL TO FOMOR

Normally, the possession of a mortal by Banes causes the mortal to slowly lose her powers (with certain exceptions for psychics belonging to Pentex's Projects Iliad and Odyssey, who have their own worries). For each month of Bane possession, a new fomor loses the highest level of her psychic, sorcerous and True Faith Numinae; the loss is permanent, although a recovered mortal may go to work building them back as usual. Note that Banes cannot possess believers with four or more True Faith Traits; their faith protects them.

MORTAL TO CHANGELING: THE CHRYSALIS

It's really very simple: When the Dreaming infuses a new changeling with Glamour and she undergoes the changes of the Chrysalis, the change washes away any previous psychic, sorcerous or True Faith Numina.

MORTAL TO WRAITH: DEATH, THE FINAL FRONTIER

If awakening into a dream is traumatic, the fall into death is more so. Mortal characters who become wraiths lose any previous psychic, sorcerous or True Faith Numinae as they become wraiths.

Jeremy pulled his coat collar tighter, trying to ignore the chill that sundown was bringing. He stared at the mounded earth, now turning to mud with the drizzle that had been off and on all day. Single flowers, crumpled and bruised from the drizzle and too much handling, were scattered on top of the mound. There was no marker yet — that would arrive in two weeks. For now, there was only the metal plate that pointed to where Stephen had been laid.

Had Stephen known they were tracking him? Was that why he'd come to see Jeremy, hoping to throw them off, or maybe to see him one last time? He thought about what Stephen had told him during the late-night conversations, or the things mentioned in passing — holy warriors who used repulsive cruelty in a campaign against creatures that sucked the blood from the living. Had anyone told him the same story the week before, he would have laughed at them. But not just anyone had told him this story — his beloved older brother who could never lie to him had told him this with a straight face. And then the three people at the loading dock, who had killed Stephen without a shred of remorse. Did Jenny try to flee them, get cut down in some corner of a dirty city, when she couldn't force herself to kill anything, not even a monster?

With his last breath, Stephen had begged him to find her, finish the job he couldn't, but Jeremy suspected there was more to it than that, just like there had been more to everything surrounding his brother. It was not enough just to find Jenny — he had to find the ones that had killed Stephen, take back the life that they had stolen. Not just Stephen's, but also Jenny's and now his.

Who's the bigger monster? The one that sucks your blood, or the one that drains your spirit?

Jeremy fingered the little Connemara cross at his throat. "You gave me a big job, big brother. I guess it's like you said — God doesn't give you anything you can't handle." He paused, feeling the sorrow squeeze his heart as one memory after another washed over him. "I just wish you didn't think I could handle so much."

CHAPTER SEVEN: STORYTELLING

Whether you're new to storytelling (and are panicking because your first game starts in three weeks and you don't have a clue as to how you're going to go about it) or a veteran of the plotline wars (and are looking for a fresh perspective on running mortal games), this chapter is for you. This section discusses the ins and outs of storytelling for mortals. It takes you through the very basics of creating and tracking plots, and into the benefits of playing mortals and building stories around them. You'll learn about developing solid story seeds for mortals, the secrets of improvisational tale spinning and how to enhance your stories by incorporating theme and mood. Finally, this chapter offers tips on using some of the most powerful but dangerous story elements.

"SO, WHO'S THE STORYTELLER?"

The players can gather at the game site, resplendent in their costumes, and play rock-paper-scissors all night long if they want, but without a Storyteller they are just a bunch of actors in search of a script. They might be able to amuse themselves for a few hours by having their characters beat the tar out of one another, but unless a Storyteller shows up, that particular session is going to be a wash. Unfortunately, it happens too often that the role of Storyteller is thrust upon an unwilling member of a troupe, conferred as a black joke on whomever failed to turn up for a meeting, or it is assumed reluctantly by a member because no one else is willing to take on the responsibility. In these groups, storytelling is perceived as a chore or a burden, and nobody really wants to do it. If you're storytelling, such groups reason, you aren't playing a character, and therefore you aren't having any fun, right? Wrong.

Storytelling is as fulfilling as any experience to be had in **Mind's Eye Theatre** games. To the right person, it's the most rewarding experience that the game has to offer. The rewards of storytelling are very real, even if they are largely intangible. If you doubt this, why not give storytelling a try on a limited basis, and see how it goes? Volunteer to run a subplot for your regular Storyteller, or offer her your services as a Narrator for an evening. It's nothing short of phenomenal to watch a game that you put together entertain your players for hours. There's nothing quite like the feeling a Storyteller gets when the game session is over for the night, but the players are howling for more. While

it's true that a lot of players won't ever understand or appreciate the amount of time and effort their Storytellers put into the game, some will, and when they thank you for it, you'll understand why storytelling is the best gig in the game.

FROM THE GROUND UP: THE BASICS

Anyone can throw a random antagonist at her player characters or track Experience Traits, and call herself a Storyteller. Sadly, that's exactly the sort of thing that passes for storytelling in some groups. Good storytelling, however, is more than just administering mob scene combats and recording Experience Traits. A good Storyteller possesses capabilities such as patience, diplomacy and flexibility. Good Storytellers are comfortable with the rules of the game but don't let the rulebooks limit their creativity.

THE TWO COMMANDMENTS OF GOOD STORYTELLING

KNOW THY PLAYERS

Before you start a new chronicle, make an effort to learn what your players want (or think they want) from the game. The players have as important a hand in creating and developing the story as you do, so don't sell them short and don't try to railroad them into plots or stories they don't care for. Maybe you want to tell an action-oriented story that involves a crossover between several different character types, but maybe your players would rather play in a more thoughtful story that's about love and vengeance. When such discrepancies in story preference exist, one side or the other is going to be disappointed. A little communication can prevent this problem from occurring, and diminish its effects if it has already occurred. It's never a mistake to poll your players, either before or during a chronicle, and ask what kind of things they want to see in the game.

During the game sessions, make another effort, this time to figure out by observing their actions where your individual players fit on the scale of active-reactive. Neither extreme is inherently better or worse, and most players will fall somewhere in between. Reactive players prefer to observe the game as it unfolds, and they normally involve themselves if they see something personally interesting. Even then, their response may be relatively low-key. Active players are never at rest, even when they probably should be. They tend to follow their own schemes and plans as often as they follow the offered plots. If you can determine where on the active-reactive scale a given player falls, you'll be able to make the game more meaningful to her, and you'll also be better able to cope with any problems that may arise.

KNOW THYSELF

If you're new to storytelling, realize now that the task will eat up a staggering amount of your free time if you allow it to do so. The responsibilities and duties of the Storyteller creep into your life nearly every day — whether it's answering email from players or just thinking about the plots you're currently juggling, you'll find that the work of storytelling expands to fill the time you're willing to give it. If you're not willing to commit this kind of time and effort to storytelling, or if your other obligations don't leave you enough time to do the role justice, you may want to consider passing the torch to someone else or getting some help. To most groups, the latter is, usually, preferable to the former.

When you find your head spinning, your blood pressure rising and your temper shortening because you've just got too much to do and too little time to do it in, try delegating some of your Storyteller responsibilities to Narrators. Does your next game session require you to create statistics and character sheets for a dozen Narrator characters? Ask a Narrator to write up half of them for you. Are characters' Influence Trait actions coming in faster than you can handle them? Try recruiting a Narrator just to handle those tasks. Can't decide which direction a particular plot should take? Bounce some ideas off your Narrators and see what you come up with together. Need two Storyteller characters to show up simultaneously in your next game, but you can play only one? Delegate the other to a Narrator.

GOT GAME?

The most basic function of the Storyteller is to provide stories for your playing group. This section explores the fundamentals of devising good mortal stories.

BUILDING STORIES

If you're new to storytelling — and even if you're a veteran — it might seem that the best way to go about starting a new hunter game is to ask your players to create some mortal characters, and then walk into the next game session armed with a few plot notes jotted down on an index card, and maybe the statistics for a random antagonist, and have at it. While this technique might work once or twice, most Storytellers can't get away with it more often than that (and even when they do, players often note their lack of preparation and feel disappointed). It's not a sound strategy if you want to give your players your best effort, or if you want to get the most out of the storytelling experience. The best stories don't just happen: They are sought out, seized and shaped. Ultimately they are exposed to the players, who then make their own contributions, but more about that later. First, let's examine the basic ingredients of these tales: theme, mood and plot.

THEME

Think of the theme as the organizing principle of your story. It's the touchstone to which you'll refer whenever you're confused or uncertain about where the story is going next, and the underlying message that your plots support. Usually a good theme consists of just one or two words that function as the question your story strives to answer as you guide it through any number of game sessions.

Don't club your players over the head with the theme, however. While the theme should make its presence felt in the course of each game session, it needn't be completely obvious. Good themes for mortal characters and mortal games are much like those germane to other **Mind's Eye Theatre** venues, but they take on special meanings and implications when applied to "ordinary" beings. Here are some suggestions for themes, and the questions they raise, that are applicable to mortals:

Truth — Is the truth really out there? Or is there no such thing as truth? Why do we want to know the truth, even when we realize that knowing may be harmful? How many separate truths can there be?

Faith — Is faith natural to humans, or can it be acquired or learned? Why does faith sometimes falter? If faith disappears, can it ever be regained? What sacrifices do we make for our faith? What effect does our faith have on those around us?

Ethics — What is right and what is wrong? How do we decide? What are the implications of our decisions, both for ourselves and for those around us?

Love — Does love truly conquer all? How does it affect our behavior, hopes and aspirations? What will we do for love? What happens when the object of our love doesn't love us in return?

Hate — How does hate develop, and what does it do to us? Can we ever purge ourselves of hate? Is love truly the opposite of hate? How does hatred distort our perceptions?

Vengeance — Can a desire for revenge ever truly be sated? To what lengths will we go to avenge ourselves? What does the need for revenge do to a person's perceptions of the world?

Freedom — How far will we go to obtain freedom? What does it mean to be free? Is true freedom possible, or is it merely an illusion? What happens to our hearts and minds when we are denied freedom?

Mortality — How does the knowledge of our impending death affect us? If offered a chance to cheat death, would we take it? How do the deaths of others affect us?

Betrayal — Why is loyalty so hard to find and keep? What prompts us to be disloyal? Why do we betray the people and things we love, or that we are sworn to protect? Once we start betraying, can we ever stop?

Trust — Can we ever really trust anyone, or anything? What are the benefits and drawbacks of trust? How is trust used against us? Why do we abuse trust?

Fear — What does fear do to our ability to function? Can we overcome our fears? Do we have the strength to confront our fears? Mortals are typically afraid of the supernatural, but the tables can be turned: What happens when the monsters are afraid of the hunters?

Redemption — Can we ever be redeemed for the terrible things we've done? Why do we seek redemption, and from whom (or what)? What happens to us if we finally gain redemption?

MOOD

If theme is the organizing principle of your story, the mood is the general feeling or atmosphere your story evokes. Think of it as your story's mental or emotional state. It's one of the most difficult story elements to work with, and once captured it can be hard to sustain, but the payoff is worth it so persevere. Here are some appropriate moods for mortal characters and stories:

Mysterious — Nothing is what it seems. Every shadow hides potential dangers, and each answer seems to lead to more questions. Nobody is sure whom, if anyone, they dare trust. Characters may experience paranoia and desperation as they peel away layer after layer of the mystery, seeking its final solution. This is a great mood for mortals, but don't forget that no mystery can endure forever and still be enjoyable. Eventually, the characters should discover some hard information and be able to put the pieces of the puzzle together.

Anxious — The air is charged with electricity. Everyone is tense. Something is going to happen, even if nobody is certain exactly what it might be. Everyday occurrences take on an ominous feeling. This can be a difficult mood to evoke and sustain, but it can have a big impact on the story (not to mention the characters' nerves).

Thrilling — A roller-coaster ride of events sweeps the characters along, rarely giving them time to catch their breaths. The action seems relentless, and characters must remain alert at all times or risk being steamrolled. Obstacles, enemies and threats follow one another in a seemingly nonstop parade. Be sure to plan at least periodic, if brief, respites from the activity, however, if you don't want your players to grow frustrated at their inability to react to events.

Desperate — There's a lot at stake in this story. Maybe the life of a friend or loved one is threatened, or perhaps the fate of an entire city hangs in the balance. Characters should be increasingly willing to take risks as the tension rises. This mood is well suited to a story that has personal involvement for the characters.

Hopeful — Things are dark, but they aren't yet hopeless. Tiny victories and small triumphs give the characters genuine reason to think that they might be able to succeed. This is a good theme for chronicles involving mortal hunters who strive to hold back the darkness.

Temptation — The world, and many of the people and things that inhabit it, can be seductive. The thrill of casting that first ritual, the ecstasy of the vampire's Kiss, the thrill of running with the werewolf's pack, the dreamlike halls of the fae — all these things can overwhelm the mortal senses and threaten to rip the hunter from her own world and into the one she's discovered.

PLOT

"So what happens next?" Any time you ask yourself that question, you're thinking about plot. When players discuss among themselves the antagonist that appeared during the last game session, or what the discovery of a new clue might mean, they are mostly talking about plot. A plot is the series of events that moves the story along from game session to game session. It's the framework on which you'll build a great portion of your story, and the part of the tale that is usually the most visible to your players and their characters.

BIG PLOT, LITTLE PLOT

Plots come in all shapes and sizes. They can be as large or small as you like, and can incorporate any themes and moods that you think will entertain and interest your players. Main plots are the central events of your story, the major activities and happenings that propel the game toward its climax. That is not to say that every character must necessarily participate in each main plot; they should at the very least be aware of a main plot's existence and understand that it could have an impact on their characters' lives whether they desire it or not. Main plots for mortal chronicles almost always focus on the manner in which the characters interact with the world around them, and very often that means the supernatural. This is especially true for hunter characters.

An example of this type of plot in a hunter story might be the search for a werewolf's lair. The hunters are seeking the lair with the intent to destroy the werewolf, and most of these characters will be affected in some way by this plotline as it moves forward. The search for the lair will probably take a while, and require some effort from the characters. How exactly does one go about sniffing out the haven of a savage monster that can also look like a normal human? Do the characters conduct research in the city's libraries and public records offices, or do they plunge into the city to follow the werewolf? If the

hunters locate the lair, how will they deal with the creature that dwells within (not to mention its servitors and any traps it may have prepared)? If they don't locate the werewolf's hiding place, how will they deal with the displeasure of their superiors?

Main plots for mortals need not be so simplistic, however. Consider the possibilities of a plot that centers on a small cabal of mortal sorcerers that is slowly taking over a mid-sized city by gaining influence over key mortals. The protagonists must face not only these antagonists, but also their sorcerous powers and any mortal minions that may be in their employ. Some mortal characters may be affected directly by the sorcerers' machinations, while others encounter only indirect evidence of the cabal's plan. Many of the characters might be forced to come to grips with the fact that, despite being manipulated by the sorcerers, many of the mortals they encounter don't know what's going on and aren't truly responsible for their actions. The game setting itself (the city) can change as the cabal's control waxes, and every character will eventually feel the impact of this plotline.

Occasionally, a player will remain willfully ignorant of plots, and even attempt to avoid them in concern over the Storyteller "messing" with his character (as if that was not one of the Storyteller's roles!), a fear of a character's death or just plain contrariness. Don't give these players any slack or do them any favors. Let their characters suffer the consequences of remaining purposefully ignorant of the plot, and let that be a warning to them in future stories.

WHERE DO YOU GET YOUR IDEAS?

Many of the best stories begin with nothing more than the germ of an idea that grows when time and effort is invested in it. Initially, you'll want to spend a respectable amount of time planning your plots, particularly at the beginning of a new chronicle. If you're having trouble thinking up plots or generating story concepts, look no farther than your media resources for inspiration. Humans live in a world comprised mainly of stories — that's how we communicate with one another. Newspaper articles, evening news broadcasts and Internet wire services are all filled with the seeds of terrific stories, many of which have the potential to become great plots if you look at them with the right perspective. The same is true, of course, of books, magazines, movies and Web sites. Even if you're not yet skilled at recognizing viable plots from media sources, you soon will be given sufficient practice.

Eventually you'll be comfortable enough with your plotting capabilities to leave a few things to chance, particularly once your chronicle is up and running. Sometimes the most memorable plots arise not from what the Storyteller orchestrates, but from what the characters say and do. Character interaction is the most fertile source of plots, bar none, and you'll want to keep your eyes and ears open for hints and ideas that spring from the activities your characters undertake. For example, you might be telling a story about a cenacle of Inquisitors and their search for a vampire's haven. During a game session, and apropos of nothing, one of the characters remarks to another that something about their task reminds her of a knight's quest for a holy relic. Suddenly, without warning or prompting, an interesting plot element has just been dropped in your lap. What if the vampire has in his possession a holy relic? How might that affect the current story? You could decide that when the hunters finally locate the vampire's lair, they find the aforementioned treasure instead of their quarry. Is the relic a fake, or is it genuine? If the latter, what properties does it possess? And more importantly, what

in the world is it doing in a vampire 's lair? The wise Storyteller keeps a notepad and pen (or PDA, or wax tablet and stylus, etc.) handy during game sessions so that she can jot down plot ideas and concepts on the fly.

BEHIND EVERY GOOD STORY

Encourage your players to give adequate attention to their characters' background stories. No character should be permitted to enter the game tabula rasa — at the very least, each character needs to account for his or her immediate past. What did the hunter character do before hunting? How and when did the medium first experience her initial brush with spirits? What experiences shaped the way the bartender deals with the world around him? How does the character feel about her organization, her peers and the world in general? What is her favorite color? Answering questions of this sort and compiling the answers into a background history is important both for the player and the Storyteller.

Encourage your players to use the character's background history as guide to roleplaying the character's reactions to various events, and as a source of inspiration when developing the character over the course of play. Was the character's younger sister a medium who became the victim of a wraith's ill will? The character might then well harbor a bitter hatred toward the Restless Dead and nurse a violent grudge against the particular ghost who tormented her sister. Has the character always been possessed of a deeply seated sense of curiosity about the occult? Her first actual meeting with a vampire might then be marked by a desire to question the creature rather than fight it, contrary to what her superiors might expect of her. Does the character still carry the stigma of being tormented by bullies during her high school days because she was always smarter? Whenever a player is uncertain about how his character should behave, a quick mental review of her background history will usually provide a clue.

Storytellers, on the other hand, make use of character background histories in a manner that is simultaneously nefarious and fun. Background histories are fertile ground for story seeds, especially for the Storyteller that wants to give his troupe something highly personalized in the way of drama. Remember the hunter whose younger sister was the plaything of a wraith? That particular wraith could make an appearance in the story, presenting that hunter character with the opportunity to fulfill her desire to avenge her sister. And the scholar hunter who would rather conduct research on vampires rather than fight them? Present him with an opportunity to acquire some occult knowledge of a truly rare and valuable nature, but only at the risk of shirking his responsibilities as a foe of the supernatural. The character that was bullied in high school might meet up with some of the people who once made her life hell — how does she react to them now? How will she react if given the chance to get even? All characters should have a past, and that past can inform the present. Sometimes, when you find yourself completely stumped for ideas, a review of the characters' background histories will hold the key to avoiding game stagnation and player boredom. Character histories are usually chock full of unhappy love affairs, intense rivalries, dark secrets and skeletons in the closet. Feel free to make use of these things shamelessly.

Histories aren't just for characters: Your setting should have its own dark secrets, past misdeeds and surprises waiting to spring on unsuspecting characters. The story behind the story is often as compelling and important as what's going on right under the characters' noses. Whether you choose a real or fictional city as the setting for your story,

take the time to note what has occurred there before you start a new game. If your game is already well underway, you can give the story more depth by introducing nuggets of background history into the existing plots. Some aspects of the setting's background history are merely window dressing — odd events that occurred in the past but have no purpose other than to make the setting seem more lifelike and interesting (unless a character decides to focus a lot of his energy on that historical element, in which case you might want to consider converting it into something of significance after all). Other elements in the history are, on the other hand, the plot equivalent of time bombs. These "accidents waiting to happen" can be as fiendish as an elder vampire slumbering in the throes of torpor far beneath the city streets, or as benign as an ecclesiastical ally who has long possessed the means to contact an angel and has chosen this place and time to do it. Still other types of stories are those that are programmed: They activate according to the Storyteller's predetermined timeline regardless of whether any characters pay attention to what's happening. Maybe the vampire in the above example awakens from torpor immediately after the ninth game session in the chronicle, whether anyone has found her lair or not; maybe the potential ally hears about the characters' activities and decides to seek them out after their names and photos appear in the paper.

When your players realize that the game setting is filled with these sorts of hidden treasures, their characters may start jumping at shadows because the players may mistakenly conclude that all the background history they uncover is connected to some surprise or reward. Therefore you should use this plot element judiciously, so as not to derail your main plots. Conversely, you might also decide to imbue a heretofore ignored aspect of your chronicle background with story-related information if characters start sniffing around something that you hadn't considered but that you think would make a pretty good addition to the story.

PRELUDES AS BACKGROUNDS

Long utilized in tabletop roleplaying games, preludes make great sense for **Mind's Eye Theatre** games too. Consider the questions posed about the characters' backgrounds in the preceding section: Instead of having your players just write some notes about these events, why not conduct a prelude and actually roleplay some of those elements? Preludes are generally brief, usually no more than a single evening's play and often much shorter, and they usually involve only the Storyteller and from one to three characters. Think of it as if you were narrating a flashback sequence for the character. Even if you don't have the time (many groups are simply too large for the Storyteller to conduct a prelude for every single character), asking the player to answer the question "How did your character first get involved with the supernatural?" is an essential part of building your story. The players' responses will vary, encompassing everything from "Vampires are just a bunch of kids who read too much Anne Rice and listen to bad music" to "It's my sacred duty to stomp the holy bejeezus out of God's enemies." Regardless, the answers to this question will give you one more hook on which to hang plots.

STORY SEEDS

If you need help getting pointed in the right direction, or need a plot idea quickly, here are some examples of good mortal story concepts that could each blossom into full-fledged chronicles.

Crisis of Faith

This is a basic story seed that acts as a framework to which you can attach other plots and subplots. It works best with a group of Inquisitors. Acting on a tip, or perhaps alerted by news stories that imply supernatural activity, a cenacle comprised mostly of novice members of the Society of Leopold arrives in the city. The Inquisitors begin hunting for evidence of nocturnal monsters and discover clues that lead them to believe that a vampire is active in the vicinity. The *auto-da-fé* begins in earnest, the cenacle bending all its energies to tracking the monster and discovering its lair. Early confrontations are with other mortals who, willingly or otherwise, serve the vampire. Later, the cenacle comes to grips with the vampire's ghoul servitors in a pitched battle that brings home to the hunters the power and danger of that which they seek. Along the way, the cenacle obtains clues that hint at the vampire's identity. They are shocked to discover that the creature was once a nun, a Bride of Christ, who, despite her current state, still believes wholeheartedly in many of the Church's most precious teachings. How the members of the cenacle deal with this revelation, and its implications, informs and energizes the final stages of the story.

Come Out, Come Out, Wherever you Are

The characters are worried because one of their friends have disappeared recently and cannot be found. Despite all efforts — the missing persons reports, the late nights combing the streets, and the posters reading "Have you seen this girl?" — there has been no progress. As far as the characters are concerned, the city might just as well have swallowed up the missing one (and maybe it did, you never know). The characters begin searching for clues in the accustomed and expected places: The missing person's home, her offices, her favorite recreational places such as dance clubs or parks. Gradually, the characters build a picture of what their friend was really like and discover clues that help them piece together the puzzle. Maybe they find out that their friend was into some weird stuff she never mentioned. Who is this strange man who left a dozen messages on her answering machine, and why was she hanging out at that freaky gothic-industrial club? Eventually they discover the exact fate that befell their associate — but will they be able to prevent the same from happening to themselves? This is a good story to run if you have a small number of player characters (say, a six or less).

All Alone in the Night

This sort of story works best for one-night or one-shot game sessions. Basically, all the characters are normal people — perhaps patrons at a nightclub, or passengers on a cruise ship — who are the victims of a supernatural creature's depredations. The marauding enemy is usually a vampire or werewolf, but it could also be a wraith or even a mage. The main plot involves the supernatural baddie stalking and slaying the characters, one by one, leaving the surviving victims with no choice but to attempt to discover the identity of the killer and stop her. Naturally, this tale may not have a happy ending: A clever antagonist may well pick off all the players' characters, or the big combat at the end — as the survivors confront their enemy — might result in the deaths of all the characters. Build characters for this story with the basic mortal template, and do not add any Numinae or other Traits (including Merits and Flaws) that are connected to the supernatural world; the characters should be completely mundane people.

A game like this can be a very interesting way to begin a new mortal chronicle. It can act in the same manner as the prologue of a novel or the foreshadowing in the

opening scenes of a film or play. Start the story by running this game, but ensure that the antagonist either prevails over the victims or escapes before she is killed. The subsequent games involve the surviving characters' quest to figure out what the hell happened, or the arrival of a group of hunters who examine the evidence that the supernatural creature left behind (i.e., the victims), and set about trying to find it before another massacre occurs.

Mean Streets

Supernatural beasties aren't the only threats that a hunter must deal with in her line of work. The cities in the World of Darkness are populated by a variety of monsters that are, despite their vicious and callous deeds, all too human. Corrupt politicians, insensitive industrialists, uncaring bureaucrats, violent street gangs and psychotic killers are all members of the city's cast of thousands, and hunter characters could meet any number of them during the course of their investigations. While supernatural creatures commonly have allies, contacts and minions among a city's mortal population, the monsters don't control everyone. It's quite possible that a mortal may run afoul of another mortal who, for reasons of his own, decides to make the character's life miserable. This story, which works with nearly any size group and can suit organized hunters or normal people, demonstrates that evil resides not only in the supernatural but the natural as well. It is best suited as a subplot to be run concurrently with a major plot and targeted at a smaller number of characters (from one to three characters usually works best).

Enemies Within

In this story for organized hunters, one of the members of the hunter group is a traitor. There are two ways to handle this type of story. The first is for the traitor to be a plant or a mole: a Kinfolk, for example, who infiltrated the association specifically to spy for and provide inside information to her werewolf friends. The other is for the traitor to be a victim of circumstance: a loyal Inquisitor, for instance, who unwittingly becomes a vampire's ghoul and, once under his control, betrays her comrades. Whether or not the group eventually learns of this betrayal, and if so in what manner, depends largely on whether the traitor is a player's character or a Narrator character. If the former, it's up to the character to cover her tracks and conceal her true nature from her teammates as best she can. If the latter, the Storyteller should orchestrate the progression of clues (if any) that lead the players' characters to this discovery. This can be an intensely personal story, both for the traitor character and the players' characters.

Hunting Party

This story reminds the players that their hunter characters don't exist in a vacuum any more than the creatures they pursue. The characters in this game are organized hunters. The antagonists in this tale are the hunters' supernatural foes *and* another group of hunters from an unaffiliated agency. For instance, if your characters are all members of the Sons of Tertullian and are intent on cleansing a wraith haunt, the hunter antagonists of the story could be a trio of federal agents who arrive on the scene — not to expunge the spirits, but to communicate with and recruit them for a specific task. The players' characters must figure out how to deal not merely with their original quarry, but how to cope with the presence of the government spies as well. Do the Sons and the feds team up and take on the wraiths together? Or does one side attempt to undermine the other?

Everybody Comes to Rick's

Hunters are not particularly suited to crossover games, but sometimes that's the only sort of game in town. For the Storyteller who runs a crossover game and wants to include some hunters, this story offers a departure from the standard hunter tale. The story presumes the existence of a place (such as a nightclub or museum) located in the characters' city that functions as "neutral ground" for the vicinity's supernatural creatures. Vampires, werewolves, the fae and even hunters are all welcome to visit this place, and in some fashion best left to the imagination of the Storyteller are either willing to refrain from spilling one another's blood or are barred from doing so by a greater power or authority. This type of story can stretch credulity, but for some troupes it's the only way to account for the relatively peaceful coexistence of so many different types of supernatural creatures — who should be either fleeing in fear or ripping each others' throats out — in one small area. The hunters are merely one more group among many others, and they try to carry out their tasks through trickery, bribery and luck.

Trust No One

In this story, the characters are organized hunters who discover that their own organization has set them up or betrayed them, for reasons of its own. Maybe the characters are federal agents who barely escape a surprise encounter with a werewolf, only to discover that their boss fed the monster clues that led him right to the hunters. Perhaps the characters are Inquisitors who, during a confrontation with a vampire, discover that the equipment sent to them by their superiors does not function properly. Examination of the equipment suggests strongly that someone has tampered with their gear. As if the characters didn't have enough problems in thwarting the evils of the night, now they have to figure out who in their own organization is trying to get them killed.

Humble Origins

In this kind of story, best suited for small groups of players, the characters all begin as normal people whose lives are impacted in some fashion (usually unpleasant) by a supernatural occurrence. They come together, driven by a common purpose or desire — curiosity, paranoia, revenge — and proceed to uncover the facts about what's really happening out there in the night. Build characters for this story with the standard mortals template, and don't add any Numinae or other Traits related to the supernatural. The characters may eventually gain such abilities and powers, however, depending on who and what they are exposed to during the course of play. Maybe they meet a priest whose strong faith encourages one of the hunters to follow in his path, thus developing True Faith over time, or perhaps they encounter a kindly but crazed old witch who teaches some of them the rudiments of hedge magic.

You and Me Against the World

The story revolves around the activities of hunters who are neither part of an organization nor ordinary Joes. They are individuals who have devoted their lives to hunting down the supernatural for reasons of their own, and are reasonably informed and skilled with regard to their chosen occupation. Some of the characters could be former members of hunter organizations who were expelled or left for various reasons (for example, an Inquisitor who suffered a crisis of faith or a federal agent who was betrayed by his parent organization). The hunters engage in a kind of haphazard, seat-of-their-pants operation, and as often as not end up coming to terms with the creatures that they might try to destroy in other circumstances. This kind of story is excellent for those occasions when you want to drop hunter characters into an existing chronicle that is populated primarily by other supernatural creatures. Be cautious about the power levels, however. It's tempting to load up the mortals with lots of Numinae and equipment, but the result could be disastrous for your story. Of course, a great way to "clean house" in a chronicle that's gone awry is to do exactly this.

Guess Who's Coming to Dinner?

This kind of story works best with a limited number of mature players, and it requires quite a bit of preparation, but it's terrifically satisfying if done well. Tell the players to create one mortal character each. Prior to the beginning of the game session, arrange for each character to receive a strange email or letter that includes an invitation to dinner. Not realizing what is in store for them, the characters arrive at the location in the invitation. The plot commences at that point. A mysterious patron who desires their assistance with a situation has selected the characters. Perhaps the characters are famous or infamous hunters, or they possess certain talents or skills that will be useful in solving the patron's problem. Perhaps each of the characters has a connection to the host (who should be played by a Narrator). The beauty of this game is that you can actually stage it in a public place, such as a restaurant, shopping mall, art gallery, museum or what have you. In such a place, preserving secrecy of the supernatural (the Masquerade, the Veil, etc.) becomes essential, so the chances of the characters duking it out with a supernatural baddie right away are small indeed. You can leave the public location and repair to more private quarters (somebody's apartment or house, a quiet café, etc.) if the story demand lots of Physical Challenges. The game should focus on character development through roleplaying and solving the puzzle of what is going on.

PLOTTING

The Storyteller does a tremendous amount of work before the first game session of a chronicle ever begins, but he doesn't do it alone. He needs the players, as well as their creativity and energy and goodwill, to tell successful stories. The Storyteller provides what might be considered the foundation on which the players build the rest of the structure, and the result is a story. However, your players can't build upon your foundation with their bare hands. You must give them enough tools and adequate materials so that they can set to work on the story the minute you announce the start of each game.

SUBPLOTS

It might not appear so at first, but subplots can drive a story as surely and strongly as all but the most forceful of main plots. Subplots are essential to giving your story the spark of life, for they are the minor victories and failures that mark the mortals' lives. You need not create a separate subplot for each individual character, but you should probably create several, and you should be prepared to introduce more as the story progresses (particularly if the characters wrap up subplots during the course of play). Character background histories are fantastic sources of subplot ideas, and the best thing about such subplots is that they invariably grow to involve multiple characters without anything much in the way of prodding from you.

Subplots are essential to keeping players happy, particularly those players who aren't interested in the main plots despite your best efforts. Because character subplots can and do sometimes develop into main plots, don't discourage players from allowing

their characters to pursue personal agendas to the exclusion of Storyteller-introduced plots. Conversely, don't go easy on a character just because the player disregards a main plot in favor of a personal subplot. If the mages decide to kick the hunters to the curb in a fit of irritation, don't spare the hunter who was off chasing down the only extant copy of *The Necronomicon* if he had ample opportunity to be aware of and get involved in the main plot.

Characters often create their own subplots, and you'll be grateful for this. Allowing the characters to jump all over a subplot for a game or two can also give you some breathing room if things are getting difficult. Here are some common signs of character-driven subplots:

• Two characters begin arguing frequently about the direction the hunters are taking or the methodology they employ.

• One character starts to go his own way, working solo as much as he cooperates with his fellow hunters.

• A character has the opportunity to destroy an antagonist but deliberately stays her hand.

• Multiple characters begin pursuing the same goal from different angles, or from different motivations.

Don't hesitate to capitalize on these warning signs! When you see a good subplot in the making, it's okay to give it a little nudge, as long as you can do so unobtrusively (if you're too obvious, the players may decide that they were doing something wrong and shut down the potential source of drama).

You can ease the transition of a new character into the game by introducing a subplot connected to her. Give the newcomer a connection to one or more of the other characters, and let events run as they may. Enlist the aid of an experienced and willing player and give his character and the new player's character some kind of link (family relation, mutual friend, college chums, etc.) that establishes a relationship. The characters therefore have a reason to interact with one another, and the new player will learn the ropes quickly without being thrown to the sharks. (Make sure that you alert your Narrators whenever you introduce a new subplot!)

MORTAL NOIR

Subplots are also an unbelievably rich source of material that can potentially rock your chronicle to its core. If you're seeking some inspiration about the kind of atmosphere and stories that can really shove mortal chronicles into overdrive, check out a couple of the classic movies from the film noir genre. Some notable flicks in this category are *The Maltese Falcon*, *On the Waterfront*, *To Have and Have Not* and the quintessential masterpiece *Casablanca*. The hard-edged realism and murky ethics of these stories are the touchstones of terrific mortal chronicles.

Consider a mortal chronicle that includes a couple of characters who become friends during the course of play. One is a disgraced federal agent who hunts vampires, and the other is an Inquisitor who does likewise. Scanning the agent's background, you note that his motivation for hunting comes from an incident in his past: His sister was attacked and killed by a vampire, and he witnessed her death. Since then, he's tracked down several Leeches and destroyed them. You decide to put this little tidbit of character history to good use and determine that the agent's sister isn't actually dead: What the agent saw was her Embrace, not her demise. His sister is actually still out there

in the night, living the immortal version of the good life. In fact, she's still in the same city but has been very careful to stay out of her brother's way so that he will think she is dead. The Inquisitor, on the other hand, sees his mission as nothing less than a directive from God Almighty Himself. He's been tracking a particularly vicious vampire for a few months, and eventually he discovers her lair. The Inquisitor proceeds to capture the vile creature and contacts his friend the agent for help in sending her forever to the fires of perdition. The agent meets his buddy and discovers (you guessed it) that the Inquisitor has caught not just any vampire but his sister!

Now what happens? Does the agent rescue his sister from the Inquisitor? Does he permit his friend to persuade him that his sister must die because she's now nothing more than a tool of the Devil? Does the Inquisitor show mercy and permit his friend's sister to go free, risking not only the ire of his superiors should they ever find out but his own immortal soul as well? And what about the sister, who is now a vampire? Does she revel in her newfound immortality and powers, or does she experience horrible guilt and dismay at what she has become? How will she react to coming face to face again with the brother who thought she was dead?

Note that while there are no "right" answers to these questions, they are no less powerful for their ambiguity. Quite the contrary: It's the very lack of definitive morality in this situation that makes it so meaningful. Strive to include similar questions of ethics and morality when you can, and start looking for opportunities within the characters' background histories. If you can't find any (unlikely, but possible), then make some up.

STORY CONSIDERATIONS

The following game elements are also part of building good stories, but they are usually easier to establish than the key ingredients. Their impact on your game is also normally less significant, though neglecting them entirely can take apart your careful work with surprising speed.

SCALE

The relative size of your story is partly defined by the number of players who want to participate. You can run stories for three people or 300, but hunter stories generally work best with fewer than 20 players. You must necessarily be flexible about your story's scale, because the total number of participating players will vary according to a number of factors. Most groups are comprised of a number of "core" players who habitually attend every game session, and a number of players who either attend infrequently or with unpredictable frequency. The latter type of player can be frustrating — few things are more irritating than building plots around characters that don't show up regularly — but they are a fact of storytelling life. Players, just like Storytellers, often have commitments and responsibilities outside the game, and their attendance will be affected sometimes by circumstances beyond their control. Meanwhile, new players will join your game after it's started, and others will drop out while it's in progress.

If you're the only Storyteller in the group, scale can quickly become a major problem if you gain too many players too quickly. Fortunately, you can usually see this problem coming and take steps to minimize its impact. If you are reluctant to impose a cap on the number of players that the story can handle, you'll need to start delegating tasks to Narrators pronto. Otherwise you'll be drowning in player questions and rules adjudication in a matter of weeks. Scale affects more than just your ability to handle your

Storyteller responsibilities. It also has (or should have) an impact on the plots you choose to run. The larger your total number of players, the more broad and encompassing your plot must be. If you have 30 mortals all hailing from several different associations, your main plot should be more flexible than if you are telling a story for only five characters. You might have to consider broadening the story by including a larger number of differentiated antagonists, making greater use of character background histories, and tasking Narrators with developing plotlines that are targeted at the individual character organizations. In such cases, it's also helpful to establish some kind of "Storyteller council" so that you and your Narrators can touch base regularly to discuss story continuity, plot development and character activity.

The scale of your story also influences the decision of whether to run an open-ended chronicle that continues forward regardless of other considerations or a closed chronicle in which the game sessions end when the story concludes. If you choose to tell a story that you know will require multiple game sessions and months of continuous play to create, unexpected changes in scale can derail the entire story. A main plot that focuses on the efforts of a quintet of mediums to deal with some particularly troublesome wraiths falls apart if 20 more players join in the space of a few short months. Likewise, a main plot that deals with the quest of 40 Inquisitors for a powerful holy relic can take a sharp left turn into disaster if half the players decide to quit midway through the story. Ongoing games are by their very nature an ambitious undertaking, because they may include multiple main plots that run concurrently and thus demand a greater bookkeeping and tracking effort from you and your assistants. Individual character goals become extremely important in open-ended games. The factors that motivate the hunters to go about their work can carry the story when the plots aren't immediately apparent.

If you aren't certain about the stability of your scale, you might try running one or more one-shot games. These are self-contained events that usually take place over the course of one single game session, and although the plots of multiple one-shot games can be linked together, the action of each game session concludes when the game itself does. These single-session games can mean a little more work for the Storyteller and Narrators, because events must be scripted a bit more tightly than those of open-ended or continuous stories. Each character needs a strong and immediate reason to participate in the game session's events as well as to interact with the other characters, and all the loose ends should be wrapped up by the time the game session is over. Such events are often well suited for conventions, demonstrations, recruiting nights and similar venues that are unlikely to spawn subsequent game sessions. One-shots are a terrific way to introduce new players into the game, to provide bored players with a break from the tried and true, and to attempt different kinds of stories that don't always fit neatly into the customary styles of play.

SCOPE

The exact nature of what is at stake in your story is its scope. Scope describes the range of possibility for character action and impact on the game environment. Do you plan to tell a story about a medium who is trying to stop a single wraith from terrorizing a remote alpine village? Does your story concern the struggle between an entire cenacle and a city full of vampires? Or could the consequences of the characters' actions possibly affect the lives of every single person living in an entire country? These are all questions of scope, and you'll need to think about this as you develop your main plots.

Scale and scope are intertwined, at least partially. Smaller scale stories naturally lend themselves better to smaller scopes. The smaller the scope, the more likely the story will feature an "us versus them" plot that pits the hunters against a single antagonist. Likewise, the larger the story, the greater the stakes are likely to be, especially if the characters are at all inclined to work against one another during the course of play. This isn't a universal truth, however: It's quite possible to concoct a main plot about three characters or 50.

Open-ended and extended chronicles can generally handle plots with larger scopes than can stories of a more limited duration. You needn't allow the characters to catch on that the stakes are high until well after the chronicle has started. Build dramatic tension by slowly upping the ante each game session (or even less frequently if you and your players are really in for the long haul), introducing hints and clues that point to greater plot importance. Be sure to watch character and player reaction carefully: If the fate of the world hangs in the balance, you can be certain that some characters will be paralyzed with indecision. Fortunately, not every loose end need be tied up at the end of each game session in an extended chronicle, so you have greater plot flexibility. Feel free to retrofit and adjust the plots to reflect the characters' decisions, especially if you wish your players to give your game setting a sense of verisimilitude. If a character mistakenly kills a police officer, thinking incorrectly that he was an antagonist, the game environment should react to that event, and so should your plot. Plots usually advance more slowly in open-ended chronicles, though, so keep a careful eye on your story pacing even as you're fine-tuning the main activities for each game session.

RETROFITTING

Because of the mutable nature of scale and scope, you may discover that the plots you originally planned are no longer as suitable for your group as they were when you initiated them. Don't panic: Retrofitting the plot — that is, adjusting the established plots to take into account new factors — is a time-honored storytelling tradition. Storytellers who refuse to alter their plots to account for character activity are doing their players a disservice. Players who invest time and energy into playing their characters well and interacting with the plots deserve to see the fruits of their labors. Likewise, you don't have to let a problem player destroy a given plot when you have the alternative of changing its details in midstream.

Presume that your current plot features a key antagonist who is discovered and killed much earlier in the storyline than you had planned. You now have two options: That plot can end, or it can continue after some tweaking. If you choose the former, you might have to create a new plot on the spot without adequate preparation and hope that it works. If you choose the latter, you'll probably get more mileage out of the plotline. Using the above example, you could retrofit the plot in any number of ways. Maybe the antagonist had a friend or relative who learns of her death and seeks to avenge her. Maybe the antagonist has only appeared to die, and will return after nursing her wounds. Perhaps the death of the antagonist attracts other agencies or powers that had an interest in her and will be curious to know who had a hand in destroying her. You can even get really nasty and have the spirit of the deceased antagonist possess one of his killers, and hide in his body, spying all the while on the characters as they go about their business in the belief that their enemy is dead.

PLAYER INPUT

Don't be hesitant to ask your players for their opinions about the game. On the contrary, soliciting player input is one of the most overlooked and underutilized methods of ensuring that your story will be fun and interesting. If you intend to start a new story, share the gist of your idea with your players and check their reactions. They will almost certainly have ideas and suggestions that didn't occur to you when you conceived your plot — not because you aren't a thorough Storyteller, but because the collaborative effort between Storyteller and player almost always yields superior results than solo preparation. You might be surprised to learn that what you thought was a stellar idea for a story doesn't pique your players' interests. Ask your players some key questions as you're about to start work on a new story:

• What kind of story would the players enjoy most — do they want a game that involves specific types of hunters and specific types of supernatural antagonists?

• What sorts of plots would the players like to see in the story — do they want stories based on internal agency rivalries or events driven by action?

• What should the scope of the story be — do the players want to portray characters that save the world, or would they rather keep the scope limited to more immediate consequences?

• Should all the characters be members of the same hunter agency, should they all be independents, or should they be from mixed associations? (Remember that one of the advantages of single-association stories is all the politicking and intrigue that seems to inevitably breed in these sorts of places.)

• What power level should the story feature — do the players want to portray top-level federal agents armed with the latest high-tech gadgetry and weapons, or would they prefer to portray fledgling hunters who are up against their first quarry?

STORY STAGES

A good story has identifiable stages — an opening, climax and denouement. These stages are the road markers that help you determine where the story is and where it should go next, and incidentally will keep your tale moving in a direction that entertains you and your players.

OPENING

Invest plenty of time and attention in your story's opening. Even if you have a veteran group of players, don't rely on their understanding of the game's conventions to jump-start your story — that's your job. All too often, hunter stories begin with the characters sitting around an office or a graveyard, waiting for the antagonist to make an appearance. You can give your story a boost by establishing the conditions of your story and making the events of your first few games truly meaningful to the characters. Think about why the characters are all together in the first place. Do they all work for the same agency that has sent them to this area as part of an investigation, or have they each come to this place on their own and are meeting one another not only unexpectedly but also for the first time? It's helpful to hand your players a briefing that outlines the impetus for the characters' first gathering.

CLIMAX

The story reaches its climax when the characters are ready to resolve the main plot. When the hunters have learned all they need to know about the haunted mansion or have discovered the identity of the traitor in their midst and are ready to expose him, you've reached the story climax. This is the high point, the big pay off, when the players' mutual goal is finally in sight. Tension runs high at this point, and anything can happen. You and your Narrators should be ready to get involved at a moment's notice, because things can start to happen with frightening speed when the story arrives at this sign post. Provided that your opening games were strong and your plot well designed, the characters should be able to reach the climax with minimal assistance from you. But sometimes players miss vital clues or misinterpret key data, and you need to give their characters a helping hand. You might, for instance, be obliged to place a missed clue someplace else (if the hunters didn't find the personal computer disk in the vampire's haven that contains the occult formula they need to prevent the demon from manifesting on Earth, you might want to move it to the vampire's car which you know they will search next). Try to interfere, if you must do so at all, unobtrusively as possible. Being heavy-handed at this point usually stifles the players' sense of achievement and thus diminishes their enjoyment of the game.

DENOUEMENT

Once the story reaches its climax, it begins to wind down. Tension disperses, the drama subsides and most of the key pieces of the main plot puzzle are visible and assembled. Most players enjoy feeling as though their characters accomplished something, whether it be their association's ultimate goal or something more personal. Try to foster that feeling among your players so that they are satisfied with the story outcome and are willing to participate in future stories. That doesn't mean that each and every character must get everything she wants. On the contrary, some of the most poignant hunter stories drive home the lesson that you can get what you want and still not be happy.

A WORD ABOUT ENDINGS

Resist the temptation to script the end of your story. Allow the actions of the characters to inform and affect the direction the story takes, and how it ultimately concludes. It's no secret that when a Storyteller predetermines the fate of a given plot, her players pick up on the fact that nothing their characters do will alter the course of plot action in the game. This realization often robs the players of their enjoyment and reduces their incentive to play the game with enthusiasm. It's okay to sketch out where you think the story will go, but don't railroad your players toward the conclusion that you prefer.

Stories rarely end the way the Storyteller thinks that they will.

You might labor on your plot in the belief that the hunters will eventually confront and destroy the diabolical wraith antagonist, but you might be disappointed when they decide that the wraith should be allowed to survive. And that's okay: One of the best things about being the Storyteller is watching how the players take your ideas and run with them. Not long after you introduce a new plot, the players will have made it theirs. The combination of Storyteller and player participation makes **Mind's Eye Theatre** a cooperative project that is richer and more rewarding for the union of effort.

TELLING THE TALE

Okay, you've got your players, and they have their character sheets and personal props. You've acquired a game site, and your Narrators are ready to leap into action with their antagonist characters. You have nothing else to worry about, right? Nope — there are still a few things for you to worry about.

BOOKKEEPING

You can't underestimate what the habit of regular and accurate bookkeeping means the success of your story. Because there are so many other demands on your time before, during and after game sessions, you might be tempted to let the paperwork slide. Don't fall for this trap. Taking it easy on yourself now only leads to hard work and grief later. Players want to know (and have a right to know) exactly how many Experience Traits their characters have gained, whether or not that new equipment they requisitioned from agency headquarters has arrived yet, and how their last Influence Trait expenditures turned out. You should be able to answer these questions because you have all the necessary information tucked away in a notebook, PDA or computer disk. If you don't do your bookkeeping, however, you won't be able to answer these questions and your players may get upset with you. Some or all of them might even leave the troupe if you can't deliver on this very basic expectation. If you don't have the time or resources to track all this information by yourself, get some help. Some troupes engage Narrators whose sole responsibility it is to keep track of the paperwork so that Storytellers can focus on the plots (see "Narrators"). But at the same time, don't let yourself be bullied by unreasonable demands from players. If you've told your troupe that you'll give them the results of their Influence Trait actions at the first game of each month, don't feel pressured to provide the information earlier than that to a player who insists that he simply "has to" have it sooner than promised (see "Problem Players"). Provide your players the results of your bookkeeping when you promise it, and everyone should be reasonably satisfied.

CHARACTER SHEETS

Insist that each player give you an accurate copy of his character sheets, and under no circumstances should you allow a player to participate in the game until you have that copy in your hands. Keep a copy of each player's character sheet on file and bring a hard copy of the character sheets to each game. If you use your personal computer for record keeping, you might be tempted to leave all the character sheets at home on your hard drive, but don't. Sooner or later — probably sooner, in fact much sooner than you would have dreamed — a player will show up at a game session sans character sheet. If you don't have a hard copy for her, you're faced with several options, all undesirable: Allow the player to participate in the game without her character sheet, which will almost certainly lead to problems when she can't remember whether she had five or seven Physical Traits at a crucial moment; oblige the player to sit down with a copy of this book and recreate her character, which reduces the player's involvement in the game and usually results in a character sheet that doesn't jibe with the official record; or refuse the player permission to play, which creates hard feelings and deprives your troupe of a participant.

Be absolutely certain to make time between each game session to update the character sheets, noting as the story progresses how many Experience Traits each player has earned, what Traits each may have gained or lost, and other changes that may arise in the course of play. Get into the habit of making this procedure a regular part of your storytelling regimen — reviewing the character sheets a day or two before each game session might work, depending on the number of players in your troupe and the amount of available time you have. If you see a discrepancy on a character sheet (maybe a player claimed to have a Numina power during the last game session that doesn't seem to be accounted for on your copy of his character sheet), note it so that you can contact the player and talk to him about it later.

If you're starting a brand-new game, think about the character sheet policies you want to have in place before the first game session. It's a good idea, for example, to establish a policy that if there is ever a discrepancy between something appearing on a player's character sheet, and what's on the Storyteller's copy, the Storyteller's copy takes precedence. Another good policy is one that tells a player what she can expect when she forgets her character sheet. Some troupes oblige the absent-minded player to portray a Narrator character for that game session, while others require them to copy the Storyteller's information onto a fresh character sheet, taking whatever time is necessary out of game play for that task. Many Storytellers also demand appeasement from these players, in the form of snacks or other small tributes.

EXPERIENCE TRAITS

It's a good idea to determine, before you run your first game session, exactly how you will award Experience Traits. Many Storytellers err on the side of conservatism or liberality in the matter of Experience Traits, and the results of either extreme are quickly visible in the game itself. Award too many Experience Traits, and characters will reach their maximum potentials far too speedily. Award too few, and your players will be frustrated at their characters' inability to develop new skills and powers. Try to strike a balance between these extremes. It's not always easy to know exactly how many Experience Traits is fair, but here are some helpful guidelines.

Every player should get one Experience Trait for participating in a game session, even if his character didn't do anything particularly noteworthy or interesting. Give an extra Experience Trait to those players who roleplayed their characters exceptionally well, but use caution in determining how and where to bestow this award. Beware of the perception of favoritism, however, and to counteract that possibility consider accepting nominations (publicly or privately) from the troupe and awarding extra Traits for roleplaying to those players who receive popular acclaim. Think about limiting the number of extra Traits of this sort that a given player can receive in one month. And while you should be certain to congratulate the players who earn this award, you should also make sure that you maintain increasingly higher standards in its receipt so that you don't encourage players to coast along without continuing to challenge their own roleplaying capabilities.

You might want to award an extra Experience Trait to players whose characters achieve something truly significant during a game session. Some troupes award Experience Traits, or even fractions of Experience Traits, to those players who contribute to the game's success by taking on extra duties outside the game itself, such as maintaining the game site, providing refreshments, creating advertising flyers for the

game, mentoring new players and the like. It's your call whether or not to award Experience Traits in this fashion, but if you decide to try it, remember that one day you're going to have a player whose character reached all his Trait maximums not through participating in the story but from buying cookies and punch.

Once you decide how you're going to award Experience Traits, be sure that all players are aware of your policy so that they can know what to expect. If they understand that you're awarding extra Experience Traits for good roleplaying and the accomplishment of goals, your players will be encouraged to pursue these things and thus contribute to a more enjoyable and successful story. When a game session concludes, inform each player as soon as possible thereafter how many Experience Traits her character earned, and be certain to note the award on your copy of the character sheet (as well as how many of his Experience Traits a player expends in acquiring new, different Traits).

INFLUENCE TRAITS

Tracking Influence Trait usage in hunter games is sometimes less time-consuming than in other types of stories, because the hunters are often working in concert with one another to accomplish the same or similar goals. Each hunter character probably has different Influence Traits in different categories — some with *Church*, some with *High Society*, and so on — and will therefore approach accomplishing goals in different ways. But the chances that the hunters' Influence Traits will clash directly with one another are smaller, unless some of the characters are working against one another intentionally. That said, tracking Influence Traits could still take up as much if not more time than any other single aspect of bookkeeping, because Influence Traits are often used for complex activities that require extended periods of time to accomplish. It's important, therefore, that you know exactly what everyone's Influence Traits are doing at all times. This can be a huge headache if there are more than about 15 players in your troupe. If that's the case, do yourself a favor and get some help before the trouble starts: Give control of some or all the Influence Trait bookkeeping to a trusted Narrator, or you may well find that the demands of Influence Trait tracking suck up far too much of the time you should be spending on plot and story development.

STORY LOG

Has this ever happened to you? A player walks up to you during a game session and says that she wants to use that piece of really nifty information you gave her last week to solve the puzzle that's been plaguing the hunters all night, and you draw a blank. If so, this problem probably arose because you weren't keeping a story log. A story log is simply a notebook in which you record your notes about how the story is progressing.

When a character accomplishes something significant during a game session, like gaining a clue that will ultimately lead her and her associates to the antagonist's lair, make a note of it. If a character makes a remark during a game session that sparks a great idea in your head for a new plot, make a note of it. When characters do or say things during games that you think should come back to haunt them later, make a note of it. Then review your notes after each game session. This will help you prepare for the next one.

It's perfectly acceptable to approach individual players and ask them to provide a brief summary of what their characters did during the game session so that you can track

story developments. Some troupes even require players to submit some kind of "game report" following the conclusion of each game session. The Storyteller can't be everywhere at once, after all, and chances are good that you'll miss some important developments that occur in one room of the game location because you were busy adjudicating or narrating in another area. Game reports need not be elaborate: You don't want to burden your players unduly by making this part of the game a chore. Reports should contain a brief and accurate account of anything significant that the character did during the game session, and anything important that he heard or saw, from the character's perspective. You might even decide to tie these reports to Experience Trait awards (see "Experience Traits"), awarding an extra Trait to those players who turn in exceptionally useful game reports.

PACING

No Storyteller wants to look up from his notes halfway through the game session and see the majority of his players leaning against the walls, chatting with one another about the movie they saw last night on television, or worse about how boring tonight's plot seems. Visible player boredom during games is a sign of poor pacing (at the very least). It's a good idea to walk into each game session with at least a rough idea of what's going to occur that night. Some Storytellers make some rough notes along these lines: "8 p.m. - start game; 8:30 p.m. - ghouls arrive; 10 p.m. – bomb explodes." Others make more elaborate notations: "8 p.m. - start game; 8:30 p.m. - ghouls arrive; two distract the hunters while the third plants the bomb; 9 p.m. - any ghouls still alive flee; 9:30 p.m. - Marcel gets phone call from cenacle leader; 10 p.m. - bomb explodes." Use whatever method works best for you, but don't just rely on your memory: You'll find that the game goes more smoothly and has a better chance of providing your players with a fun evening if you're at least organized enough to make a few notes about what's happening.

The downside of making these kinds of preparations is, unfortunately, that nothing ever goes exactly as planned in a live-action game. There are simply too many variables at work, and any one of them can alter the night's events completely. And just because it hasn't happened to you yet is no reason to feel smug: You're storytelling on borrowed time! Eventually, no matter how meticulously you prepare for what you believe is every conceivable eventuality, a player will surprise you by doing something totally unexpected that rattles your nerves, confidence and sanity (sometimes all three simultaneously). Some players are disturbingly good at solving your most fiendish puzzles in record time, so that a mystery you hoped would occupy all of the characters for the better part of an entire game session actually occupies one character for a half hour, leaving you with hours of game time to fill and nothing planned. Sometimes your players will miss vital clues, no matter how enticingly you dress them up or how obviously you plant them, and the night's game session will start to seem like a forced march through a swamp: Dull and interminable. What can you do to avoid these problems? You can learn to pace your stories well.

Before you start a game session, you should have some idea of how quickly or slowly you want the events of the night to progress. If you want your game session to have a fast pace, be sure that you've prepared enough activities and events to introduce into the mix so that your players don't get bored. If you want your characters to slow down and focus on one or two particular aspects of the story, don't plan too much for the game session that's not connected with those elements. It's okay, even desirable, to vary the tempo of your games, so that some sessions are paced quickly and others more slowly. You can even alter the tempo within a single game session, although that calls for you to be something very like a film director in your timing. But even if you're a master at planning the pace of your games, you'll still face situations in which the game session is going either too slowly or too quickly. Fortunately, you can help yourself considerably by learning to improvise.

An ability to improvise is perhaps one of the most important characteristics of the good Storyteller. Improvising — or "winging it" — means narrating stories without the benefit of knowing exactly what comes next. Almost all Storytellers do it — it's not possible to plan for every contingency — but not all Storytellers do it well. The best Storytellers make their improvising look so easy that it's often not possible to be certain that they are doing it: If you know such a person, study her technique carefully, or better yet ask for some pointers. If you don't know a good improvisational Storyteller, there are some things you can do to improve your own skills at narrating by the seat of your pants.

You'll want to lay in supplies for the improvisational journey. Remember that story log you're supposed to be keeping? You can also use it to note interesting plot threads that you might like to introduce, but that don't necessarily fit into the game right at the moment you think of them. Keep this list of plot catalysts handy so that you can introduce one on the fly when game sessions bog down or need a lift. "To improvise" does mean the equivalent of "making it up as you go along," but you'll find that making up stories on the spot is a lot easier if you've left yourself a cache of tools.

A plot catalyst can be nearly anything that is unexpected and sparks the characters' interest. If you see a lull in the game and you think that it may go on for a while (maybe some of your more active players banded together and resolved the plotline you had planned for the game session in record time), pull out one of these plot threads and let the characters tug on it for a while. Examples of good plot threads:

• The characters receive a phone call or wire from their superiors that contains a cryptic message they must decipher right away;

• The characters are visited by an unforeseen antagonist;

• Police officers stumble onto the hunters just as they are concluding a successful hunt, and suddenly the characters are in serious legal trouble;

• The characters discover a bizarre item that defies explanation while ransacking a location connected with the main plot (this one can be tricky, so don't overuse it — introducing big, scary artifacts and relics can send the plot off the deep end);

• Several of the antagonists' bully boys pay an unexpected call on the hunters at a very inconvenient moment;

• A character experiences a terrifying vision that is clearly connected to the story, but is so vague that it may have several meanings.

The danger inherent in utilizing story threads of this sort is that they can blossom suddenly into separate, full-fledged plots that you must then maintain if you want to certain that your story remains cohesive and consistent. Keep track of the plot threads you introduce, and how the characters react to them.

ANTAGONISTS

Obviously, mortal stories need antagonists. Hunters need a quarry: They wouldn't be hunters without something to hunt. In the early stages of a story, this game element usually presents very little problem. Lots of supernatural beasties haunt the night, after all, and most of them are probably ripe for a little righteous butt-kicking from the friendly neighborhood hunters or are eager to make life very unhappy for the Average Joe who stumbles on their existence.

The type of characters that your players are portraying should inform your selection of antagonist. The Dauntain should probably be hunting some fae initially, and the Society of Leopold is the traditional foe of vampires. But that doesn't mean that you have to limit your menu of antagonists to just what the characters (and players) expect to face. Consider the delicious possibilities that could arise when a group of members of the Order of Saint Peter, fresh from their defeat of a minor magician and feeling all smug about their victory, come face to face with a powerful wraith. How do they cope with something they know very little (if anything) about? Using different types of supernatural antagonists keeps characters on their toes.

TROUBLESHOOTING

You will, unfortunately, need this section at some point in your story. Here are some common problems that can befall chronicles. Take heart: None of them, if addressed promptly, are fatal to a chronicle.

Stagnation: Eventually, the characters may achieve all of their goals. Hunters, for example, may run out of things to hunt, at least as far as you are concerned. Even the best Storyteller can sometimes be hard-pressed to think of new ideas quickly enough to prevent a chronicle from stagnating. Sometimes it's hard to keep a hunter game fresh over long periods of time. The solution, as intriguing as it might seem, is not to pile on ever more antagonists in the hope that your players will find joy, or will be sufficiently distracted, by mindlessly slaughtering the supernatural hordes you throw in their paths. Fortunately, there are alternatives to this desperate course.

If the problem is Storyteller burnout, try staging your game sessions farther apart in order to give yourself more time to create plots and prepare for individual games. Try taking on some Narrators or assistants, and delegating to them some of the work you've been doing yourself (this is also a great way to train Storytellers who may one day be interested in running stories of their own, giving you not only a break but a chance to play!). Above all else, remember that running the game should not take precedence over your life. Do not neglect your health, your job or your relationships with friends and family in favor of running games. When you see this happening to you (and if you're a conscientious sort of Storyteller, it just might), take a break and hand over the reins to somebody else for a while. Chances are excellent that, once you've got your second wind or recharged your mental batteries, the game will still be there and waiting for your return.

Boredom: This is similar to stagnation. Players get tired of the same old thing, but they also sometimes get tired of things that may seem fresh and interesting. If you are careful about the players you invite into your group and spend adequate time preparing for game sessions, this won't often be a problem. But even if you do hear players complaining "There's nothing to do in this game," don't panic. You're responsible for providing the story, it's true, but the players are responsible for making a good-faith effort to interact with the tale you are trying to tell. They have some responsibilities as well, and you can help to emphasize their role in the story equation by taking their complaint seriously and investigating its causes. Sometimes, players say that they are bored even when that isn't really the problem, but boredom sometimes becomes a catchall complaint. You might have to do some digging to figure out what's really wrong. Here's a list of questions that you might want to ask players who say that they are bored, all of which emphasize different aspects of the game and highlight the players' responsibilities:

• Are they pursuing their characters' goals actively?

• Are they hoarding information they should be sharing with other characters?

• Are they being willfully ignorant of the plots and subplots?

• Are they making an effort to interact with other characters?

• Are there elements about the story that the player doesn't like or doesn't understand?

• Is the game's pace too slow or too fast for the player's taste?

If your players still feel bored, running a one-shot game (such as the *All Alone in the Night* plot: See "Story Seeds," p. 289) can sometimes do wonders for a group's creative energies. Alternatively, you may have to make a drastic shift in the focus of your stories in order to maintain player interest. For example, if you're running a chronicle about organized hunters who have been stalking dozens of supernatural baddies, give them something new to think about by introducing problems that they can't solve by killing, such as an internal audit of their methods by their association, or the impact of a sudden schism within their order. If all else fails, it's perfectly reasonable to switch to a different type of game for a while. Try a **Masquerade** or **Apocalypse** game, and allow your players to enjoy the view from the other side of the supernatural fence for a while.

Metagaming: Some players seem perpetually confused about the difference between what their characters know and what they know. These players continuously allow their characters to use knowledge during game sessions that they (the players) possess, usually because they picked it up during a chat with the other players, but that their characters cannot possibly know. When this happens, communicate promptly to the metagaming player that using information gained outside the context of the game isn't permissible. At best it's bad form and unfair, and at worst it's cheating. Recommend that the player try remaining in character at all times when he's participating in game sessions, and that he make a strong effort to separate what he knows from what his character knows. If he can't or won't do this despite your repeated attempts to correct the problem, you might be left with no other alternative than to ask the player to leave the game.

Cheating: Cheating can be a difficult problem to deal with, because it's not always apparent that a player is actually breaking the rules. A player whose character uses a Numina power he doesn't yet have might have legitimately forgotten that he hasn't yet expended the Experience Traits to acquire it, although he meant to. Did the player cheat? It's your call.

That said, don't let cheaters ruin the enjoyment of the other players. The sad fact is that some players will cheat, and that some of them won't stop just because you ask them to. Cheating can take many forms, from a player who uses Traits that his character doesn't possess, to players who "forget" to cross off expended Willpower Traits during game play. You can counter some of these common types of cheating by instituting policies that make it harder to engage in the specific sort of cheating — such as by making spot checks of character sheets during games, monitoring challenges, or using tokens to represent expendable Traits — but these measures can have the undesirable effect of making you feel like a hall monitor or jail guard rather than a Storyteller. When a player cheats despite your warning, you really only have two options: Allow the cheater to remain in the game or throw him out. Usually, your other players will thank you for doing the latter, which is generally the most sensible solution.

Problem Players: It's important to remember that the main goal of all players, problem and otherwise, is to have fun. But a player need not be a cheater in order to cause you, and the rest of your group, immense headaches. Problem players come in a bewildering variety of guises: There's the Rules Lawyer, who has memorized every single rule in every single **Mind's Eye Theatre** book and insists that you follow each one to the letter. There's the Beatdown Squad, who live to instigate massive combat scenes for no adequately explored reason. The Equipment Mongers think that their hunter characters should be able to easily obtain the most expensive and powerful paraphernalia in existence. The Powergamer believes that her character's statistics are the most important thing about her. Each problem player has a different impact on the game, mostly negative.

Sometimes, if you take the time to search for the root causes of the problem and work with the player to correct it, a former pain-in-the-neck can become a valuable contributor to the story. Communicate your concerns clearly and civilly, and leave the door open for cooperation in finding a solution to the problem. Chances are good that the problem player didn't know that his behavior was an issue, and he'll be happy to work with you to change it if it means having more fun. Unfortunately, there are always a handful of players who cause problems intentionally, and some of these even appear take great pride or pleasure in it. For them, there's no other alternative: Either they reform (and demonstrate their good intentions) or find a different game.

NARRATORS

You need Narrators. You might not think that you do, but you do. It's simply not possible for you to do everything by yourself, no matter how much you might want to. You might be the very best Storyteller ever to pick up a copy of this book, but unless you have only a handful of players you will be overwhelmed if you try to run every aspect of your game personally. And if your game is growing in scale, gaining new players with regularity, you'll have less time to personally take care of all the necessary duties. Thus, you need Narrators.

A Narrator is an assistant to whom you can delegate tasks. The larger your group, the more Narrators you'll need. A good rule of thumb is one Narrator for every ten players, but this ratio varies wildly with the type of players, sorts of stories, and individual preferences that make up your group. Some large groups find it useful to maintain an entire staff of Narrators, assigning each one a particular area of responsibility, such as Influence Traits, Antagonists, Rules and Challenges, Downtimes, Bookkeeping, etc. Try to allow your Narrators to work with the type of things that interest them.

Encourage players to make use of Narrators, and encourage them to go to Narrators first with their questions. Narrators can help new players create characters, facilitate the use of Influence Traits during game sessions, handle situations in which a character uses a Numinae power over an extended period of time, and help you corral problem players who are running amok. They can also portray Storyteller characters who are important to your stories. In some larger games that occupy a big game site, or that are spread out across larger spaces like a park or college campus, the storytelling staff makes communicating during games easier by investing in inexpensive two-way radios (available at many toy stores, electronics shops and military surplus stores). It's a lot easier to radio for assistance ("I need three ghouls over by the parking lot, pronto!") than it is to run half a mile to ask for it.

One of the most significant contributions a Narrator can make is in the realm of rules adjudication, particularly during game sessions. It's not fair to your players if they have to freeze an exciting scene in order to track you down for a ruling. Far better if there are one or more Narrators who can step in and adjudicate the action while you are dealing with another aspect of the game elsewhere. Narrators should therefore be comfortable with the rules, but they should also be able to ask you for help if they should get in over their heads. Don't contradict your Narrators rulings publicly if you can avoid it, because doing so undermines their authority and reduces their effectiveness. Therefore, strive for clear communication between your Narrators and yourself. Let them know what you expect from them, and show them that you respect and trust them. Establish the boundaries of their responsibilities and encourage them to use you as a resource and backup when things threaten to get out of control.

ONE NIGHT'S EFFORT: MAKING IT HAPPEN

Pre-Game Issues

Make sure that you have all the materials, props and information you need to run the game smoothly. Contact your Narrators who are playing Narrator characters, make certain that they understand what's expected of them, and be certain they, too, have everything they need to meet their goals. Meeting with your Narrators to go over last-minute questions can save a game from an avoidable problem. If you have time, glance over the character sheets and make any final adjustments to the night's plot events. Above all, find a few minutes to relax and prepare yourself mentally for the task ahead.

Setup

You'll be doing yourself a big favor by being one of the very first people to arrive at the game site, because you'll almost certainly be in demand from the moment you show up. Give the site itself a once-over. Is everything safe and where it should be? Keep an eye out for players who try to smuggle in unsafe props. Keep your character sheet copies and story log handy, and try to set aside some time for players who will wish to ask you questions (here's where Narrators come in very handy).

Starting the Game

Gather all the players together and give them a minute or two to shift gears. Most people need a little time to get into character before a game session actually begins. Remind them that once they are in character, they should remain so unless they have a question that a Narrator or the Storyteller must answer, or unless they step into the area designated for "reality" (if your game site is large enough to offer such an amenity). Go over any safety rules concerning the game site and invite questions. When all questions are answered, inform the players where the game is taking place and give them any special knowledge they might need about the game environment. Adjust the

lighting if the game is meant to be taking place in a darker or lighter area, and announce the start of the game.

Steady as She Goes

Your personal storytelling style and preferences generally dictate how you spend the hours during the game itself. Some Storytellers like to walk around the game site, observing the characters' interactions. This can be a particularly useful way to spend your time if you're running a complex story, because it affords you the opportunity to see and hear what the characters are doing. Other Storytellers prefer to sit at a table where the players can find them easily. Regardless, chances are very good that you'll be pulled into service suddenly to answer rules questions, describe a scene or object, or adjudicate a challenge.

The Curtain Falls

Just as you did before the game started, gather your players together again before they leave. Live-action roleplaying can be an intense and exciting experience, and players sometimes benefit from the opportunity to "cool down" and be guided gently back to reality when the action stops. Solicit feedback from your players. Do they have any comments or suggestions about the game session? Did anybody see any really great roleplaying, or exceptional drama, that they would like to share? Did everyone enjoy themselves (don't let the players off the hook with a "yes" or "no" answer to this question — ask for specifics and clarifications)? Make any necessary announcements at this point, and then turn everyone loose.

MISTAKES YOU'LL MAKE, AND HOW TO LEARN FROM THEM

Every Storyteller makes mistakes. Those who claim to be perfect are either lying or selling something. Nobody is perfect, and you'll only waste your time if you beat yourself up over your mistakes. Instead, strive to learn from them, and in doing so you'll find that you'll become a better Storyteller. Here are some of the common mistakes that plague Storytellers everywhere, and what you can do about them.

Forgetting Something Important

Sooner or later you will neglect to remember something important. Maybe you'll forget to bring a key prop to the game, or maybe you'll contradict a ruling that you made at the previous game session. Perhaps you'll forget to give a Narrator a vital piece of information she needs to portray a Storyteller character effectively, or you won't remember to respond to a player's downtime actions by the deadline you set for yourself. Regardless of what you forget, make a point of apologizing as quickly as possible to the affected party (or parties), and then evaluate the situation. Ask yourself, "Will the game come to a crashing halt without the misremembered thing, or can we carry on and rectify the problem later?" If the answer is the former, you're in a bit of a bind because you're faced with the unattractive proposition of either departing the game site to go fetch whatever you forgot or convincing someone else to do so in your stead. If the answer is the latter — and nine times out of 10 it is — don't let your mistake distract you from the other duties you have. Run the game as best you can and attempt to make things right later. If this problem becomes habitual, however, you should consider inventing a system to remember all the important things you need at game sessions. Try making a checklist and reviewing it before leaving home for the game site, or using some other organizational system that you can access quickly and easily (like a notebook, laptop computer or PDA).

Telling a Story That Blows

You will, eventually, tell a story that for any one of a number of reasons just doesn't go off correctly. Maybe the players weren't as intrigued by your choice of antagonist as you'd hoped they would be. Maybe you didn't make the mystery challenging enough. Perhaps you just had an off night. Keep your ears open, because your players will complain when these things happen (to one another, at least, if not always directly to you). Although players sometimes complain for no readily discernable reason, player reaction is also an important gauge that will help you determine how successful your stories are. No matter how badly things go at any given game session, don't be discouraged from telling more stories! Try to examine exactly what went wrong with the game and learn from the mistake. Talk to your Narrators: They might have seen warning signs that you missed or have suggestions for improvements in future tales. Talk to your players, too: The more feedback they give you about what they like and don't like in game sessions, the better able you will be to give them the kinds of stories they enjoy.

Favoritism

No matter how carefully you strive to maintain your objectivity, you'll eventually be accused of favoritism from some quarter. Sometimes these accusations are completely groundless and arise from nothing more substantial than jealousy, pettiness, egotism or sheer immaturity. Some players refuse to accept any responsibility for events that displease them, and they look for others to blame. When this happens, confront the accusation directly. Take the accuser aside and discuss the situation, asking her to explain why she feels that she's been the victim of favoritism. As unpleasant as it might be to admit it, there's always the chance that she's right and that you've unwittingly practiced favoritism. If that's the case, correct your mistake accordingly.

The best way to assure yourself that you'll be able to deal effectively with such accusations, of course, is not to practice favoritism in the first place. Explain to your players how you make decisions about who gets to play what sorts of characters, how you award Experience Traits, when you're available to help them with story matters and the like, and then stick to these policies. Police yourself when you're in the process of making decisions about the game. Ask yourself if you're being as impartial as you should be. You'll find that your players expect you to avoid giving even the appearance of favoritism, as well as to refrain from practicing it.

Bad Rulings

From time to time, you'll make a mistake when adjudicating a scene. Maybe you forgot a certain rule that would have altered the scene's outcome had you remembered it. Maybe you unilaterally declared a shift in a game policy without thinking through its implications. Sometimes you won't know what the best answer is for a given situation (presuming that a "best" answer for it even exists), and you'll be obliged to wing it and make a judgment call. Sometimes these instances result in bad rulings that you later regret.

Handling bad rulings can be dicey. It's natural to want to correct a mistake, and sometimes you can do this. If you discover that you made a mistake in adjudicating a rule or challenge, but the effect of your mistake was relatively minor or negligible, often the best thing to do is notify the concerned parties of the mistake and apologize. If you can

make minor adjustments to the outcome of the scene without unduly disrupting the flow of the story, go ahead and do so. But if, on the other hand, your mistake seriously biased or even altered the potential outcome of a scene, fixing the result is almost never easy.

It's an unfortunate fact about the nature of live-action roleplaying chronicles that repairing the result of a significantly mistaken ruling can cause more damage to the story than letting it stand. A misapplication of the rules that results in the overthrow of a character from a position of authority (such as the leadership of a hunter organization) can be very difficult, even impossible, to repair without irreparably damaging the story's integrity. Before you reverse a judgment for such an instance, take the time to think it through. Consult your Narrators — perhaps they have some suggestions or alternatives that you might have overlooked. Talk to the players involved and try to assess what the damage to their enjoyment of the game will be if you reverse a bad ruling. In many instances, you and your story might be better off in the long run if you allow your mistaken ruling to stand, apologize to all parties, allow the story to continue unimpeded, and try to learn from the error.

The Inappropriate Character

After you've made this mistake once, you'll probably make it again some day. It's sometimes difficult to gauge the exact effect that certain types of characters can have on a story. The Gladius Dei ghoul might have looked good on paper, but shortly after you allowed it into the story you probably noticed the deleterious effect it had on your plots. Ditto for the Kinfolk/kinain sorcerer that you, in a moment of weakness, allowed a player to talk you into approving after months of begging. Maybe your brain was on vacation when you decided to allow a player to create a 103-year-old, wheelchair-bound, ex-soldier with Tourette's Syndrome. It's no secret that many players feel that if their characters don't have all the best powers or most lethal abilities, they aren't having fun. You could save yourself some grief by suggesting that these players find a different game, but if that solution isn't to your taste, there are a couple of other solutions.

First, make certain that your players understand that you acknowledge your own fallibility. Warn them that although you want to help them get as much fun and enjoyment out of the story as possible, you'll make mistakes just like everybody else. Be sure that your players comprehend that they don't have a "right" to play any given character. The U.S. Constitution says nothing about being able to play a Brujah-Bastet abomination with Spheres. The Storyteller is the final arbiter of whether a character meshes well with the story environment, and you have a responsibility both to your story and your other players not to allow one of your mistakes to drag the entire shebang into the mud. If you find yourself in a situation in which you must withdraw a character from the story, at least your players cannot assert that they were not given fair warning of your privilege to do just that.

Unfortunately, about the only reasonable solution to this problem is to inform the player who's got the über-character that you made a mistake, and advise him that you're withdrawing the character from the chronicle. He won't like it, of course, but try to appeal to his sense of responsibility. The only other alternative is to leave the character in place and take whatever comes next.

CROSSING THE STREAMS

Maybe you aren't running a hunter game at all, but are instead running a game with characters that are primarily supernatural creatures, such as vampires, mages or changelings. Some of the most exciting stories arise when hunters move into your chronicle and begin stalking, and perhaps even taking down, your regular characters. There are two means of creating this type of story. The first utilizes Narrators to portray the hunter characters, and the second presumes that other players will be the hunting folk.

The former method — hunters as Narrator characters — is the most appropriate if your chronicle consists primarily of vampire or werewolf characters. It's reasonable to presume for example that, eventually, the Kindred in your **Masquerade** story will probably come very close to breaking the Masquerade, if they don't actually shatter it into embarrassingly tiny pieces. When this occurs (and it will), it's equally reasonable to presume that mortal hunters might get wind of what's happened and arrive in the vampire's city for the specific purpose of tracking down the bloodsucking idiots and eradicating them like the vermin they are. Some vampire characters are so arrogant about their invulnerability that they practically hang signs outside their havens that read "Here is the Vampire" just for the hunters' convenience. Likewise, the characters in your werewolf chronicle will probably make the monumental mistake of leaving clues behind after some act of destructive mayhem that would lead a federal agent (even if he had been blinded in a freak espresso accident) right to their caern.

Narrator hunters should be planned thoroughly, and the arrival of hunters in the vampire or werewolf chronicle should be a carefully orchestrated affair. Don't make the hunters so powerful that they can thumb their noses at the Licks and furballs, or your players will be royally irritated and complain that you are trying to "screw them over." On the other hand, don't make your vampire and werewolf hunters so weak that a freshly Embraced neonate armed with a tongue depressor could make mincemeat out of them. Stories in this mold should be tense, dramatic and above all brief. Don't make the hunters a constant threat to the characters, or you won't be able to enjoy your storytelling tenure much.

Other types of supernatural creature chronicles, however, can be better suited to players taking on the roles of the hunters. Limited crossover for mediums and wraiths, Dauntain and changelings, and sorcerers and mages, for example, can usually be sustained. Such plots should also be carefully planned, but they usually require less micromanagement than the vampire or werewolf plots that feature hunters.

Do not — no matter how cruelly your players may beg you — take seriously the idea of dumping player-run hunters into your vampire or werewolf chronicle, and vice versa. Resist the urge to place "just a few" player vampires or werewolves into your hunter chronicle, even if your hunter players remind you hourly "There's nothing for us to hunt!" When the story involves vampires or werewolves on either side of the equation, Narrators should always portray the minority population. Inquisitor characters can derive a great deal of enjoyment from conducing research on the location and activities of vampires, and mediums will get an eerie thrill from "making contact" with their quarry. But allowing players to hunt one another's characters is an invitation to disaster in the form of deeply hurt feelings on both sides of the fence. Live-action roleplaying can be an intense experience for players, and few things can be quite as bruising to the player's feelings as the knowledge that it was another player — rather than the

Storyteller or a Narrator — who invaded his vampire character's haven and burned it to the ground while he was sleeping inside it, killing his character.

THE INFERNAL AND THE DIVINE

"What happens if my character summons up a demon, huh?"

"Does my character's True Faith allow her to communicate with angels?"

"Can my character make a deal with the 'dark powers' to gain more Ability Traits?"

If your players are asking these types of questions, relax: It's perfectly normal in hunter stories. Your players will eventually expect their characters to mess with the holy and unholy powers, and their respective provinces. That expectation is even more likely if the characters are members of certain hunter associations, such as the Inquisition, or if they are Hermetic-type sorcerers. That puts you in what may feel like an uncomfortable position. On the one hand, you want to meet your players' expectations, but on the other, telling stories that involve angels or demons can make Storytellers cringe with the dread of either offending their players or blowing their games into tiny pieces.

Storytellers usually don't want to offend or mock anyone's religious beliefs, and they obviously don't want to see their game derailed by the introduction of what might appear to be uncontrollable forces. But with the proper care you can add these potent elements to your stories without making your players angry or trashing your game. Before introducing holy or unholy creatures into your game sessions — or, better yet, before you run your first game in a mortal chronicle — talk to you players about how they perceive their characters' relationships to the great powers that be. Chances are good that, if your characters are playing religiously motivated hunters, they'll perceive a strong, positive connection to the divine and a loathing for the infernal. If the characters are Hermetics, they're likely to be intensely curious about both ends of the spectrum. Sometimes, even those characters with lapsed beliefs can make pretty good fodder too. In any event, discuss this topic with your players in an informal, nonthreatening setting. Your goal is to get a sense of the players' comfort zone when it comes to roleplaying interactions with such culturally charged and iconic forces. If they make it plain to you that they aren't comfortable going down that road, don't force them. If, on the other hand, they indicate that they are interested in and willing to bring the holy and unholy into the game, you have a rare opportunity to generate some stories that you and your players will remember for a long time.

Do Your Homework

Even if your players tell you that they are prepared to have their characters plunge headlong into the nearest portal to the netherworld and grapple with a horde of demons, it behooves you to treat this subject matter with a degree of respect. This is heavy stuff, and if your players see you taking a cavalier attitude toward the belief systems held near and dear to untold millions of people, they and their characters will probably feel free to treat it lightly. That's not a good idea, because doing so diminishes the impact that these elements can have on your story. So do your homework. Make use of just a few of the staggering number of books, magazines, pamphlets or Web sites that cover these topics. You'll want to do this not only to help you understand the material, but to bring some extra realism and punch into your plots. An encounter between Inquisitors and an angel works far better if the angel quotes the Scriptures.

Exercise Restraint

Use the divine and infernal sparingly. If you include them too frequently in your story, both your players and their characters will grow blasé ("Oh look, it's another angel. I am so sick of these things popping up every time we visit the mall!"). Once per chronicle is generally sufficient for any significant appearance by a holy or unholy power.

UNHOLY TERRORS

The demonic side of the formula will probably come easier to you, simply because of its prevalence as a plot device in modern media. There are at least a dozen recent films that tell stories about demonic possession or mortal incarnations of the Devil, and you can use these as inspirations for bringing the forces of Hell into your stories. Demons and their ilk are generally one-dimensional in their goals: They want to corrupt, convert, steal or otherwise obtain power over the souls of living mortals. The reasons they wish to do so can be anything that you think is appropriate to your story. Maybe his unholy master sends the demon in question, or maybe the creature is engaged in a contest with others of his kind (he who dies with the most souls wins). The reason doesn't usually matter, unless you want to build a main plot around it; otherwise it's worthy of a subplot at best.

Try to avoid demonkind that tend to look something like the cartoonish or medieval interpretations of such creatures — huge, overly muscled, with brick-red skin and cute little horns (save the cute little horns for the succubus plotline!). The modern demon should be subtle, suave and sophisticated. Like vampires, demons are immortal and must change with the times if they hope to interact successfully with the mortals who are their targets. The modern demon is far more likely to be wearing an Armani suit or a leather miniskirt than chain mail or a toga. Like their appearance, demons also take more subtle approaches toward achieving their goals than appearing in a puff of smoke and blasting their enemies with jets of hellfire. Save that for later, when the demon has been revealed for what it is and it must either fight the hunters openly or be defeated. Try to describe encounters with the infernal so that the characters experience mixed sensations of dread and desire. They cannot fail to feel the primeval power of unrepentant evil, but at the same time they also cannot help but feel somewhat inclined to listen to whatever it has to say. This mixture of fear and attraction can be quite powerful. Here are some examples of infernal plots:

The Botched Summoning

This plot is triggered when a character makes an attempt to summon a creature or conduct some other ritual, and instead ends up bringing a completely unexpected power into this world. These types of encounters generally proceed in one of two ways. The first is that the summoned nasty breaks free and runs amok, obliging the character to hunt it down and dispose of it. In these cases, the general population that is terrorized by the unholy beast isn't normally aware of its infernal origins, and instead writes off its depredations to the likes of a wild dog pack, a marauding biker gang or a serial killer. The second, and often more enjoyable, story occurs as a cautious interaction between the summoner and summonee that may lead to intense roleplaying as the two fence verbally with one another. Again, subtlety is the watchword here: Demonic forces, even when summoned accidentally, combine attitudes of both controlled menace and seductiveness. The demon will be seeking an escape from its confinement if it is magically imprisoned, and even if it's not, it will be intent on pursuing its personal agenda at the expense of the summoning character.

The Unwitting Apprentice

It's possible that a character may become allied, or even friends with, an infernal creature without realizing its true nature. Consider the implications that arise when a hunter, perhaps a freelancer, meets up with an individual who appears to be relatively normal, if a little weird, and who gives the hunter some valuable information that proves useful in tracking down a target. The hunter is likely to return to the source of information and initiate some kind of relationship (casual, professional or otherwise) in order to acquire more. The hunter might even take his newfound ally into his confidence. The source of information doesn't dry up — on the contrary, she'll continue to supply valuable aid and assistance periodically, but soon her favors will come with prices. She'll want small stuff at first — help with tracing a missing person, for instance, or clandestine acquisition of a rare occult tome. Eventually, her requests will grow more demanding, and if the hunter doesn't figure out what is happening he may find himself deeply indebted to a demon. The story then shifts to focus on the hunter's predicament. Does he tell others or seek to find help? What avenues of escape are open to him? Will he try to kill the unholy creature, or will he simply try to escape its influence?

ON HOLY GROUND

Believe it or not, making the divine work in a hunter story can be a lot harder than doing the same with the infernal. There are fewer useful media references to use as touchstones, and the nature of the subject matter makes some people reluctant to go anywhere near it. And for some reason, players sometimes tend to treat the divine as if it were somehow less dangerous than the infernal. If your characters are members of organizations that are affiliated with any ecclesiastical society, however, you'll need at the very least to bone up on the basic tenets of the appropriate religion. The motivations of divine creatures can be obvious, such as protecting the innocent, combating infernal forces or conveying messages from a higher power. Their goals can also be as subtle as those of their opposites: An angel might be sent to judge a character who has, through her actions, found herself on the threshold of jeopardizing her immortal soul or has started trafficking with demons, or the characters might discover a genuine holy relic that provides them with an important clue or means of fighting their adversary.

Angels and their like tend to manifest as best befits their mission. If they are meant to deliver a message from a higher authority, strike fear into the heart of a malefactor or reward the faithful, they tend to appear in a formidable guise. Their appearances on such occasions usually incorporate light in some fashion, and in some instances a holy power may appear as nothing more than light. Should an angelic mission require that the creature move among mortals without attracting undue attention, the hunters will discover that demons aren't the only ones who can adopt disguises. An encounter with an angel that is undercover might seem nothing more than a chance meeting with a particularly insightful child, a wise street musician or a benevolent professor. These creatures probably will not reveal their true nature until the climax of the story is reached, or unless forced to do so by difficult circumstances. Keep in mind that not all angels are from the Bible: They also appear in the Koran and the Torah, and feature in many different faiths. Each of these various angelic beings looks and behaves quite differently, too.

Be sure to portray any kind of divine manifestation as suitably awe-inspiring, unless you have a specific reason for making it seem mundane and ordinary. Angels can be just

as terrifying as demons and devils — perhaps more so, because they represent a terrible, omnipotent power that has a rather unforgiving and extreme point of view. Angels in holy works tend to appear as messengers (the Annunciation) or as the bringers of God's test (the angels that Lot hosts), occasionally as guardians (the Apocryphal story of Tobias or the angel who bars the entrance of Eden) or as holy warriors (Christian folklore places St. Michael as the general of the Heavenly Host). An angel's appearance can also be used as a herald for those Faith-based characters who are working their butts off on whatever purpose and need a shot in the arm, or as the last sight of a Faith-based character whose good fight is coming to an end.

Here's a sample divine plot:

Crisis of Faith

The hunters pursue a vampire that was, unbeknownst to them, a devout member of the clergy before the Embrace. The creature might have been a priest, nun, monk, rabbi, altar boy or whatever seems appropriate. And since the time of his Embrace, he's struggled long and hard against the Beast, striving to remain on the Path of Humanity without slipping off like so many vampires tend to do. This vampire's Humanity is so high, in fact, that he may seem more human than most "normal" mortals. The hunters destroy him, as they would any hell-spawned fiend, but as they do so one of the hunters experiences a divine vision that reveals the error of her actions. Too late to stop her associates from carrying out the execution, the hunter is now left with doubts about the rightness of their actions. How will this revelation affect her, and her fellow hunters?